Public Culture

Public Culture

*Diversity, Democracy,
and Community in the United States*

Edited by
Marguerite S. Shaffer

PENN

University of Pennsylvania Press
Philadelphia

Copyright © 2008 University of Pennsylvania Press

Published by
University of Pennsylvania Press
Philadelphia, Pennsylvania 19104-4112

Printed in the United States of America on acid-free paper

10   9   8   7   6   5   4   3   2   1

A Cataloging-in-Publication record is available from the
Library of Congress

ISBN 978-0-8122-4081-8

In memory of Hal Rothman (1959–2007)

Contents

Preface
Why Public Culture?

Marguerite S. Shaffer

This book began as part of an extended reflection about the current status of American studies. The process of redesigning the curriculum for the American studies major at Miami University and developing an introductory American studies survey forced me and my colleagues to ask fundamental questions about the field: specifically, what could American studies offer to students and scholars confronting a politically polarized, increasingly privatized, corporate, global culture? For me these are deeply personal questions about my responsibility and identity as an American studies scholar. In developing and teaching the introduction to American studies, I have struggled to promote both cultural competency and cultural agency. Similarly, in thinking about the curriculum for the major, I have wondered how to move students from detached cultural analysis to active cultural engagement. And as a scholar, I have questioned the insularity and public relevance of purely academic work. I have pondered how to integrate cultural critique with culture change—cultural analysis with cultural agency. Ultimately, these questions are about public culture.

Literary critic Terry Eagleton, in his recent book *After Theory*, begins with the pronouncement "The golden age of cultural theory is long past."[1] Eagleton traces the development of postmodern theory from the 1960s through the 1990s, detailing a shift from a politically engaged, intellectual commitment to egalitarian social change to an increasingly insular, elitist, academic focus on subaltern subjectivity. Although his critique is aimed broadly at the humanities, specifically cultural studies and literary criticism, it is also suggestive for the field of American studies. At a time when globalization has dramatically expanded the power and reach of multinational corporations, and the war on terror and ideological and political polarization challenge the core principles of participatory democracy in the United States, American studies can benefit from a reconsideration of its organizing topics, themes, and questions. The concept of public culture presented here serves to reframe the work of American studies. Specifically, public culture has the potential to shift the focus of the field beyond its current interest in issues of difference and identity toward new and varied concepts of belonging, collective life, and community as they are played out in multiple forms within a diverse and increasingly global culture.

In *The Human Condition*, political philosopher Hannah Arendt provides a powerful metaphor for this concept of public culture. She writes, "To live together in the world means essentially that a world of things is between those who have it in common, as a table is located between those who sit around it; the world, like every in-between, relates and separates men at the same time. The public realm, as the common world, gathers us together and yet prevents our falling over each other, so to speak."[2] This image of a table that connects diverse individuals in a shared endeavor elegantly encapsulates the very complicated intersections between individuals and diverse communities as they come together in the public realm. Arendt explains, "Only where things can be seen by many in a variety of aspects without changing their identity, so that those who are gathered around them know they see sameness in utter diversity, can worldly reality truly and reliably appear."[3] In many ways, Arendt's "famous table around which people gather in public life"[4] inspired this volume and the idea of public culture it seeks to promote. What Arendt calls the public realm and others have called the public sphere,[5] or public work,[6] is particularly relevant to and offers a range of possibilities for the field of American studies and its ongoing effort to examine and understand American culture.

American studies scholars have long considered public questions, as evidenced by the field's originating focus on issues of national identity and its history of interest in the idea of a "usable past." The field also has an established tradition of scholarship based in activism and issues of social justice. However, in the past decades as American studies scholars have moved beyond a problematic Cold War interest in American character, national identity, and American exceptionalism, and shifted toward cultural studies and ethnic studies, the field has retreated from any formal or acknowledged examination of shared public culture in the United States.

That said, "the public" has recently provided a galvanizing theme within the field. Michael Frisch, in his presidential address to the American studies Association in October of 2000, identified four core trajectories that have defined American studies: (1) interdisciplinarity; (2) the discourse of nation; (3) multiculturalism (including ethnicity, race, class, and gender); and (4) engagement, praxis, and activism.[7] Contrary to the established conceptualization of American studies, which centers on a linear history that began with what Frisch called "a national project informed by a limited literary-historical interdisciplinarity" and then evolved into a more multidisciplinary multiculturalism informed by cultural studies and transnationalism, he argued that the history of the field is much more multivalent and prismatic.[8] His assessment suggests that interdisciplinarity, national identity, and multiculturalism have come to be recognized as the dominant narratives of American studies. But he went on to argue the case for the significance of praxis, which he described as "a scholarship with the intellectual capacity to both *describe* and *engage* the world more usefully."[9]

In 2001, following the September 11 attacks, then ASA president and ethnic studies scholar George Sanchez followed Frisch's lead, calling for increased public engagement in the field. Building on the conference theme of crossing borders, he noted, "I am now constantly reminded that one of the most significant borders to cross is the one that separates the academic community from the wider public." He went on to conclude, "The issue of preparing students for a multitude of possible interventions in public discourse should be a priority for us in American studies."[10]

Extending from this dialogue, the essays in this volume are a call to consider the public realm, to examine public discourse, and to define or conceptualize public culture. I use the term "public culture" to blend the distinctly cultural work of American studies with some of the more focused examinations of civic engagement.[11] The organizing concept of public culture articulated in this book is grounded in the political theory of Hannah Arendt and John Dewey and also informed by the work of a handful of other scholars, including Harry C. Boyte, Clifford Geertz, Jürgen Habermas, Stuart Hall, and Michael Warner, who are all interested, in one form or another, in the public and the process of creating shared meaning.[12] Drawing from this body of work, "public culture" refers to the process of negotiating shared meaning among a diverse group of individuals. As Dewey explains, publics emerge when "the consequences of conversation extend beyond the two directly concerned," expanding out to "affect the welfare of many others."[13] This strand of political theory offers at least some alternative to postmodern theory, which effectively denies the possibilities of public culture in a society bounded by hegemonic forces struggling for power over all forms of cultural production, representation, and signification. As Terry Eagleton has pointed out, cultural theory in its current state actively promotes "the absence of memories of collective, and effective, political action."[14] From the perspective of current cultural theory, "Human history is now for the most part both post-collectivist and post-individualist," according to Eagleton. He concludes, "if this feels like a vacuum, it may also present an opportunity. We need to imagine new forms of belonging, which in our kind of world are bound to be multiple rather than monolithic."[15] All of the essays in this book, in one form or another, draw on the concept of public culture to explore these issues of collective identity and social belonging, cultural agency and cultural change.

This book grew out of a conference held at Miami University in Oxford, Ohio, in March 2003 entitled "The Transformation of Public Culture: Assessing the Politics of Diversity, Democracy, and Community in the United States, 1890 to the Present." The idea for the conference emerged from a larger reassessment of the American studies Program at Miami under the auspices of an NEH Humanities Focus Grant in 2002–3.[16] The driving intellectual question that had inspired our curricular reexamination focused on a central tension in American studies that existed between acknowledging and understanding the diversity of American culture and defining a collective identity for American culture. We began with a broad question: How, if at all, do the diverse peoples and groups in the United States come together to create a set of shared values, common experiences, and a shared public culture?

Our premise was that despite significant differences, Americans do come together in public to discuss, to negotiate, to debate, and to protest common values, issues, and concerns. Through this process, people form and reform collective identities and shared public cultures, though provisionally and temporally. Specifically, we sought to address issues of multiculturalism, the formation of social identities, the creation of community, and the construction of collective public identities as they have intersected in contested and complementary ways in localized and national cultures in the United States.

Although curricular interests provided the impetus for the NEH project, I was also interested in recent scholarly work addressing issues of public culture as they had evolved in the United States over the past century. I invited a group of interdisciplinary scholars from a range of fields that intersected with American studies—mass communication, cultural and social history, urban sociology, urban studies, ethnic studies, cultural studies, and American studies—to share their ideas about public culture. Specifically, I asked participants to explore the period from 1890 to the present: a historical moment notable for the rise of widespread democratic movements, the emergence of a corporate urban-industrial consumer culture, the expanding dissemination and influence of mass media, the increasing ethnic and racial diversity of communities throughout the United States, and the decline of traditional political action and notions of republican citizenship. Focusing on four defining themes—public action, public image, public space, and public identity—I hoped to generate a conversation about the shifting structure and vocabulary of public identity and public interaction. Who and what constitute the public or publics? How is public action played out in a modern, corporate, bureaucratic society? Where is the public realm in an increasingly privatized culture? And how is public identity fashioned and represented in a diverse, fragmented, mass-mediated society? Participants were invited to explore these broad questions through their specific research.

Although none of these scholars distinctly identified public culture as the central focus of his or her work, they all acknowledged that conceptions of the public underlay their research. Some scholars, such as Mary Ryan, who has written about the history of civic engagement and participatory democracy, and Ed Linenthal, who has examined issues of public memory and commemoration, have been much more explicit in claiming the public as an overarching concept in their work. Others, such as Suzanne Smith, who has written about popular culture and the construction of racial identity, and Catherine Gudis, who has examined the development of the commercial strip, felt less certain about the centrality of public culture in their work. However, the conversation that ensued was inspiring, offering a range of perspectives on how publics are formed, imagined, positioned, and defined. The essays here reflect the collective thoughts that emerged on the topic and serve as an invitation to further explore and expand the concept of public culture.

The essays also speak to the implicit tensions within American studies between the originating focus on shared national culture and the current interest in social and cultural identity and issues of race, class, gender, and ethnicity.[17] American studies scholarship grows out of these dual and sometimes competing traditions. On the one hand, American studies scholarship from the post–World War II period originated in questions about the common experiences and ideas that defined and shaped a shared culture in the United States. On the other hand, a revisionist trend that has dominated the field since the 1970s has focused on issues of diversity of peoples and experiences—the multiplicity of cultures that interact with each other in the United States and the underlying debate and conflict between cultures that challenge the notion of a unified U.S. culture. For the last three decades, American studies scholars have been debating these opposing views of consensus and conflict, probing this issue of shared culture in the United States.

In recent years, theories of multiculturalism and hegemony have become the norm, so that even studies of national culture look at the constructed and exclusionary process of defining a shared national identity.

The essays in this volume both add to and expand from these theoretical positions. Each essay addresses the question of how disparate Americans have come together to negotiate shared meaning. Some of the essays detail the ways in which shared meaning is circumscribed by hegemonic forces, drawing attention to the limitations of public culture; others explore the negotiations of civic engagement and the construction of collective memories, highlighting the possibilities of public culture. Together, all of the essays implicitly and explicitly build and expand on Arendt's notion that "being seen and being heard by others derive their significance from the fact that everybody sees and hears from a different position. This is the meaning of public life."[18]

This volume is not meant to be a comprehensive overview of public culture as it has evolved in the United States. While the essays touch on a number of key issues related to the larger theme of public culture—the evolution of public action, public memory and commemoration, corporate sponsorship and mass-mediated public discourse, the market place and privatized public space, and the construction of public identity—many key topics and issues have been left out. There is no essay that overtly addresses political engagement, nor is there anything about public work. The volume also does not provide a formalized definition of public culture. Rather, it uses the concept of public culture to open up discussion and new possibilities for thinking about American studies and its responsibility to help understand, foster, and sustain a diverse and democratic culture in the United States. Finally, the volume does not seek to retheorize the idea of the public, but it does seek to examine and draw attention to the ways in which diverse groups and individuals have come together to discuss, debate, negotiate, create, claim, and control shared public meaning and discourse. I use the phrase "public culture" because I believe it best reflects this process as just that, an ongoing process, rather than an end in and of itself, or a tangible entity, or a concrete, identifiable thing.

The essays that follow shed light on the complicated and conflicted process of negotiating new forms of belonging in a diverse society. Divided into five sections—public culture, public action, public image, public space, and public identity—the volume provides a series of scholarly snapshots that highlight public culture as a process, taking very different stances on issues of agency, hegemony, democracy, and identity.

In "What Is Public Culture? Agency and Contested Meaning in American Culture," Mary Kupiec Cayton surveys the various theories of the public, situating the concept of public culture in the larger framework of cultural theory. This essay provides a broad theoretical overview of the concept of public culture.

Part I, "Public Action," examines how Americans have come together in public, looking specifically at civic engagement, collective memory, and public sentiment. In particular, the essays draw attention to the ways in which diverse individuals have acted in public in an attempt to achieve some common understanding. They reveal how social divisions and power differentials get played out in conflicting public actions and contested public meanings. Mary Ryan focuses on the Los Angeles Plaza to explore how the public has come together in collective action from the eighteenth century to the present. Edward Linenthal examines three sites of public commemoration in Oklahoma—the Washita Battlefield National Historic Site, the Alfred P. Murrah Federal Building in Oklahoma City, and Tulsa, Oklahoma, the site of the Tulsa Race Riot of 1921. John Bodnar traces shifting public sentiment about World War II and how the memory of the war has been used to unify the American public.

Part II, "Public Image," examines the way in which the public has been imagined in the context of a modern, media driven, consumer culture. Specifically, the essays consider how mass marketing and mass media have recast the public as consumers, as audience, as spectators, and as voyeurs. In doing so, they raise questions about cultural agency and public engagement in a society that increasingly revolves around entertainment, advertising, consumption, spectacle, and image. Susan Strasser focuses on early medicine shows and the marketing of patent medicine to explore the history of commercial sponsorship and the construction of a buying public. Lynn Spigel analyzes the television response to 9/11 in order to assess the role of television in defining citizenship. And Wendy Chun examines the issue of cyberporn, exploring the ways in which the Internet has publicized private life.

Part III, "Public Space," focuses on the tensions between public space and the marketplace, exploring the public view, the social space of shopping, and privatized public space. The essays included here explore the ways in which mobility, commercialization, incorporation, and privatization have redefined traditional notions of place and how individuals shape, claim, and understand public spaces. Catherine Gudis focuses on the development of the public road during early twentieth century, detailing the battle over outdoor advertising and control of the roadside landscape. Sharon Zukin explores the shifting social spaces of shopping and the role they play in shaping public identity. Hal Rothman examines the privatization of public space in Las Vegas.

Part IV, "Public Identity," considers the social, cultural, and political production of public identities. Specifically, the essays examine issues of transnational identity, the intersections of race, entrepreneurship, and civic agency, and the construction of civic identity. They reveal how public identities are constantly negotiated and renegotiated in a diverse and conflicted culture. Suzanne Smith traces the history of African American undertakers, highlighting their role as professional, social, and political entrepreneurs. Rachel Buff applies the idea of denizenship to examine the public position of Latino immigrants in Toledo, Ohio. Mary Frederickson examines the role of museums as public institutions that sought to define and promote specific visions of civic identity in Cincinnati, Ohio.

Finally, in the epilogue Sheila Croucher considers these essays in the context of the larger debate about civic engagement in the United States and the possibilities for civic revitalization in an increasingly globalized culture. Her analysis points to the larger issues at stake in considering public culture: issues of democracy, diversity, identity, community, citizenship, and belonging in "a postmodern, possibly postnational, world."

Although these essays range over a broad array of disparate topics, together I hope they bring the concept of public culture to the forefront of American studies scholarship.

What Is Public Culture? Agency and Contested Meaning in American Culture—An Introduction

Mary Kupiec Cayton

Culture is the name for what people are interested in, their thoughts, their models, the books they read and the speeches they hear, their table-talk, gossip, controversies, historical sense and scientific training, the values they appreciate, the quality of life they admire. All communities have a culture. It is the climate of their civilization.

—*Walter Lippmann,* A Preface to Politics *(1913)*

The public is one thing, Jack, and the people another.

—*Spoken by the poet Lemsford to Jack Chase in Herman Melville,* White-Jacket *(1850)*

All culture is in some sense public. Who of us would dispute it? As human beings, the meanings we attribute to our individual experiences emerge only through the use of shared codes, some verbal and some nonverbal. Culture is about the patterns of meanings we use to organize human behavior. As such, it always has a public—that is to say, a shared and suprapersonal—dimension. Meaning is never the product of individual experience considered in isolation from other human experience. What we know and experience can only be known and experienced through the prism of what we share with others, and the something that is shared is always based on shared codes and languages.

All culture, then, is by definition public.

In addition, "public" is perhaps the term most commonly used, at least in the Western Enlightenment tradition, to talk about what some general "we"—often defined in national terms—have in common in the realm of cultural interaction made visible through discursive articulation. The United States in particular, from its embodiment as a nation during the late Enlightenment, was born as a *res publica*, a thing of the people, a realm of human activity where the good of the whole could hypothetically be paramount. Derived from the Latin *populus*, the notion "republic" marked the discursive site where duly constituted deliberative bodies ("citizens") deliberated rationally to produce a metadiscursive realm apart from everyday life—one where the variety of private concerns that comprise everyday life were defined, regulated, and protected, for the good of the whole (or alternatively, for the "commonweal"). Simultaneously both a place or space as well as an abstractly constituted group of people, "the public" represented both process and product—the place where a common good transcending the particular and private was discussed, ratified, and promoted, as well as the result of those deliberations.

It is to the nature of this *public* deliberation and the culture it produces—or purportedly fails to produce these days in the United States (as some significant contributors to the conversation about the vitality of the *res publica* would have it)—that I turn in this essay. The propositions that this *public* is in crisis, that this crisis in *public culture* has significant ramifications for the welfare of *citizens*, and that significant interventions into this culture are necessary to preserve or restore its health are widespread. The most visible such case in recent years has been made by Harvard political scientist Robert Putnam, whose discussion of the decline of social capital and the civic enterprise has found a receptive audience not only among scholars, but also among national leaders such as Bill Clinton, George W. Bush, and Tony Blair.[1] Efforts such as Putnam's emphasize the importance of civic engagement as a way of overcoming the fragmentation of values and identity associated with postmodern America—that is to say, with a perceived disintegration of *public culture*. Putnam's civic engagement model and those like it address the importance of civic intervention in maintaining liberal democracy as it has flourished in the United States.

They leave out, however, questions about how inequalities of cultural power get created, established, sustained, contested, and transformed—and the effect of those inequalities of power on a public realm designed to promulgate and promote the common good. Or put another way, such liberal political models of citizenship feature a totalizing rhetoric that makes citizenship a category that transcends other identity categories and which subsumes them. Such "official" conversations, which privilege citizenship as a transcendent category of value, obscure the degree to which national conversations utilize an open-ended set of meanings or processes, which, far from being agreed upon and uncontested, are negotiated, disputed, accommodated, and modified over time. Whatever ongoing national conversations exist now take place in many forms and forums, and most are not solely or even mainly defined by citizenship. Nor do these conversations necessarily share common cultural meanings, assumptions, or values anymore, if ever they did share them.

In a world where cultural identity proves far more complex than any simple reference to national identity or citizenship can capture, we fragmented selves mark meaning through no single, constant, shared inventory of assumptions. We use many languages and codes to identify ourselves and delineate the contours of experience in our multiple cultural communities and contexts. I am an academic, for example, but also a wife and a mother; straight (at least performatively, at least at present) and not gay, transsexual, or bisexual; a third-generation American of European descent, not an immigrant or a member of a (recognized) racial minority; a woman, not a man; an adult, not a child; progressive politically, not conservative, libertarian, or anarchist. I watch reality television, shop online, download iTunes, attend the Episcopal church most Sundays, read the *New York Times*, and live in a small, Midwestern college town. My telling you about myself really is a statement about some of the different subcultures to which I am cognizant of belonging at this moment in my life. (Several of them may overlap, although certainly not in their entirety). In my lifeworld, I experience myself in ways that lead me to use language and tropes generated by and associated with specific groups such as these in order to live my life. I define much of my identity with reference to them. My citizenship does not suspend the many ways I identify myself in order to allow me to speak from some abstract identity position called "citizen." To the contrary, I am the variety of my lifeworlds—and they may differ enormously from those of others who also claim the right to inhabit the category of "citizen."

Though we may not share common funds of lived experience and the tropes they generate, what we do share is a historically determined lexicon for speaking as citizens of the United States. That lexicon includes such concepts as freedom, equality, and justice. It suggests that these qualities must inhere in any *public sphere* where a common American identity is defined and (re)interpreted. It does not demand that agreement exists on the origins and nature of any crisis of the *res publica*, or of any public(s) that embody its deliberative processes. Neither does it require us to agree on which interventions, if any, will be most likely to restore the health of the public body, if in fact we deem it to be ailing in the first place. But our shared civic lexicon does stipulate as a sine qua non that conversations exist where issues that transcend the particular and private experiences of individuals, however these identify themselves, are admitted for consideration and deliberation. How that happens—along with understandings of how it can or should happen, and why it is not happening today as much as many of us would like—depends on the assumptions we bring to the table about what "public culture" is, what it does, and what might be its possibilities in a globalized, mass-mediated age.

Where Public Culture Happens: Competing Models

"Public," however the notion gets deployed, nearly always signifies those places where cultural meanings are made and negotiated. "Public culture" most often signifies the pattern of signs, symbols, languages, and codes through which such meanings are negotiated. However, where the publics that count are located—along with questions of who might legitimately participate in them, in what ways, and what sorts of things they do that count as public actions—all of these are historically contingent and contested questions. The problem of defining public culture in a culturally useful way depends on identifying (1) the sites where contestations for meaning take place, and (2) what forms those contestations may take.

The Liberal Democratic Public

The most commonsense meaning for "the public," at least in contemporary American culture, calls to mind government or quasi-governmental structures and organizations, and their various activities (for example, the state of Ohio and its official political structure, representatives, and agencies). Publicly sponsored institutions such as schools, parks, and museums may also be associated with this area of human activity. The nation-state remains the representative par excellence of public deliberation and action, but significant nongovernmental organizations (NGOs) such as the United Nations or the Red Cross, equally are meant to act to further the general welfare and might qualify as well. The descendant of the Greek *polis*, contemporary public institutions of this variety exist to serve the "public good," however that may be defined. The "public culture" associated with this public is most nearly synonymous with political culture, a term that (as social historian Robert I. Rotberg puts it) "describes how a society and a collection of leaders and citizens chooses, and has long chosen, to approach national political decisions."[2] Though Rotberg specifies political culture as inherently national, it seems to me that institutionalized political activity at both local and international levels might qualify just as easily. Or alternatively, such a culture might be viewed as synonymous with civic culture: that culture which emphasizes the nature and values of citizenship and the practice of it.[3]

This arena of public culture has been perhaps best described by the political philosopher Hannah Arendt, who uses the Greek *polis* as the model for the site where citizens actively come together to exercise agency through speech and communicative action. "According to Greek thought," she writes, "the human capacity for political organization is not only different from but stands in direct opposition to that natural association whose center is the home (*oikia*) and the family. The rise of the city-state meant that man received 'besides his private life a sort of second life, his *bios politikos*. Now every citizen belongs to two orders of existence; and there is a sharp distinction in his life between what is his own (*idion*) and what is communal (*koinon*).'"[4] Such a concept of "public" implies its opposite, as Arendt indicates: that is, the private. The private realm as invoked here is the arena associated with the household, where the biological processes necessary for human existence are sustained and carried on. The "public," in contrast, is the arena of communicative action where collective judgment leads to informed action that transcends private need and desire—for example, collective provisions for health and welfare, not individual ones; regulation that allows an economy as a whole to flourish, not measures that benefit a few at the expense of the many. To speak of "public culture" in this sense is to contrast it with something it is not—culture that principally confines itself to and concerns a more partial, private realm.

Although Arendt is fairly clear about what she means by the private sphere, her definition by no means is the only one, or even the one most Americans have commonly used in thinking of divisions between public and private.[5] The philosophy of classical liberalism strongly influenced the thinking of Americans about their political culture throughout much of the nineteenth century, and it is still the model of choice that many Americans apply, consciously or unconsciously, when we think about what the opposition between public and private means. Only the state and institutions closely associated with it, realms of political deliberation and decision-making, are public; outside it, operating according to rules and codes of various sorts, lies the variegated territory known as the private. The public best orients itself to the common good through insuring that the realm of the private—that which is off limits to the state and no one's business but one's own—is protected from encroachment and interference. Or, as the Enlightenment philosopher John Locke put it, "[M]en, when they enter into society, give up the equality, liberty, and executive power they had in the state of nature, into the hands of the society, to be so far disposed of by the legislative, as the good of the society shall require; yet it being only with an intention in every one the better to preserve himself, his liberty and property."[6]

In Aristotelian thought, the private was the realm of the personal, the passional, the particular, and the necessary, as opposed to that of the political, the rational, the universal, and the freely and deliberatively chosen.[7] Aristotle saw the public as superior to the private, in that it represented freedom and rational choice. Classical liberalism, as articulated by political philosophers such as Locke and John Stuart Mill, turns the hierarchy of values on its head: important initiatives come from the private, and it is privileged as the arena of choice and freedom. The public, in contrast, exists to protect the rights of individuals and groups to operate free of unnecessary interference with regard to issues of family and property.

In classical liberal thought, the political or civic public stands in sharp contrast to a number of other realms normally seen as private. The domestic realm, of which the family is the primary functional unit in the private sphere, is the one Arendt identifies as the site of biological reproduction and sustenance. Economic activity and enterprises external to the household, which are necessary to their survival, are located as an outgrowth of them, as are the groups that in liberal democratic society represent interests and values of significance to the public but which arise from private concerns and efforts.

In other words, a classical liberal view of "public culture" would see it as the system of behaviors, codes, and languages associated with state-related deliberative action and the meanings generated there. Agency in this model involves citizens: active participants (1) who understand the political culture of the state, (2) who are prepared to make their influence felt there through rational action, and (3) who utilize the mechanisms through which such decision-making occurs to effect change. Such a view of liberal democracy implies an educational agenda that prepares free citizens (those possessing freedom and agency) to participate using the political apparatus at hand. According to this model, effective forms of civic participation in contemporary society might include such activities as "get out the vote" and voter registration drives, as well as forums that educate voters on the positions of candidates.

Classical liberalism assumes a cohort of informed citizens who are relatively equal in the power they have to make their voices heard in deliberative processes and to influence decision-making processes. It assumes as well that issues and problems of public concern can effectively be sorted out from those that should remain within the purview of the private citizen. Perhaps most important, classical liberalism envisions a world where systematic differences of cultural power do not exist.

Hegemonic Culture, Mass Culture, and Public Culture

The Marxian tradition, in contrast, contemplates a world where differences in cultural power do exist. These differences, not rational discourse, become the primary arbiters of decision-making and the drivers of social and cultural change. Marxian thought provides two models in particular that have influenced scholarly thinking about the shape culture assumes: Antonio Gramsci's model of cultural hegemony, and the Frankfurt School's model of the production of mass culture by the culture industry.

Gramsci's model, most famously used in historical work by scholars such as E. P. Thompson and Eugene Genovese, describes culture's role in legitimizing the power of those who own the means of production.[8] Classical Marxist theory saw a direct relation between the rule of those in control of the means of production and the ideology that provided the codes and language through which ideas were communicated and experiences conceived. That is, those in charge of the means of the production controlled the *Weltanschauung* as well as the material resources of a culture. The supposed common coin of the realm, "common sense," was anything but. Rather, it was a legitimation of the way of framing the world of those in power. By skewing conversations in a way that made life in the existing order seem good, right, true, natural, and inevitable, it distorted and misrepresented the life experiences of all but those with a vested interest in maintaining the status quo.

The laboring classes, dispossessed not only of their share of the wealth but also of means to challenge the legitimacy of those in power, could only come to constitute themselves as a separate group through the realization that the ideology of the bourgeoisie was specious as a purported representation of all experience. Gramsci's model modified the economic determinism of classical Marxist theory, elaborating on the ways dominant orders secure legitimacy through cultural means as well as by force. According to Gramsci, cultural hegemony—that is, the legitimization of power of the ruling classes through intellectual and moral leadership—rests not (only) on physical coercion but on social consensus, or at least on the appearance of it. Through the exercise of cultural hegemony, a ruling class both establishes its authority and makes its worldview seem commonsensical and indisputable. This hegemony was legitimized and perpetuated by the variety of cultural institutions within a society—schools, churches, arts organizations, media outlets, and the like. The revolution in social condition that Gramsci sought could only be accomplished by first building counterhegemonic cultural groups and dialogue. These could articulate alternatives to the "common sense" of the ruling elites. Such a movement, Gramsci believed, would be led by a self-conscious cadre of intellectuals, who would be able to articulate alternatives to the hegemonic cultural understandings provided by those in control. Intellectuals coming to consciousness from among the revolutionary classes would develop ways of talking about and explaining experience that would allow the disadvantaged (in Gramsci's articulation, rural laborers and workers) to escape the burden of false consciousness.

The differences between classical liberalism and Gramscian Marxism with respect to what does count—or should count—as public culture are immediately apparent. The difference is no longer between what is public and what is private; it is rather between the ways of seeing that power legitimates and those ways of seeing which stand as challenges to power. In this model, virtually *all* aspects of lived human experience become open to public scrutiny and discussion, since even the most personal parts of life are seen through the lens of a dominant ideology that supports the dominant capitalist order. Or, as the feminist critique in the 1960s and 1970s would put it, to this way of thinking, "the personal is political." *All* parts of culture are problematized as objects for scrutiny and discussion, since all contribute to maintaining or challenging the ruling capitalist order. In order to effect significant change in the realm of public power, the counterhegemonic class will need to challenge business as usual in every part of life. Those seeking serious cultural change are challenged to help to define an ideology and praxis for the counterhegemonic class to set it in sharp opposition to hegemonic culture. Significant culture change from this frame of reference means defining oneself in opposition to the commonplace understandings of capitalist culture, not accommodating them. There is no public, there is no private—only the spaces in life where power operates, and those where the operation of power is resisted.

Several decades after Gramsci—and without apparent influence from his work—the Frankfurt School, a Marxian group of critical theorists, also focused on the power of capitalist producers to define the terms of culture. Their focus, however, was explicitly on mass-mediated culture. Theodor Adorno and his collaborator, Max Horkheimer, produced a vision of a common culture where citizens, rather than engaging in genuine deliberative action designed to solve common problems, instead merely chose between prepackaged alternatives that represented virtually no choice at all. Their most significant work, a sober examination of mass culture first published in 1947, was entitled *Dialektik der Aufklärung* (*Dialectic of Enlightenment*). In it, Adorno and Horkheimer describe the modern system of standardized production, whose aim is to transform citizens into consumers, which they call "the culture industry." Everything in the world of mass culture, including ideas, becomes commodity. Adorno and Horkheimer argue that the mass culture generated by the culture industry has the power to insure capitalist hegemony, for those who hold economic power are ones with the power to establish the common language and tropes that form the basis of culture in common. Moreover, this culture industry undermines the power of critical thinking in society. By replicating the same product over and over with minor variants, it thereby deceives potential consumers into thinking they are making choices when their choices are in reality very narrow indeed.

Mass media, the focus of much of Adorno and Horkheimer's analysis, provide only the most important example of the ways in which the machine of capitalist production standardizes not only products but culture itself. In response to sociologists who see modern life as being characterized by cultural chaos and fragmentation, Adorno and Horkheimer argue that, to the contrary, "culture now impresses the same stamp on everything. Films, radio and magazines make up a system which is uniform as a whole and in every part." Cultural producers churn out standardized products differentiated in only slight ways in order to satisfy different consumer niches. Neither reason nor the common good drive action, only profit. Ominously, Adorno and Horkheimer see the logic of consumerism extending to the political arena as well—in classical liberalism, the place where the individual rights are presumably protected and the common good honored: "The ruthless unity in the culture industry is evidence of what will happen in politics. Marked differentiations such as those of A and B films, or of stories in magazines in different price ranges, depend not so much on subject matter as on classifying, organizing, and labeling consumers." In the end, citizen-consumers choose among prestructured alternatives that in fact offer very little choice. "How formalized the procedure is can be seen when the mechanically differentiated products prove to be all alike in the end," they write. "That the difference between the Chrysler range and General Motors products is basically illusory strikes every child with a keen interest in varieties."[9] So too with politics. A system that ideally exists to solve citizen problems is replaced by one designed to maintain the status quo as the only possible alternative, with the choices offered citizen-consumers running a narrow gamut from A to B, but prepackaged to look as through they provide a wide range of alternatives.

From the perspective of Adorno and Horkheimer, the liberal distinction between public and private spheres is specious. Power inheres in those entities, corporate more than individual, that wield economic power and that have the ability to establish both common agendas and the languages and tropes through which they will be addressed. "Public culture" in essence becomes the patterns of meaning established by mass culture and its corollary, consumerism. Though independent spheres seem to exist, they are finally reducible in their most significant attributes to the patterns of meaning and ideation provided by the culture industry. Even state power begins to be overshadowed by that of the mass market, they imply, anticipating contemporary commentary on the shifts in power that accompany globalization.

Finally, Adorno and Horkheimer's model provides very little room for self-conscious agency within the public sphere. Hegemony (although they do not call it that) is established through the action of a market that has its own dynamic and that finally becomes systemically totalizing. A naive activism might assume that consumer boycotts and economic actions might cause the operation of the market to change ever so slightly. In the end, however, the totalizing system of commercial mass culture is self-adjusting and self-sustaining, absorbing and co-opting both vernacular culture and what Gramsci might see as counterhegemonic culture. It can take a protest genre such as rap, for example, and convert it to an engine of profit in almost the blink of an eye, or it can make a political contest not much more than an advertising duel. By the end of his life, Adorno could offer no advice to the "actionist" at all. The critical intellectual alone opposed the tendency of mass society to eradicate rational thought. "[T]he uncompromisingly critical thinker, who neither signs over his consciousness nor lets himself be terrorized into action, is in truth the one who does not give in," Adorno wrote. "Thinking is not the intellectual reproduction of what already exists anyway. As long as it doesn't break off, thinking has a secure hold on possibility."[10]

Habermas, the Bourgeois Public Sphere, Civil Society, and Communicative Action

It was the pessimism of the Frankfurt School's vision of culture that impelled Jürgen Habermas, a student of Adorno's at the Institute for Social Research, to formulate his models of the bourgeois public sphere and communicative action. Although Habermas has been one of the most important and productive of contemporary philosophers and social theorists for over four decades, the heart of his work—at least as far as this examination of public culture is concerned—lies in two major works: *Strukturwandel der Öffentlichkeit*, originally published in 1962 and translated into English as *The Structural Transformation of the Public Sphere* in 1988; and *Theorie des Kommunikativen Handelns*, originally published in 1981 and translated into English as *The Theory of Communicative Action* (1984, 1985).[11] Habermas moved to a post-Marxist model and away from a material determinism that viewed the means of production as socially totalizing. His work emphasizes the possibility for rational human action despite the presence of systems that limit human choice and freedom in pronounced ways.[12] Capitalism has spawned systems of organization and ideology that have "colonized" the lifeworld (reality as experienced and lived by persons), he posits. Yet through a process he calls "communicative action," it is possible to affect and to alter the operation of the system to more closely reflect the realities of lived experience.

In *The Structural Transformation of the Public Sphere*, Habermas describes the development of a critical public during the eighteenth century in much of the West.[13] Its role was to provide a space for rational criticism of the state from a place outside it. This bourgeois public first arose from a literary public, as print provided a vehicle for strangers to engage in rational-critical discussion. The initial ground rules of this literary sphere of discussion privileged the pursuit of truth (which Habermas elsewhere defines as intersubjective understanding) in the form of common agreement on claims. Out of this literary public sphere grew a political public sphere—educated, informed, and propertied—that provided steering for government and correctives to its actions. Its critiques and direct political action were geared toward supplying or withholding legitimation of state authority. Through this public sphere, civil society (that is, the world of the private, including the family, the household, the economy, and institutions arising therefrom) most effectually expressed itself and made its force felt by the state. As such, it functioned as a kind of halfway house between state and society. Habermas's model of society resembles in many ways that of classical liberalism, but with a significant difference: Habermas interposes an intermediate, quasi-public realm between public and private. It is in this public sphere that individuals and groups articulate the reality of their lifeworld to the state, a critique to which the state must accommodate or respond if it is to retain its legitimacy.

Habermas parts ways with liberalism significantly, however, when he describes what happens to the structure of the public with the development of capitalism in the nineteenth century. By the late nineteenth century, he sees the developing social order almost entirely eroding the separation between public (the state) and private (civil society). The state begins to intervene more forcefully in the economy. Society at large assumes more responsibility for educating the young. Work moves outside the home. Moreover, the capitalist economy evolves into a machine for mass reproduction of products and ideas, and its purposive action begins to permeate other areas of social functioning. As the private sphere vacates (or loses) many of its former functions (for example, education, work, social welfare), what is left to it is leisure, and its discourse becomes dominated by that of mass consumer culture. In other words, Habermas's model in some measure is an attempt to provide a developmental foregrounding for the Frankfurt School's critique of mass culture. Modern culture as it has developed under the auspices of capitalism has bankrupted the individual (when taken in isolation, at least) of a good measure of his (or her) rational, deliberative power, as individuals experience life through the lenses supplied by mass culture.

But not entirely. In contrast to Adorno and Horkheimer, Habermas retains enough of the liberal model in his analysis to locate a space for communicative rationality within it. Rationality, as Habermas redefines it, becomes a particular kind of discursive process, not a property of individual being. Where Enlightenment thinkers had seen human beings as rational animals, Habermas sees people as capable of participating in rational processes in liberal democracies in which the state and the media are sufficiently restrained. In order to understand how this may be the case, imagine capitalist society (as does Habermas) as not a single social totality dominated by a single mode of production, but rather as a conjunction of relatively autonomous spheres that, while ineluctably shaped by capitalism, also develop their own characteristic organizations. Habermas believes such organizations to be indispensable in the kinds of complex, fragmented cultures that capitalism produces. Unless we have shorthand ways of communicating the most basic features of the system, individual decision-making would become unmanageable, as every aspect of life would need to be rethought over and over. "Survival imperatives require a functional integration of the lifeworld," he writes.[14] Rather than continually inventing ways to respond to the lifeworld, the system fixes ways of thinking and behaving through investing them with money, power, influence, or value. Ways of thinking and behaving are conditioned by monetization, bureaucratization, and politicization.[15] Or in Habermas's language, the lifeworld becomes "colonized" by systems that constrict thinking and fragment consciousness. "Fragmental consciousness" replaces "false consciousness" as the chief form of cultural distortion.[16] Social worlds are constructed by systems of nondiscursive instrumental rationality. Lifeworlds become structured so that domination masquerades as something natural, and human needs are translated into systemic needs.

Nevertheless, such a system (according to Habermas) cannot completely obscure the reality of the lifeworld nor annihilate an innate impulse toward rational communication. Humans are fundamentally communicative animals, Habermas believes, and this impulse entails—at least some portion of the time, under certain conditions—a desire to achieve mutual understanding and agreement free of distortion, manipulation, or oppression. Not all communication is rational. Some is strategic; some is instrumental. Neither of these is what Habermas means by communicative rationality. Rather, rational communication as Habermas defines it is unconstrained, interpersonal, and related to something in the lifeworld of the participants in the conversation. Claims are evaluated on the basis of a validity drawn from lifeworld experience rather than from norms based on influence, status, or power. Communicative rationality hinges on open discussion and debate. Hence, rationality comes to reside in the process for reaching intersubjective agreement rather than in the consciousness of the subject.

The process of communicative rationality, for Habermas, defines the public sphere in its modern incarnation. One of its principal embodiments includes civil society—that is, "those more or less spontaneously emergent associations, organizations, and movements that, attuned to how societal problems resonate in private life spheres, distill and transmit such reactions in amplified form to the public sphere."[17] Here is where issues and problems related to the lifeworld, *not* to the instrumental rationalities of the systems that colonize it, are articulated, focused, discussed, and raised. These can serve as challenges to respond to various components of the system. Habermas is under no illusions that such communicative rational action always, or even often, bears fruit in terms of systemic change. But in periods of crisis and mobilization, such vehicles for discursive rationalization can force components of the system to change in order to maintain systemic legitimacy.

Habermas's model provides a way of viewing public culture in multifaceted ways: it can be seen as the culture of the state and state bureaucracies; the cultures of status, value, and prestige that are established by reified systems of evaluation created by the economic sphere; or as the discursive culture of communicative rationality emanating from the lifeworld. In liberal democracy, which Habermas continues to support as the form of social organization offering the greatest opportunity for freedom, it is only public culture in the last incarnation that provides opportunity for agency and cultural transformation. Like Gramsci, Habermas means to emphasize the role of rational discourse in providing challenges to pathologies imposed on the lifeworld by systemic demands. Unlike Gramsci, however, he does not see such rational communicative discourse as the prelude to distinct class formation or revolution. Because Habermas sees some form of systemic rationality as inevitable in any complex society, in his view it cannot be abolished: it can only be recognized and reconfigured.

Postmodern Public: Discursive Publics, Counterpublics, Identity Publics, and the "Intimate Public Sphere"

As in the world as seen by Habermas, postmodern discursive theory also theorizes a landscape populated by fragmented subjects. But in the postmodern discursive environment, there is only a proliferation of discourses and publics, no "master public" (such as the one Habermas theorizes) to enable communication that allows escape from the domination of the various discursive strains that comprise systems of meaning. To the extent that the subject becomes an effect rather than a cause of discourse, agency exists only to the extent that subjects so constituted are able to critically deconstruct (some) of the discursive strains that enable thought and communication. But finally there is no escape from the power of discourse to shape and determine what it is possible for us to conceive. We can come to formulate critiques. We can delegitimize and destabilize. But postmodernism's major strategy for otherwise acting efficaciously in the world is by way of cultural and aesthetic politics.[18] To visually (or virtually) depict "public" in any meaningful way in this model would require animated shapes that slip and slide into each other on the page as they do in the world of Harry Potter. Because everything of which we can conceive is discursive, it is all also public, and any division of it into relatively autonomous discursive publics is finally an arbitrary and temporally bound move. Moreover, in contrast to the liberal model, any distinction between public and private is also arbitrary, determined only by the ways in which existing discursive systems configure power at any given moment in time and location in discursive space.[19]

The cultural critic Michael Warner has been one of the most systematic and insightful of recent scholars to think about the notion of the "public" in light of discursive models of culture.[20] "The idea of a public is a cultural form, a kind of practical fiction," he reminds us, and "present in the modern world in a way that is very different from any analogues in other or earlier societies." For Warner, it makes sense to speak of "publics" in the plural, "potentially infinite in number." We live in the world with countless strangers, he explains, and our principal way of relating to them is "as transient participants in common publics." Publics "[enable] a reflexivity in the circulation of texts among strangers who become, by virtue of their reflexively circulating discourse, a social entity." In other words, a public for Warner is something of a chicken-and-egg phenomenon. A public comes to exist by virtue of its having certain cultural texts circulated among people, who, through the common texts, come to have experience in common. At the same time, however, such a public is not something fixed and stable. Rather, the way that public will be defined—or how it will come to define itself—always involves contestation. Or as Warner puts it,

> [W]hen people address publics, they engage in struggles—at varying levels of salience to consciousness, from calculated tactic to mute cognitive noise—over the conditions that bring them together as a public. The making of the public is the metapragmatic work taken up by every text in every reading. What kind of public is this? How is it being addressed? These questions and their answers are not always explicit—and cannot possibly be fully explicit, ever—but they have fateful consequences for the kind of social world to which we belong and for the kinds of actions and subjects that are possible in it.[21]

Warner has been influenced by Habermas's notion of the public sphere and interprets it as not a sphere in reality, but rather as an ideal, an interpretive fiction. "The ideal unity of the public sphere," Warner believes, "is best understood as an imaginary convergence point that is the backdrop of critical discourse in each of these [different] contexts and publics—an implied but abstract point that is often referred to as 'the public' or 'public opinion' and by virtue of that fact endowed with legitimacy and the ability to dissolve power."[22]

Warner (following feminist political philosopher Nancy Fraser), modifies Habermas's analysis, however, recognizing the existence of certain "counterpublics" that function in self-conscious tension with the larger public.[23] Such counterpublics are not exactly the same as subcultures. Generating a critical discourse that articulates and embodies new horizons of interchange, such counterpublics allow for the possibility of the emergence of new publics with new discursive styles and codes: "Dominant publics are by definition those that can take their discourse pragmatics and their lifeworlds for granted, misrecognizing the indefinite scope of their expansive address as universality or normalcy. Counterpublics are spaces of circulation in which it is hoped that the poesis of scene making will be transformative, not replicative merely."[24] Counterpublics may form around a variety of foci. If they develop agency in relation to the state, they can be said to be political movements. They may coalesce around texts, codes, styles, or behaviors centered on issues of race, gender, ethnicity, religion, sexuality, or any of dozens of other categories. These become identity publics. Nothing in one's essence or social location determines membership in such an identity public. Rather, it is one's participation in publics defined by identity-inflected discourse that does so.[25]

Conversation about difference and identity in public discourse has produced some of the most interesting critiques of Habermas, as well as adaptations and uses of his model. Feminist philosophers in particular have found Habermas's model both helpful and problematic in addressing issues of difference within culture. Habermas's public sphere has never been a neutral, equally accessible space. Rather (as Fraser has very persuasively argued), the bourgeois public sphere has traditionally been defined in a masculine way that has privileged the propertied as well as those possessing a particular cultural ethos.[26] However, as Mary P. Ryan has shown in her historical work on women and the public sphere in the nineteenth century, "The proliferation of publics—convened around concrete, localized, and sometimes 'special' interests— . . . opened up new political possibilities for women."[27] Her counternarrative to Habermas's story of the decline of the public sphere shows how that sphere has been democratized over time with the multiplication of publics. New discursive spaces opened. Over time these came to challenge the dominant (and limited) discourse. It is precisely because the public sphere is itself so fragmented, inhabited by so many different publics, that it allows space for diverse individuals and groups to recognize themselves in its discourses. Such a broadening represents—far from a degeneration of the public sphere—an enlargement of the space for critical debate within capitalism. Where Habermas seems to see the public sphere of liberal democracy as a space with a level playing field, others like the postcolonial theorist Madan Sarup increasingly see this space as one occupied by multiple publics with multiple agendas. "There is an increase, a proliferation of identities," he writes, "and this implies that there is a plurality of democratic struggles. People have begun to channel their politics by working in groups based on ethnicity, 'race,' gender, religion and nation."[28]

Not only does this pluralist public sphere allow the concerns of those who had been excluded from the bourgeois public sphere a voice. It also is the means by which those counterpublics become constituted. "[P]oliticized identity emerges and obtains its unifying coherence through the politicization of *exclusion* from an ostensible universal, as a protest against exclusion, a protest premised on the fiction of an inclusive/universal community," as the feminist theorist Wendy Brown puts it.[29] Identity is discursively constituted, according to this model, and subaltern counterpublics become present to each other, as members of a particular group with particular identity attributes, insofar as they are either actual or vicarious participants in such public discursive communities. Thus, those whose concerns are not visible in dominant (Gramsci's "hegemonic") discourse—for example, "women, workers, peoples of color, and gays and lesbians"—develop self-conscious social identity through participation in a public, which itself continually debates the texts, codes, and behaviors that constitute it.[30] This modified and pluralist public sphere becomes the space used by coalescent identity publics to articulate problems of identity and difference.

Yet the power of such discourses of identity go beyond the simply collective articulation of issues so that they may (eventually) make their way into some more general and enlarged ("mainstream") public sphere. As Warner and the feminist philosopher Iris Marion Young both argue, one of the problems with the concept of communicative reason as Habermas has articulated it is that discursive communities take shape not only around discursive dimensions, but around aesthetic and affective ones as well.[31] That is to say, as part of their tension with the wider public, counterpublics develop styles of expression, modes of address, and speech genres designed to distinguish them from that "mainstream" public. "The discourse that constitutes [such a counterpublic]," Warner writes, "is not merely a different or alternative idiom but one that in other contexts would be regarded with hostility or with a sense of indecorousness."[32] Such discursive communities, while located in what Habermas would call the public sphere, are not rational only. Rather, they also communicate via a host of symbols and styles that may render such a discursive public, at least in some contexts, a subculture as well. In such instances, rational communicative action becomes only a part of what such a discursively formed identity community is all about. Discourse generates a public, which in turn generates a distinctive subculture. Such a subculture may orient itself toward political action, or it may not. But finally it is always political in character, in the sense that it comes into being on the basis of perception of exclusion from general discourse and location of participants in a contrastive relation to that mainstream discourse.

The cultural critic and queer theorist Lauren Berlant takes this notion of publicness based on lifestyle a step further when she argues that, since the Reagan Revolution, even much of the dominant discourse defining American citizenship has been worked out in an arena she calls the "intimate public sphere."[33] Berlant's critique turns inside out earlier logics that suggested that public discourse flows from concerns experienced and articulated in separate lifeworlds to a common and more abstract sphere of discussion. Instead, she argues, in cultural milieus where the vast majority of persons experience themselves as ineluctably alienated from the corporate decision-making apparatuses that arbitrate official discourse, the notion of a common public sphere demarcated by rational discussion has collapsed. In its place has arisen an official public sphere based on sentimental conceptions of what private life for individuals is and should be. (Think of a discourse arena where the lives of Brad Pitt and Angelina Jolie, for example, become emblems of what the good and the decent may, or may not, be.) Issues of common concern and discussion now frequently are of the sort that in a different time would have belonged to the sphere formerly known as private—for example, abortion and other reproductive issues, definitions of marriage, and the like. The common denominator of this new "intimate public sphere," as described by Berlant, is its grounding in normative versions of private life, which get defined in the dominant discourse as universally good and moral. Once constructed, these definitions are deployed to delineate the parameters of "true" (authorized, empowered, legitimated) citizenship. In this version of the world, according to Berlant, the prerogatives of citizenship are seen as belonging to people whose intimate lives fit certain criteria of orthodoxy. The role of public discourse in this age of sentimental citizenship, she argues, is to celebrate and promote dominant definitions of family, sexuality, and reproduction. What was formerly private and outside the arena of public discussion now provides the very definition of legitimated citizenship.

In many ways, Berlant's reading of what public culture has become is similar—and indebted to—the work not only of the Frankfurt School and of Michel Foucault, but to queer theorists (Warner included). Berlant's "intimate public sphere" is set in a particular moment of time, the "afterglow" (as it were) of the Reagan Revolution, and is Habermas's private sphere turned on its head. Constructed out of Adorno et al.'s mass-mediated forms of culture produced by "the culture industry," this new public discourse takes the "intimate" aspects of people's lives—their sexuality in particular—and makes them the stuff of public discussion, creating thereby the new norms that form the litmus test for citizenship. In this world, "public culture" no longer works to protect a "private sphere" that occupies a place apart; instead, it works to regulate that private sphere and to insure that "normal" and "public" become synonymous.

Whence comes this inversion? Berlant seems to suggest a number of sources. First, she indicts a group whose right to define cultural norms had been unquestioned in serious ways up until the 1960s—that is to say, the white, (largely) male, heterosexual block who formed the backbone of the Reagan backlash. Their presumed right to enjoy a normative intimate sphere (according to their own definition of it) had been violated by groups of (gendered, racialized, sexually dissident) Others who had entered a public sphere formerly closed to them. These latter brought to the table defenses of their own right to conduct business in the intimate sphere in ways they thought appropriate. But their doing so, according to this Reaganized narrative of America, blurred the gap between "public" and "intimate" in dangerous ways, threatening the ability of "normal" citizens to live lives in "normal" (that is, reproduction-centered) ways. Berlant's counternarrative argues that this group of Reaganized citizens clashed with gendered, race-conscious, and dissident sexual groups, who had begun to crystallize identity positions in opposition to "normative" assumptions regarding life in the intimate sphere. Prior norms of citizenship based on orthodoxy in the "intimate public sphere" were in fact arbitrary creations of the heretofore dominant groups and artifacts of power rather than anything natural. As differing cultural assumptions took concrete form in heated debates over such issues as the rights of fetuses and the prerogatives of queer culture, the "public sphere" and the "intimate sphere" began to converge into an "intimate public sphere" where orthodox norms of private behavior, not rational debate over the common good, defined responsible citizenship. What had allowed the "intimate sphere" to remain separate from the "public sphere" prior to this point was an unquestioning acceptance in the "public sphere" of assumptions about what was normative in the "intimate sphere" and what was not. When these assumptions came into question in the "public sphere," one response of cultural conservatives was to move to make intimate concerns the major, defining substance of public sphere discussion—thereby leaving off the table a host of other political, economic, and social concerns that were consigned to the offices of the market to arbitrate.

The common denominator in these public culture models that speaks to the presence of plural discursive publics, then, is a concern with the ways in which publics (including identity-oriented publics and "intimate publics") form, and how they align themselves discursively with respect to the dominant culture. To the extent that such publics spawn well-elaborated subcultures that become associated with them, we might extend the parameters of liberal and Marxian public culture analysis to include examination of the ways in which communication across discursive boundaries and subcultures takes place, as well systemic changes that may result from such communication. If we see these new "publics" as arenas where lifestyle issues become the focus of cultural critique, such a perspective would suggest that we need to attend not only to the cultural and aesthetic issues within these arenas as legitimate parts of public culture analysis, but also to questions these "lifestyle publics" raise about the sorts of issues that get displaced from general discussion as beyond the grasp, reach, or interest of ordinary citizens.

Toward a Generative Model for Investigating Public Culture

What we mean when we say "public," then, differs depending on the implicit epistemological and political model on which we are drawing when we invoke the concept. In virtually every model, "public" refers to issues, problems, or topics that are discussable in nonpersonal terms, and not only within the particular lifeworlds of individual subjects involved in them. But is what is public necessarily "state-defined"? Is it essentially constituted by rational discourse? Or may discourse that is (in Habermas's schema) primarily instrumental rather than rational—for example, advertising—also qualify? Ought we to think of "public" as synonymous with the "official" or the culturally hegemonic, or is it possible also to recognize as public groups that resist a dominant cultural ethos? In what ways might placing "public" in binary opposition to "private" obscure the ways in which meaning(s) get made in mass-mediated cultures, where distinctions between the personal and the corporate often blur? Our answers to these questions imply more than an exercise in definition. For within each of the models described are embedded implicit messages about possibilities for effectual action. Each implies a question about the possibility of action: What viable forms of political and cultural intervention exist in a world where systemic forces play a huge role in determining social, political, economic, and cultural outcomes? These assumptions make a huge difference in the way we conceive ourselves as change agents (or potential change agents) with respect to culture; and how we conceive ourselves in public terms.

The question of agency is perennially a perplexing and meaningful one for us as students of culture. Specifically, how are public cultures constituted and reconstituted in liberal democratic settings? As I see it, various kinds of possible "publics" are grouped together without specifying a fixed hierarchy of influence.

The two spheres, which Gramsci might have called hegemonic, are associated with the state and "official" organizations and with socially legitimated professional cultures and mass commercial cultures. That is to say, they are conceived as embodiments of public culture, possessing the power to dominate discourse. In consequence, they represent the most widely disseminated versions of public cultures. Although Adorno and Horkheimer's model sees the two overlapping substantially, and although Habermas follows suit by exploring the ways in which the state public increasingly reflects the influence of commercially developed modes of discourse not primarily rational in character, the two spheres still seem to me different enough from one another to be distinguishable conceptually. The state, as well as state-sponsored institutions and agencies, have their own relatively autonomous discursive spheres, and these resist complete domination by the world of mass culture, consumerism, and professional authority. Likewise, transnational corporate interests today have power on occasion to override the influence of state policy in shaping global cultural trends, but these corporate bodies are not synonymous with the state, however much they may influence its workings. Likewise, professionally sanctioned cultures enjoy a relatively autonomous existence, though affected by both state and commercial interests. In other words, I do not see capitalist society as monolithic and immune to conflict, even among the spheres that I am conceptualizing as hegemonic. Although, as Marxian theory claims, dominant economic interests exert disproportionate influence in all spheres, that influence is not totalizing. Or, as Nancy Fraser has theorized in her post-Marxian approach to culture,

Certainly, we should reject the untenable view that collective social identities are somehow secreted by the structural positions of social actors. Instead, we should assume that identities are culturally *constructed*. By this I mean that they arise from relatively autonomous, contingent cultural processes that escape structural determination. Thus, where Marxism posited convergence between structural position and group mobilization and affiliation, we should assume instead the relative autonomy of identities from structure and the relative contingency of processes by which affiliations are formed and groups mobilized.[34]

Two additional spheres focus on areas where social identities are constructed around nonprofessional characteristics that distinguish the discursive publics thus constructed from a public "at large." One of these spheres is associated with identity- and movement-oriented cultures, discursive publics that take shape according to particular characteristics. They may be identity-defined, for example, groups defined discursively by race, gender, ethnicity, sexual orientation, or, in liberal democracies where church and state are separate, by religious affiliation. In addition, social movements such as Greenpeace or Mothers Against Drunk Driving, groups that organize strangers to achieve specific, project-oriented results, would also occupy this sphere. Part Alexis de Tocqueville's world of "voluntary organizations," part Habermas's "public sphere," part Fraser's "subaltern counterpublics," this group of publics might be distinguished by their public purpose but private standing (as defined in traditional liberal democratic terms).

In the other sphere, which I envision as that of "potential publics," discursive cultures coalesce mainly around commonalities in local lifeworlds. They are the coffee klatch that meets once a week in the local coffee shop and whose members develop rituals and customs of their own, as well as a shared past. They are the condo association, or the corps of regular volunteers at the town food pantry. They are swim team parents and online chat room buddies. They are the singles who gather every Friday night at a downtown watering hole. In other words, they are groups, often ad hoc but sometimes not, who develop languages and codes for relating to one another through lifestyle considerations and common concerns. Though they never exist in complete autonomy from other spheres of public influence, they are mainly local cultures. And though they do not exist in order to have an impact on any of the other spheres, they may mobilize members on occasion to attempt to do so—for example, to lend support to an organized effort elsewhere, or to participate in the articulation of a common problem that may "go public." They can be, in other words, seedbeds for translating mainly local lifeworld concerns into something more than that. Berlant's "intimate public sphere" arises from this sphere and is distinguished by its blurring the boundaries between identity-oriented cultures and lifeworld cultures. Lifestyle concerns are translated into movement concerns, with these in turn mobilized in efforts to intervene in both.

It might be asked, and with some justice, whether such particularistic and evanescent cultures are in any sense really publics, given their existence largely in what liberal theory would call the private sector. One response might be that to the extent that all cultures involve some public component—that is, a sharing of codes and languages that enable communication—they could be conceived of as public. However, if we use Michael Warner's definition of "public," that which "enables a reflexivity in the circulation of texts among strangers who become, by virtue of their reflexively circulating discourse, a social entity," such cultures, no matter their shared languages and customs, are *not* exactly public.[35] That is why I choose to think of them instead as *potential* publics—groups sharing enough by way of cultural commonality in the lifeworlds they inhabit to have the potential to become publics if something catalyzes them into doing so. To move into a public realm as I am defining it (following Warner), such a group would need to translate its particularist discourse into modes that would make it available to strangers. For in the end, a public culture distinguishes itself from a potential public by its potential permeability to strangers not part of regular face-to-face interaction.

As an example of how these different types of public spheres might relate to one another, let us take the example of sexual orientation.[36] One may engage in same-sex intimate relationships without defining oneself as gay, as the historian George Chauncey (among others) has shown us.[37] It is entirely possible for a number of individuals to engage in particular kinds of sexual behavior without adopting any particular sense of themselves as part of their identity definition. However, at a particular historical moment when certain kinds of intimate behavior become discursively marked as characteristic of individual identity, a group may be singled out (or single itself out) as sharing a common identity on the basis of those behaviors. Further, such a group, if marginalized by dominant cultural discourse, may come to form a counterpublic based on a discursively constructed and oppositional common identity. Private behaviors that do not generate a discursive field around them remain private; identity, in contrast, requires discursive articulation. In other words, to engage in intimate activity with a member of one's own sex (or even to share expectations about same-sex activity with a group of local others) becomes public only when a public discourse surrounding it develops. Perhaps the most salient example of such a process is that associated with the social construction of "race" in Western culture. A category having no basis in biology, the discursive construction of the identity category has had consequences that have been among the most culturally far-reaching in Western history.

Such discourses, though initiated in response to discourses of power, do not necessarily remain forever subjugated. To form a counterpublic is to oppose the dominant cultural understanding, through a discourse that is often rational, cultural, and aesthetic at the same time. Once such a counterpublic is discursively articulated, it may affect not only behaviors in the lifeworld; it may also intervene in new ways in the dominant realms of the state and of mass culture. All one has to do in order to see such influence (to return to the example of sexual orientation) is to look at current controversies surrounding gay marriage, an issue that could not have been articulated before the existence of a gay public, or to look at the degree to which commercial mass culture has both incorporated representations of gay subjects (for example, *Will and Grace, Queer Eye for the Straight Guy*) and marketed to a gay niche (for example, sexually ambiguous Calvin Klein advertisements). To note the presence of such issues and representations is not to claim that the balance of power has changed in significant ways nor that counterpublics have been embraced in significant ways into dominant cultural forms. Rather, it is to observe that such counterpublics may force dominant modes of discourse to change, and to a greater or lesser degree, to accommodate challenges.

What approach(es) to public culture can prove most useful to us as students of American (and transnational) culture at the beginning of the twenty-first century? I propose that one response to the complex of issues raised for us by the notions "public" and "public culture" involve the exploration of interactions between and among the different types of publics inhabiting the different types of public spheres described above. These interactions produce cultural transformation of various sorts—resistance, articulation of new problems, accommodation, political and cultural realignment, and the like. They involve changes in the way "we" live (with the definition of "we" depending on the discursive situation at issue and the particular "public" invoked) and the kinds of choices it is possible for "us" to make. This model presumes the existence of multiple publics defined by the processes through which they make discursive meaning. The state realm is that of system-driven political processes. The realm of professional and mass culture produces public meanings that are as much aesthetic and cultural as rational; their value is most often determined by monetary return or prestige, not necessarily by efficacy in solving lifeworld problems. Political critique of the two dominant realms occurs in the sphere of movement- and identity-driven public culture, and it is there that new problems arising from various disparate lifeworlds most often get articulated. Finally, in the sphere of potential publics, local groups generate cultures and discourses that have the potential to move into discursive articulation involving larger movement- or identity-oriented publics or to effect changes in the world of state institutions, mass commerce, and culture. For it is the interaction among the publics of various spheres—fragmented, multiple, and contested in nature—that provides the impetus for larger social and cultural transformation. That is not to say that each of these spheres possesses equal power to effect change, only that it is worth considering the possibility that there is more permeability among the spheres than any one of the models of "publicness," when taken in isolation, might imply.

In a world of almost unimaginable complexity, neither the simplistic world of classical liberalism nor the hopelessly fragmented world of post-modernism will do. We are no more the products of mass media alone than we are individuals able to act freely in an arena of untrammeled rational discourse. In different areas of our lives, we participate in publics differently constituted and constantly contested. We contain within ourselves the tensions, conflicts, and complexities of each of the public cultures in which we participate—as well as those tensions that are implicit between the various cultural publics of which we are a part

The study of public culture as envisioned here, then, involves investigation of the process by which public meanings (in each of the public discursive spheres) are defined, debated, adopted, accommodated, contested, opposed, and transformed. Though it is informed by models, it is not model-driven. Its purpose is finally a humanistic one: to investigate avenues for human agency in a world where culture both makes us human and is made by us. For when all is said and done, what matters for us—people who inhabit flesh-and-blood worlds and not just abstractly theorized spheres—is not just to explain these various worlds we inhabit. We need to know when and how to intervene, when necessary, to change them.

PART I

Public Action

Chapter 1

Looking for the Public in Time and Space: The Case of the Los Angeles Plaza from the Eighteenth Century to the Present

Mary P. Ryan

On July 1, 2005, a jubilant procession marched through downtown Los Angeles to celebrate the inauguration of Antonio Villaraigosa, the first person of Mexican descent to be elected mayor in over a century. The parade route went from City Hall to the Catholic Cathedral of Our Lady of the Angels, where an interfaith service, representing Christians, Muslims, Jews, Buddhists, Sikhs, and Hindus, had just been conducted. Fortuitously, this event seemed to proffer a positive answer to the questions raised by the conference on public culture, which met at Miami University in Oxford, Ohio, the spring of 2003. "Is there an inherent and unbridgeable tension between cultural diversity and civic community?" The new mayor exhorted a gathering of a few thousand citizens to "dare to dream together. Let's dare to work together."[1] The hopeful words spoken on this occasion are too evanescent to sustain an argument about the variety and vitality of American public culture. I look not to the words heard on this occasion but to the place where they were spoken in order to fulfill my assignment in this volume: to ascertain the "historical roots of this conflict between cultural diversity and public community." It is on the public spaces of downtown Los Angeles that I have attempted to plot out the relationship between cultural differences and the public realm. The space that most interests me as a historian is the old plaza found just across the freeway from Mayor Villaraigosa's line of march to City Hall. A few acres laid out more than two hundred years ago on Spanish principles of town planning serve as my laboratory, a specific space in which to put public culture to an extreme test. Can the space between City Hall and the Plaza be bridged? Do the political and ethical values we invest in the term "public culture" have any meaning, any chance of survival, in such a seemingly hostile environment as Los Angeles, reputedly the epitome of sprawl, solipsism, and the facile commonality manufactured by Hollywood.

By pursuing a method that is empirical, historical, and spatial I hope to steer clear of the theoretical impasse and conceptual confusions that plague the literature on public culture. By focusing on a narrow space and looking through the long lens of time, I will foreground the political and ethical stakes that make the concept of public culture so important to us. The debate around various permutations of the term "public" that began in earnest among American scholars more than twenty years ago has not abated: it has not been resolved and cannot be put aside. On the one hand, proponents of Jürgen Habermas's philosophy of the public sphere persist in a quest to find some universal, rational, or at least procedural, foundation that will under-gird the public good. Critics speaking from positions of subaltern status or sexual differences, on the other hand, tenaciously resist the pull toward a unitary public that would suppress both the aesthetic and the social diversity of contemporary culture. The persistence of this debate testifies to the irreducible tension at the heart of the concept of the public. Most parties to the debate gravitate between two equally valuable political goals, to find, on the one hand, some way of bringing together all the fractious people and conflicting interests of our small planet, and, on the other, to give full expression and strong voice to every possible cultural and social difference. It is in the space between these poles that the substantive civic action that concerns me takes place, the pursuit of justice and the practice of democracy.[2]

This combination of political urgency and intellectual stalemate that surrounds the question of public culture warrants a pragmatic research strategy and a look beyond both Habermas and his postmodernist critics to the writings of the premier American pragmatist John Dewey. The closest Dewey ever came to a definition of "the public" was "the objective fact that human acts have consequences upon others." According to Dewey, the boundless terrain of shared consequences could only be given concrete meaning in specific times and places. The consummate public intellectual, Dewey looked to very specific social institutions through which to shore up the democratic public process, especially voluntary associations and the protection of free speech and association. Dewey grounded the public in commonsense notions of the social, the historical, and the spatial. Late in his life he confessed, "I am inclined to believe that the heart and final guarantee of democracy is in free gathering of neighbors on the street corner to discus back and forth what is read in uncensored news of the day." Taking a cue from Dewey, I will search out public culture not just on the street corners, but also in a space dedicated to civic assembly, the Plaza of Los Angeles. My investigation touches on all four themes on our program: action, image, space, and identity. I have carried my pragmatic methodology a step further by privileging photographic rather than literary evidence in my search for public culture. Tracking public culture over time in this one small space will reveal a succession of very different historical manifestations of the public, characteristic first of imperial Spain, next a hybrid Mexican-American town of the mid-nineteenth century, and finally the modern California city.[3]

The Mexican-Spanish Plaza

The pueblo of Los Angeles was founded in 1781 on a model of centered publicness first codified by the Spanish Crown in the sixteenth century. According to the Law of the Indies, colonial settlement was to be anchored in a public plaza, whose minimum and maximum dimensions, alignment with the cardinal points of the compass, and essential buildings were all prescribed. In 1779 Felipe de Neve, the governor of Alta California, translated these colonial directives into a plan for a pueblo to be situated along the trail from the San Gabriel Mission to the Pacific Coast near an Indian village named Yangna.[4] While they claimed title to the whole Los Angeles basin, the emissaries of the Spanish Crown corralled the first settlers into a narrow spatial radius. Although the land grant extended two leagues on each side, or over ten miles, individual plots could be claimed only after taking up residence around a plaza measuring 200 by 300 feet. Three years after their arrival in Los Angeles the first families received formal title to the farmland that surrounded their adobe huts in the pueblo's center. The colonial governor journeyed south from the presidio at Santa Barbara and summoned the first Angelenos to the Plaza, where each head of household stepped forward, signed a promise to pay taxes, and in one public gesture was granted citizenship and the means of a livelihood. Even then the Spanish reserved much of the landscape for public purposes, for pasturage, common fields, and communal functions, public buildings as well as the central open space of the Plaza itself. The interdependence necessary to sustain a population in Southern California was anchored in the Plaza (Figure 1.1). The centerpiece of the Plaza was the main reservoir of the Zangra Madre, which channeled water throughout the pueblo lands. The city of Los Angeles took deep root in a central public space.[5] Indeed the polity of Spanish Los Angeles was public by definition; it only came into being when the inhabitants came together in one

Figure 1.1. The Los Angeles Plaza, circa 1865. From Godfrey's Sunbeam Gallery, Huntington Photographic Collections. Reproduced by permission of the Huntington Library, San Marino, California.

space. Those who gathered in the Plaza in 1784 signed their pledges of mutual support with a crude cross. Unable to communicate in writing, the inhabitants of Los Angeles wove whatever common identity they shared from ritualized actions in the public space of the Plaza. The social life of the pueblo centered in the Plaza, where each landowner was required to establish a home, attend church, and practice the social obligations of a civilized community. Perhaps the predominant expression of commonality was religious, but it extended far beyond the pueblo's small chapel, which has been in continuous use since 1822. On the feast of Corpus Christi the families who resided along the Plaza erected altars draped in fine fabrics and costly jewels in front of their homes. Children dressed in white, accompanied by men costumed as the apostles and carrying great burning candles, paraded through the Plaza and the surrounding enclave of adobe residences, sometimes taking two hours to complete their circuit. The same streets were witness to another elaborate procession on Christmas and a promenade to church each Sunday. The Los Angeles community was knit together by more secular performances as well. Ranchers tarried at the center of the pueblo for a good portion of the year, occupied with marketing produce and playing at bullfights, cockfights, and horse races, all mounted on the Plaza. Political life centered in the same space, so thoroughly public that it sometimes occluded the private. The deputies of the Spanish Crown and the local leaders governed from their homes on the Plaza. After Mexican independence, Governor Pío Pico administered the republic of Alta California from his adobe on the Plaza while local politics operated out of the home of the alcalde Ygnacio del Valle just across the way.[6]

This bucolic portrait of early Los Angeles appears altogether too quaint to be relevant to the complex contemporary questions before us. With a population that never exceeded three thousand souls, the pueblo of Los Angeles seems too intimate, and its population too homogeneous, to justify the term "public culture." Yet several aspects of social life in Los Angeles early in the nineteenth century qualify it as a useful case in point and counterpoint. First is the fact that Los Angeles was never a "natural" community where every resident shared common ancestry and values. The majority of the population did hold one characteristic in common, but it is an unusual index of homogeneity: among those first eleven families there was not one purely Caucasian domestic unit. If not Indians they were of mixed races, at least one of whose parents was either Mexican, mestizo, mulatto, or African.[7] But second, and more important, the differences that came together in the common, emphatically public space did not share equally in the privileges of the commonweal. While they might be exonerated from the charges of ethnic and racial intolerance per se, the ruling classes of early Los Angeles were downright oppressive on other scores. Although men of Indian or African blood, like Governor Pío Pico, may have risen to positions of leadership among founding families, most native Californians or Mexicans were not so fortunate. Indigent men and women found loitering around the Plaza could be forced into labor on the ranchos. Indeed half of the population occupied this servile, slavelike status, designated in the census by the term "domesticated Indians."[8] Early Los Angeles, like the Europe that spawned it in the eighteenth century, was not built on free labor, but on the work of serfs, servants and that other "domesticated population," women. Indians were prey to "young men [who] ride on horseback through the Indian villages, soliciting women for immoral acts," while elite wives were under a genteel house arrest, denied access to the Plaza unless chaperoned by kinsmen or on their way to and from church.[9] For the most unfortunate and unprotected women, the Plaza could be a place of public shaming. Such was the fate of two women accused of "slanderous behavior." They were sentenced to stand outside the church door, exposing their shaved heads to the passersby.[10]

The point is obvious: a public culture, even a relatively diverse one, is not necessarily just and inclusive. It may be built on hidden exclusions, like those of gender that are buried beneath the public sphere and dismissed as private matters. In fact publicness and public space can be very effective instruments of subordination. The Los Angeles Plaza as ordained by the Law of the Indies was a mechanism of imperial rule. Indeed the plaza as a town plan traces it origins from imperial Roman bastides, spaces designed for the observation and control of conquered populations. The Roman Catholic Church colluded with the Spanish Crown in staging its cultural hegemony in the plaza, from the extreme of the autodafé conducted in Madrid's Plaza Mayor during the Inquisition and extending to the New World as a summons of Indians and peasants to the church of La Reina de Los Angeles. Habermas called these totalitarian possibilities lurking in public space "the representative public sphere" where the power of the monarchy imposed its will on the masses.

Mexican American Spaces: The Plaza Meets Main Street

Whatever its virtues or liabilities, the old public regime was not to endure for very long. Bourbon reforms had tempered the absolutism of Spain beginning in the eighteenth century and in 1812 Mexico won its independence and ushered liberalism into Alta California. Then in 1846 the Plaza was the setting for a transfer of national sovereignty from Mexico to the United States. It was a rather civil public exchange. The Mexican loyalists assembled in the Plaza under Pío Pico and marched off to put up a desultory resistance to the U.S. Army, which finally raised the American flag on the hill above the Plaza on July 4, 1847. The conquering general, Robert Stockton, marched down into the Plaza and seized the adobe residence of the Avila family as his headquarters. Meanwhile Pío Pico agreed to the terms of surrender: he would journey to the Los Angeles Plaza for a ceremonial dismissal of his troops and enjoin them to return to their homes to "live as peaceful, good and hardworking citizens." By another account local resistance to the Americans was silenced by a rousing rendition of "The Star Spangled Banner" that brought the local population back to the Plaza for a reprise of their customary public festivity.[11]

Over a period of nearly forty years, under the flag of Mexico and then the United States, Los Angeles would reach a zenith of diversity. Mexican Californians traced their origins to different nations as well as races. Only 50 percent of those who gathered around the Plaza at midcentury were Mexicans by birth, the rest were either conquered native Californians or émigrés from the United States or Europe, including significant represen-

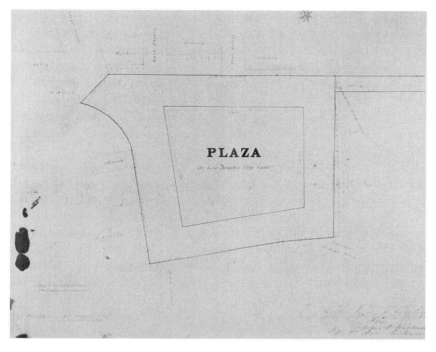

Figure 1.2. Plat map of the Los Angeles Plaza. From Solano-Reeve Collection, map 418, Photographic Collections, 74.485. Reproduced by permission of the Huntington Library, San Marino, California.

tations of Frenchmen and Jews. Neither the Spanish government nor the Mexican one that succeeded it in 1820 imposed significant restrictions on these diverse "foreign" populations. For more than a decade after the American conquest life in the old pueblo would go on much as usual. The first generation of American sovereigns adapted readily to the Californios' modus vivendi. The Plaza, "long the nucleus of the original settlement, was the center of life in the little community," wrote Harris Newmark, who arrived from Prussia in 1848. John McGroaty who hailed from Massachusetts recalled that "Life in old Los Angeles centered around the Plaza. . . . The old Plaza was the center of everything, social, religious and commercial."[12] The American conquest did not trample on Mexican public space. Quite the contrary, it embellished it. The Plaza was resurfaced, fenced, and landscaped in 1859 while surveyors were busily straightening and extending the surrounding streets (Figure 1.2). The pioneer American generation also paid respect to the cultural diversity of Los Angeles. Natives of the United States remained a minority well after they had claimed political sovereignty: at the midpoint of the nineteenth century the population was divided about equally between the Spanish-speaking Californios, United States citizens, and European immigrants. A visitor from abroad observed as late as 1876 that "despite the cosmopolitan nature of the inhabitants—on the streets are heard spoken English, French, Spanish, German, and Italian—the community spirit predominates, being strengthened by a mutual interest in the city's Advancement."[13]

A city booster of the same era, John McGroaty, waxed ebullient over the racial composition of his adopted city: "The Los Angeles of today is a city composed of people in whose veins course the blood of all the races of earth. The blood of the four great races was in their veins—red men, blackmen, yellowmen and whitemen. Can the most exacting cosmopolite ask for more?" McGroaty was perhaps a bit eccentric in his enthusiasm for racial diversity but he was a good demographer. What he lauded as cosmopolitanism was a simple transcription of the social profile of the Mexican-American town. McGroaty listed the founding families of Los Angeles one by one, appending vital statistics such as "wife mulatress," "wife Indian," or "chino," one of the many different appellations of the Spanish *casta* that was incorrectly translated as Chinese.[14] The demography of the Plaza district still conformed to this cosmopolitan standard in 1850 when only three households were said to be composed solely of Caucasians. The prominent men whose homes fronted on the Plaza represented multiple nationalities and had a decided proclivity to marry into Californio families. The major storekeepers, Abel Stearns and Juan Temple, both had spouses of Mexican descent.[15]

Juan Temple is a good representative of L.A.'s bicultural public at the midpoint of the nineteenth century. An immigrant into Alta California from the United States, Temple took a Mexican wife and acquired a Spanish Christian name. When his name was affixed to a major street in downtown Los Angeles it was not an honorific epitaph but an accurate label of Temple's place on the cultural landscape. He built the first general store, constructed in adobe on the south side of the Plaza, and then a larger multiuse brick building, which the locals called the Temple Block (Figure 1.3). An imposing structure located just off the Plaza, the Temple Block housed a city hall, a theater, and a multistalled marketplace. A rare action photograph corroborates the written testimony of contemporary observers.[16] The crowd gathered not at the commodious Plaza but at a commercial block, the tight compacted

Figure 1.3. The Temple Block. From Carleton Watkins Collection, Huntington Photographic Collections, 74.491. Reproduced by permission of the Huntington Library, San Marino, California.

space most convenient to the intersection of business and politics. The center of civic culture was moving south and transforming the cultural landscape as it went. The shift was obvious from the architecture around the Plaza: On the north in a district now known as Sonoratown, low dwellings were hidden behind adobe walls; brick and balloon-frame structures on the south were plastered with signs of Yankee enterprise. The street that jutted off to the east of the Plaza was also lined with storefronts whose mix of adobe and wood facades evoked the classic western town and supported the associated activities—saloons, gambling dens, and brothels. The Mexicans had named this quarter Calle de los Negros, a reference to the shady activities that transpired there as much as the skin color of the habitués of the place. In the 1860s the label of this slender segment of the Plaza bespoke the American language of race: it was named Nigger Alley.

Until well into the 1870s, nonetheless, many colors and cultures shared the Plaza and imbibed a common ethic, the zealous pursuit of commercial profit. The Temple Block, the more elegant Victorian structures being erected just to the south, and even the nefarious business of Calle de los Negros were all dedicated to commerce. Business thrived on bicultural marriage practices. Yankees and Europeans seeking their fortune married the daughters of Californios, who just happened to enjoy more liberal inheritance rights and land titles. One spot near the Plaza offers multilayered testimony to this practice. A busy trading post stood just a few doors south of the Plaza at midcentury, known to posterity as the Stearns Adobe. Abel Stearns married into the prominent Bandini family in 1841 and prospered near the Plaza. By the 1870s, the adobe that bore Stearn's name had been demolished, replaced by an ornate Victorian commercial structure, and renamed the Baker Block. But the Mexican roots of commercial expansion were just beneath the surface of the Plaza: Upon the death of Abel Stearns, his widow Arcadia Bandini Stearns remarried and took the name Mrs. Baker.

Crafty Anglo businessmen were not the only ones who staked their fortunes on bicultural commerce. On the north side of the Plaza Eloisa Martinez de Sepulveda converted her inheritance into a fashionable boardinghouse in hopes of prospering along with American business. While her enterprise, located to the north of the Plaza failed, the stately hotel on the south remained the fashionable address for decades to come. The Pico House was executed in the most modern style and stocked with the finest Victorian furnishings, reputedly worth $35,000. It was the enterprise of the former Mexican governor who returned to the Plaza soon after surrendering to the American army in order to invest his future in the commercial growth around the Plaza. Not far away another longtime resident was making a modest fortune of her own. A former slave named Bridget "Biddy" Mason won her freedom, practiced midwifery, and purchased several properties just off the Plaza near Broadway and Spring Street. The zest for commercial gain welled up from familiar multicultural sources. The Mexicans who won independence from Spain in 1820 were as devoted as their northern neighbors to the liberal principles of private property and free enterprise. With alacrity they converted their ranch lands to commercial plots and housing tracts and participated readily if haplessly in the remapping of the pueblo into private property.[17]

The citizens of the early American town of Los Angeles maintained two centering public spaces: a Spanish plaza and an American landscape form known as Main Street. In the short term at least, the fervent commercialism of Main Street did not prove to be a serpent in the garden of the multicultural public space. In the 1860s and 1870s Main Street and the Plaza joined together as interlocking sites for civic festivals. On July 4, Washington's Birthday, and the anniversary of L.A.'s birth in 1881, contingents of both Californios and Yankees wound their way around the Plaza and down Main Street. One pioneer fondly recalled of the 1860s: "In those days such a procession had done its duty when it tramped along Main Street and around the Plaza and back, by way of Spring Street as far as First." A somber procession wove through these same streets to mourn the death of Abraham Lincoln in 1865. The line of march linked together contingents labeled Hibernian, French, Teutonic, and "Junta Patriotica.[18]

The classic parades carried diversity and public spirit through the streets and into a thriving commercial city. What's more, the parade route around the Plaza was infused with the democratic political expectations that emanated from Mexico as well as the United States in the age of democratic revolutions. Mexican municipalities were administered by an *ayuntamiento* that was elected by a wide franchise including Indians and mestizos.[19] The American pioneers quickly transplanted their partisan loyalties to the Plaza and Main Street. They issued calls to public meetings in Spanish and English and plastered storefronts with political notices. Angelenos deposited their ballots at the same location where they stored their cash, at Juan Temple's store. Los Angeles politicians were not restrained in their search for votes by ethnic or racial scruples. Mexicans lined up and were permitted to vote without establishing their citizenship. Republicans charged that Democrats waylaid Indians around the Plaza, addressed them in their native language, and stole their votes. During the first decades of American sovereignty Los Angeles was not renowned for the civility of its public spaces, but both the Plaza and Main Street were wide open political forums, within the reach of a very mixed population.[20]

The middle decades of the nineteenth century had churned up a vigorous and multicultural democracy in the public spaces of Los Angeles, both on the Plaza and along Main Street. Democracy expressed itself, however, in ways that were often antithetical to public peace and harmony. One of the more notorious actions to occur in the Plaza dates from this period and exposes the underside of early American public culture. In 1836 a "vigilance committee" convened in the home of Juan Temple on the Plaza and claimed the title *junta de defenso de la securidad publica*. These vigilantes not only spoke the language of the public, they also represented a diverse citizenry: the call to action was signed with Spanish and English surnames in about equal numbers. Swearing that "the public will be avenged today," the early vigilantes justified their actions as the necessary assumption of authority during a civic emergency. But they were also propelled into action by the hidden tensions and deeper social divisions beneath their public rhetoric. The vigilance committee of 1836 rose to combat a breakdown in the sexual order, what they called "this abominable monstrosity who sacrificed her husband that she might enjoy the unmoral appetite which she craved, for Nature trembles at the sight of the venomous reptile . . . etc., etc." By one estimate as many as twenty different lynchings took place in the 1850s, some of them on the fence near Juan Temple's City Hall.[21]

The violence of Los Angeles in the middle of the nineteenth century might be dismissed as frontier excess, were it not for the fact that similar public actions were mounted in other U.S. cities at the time. American streets were stained by regular urban riots in the 1830s and 1840's, bloody election days and periodic lynchings in the 1850s and fierce race riots in the 1860s. When public spaces were thrown open to democratic politics the result was not necessarily civic order. Quite the contrary, democracy could sweep away the surface harmony of more hierarchical and deferential cultures. It would seem that as Americans began to practice democracy in public space, civic disorder increased apace. Civic engagement and cultural diversity coexisted in the public spaces of Los Angeles over a century ago. But these terms of analysis don't align in quite the way we might anticipate. Open public engagement was not always a civil affair. Public space, particularly when host to both social diversity and a democratic political culture, runs considerable risk of civil disorder.[22]

To hold public culture to exacting standards of civility may obscure, or suppress, democratic expression of differences. That vigilance committee of 1836, for example, was a genuinely bicultural group taking direct action in what according to the local consensus was the public good. This delicate balance between democracy and public consensus still held twenty years later, after Los Angeles had become U.S. rather than Mexican territory. Another vigilance committee formed in 1856 in response to a presumed threat to life and property that emanated from Sonoratown when angry residents were rumored to be plotting retribution for the shooting death of Antonio Ruiz by a deputy constable named William Jenkins. The Plaza became a vortex of public contention. A large crowd of Mexicans journeyed into the Plaza church for Ruiz's funeral and lingered to consider how to insure that his killer be called to justice. Fearing violent reprisals the Anglo sheriff placed Jenkins in the city jail, just off the Plaza. An anonymous "mob" lead by a mysterious "Frenchman" named Fernando Carieiga threatened to lay siege to the jail and lynch Jenkins. At this point the public was called to the task of keeping civic order. One thousand copies of a public announcement were distributed, five hundred in English, five hundred in Spanish. At the top of the broadside in bold black letters were the words "Junta Publica." The signatures at the bottom were in Spanish, English, and combinations of the two, like Juan Forster and Juan Downey. Elite Californios joined Anglo leaders in a public meeting, a call for order, and a walk through the streets making personal appeals for calm.[23]

The whole tense procedure for dealing with the conflict endemic to the heterogeneous populations of antebellum cities recalled standard practices in northeastern cities before the establishment of professional police forces. In this southwestern example, a kind of détente between mobilizations of conflicting ethnicities formed around the Anglo-Mexican center of public space and prevented either a lynching or a riot, though it could not extract justice: the killer of Antonio Ruiz was acquitted after fifteen minutes of deliberation by an all Anglo jury. Historians' hindsight has rightly emphasized the power of American institutions and the virulence of American racism that would eventually suppress the Mexican culture of the Plaza, but for several decades in the nineteenth century the central space of the *ciudad* of Los Angeles was a kind of urban "middle ground."[24]

An American Downtown

This détente between Mexican and Anglo differences, this precarious balance between the order and the openness of pubic space endured into the 1870s. Thereafter both Mexican culture and the Plaza would soon recede from the center of the L.A. landscape. Civic power and public pride had been inching its way south of the Plaza along Temple and Main Streets since the 1860s. The last Californio mayor was elected in 1872, the same year that the city council refused to invest in a face-lift for the Plaza. Instead the growing American majority followed the march of commerce down Main Street and plotted a new park to the south. Private citizens promptly

Figure 1.4. "Scene of the Chinese Riot." From Godfrey Stereotypic Views, Huntington Photographic Collections, 43. Reproduced by permission of the Huntington Library, San Marino, California.

pledged $800 to create a gardenlike retreat between Fifth and Sixth streets, an oasis of Victorian urban civility washed clean of evidence of a Spanish or Mexican past.[25] The Plaza was left to languish, and worse. In 1871 it became the staging ground for a full-scale riot (Figure 1.4). The streets around the Plaza were witness to scenes like this: "[A mob] dragged the trembling wretch up Temple to New High Street, where the familiar framework of the corral gates suggested use as gallows"; "Attacks and counterattacks spread like wildfire, and a mob of a thousand or more frenzied beyond control, armed with pistols, guns, knives and ropes . . . assembled in the neighborhood of the disturbance." This was not random violence. The twenty persons killed in the riot of 1871 had all been born in China. The site was Calle de los Negros (soon to be renamed Los Angeles Street), the haunt of the marginalized, mixed population of ethnic minorities and white men returning penniless from the gold fields. The incident that triggered this human carnage was another of those eruptions of suppressed private conflicts. It all began when Chinese men were seen "forcibly carrying off of one of the company's 'female' members." The balance of diversity and public civility had tilted in a direction all too familiar in American political culture: suppressed differences, especially economic inequities, erupted in racial and sexual violence.[26]

As the nineteenth century drew to a close the city became more diverse than ever, the cause of conflict remained endemic, and the spatial center, which once brought the public precariously together, no longer held. Between 1880 and 1930 public culture took a whole new shape in the modern city of Los Angeles. By 1880 the center of public gravity had shifted toward a grid of streets that bore the unmistakable marks of that distinctively American public space, the downtown. Rapid growth took off from the old center in the 1880s and by 1930 had deposited over a million new residents far out of the L.A. basin along hundreds of miles of electric railway. Up through the 1930s, nonetheless, there was no doubt that the sprawling twentieth-century metropolis maintained a robust civic identity centered downtown. The municipal art commission report of 1901 set out on the most Olympian of public projects: "The city as a unit—with those positions which in a sense are the property of all the citizens in common, with business streets, and connecting parkways and boulevards, it may command a unanimity of interest and zeal in execution which more diffuse plans would not at this time have received. And out of such study there should incidentally arise a more virile civic consciousness, a realization of the oneness of interest in the improvement of Los Angeles, a sense of cohesiveness rather than of competition between the different parts of the city in realization that what is done for any particular section—if it be done in accordance with a broad and comprehensive scheme—is done for all."[27] This civic idealism expressed itself in a spate of plans for new parks, tree-lined boulevards, a central railroad station, a city hall, a comprehensive traffic plan, and a subway system.

Downtown development was public in inspiration and in practice. Architectural blueprints and urban plans were circulated widely from the high-rise downtown offices of the *Los Angeles Times*. Major public works were vetted through a scrupulous democratic procedure, a citywide referendum.[28] Whether it was inspired by the Progressive government or the City Beautiful Movement, the physical improvement of L.A. in the early twentieth century was without doubt a public accomplishment and the progenitor of lavish public space. It stood boldly on the landscape in two contiguous spaces: the first, a commercial district of multistory offices, department stores, and parking structures, and the second, a civic arena, which featured a monument to municipal government—a skyscraper city hall. A new breed of professional architects and planners had far grander schemes for public space than this. They imagined a whole chain of plazas running from the

Figure 1.5. Aerial view of City Hall. From Christine Sterling, *Olvera Street: Its History and Restoration* (Los Angeles: Old Mission Printing Shop, 1933). Reproduced by permission of the Huntington Library, San Marino, California.

small space of the old parish district to the broad portals of Union Station, and the grandest plaza of all, "El Paseo," to be placed astride the towering new City Hall (Figure 1.5).

The stage is set for another interrogation of the relations between public space and public action. Just what went on in the modernized spaces of Los Angeles? The most extravagant public event dates from 1894 and gestured back nostalgically to an earlier time, but it was enacted on the commercial arteries that carried L.A. southward and into the twentieth century. In 1894 La Fiesta brought an estimated 75,000 people to assemble just west of Main Street at Hill and Ninth. The crowded pavement was said to accommodate the broadest public with "no respect for age, sex or previous condition of corns." The city's multicultural heritage was represented by such icons as the Fiesta Queen, draped in a lace mantilla and wide ruffled skirt, and a troop of Yuma dancers, advertised as the "genuine Indians," who would "take part in the parade." A part of the publicity campaign designed to bring tourists and new citizens to the booster city, La Fiesta was repeated again in 1898 when the Spanish-American War cast a shadow on the Hispanic romance.

Subsequently the "riotous revelry and debauchery" attendant to public celebrations doomed this civic pageant to extinction.[29] Accounts of downtown
public ceremonies grew sparser thereafter. A crowd of 10,000 did line the
streets once again in 1905, assembled to pay homage to what was called a
"monumental structure to which the city can point with pride." The edifice
so honored was Hamburger's Department Store. An even larger crowd gathered again in 1931 for the dedication of the new City Hall in El Paseo. Massed
densely at the base of the municipal skyscraper, the crowd adopted the pos-
ture familiar to modern public space. The people stood passive and anonymous. They may have been of diverse origins, but they were faceless and
unconnected to one another. Their common identity was that of spectators
in a mass of strangers, or shoppers filing past one another with their purchases and streaming on to the parking lot. The formal political space of the
monumental City Hall had similar human dimensions, a massive pile of bureaucrats, clerks, secretaries, and citizens on line. Ultimately L.A.'s administrative offices would house an estimated 20,000 public workers, served by
20,000 public parking places.[30]

   Early in the twentieth century, shopping, working, and parking had
become the primary uses of the most prominent public spaces. But still the
antiquated, old Spanish Plaza had not been bulldozed away by modernity.
As L.A. grew ever wider at its edges and higher in its center, the old public
space was not entirely forgotten. Nearly every blueprint for public works
downtown, left the antique Plaza intact.[31] When the art commission
drafted plans to beautify and revamp the whole city, it sought to "dignify
and emphasize the historic old Plaza." Architectural plans for the administrative city center drafted in 1924 maintained that "[i]t would be unthinkable to suggest any development of this territory that would interfere with
or destroy these historical monuments." When such powerful institutions
as the Southern Pacific Railroad and the *Los Angeles Times* considered
building new structures on the site of the Plaza, they were thwarted by citizens dedicated to preserving the city's public heritage.[32] Thanks to the
nearly single-handed efforts of a wily and determined urban activist named
Christine Sterling, the Plaza was refurbished, its remaining adobes preserved, and local business revitalized by the creation of the tourist attraction named Olvera Street. The Plaza also sponsored organized civic events.
A Cinco de Mayo Festival transpired there in 1917. Chinese New Year celebrations paraded around the Plaza until the 1920s when old Chinatown was
raised to make way for the City Hall.

   As high public culture and the City Beautiful Movement commandeered

Figure 1.6. Employment Office. From C. F. Saunders Collection, 106, Huntington Photographic Collections. Reproduced by permission of the Huntington Library, San Marino, California.

the public space on one side of the old Plaza, they left other places open for a more plebeian and quotidian public sociability (Figure 1.6). New immigrants—Jews and Italians, African Americans as well as Mexicans—made their homes and built their own communities in the cheap rental property to the north of the Plaza. The old buildings were reconverted to ethnic businesses and public halls bearing such names as Garibaldi, Hibernian, Maccabees, Druid, Syrian. The environs of the old Plaza also served as the platform upon which middle-class women stretched their political muscles in settlement houses, social service agencies, and Catholic and Protestant missions. One champion of the city beautiful hailed this chapter in L.A.'s history as the era of "matriotism" that would "bring together the divided units of a cosmopolitan city, including Russians, Italians, Chinese, Japanese as well as Mexicans."[33] Finally, this was the place where opposition politics could find a soapbox. Partisans of El Congresso gathered in the Plaza in the 1930s to hear fiery voices of radical syndicalism. The Plaza was the most popular and strategic place for radical organizing. When nervous lawmakers curtailed free speech in other parts of the city they kept the soapboxes open in the Plaza, even erecting concrete podiums for that purpose in the second decade of the twentieth century.[34] Although the voices had to struggle to get a hearing at City Hall and failed to stop federal deportations, they would not be stilled as long as they found open public space, a spot where they were not crowded out by commerce or overshadowed by monuments to state bureaucracy.[35]

Before departing downtown L.A. we should take note of what did not take place there in the twentieth century. Lynch mobs and massacres did not visit these public places. The marginalization of minorities and the poor and the filling up of the new center with white-collar jobs and middle-class consumption reduced the disorder and danger of the central public spaces. If the ideal public space is one that quiets social conflict then that civic goal was substantially achieved in Los Angeles early in the twentieth century. We might look back upon the skyline of downtown Los Angeles in the 1920s with appreciation of its civic accomplishments and public decorum but we should not be deceived by the quiet at the heart of the city. After two anarchists were found guilty of bombing the L.A. Times Building in 1910 and causing twenty deaths, the voice of organized labor in L.A. was repressed for a generation. The superficial good order of downtown Los Angeles testified to the concentration of economic power and the marginalization of social differences, something Henri Lefebvre might call abstract space or the colonization of everyday life.[36]

By the early twentieth century the public spaces of Los Angeles had assumed a shape that is easily recognized by contemporary cultural critics. The downtown shopping district reduced citizens to consumers; city hall turned civic responsibility over to bureaucrats; the mass and monumentality of it all concentrated power in a few corporate headquarters. The culture that circulated through these spaces during the twentieth century was often a burlesque of multicultural communication, Mexican history and heritage paraded as a Spanish fiesta or a facade on a fast-food restaurant. This may indeed be what Habermas called the refeudalization of the public sphere: public space used now to represent, not the absolute authority of the king, but the pervasive control of global capital. The best force of resistance to the power of this hegemonic public is what critics like Michael Warner call counterpublics, self-created discursive communities that link a network of strangers around common concerns and collective challenges to the dominant public. In the twentieth century the old Plaza became a spatial anchor for many such counterpublics, Asian and European as well as Mexican immigrants, women reformers and communist agitators. Even in Los Angeles, on the sprawling far side of modern metropolitan culture, there were public spaces in which diversity and dissent could concentrate. But still, some of us naively search for something more than this rapprochement between the dominant and the counterpublics, some more capacious and more central if not utopian public place, where all the differences and the common interests of the polity can face one another head on and communicate directly.

Thus to end my exploration of public culture in the Los Angeles of 1930 hardly resolves the quandary before us, even on the local level. It does not array the terms of our discussion as a simple formula for working out the public good. On one level it renders the polarized terms of our discussion somewhat beside the point. Some semblance of both diversity and public culture coexisted throughout this sketchy history of one city. Diversity is a given in almost any American city, at almost any time. Similarly, lip service to cultural pluralism is nearly a constant, even in a relatively homogeneous city like Los Angeles in 1930. Deference to a wide range of traditions served many purposes: it was a sound economic strategy for merchants like Juan Temple, good advertising copy for the Chamber of Commerce, and an avenue for political and social usefulness for educated women. Diversity per se is not necessarily corrosive of a common culture: it can, as seen in the parades and festivals of the nineteenth century, become its very substance. Neither was commerce necessarily corrosive of civic engagement. The pleasure of consumption could in fact whet the appetite for public projects from landscaping the Plaza to beautifying downtown. Public action of one variety or another is also a historical constant. Someone—some group, cabal, class, or committee of vigilance—can always be found acting in the name of the whole polity and speaking in the language of universality. It might be the Catholic priest at the Plaza church, or Harrison Gray Otis at the *Los Angeles Times*, or the ladies and gentlemen of the Municipal Arts Society.

Because public engagement and cultural diversity are locked in a tight and tense historical relationship, it behooves us to examine carefully the expectations with which we burden each term. The language of public culture, be it during the Progressive Era or today, often carries expectations for social harmony, decorum, and polite behavior. Given the competing interests and wide inequality that have persisted through most of American urban history, these expectations are at best utopian and at worst authoritarian. It might be more realistic to ask just how much inequity and injustice can and should be swept under the rug of public civility. Rather than asking for an easy rhetorical fix and expecting diversity to magically blend into a harmonious public culture, we might set about perfecting the ways to express and adjudicate the conflicting needs and rights of a diverse population. These public goals (to which, in my opinion, John Dewey is a better guide than Jürgen Habermas) are sometimes pushed to the margins of genteel public spaces like those favored by the City Beautiful Movement or imagined by architects and planners. The commonplace assumption that commerce is antithetical to civic-mindedness can also be translated into more pertinent questions. Is the public enemy the bad taste that pervades the shopping mall, like those artifacts deemed "weird and grotesque" for sale on Olvera Street or outside the Plaza church? Or is it the fact that unalloyed and unquestioned commercialism surrenders the public good to the free play of the market, with the imbalance of power that it entails?

These questions, which arise wherever public culture and social difference coexist—which is to say just about everywhere—warrant placing another term on the conference agenda: not just "space," "action," "image," and "culture" but also "politics." I have in mind governmental rather than cultural politics—that is, the practice and procedures of democratic debate and decision-making. When the population of Los Angeles was less than a few thousand persons, the public good might be determined by a consensus arrived at through face-to-face meetings in the Plaza. But even then, more than half the population (women and unenfranchised Indians) was excluded from the imaginary public while distant powers like the Spanish Crown were powerful silent partners to community. Through most of our history the public business had to be conducted by way of impersonal media of communication, colonial edicts, the press, print culture, the airways, and now cyberspace. Fortunately many contemporary scholars are skilled at interpreting this realm of public culture. More often neglected, however (confessedly in my own work as well), is that most efficient and democratic medium of public discussion ever devised, representative politics and the electoral process. In retrospect I would want to look more closely at such routine public practices as the turnout at the polling places, the debates at those city council meetings that determined to build a new park, or the referendums that made the erection of a municipal building a genuine democratic accomplishment.

The prospects and promise of democracy have been tinged with cynicism since the American misadventure in Iraq, but a look back to the antebellum period reminds us that democratic institutions can arise and function under the most difficult circumstances and diverse populations and in contentious but openly public spaces. The democratic practices developed in the nineteenth century remain the aging but indispensable bridge between cultural differences and the common good. And unfortunately they are not in good repair. The steady decline in democratic political participation coincided with a retreat

Figure 1.7. Shrine to the Virgin. Collection of the author.

from central public space. Over the course of the twentieth century downtown Los Angeles, like the old Plaza before it, receded rapidly from public consciousness. Social life and civic consciousness sped out the trolley lines and roadways, splintered into housing tracts and private lots. In the twenty-first century, however, both the old Plaza and the shabby downtown are fighting to win back the attention of citizens. Institutions of high culture, crowned by the Disney Concert Hall designed by Frank Gehry, surely a civic jewel in the city's center, are rising downtown in spaces that are not as yet particularly welcoming to those snarled in the traffic below, nor very accessible to most Angelenos. The same might be said of the new cathedral down the hill where the new mayor worshipped on his inauguration day. Its Catholic iconography and Mexican architect betokened a bicultural city but also displayed some of the same remote hauteur of Gehry's masterwork.

If one ventured across the great gulley of the freeway one can still find the old Plaza. The locals still gather there for christenings, weddings, and masses at the old church. Immigrants light candles to the Virgin beside a modest, gaily tiled shrine (Figure 1.7). Tourists join them and can watch troops of Aztec dancers and sample the wares of fruit vendors and peddlers of religious artifacts. One day each year thousands of Angelenos wind their way around the Plaza for the archbishop to bless their pets (which in L.A. range from poodles to boa constrictors). On another they celebrate the Day of the Dead. The residents of the second largest city in the United States can still gather with fellow citizens downtown and be reminded of their public ties and their civic commonality. In the Plaza, and to a lesser extent in the concert hall and cathedral, citizens can stretch their social imagination just a bit, see and touch those who appear different from them but whose fate is bound up with theirs in a common political jurisdiction. Such spaces, and the activities that enliven them, are dwindling, but not extinct, and like the Los Angeles Plaza they can serve as durable reservoirs of history, representations of diversity, and a summons to take democratic political action.

Chapter 2

Remembrance, Contestation, Excavation: The Work of Memory in Oklahoma City, the Washita Battlefield, and the Tulsa Race Riot

Edward T. Linenthal

The eminent Chinese anthropologist and sociologist Fei Xiaotong spent a year in the United States during the Second World War. He was struck by how little regard Americans had for history and tradition. "When tradition is concrete, when it is a part of life, sacred, something to be feared and loved, then it takes the form of ghosts," he said. "To be able to live in a world that has ghosts is fortunate."[1]

He recalled that after his grandmother died he could almost see her going to the kitchen to check on lunch preparations, as she did every day. Her enduring presence registered as a "ghost," but even more, changed the way he thought about time. "Our lives do not just pass through time in such a way that a moment . . . or a station in life once past is lost," he said. "Life in its creativity changes the absolute nature of time: it makes past into present—no, it melds past, present, and future into one indistinguishable, multilayered scene, a three dimensional body."

Unlike Fei Xiaotong, western historian Patricia Limerick sees an American landscape of immeasurable depth, resonating with the same palpable presence as a departed grandmother. While some of this landscape is celebrated and remembered intensely, there are other, darker stories that mark the landscape that have for too long been denied, suppressed, forgotten. For her, it is not a case of whether there are unsettling presences on the land, rather a question of who has the courage to look. Like Fei, however, she believes that the past is part of our present. Neither time nor space, she writes, "can insulate us from these disturbing histories."[2]

I too have felt the presence of the past—Fei's "three dimensional body"—at evocative sites. I will never forget my first visit to Gettysburg in 1965. It was evening when we approached the "High-Water Mark" memorial, where the famous Pickett-Pettigrew charge almost broke the Union lines. I have returned often for both personal and professional reasons to sit, to walk the field on the anniversary with my family, to study and write. I understand well the sentiments of a Gettysburg guide who years ago spoke of the "brooding omnipresence" of the site.

So I don't dismiss it as merely psychological "projection" when National Park Service employees who are Crow tribal members leave the Little Bighorn battlefield before sunset. I understand why people characterize the site of the Alfred P. Murrah Federal Building in Oklahoma City—site of a terrorist bombing in 1995 murdering 168 people—as "sacred ground," and I even forgive myself a dose of cowardice when in Poland some years ago. We visited the village of Belzec, site of a Nazi extermination center. We arrived at night, after spending a day at the Majdanek concentration camp, where the gas chamber was still changing color from the effect of the gas used to murder thousands more than sixty years ago, where a huge urn of human ash is part of the memorial, where barracks hold thousands of pairs of shoes of those murdered, a space too difficult to bear.

Belzec, however, has no ruins. It is just an open field, with a few farmhouses nearby. To reach the memorial we needed to walk through the field that had been the site of the killing center. After a few steps, however, the ground was spongy, soft, and I learned that we were walking on layers of human ash just beneath the surface. I could not continue, and returned to wait in the van. Ghosts indeed. The touch, feel, sight of the past indeed.

It has been my good fortune and an enduring challenge over the past quarter century to have had the opportunity to write about places populated by ghosts. These places are changed forever by the violent events that symbolically stain their landscape. Gettysburg will never again be a quiet farming community. Concord will never again be just a picturesque New England town. The World Trade Center site in New York will always carry the weight of the atrocity of September 11, as will the Pentagon and the small rural community of Shanksville, Pennsylvania, a constellation of sites marking a day of mass murder.

I knew in writing about the impact of the Oklahoma City bombing that I would be engaging another powerful site. What I did not yet know was that due to the kindness of Bob Blackburn, the executive director of the Oklahoma Historical Society, and Sarah Craighead, former superintendent of the Washita Battlefield National Historic Site, I would be introduced to two other places that make up part of our nation's haunted landscape. During my many visits to Oklahoma, I had the opportunity to attend two meetings of the Tulsa Race Riot Memorial Commission and speak briefly about issues of memorialization. I also visited Cheyenne, Oklahoma, to participate in the "Washita Symposium: Past, Present, and Future," in November 1998.

This essay is about these three intriguing and revealing "memory experiments" in the state of Oklahoma: the contested site of the Washita, where the razor's edge issue has been whether the conflict was a "battle" or a "massacre"—and a world of interpretive difference hinges on the choice—the excavation by dedicated folk of a site and story consigned to oblivion for too long, the Tulsa Race Riot of 1921, and the intensely and immediately memorialized site of the Oklahoma City bombing. I will think both *about* these sites—some specific issues that arise from them—and *from* these sites about larger challenges. Visitors come to these sites as pilgrims, tourists, voyeurs. They come to mourn the dead, to honor ancestors, to restore the forgotten dead to their rightful place in the national memory, to stand on historic ground and imagine themselves into the past. They come to consume these sites through the ingestion of "experience." Through acts of venerative consumption visitors continue to touch these sites through purchases of books, T-shirts, material memories of all kinds. These sites of violence are also dynamic centers of civic engagement. The processes through which these indigestible elements of America's past have become part of the national historic landscape are tumultuous. They are sites where different publics compete for symbolic ownership of the meaning of these evocative places.

The 1868 winter campaign devised by Maj. Gen. Philip A. Sheridan came amid mounting violence between whites and Native Americans on the southern plains. Treaties negotiated with representatives of various tribes were stillborn in Congress, and opposed by tribal members willing to fight. A series of late summer raids on whites put enormous pressure on Sheridan. During these raids, according to historian Paul Hutton, "110 civilians had been killed, thirteen women had been raped, over 1,000 head of stock had been stolen; farms, stage buildings, and rolling stock were destroyed; unescorted travel stopped on all major roads; troops were being engaged in numerous fights with the Indians, almost always being defeated."[3]

Sheridan wanted to separate hostile and peaceful Native Americans. Those unwilling to fight were ordered to Fort Cobb, while a winter campaign would seek out and destroy hostile groups. Since all Cheyenne were designated hostile, Cheyenne peace chief Black Kettle and his group were turned away from Fort Cobb. They camped for the winter along the banks of the

Washita but were excluded from another nearby larger camp that included members of Cheyenne warrior societies that had never agreed to peace negotiations with whites. This left Black Kettle's village vulnerable to attack.

Cheyenne peace chief and executive director of the Cheyenne Cultural Center Lawrence Hart describes the conflict at the Washita on November 27, 1868. "At dawn, with a foot of snow on the ground, the regimental band of the Seventh Cavalry played 'Garry Owen,' signaling the attack. Terror struck the Cheyenne. The initial charge through the village of fifty-one lodges resulted in indiscriminate shooting. Black Kettle and Medicine Women Later [his wife] sought escape but were shot off their horse and fell into the river. Another warrior, Little Rock, was also killed, as were eleven other men, sixteen women, nine children, two visiting Lakotas, and one Arapaho." Warriors from the nearby encampment responded, killing twenty-two troops of Major Elliott's detachment. Among those killed was the grandson of Alexander Hamilton. Hart informs us that fifty-three Cheyenne, mainly women, were captured, and a pony herd of between eight and nine hundred was destroyed.[4]

After implementation of the Dawes Act, which split reservations lands into individual allotments, "no Indian chose the Washita site," Hart writes, and "over the years, inadvertent discoveries of human remains have been made within the large area of the site, and for a period of time the remains of one victim were held at the Black Kettle Museum in the town of Cheyenne." By the 1950s the site had, fortunately, passed into private hands of people interested in preservation. By the 1970s and 1980s, Bob Blackburn writes, "people in the local community began talking about the site. Cheyenne leaders became involved with cultural preservation by trying to determine the burial sites of their people. Local archeologists . . . and Cheyenne youth . . . began looking at cultural preservation at the grassroots level." After a long and arduous process, the Washita became the first cultural site of the National Park Service in Oklahoma in October 1996.[5]

I became interested in this story for several reasons: because of the centrality of the figure of George Armstrong Custer, whose demise I wrote about in my chapter on the evolution of the Little Bighorn Battlefield in *Sacred Ground*, and because of my interest in the volatile issue of battle or massacre. So many people, Custerphiles and Custerphobes, have a vested interest in choosing the term and narrative that either strengthens their attack on Custer or their defense of him. For example, those who think of Washita as a battle consider Custer a military man following orders, launching a surprise attack as part of a military campaign; it becomes part of a larger story of the often brutal encounter between native and European cultures. Errol Flynn's Christ-like Custer in the famous film *They Died with Their Boots On* is a graphic popular expression of this conviction. For those who think of it as a massacre, Custer was an instrument of genocidal policy whose tactics reveal the atrocity-producing situations that were the inevitable by-products of a violent policy of conquest. One popular expression of this attitude is Custer as martial megalomaniac in the film *Little Big Man*.

Those who think it a battle might argue that the intent was not to kill women and children, and that the inability to discriminate in combat was a dreadful result of a particular kind of warfare. For those who think it a massacre, the distinctions about intent and discrimination are at best splitting hairs and at worst an offense against the dead, a way to excuse atrocity.

I joined University of New Mexico historian Paul Hutton and Henrietta Mann, Montana State University professor of Native American studies and a Cheyenne tribal member, on a panel at the symposium focused on just this issue of battle or massacre. I continue to think about how our conversation revealed different voices, each emerging from different worlds of memory and experience. In her remarks, Henrietta Mann made clear the location from which she spoke: "I have come back to this same site that constitutes my body as a Cheyenne person, to this very sacred ground for us as a people." "I look at this from the heart . . . from the people to whom I belong as a Cheyenne woman." For her, this was clearly a massacre. "How can a battle be fought," she asked, "against women and children, young and old alike?" Custer, she said, "was carrying out the military policy of his time in which the prevailing philosophy was total extermination."

Paul Hutton thought the term "massacre" was problematic at the Washita. He characterized the event as different from the massacre at Sand Creek, or Santa Anna's slaughter of Texans at Goliad during the Texas Revolution. Washita revealed, he said, the "sad nature of Indian warfare in the far west, government troops assaulting villages at dawn."

I took issue with Professor Mann's claim that total extermination was government policy. Genocidal episodes, yes, exterminationist rhetoric, yes, attempts at cultural genocide, yes. But, I said, "had it been the SS riding over the hill into a village of Jews, there would have been no prisoners." Professor Mann's aunt, sitting in the audience, responded, "I notice, as some of you must have, that the two gentlemen on the panel do not have any ties or feel the way the Cheyenne feel about the Washita; it should be 'the massacre' of the Cheyenne people at Washita. And I have noticed there is only one Indian on the panel with two white men. This is the way we have been put all through these years." Paul Hutton responded graciously, "I believe Dr. Mann has us outnumbered though, in every way."[6]

Thankfully, the symposium did not devolve into argument and bitter feeling, but the interesting mix of people in attendance worked hard at listening to and talking with one another. I have thought often about this exchange, about the power of felt history, and whether there are, perhaps, places or times not to challenge it out of respect for the suffering out of which that voice speaks. Or is the issue of language, particularly the use of volatile terms like "genocide," "extermination," "massacre," important enough that people need to struggle with the issues, particularly in a symposium setting? Was my voice simply "out of place," a voice speaking out of the privilege, the luxury, the emotional distance in which supposedly important distinctions become clear? I certainly did not represent any significant "stakeholder" group in the interpretive process at the Washita, I was just an invited conference participant. To one of the publics in the room my words were flat, devoid of the wisdom of oral tradition and shared suffering out of which such words would not come. Perhaps my comments would have been appropriate in the presence of other publics: in the classroom, in a book or article, or in a lecture somewhere. But in that room, near that site, during that occasion, they were words that spoke not at all to the impassioned ownership of a tragic story. They simply registered as insensitive and offensive.

In his own gentle and incisive manner, Lawrence Hart offered yet another reading of this vexing issue, suggesting that the term "massacre" is appropriate for the first attack when women and children were killed, and "battle" the appropriate term for the ensuing struggle between Custer's troops and the warriors who responded.

However, the relationship between Native Americans and the National Park Service at the Washita is not frozen in an endless debate over this emotionally charged issue. Founding site legislation declares that one goal is to "provide opportunities for American Indian groups including the Cheyenne-Arapaho tribe to be involved in the formulation of plans and educational programs." The tribe and the Park Service jointly hired a cultural liaison to increase conversation. There is also cooperation on a program called the Cheyenne Heritage Trail, the brainchild of Lawrence Hart. Former NPS superintendent Sarah Craighead describes the program: "we worked with [Hart] on this trail concept which would take visitors throughout western Oklahoma to various sites that were historically important to the tribe." Partnerships were established with "federal, state, tribal, and private" groups. The trail is a "420-mile route and includes twelve sites that interpret significant portions of the Cheyenne story," placing it in a context of western history. Craighead informs us that each year approximately 20,000 visitors see "some or all" of the trail, and the numbers continue to increase.[7]

Washita is a dynamic site. It is a place of mourning, a place where preservation of the land is a sign of respect for those killed. It is, by virtue of inclusion in the National Park Service, a site that complicates triumphalistic narratives of the "taming" of the West. It is a site where conversation over contentious interpretations of the past continues, and it is a site that refuses to freeze meaning on that November day in 1868, but transforms a painful living memory of violence into an activist program of cultural education. The meaning of the Washita will continue to evolve as Native American voices now help shape the National Park Service's narrative. Where one stands determines what one sees, and visitors will now "see" this place through richer, more fully textured stories.

It has always been difficult for us to find a central place in our national stories for the sobering narratives of slavery, white terrorism during Reconstruction, and the chronic violence of the Jim Crow years. In his seminal essay "The Deforming Mirror of Truth," the late Nathan Huggins reminds us that American historians have too often been complicit in this denial. "They have chosen to see American history from even before the Revolution as an inexorable development of free institutions and the expansion of political liberty to the broadest possible public. Like the framers of the constitution, they have treated racial slavery and oppression as curious abnormalities—aberrations—historical accidents to be corrected in the progressive upward reach of the nation's destiny." He calls for a new national history that will locate "racial slavery as a structural part of the foundation of the edifice."[8]

As in our written history, so too on our national landscape, where only recently have numerous African American historic sites of slavery, Jim Crow, and the civil rights era been uncovered, reconstructed, preserved, and interpreted for a wide audience. This is not so difficult with sites and stories that reveal the progressive narrative of our history—the story of the Underground Railroad, or inspiring sites of the civil rights movement, for example—but it is more difficult with toxic sites that reflect harsher stories.

Significantly, even sites of race hatred, so painful to confront, are being brought back from willful oblivion. Such is certainly the case with the Tulsa Race Riot of 1921. Historian John Hope Franklin—whose father was in Tulsa during the violence—and Tulsa Race Riot Commission (TRRC) member Scott Ellsworth, author of *Death in a Promised Land: The Tulsa Race Riot of 1921*, offer a moving introduction to the event. Reminding readers of the horror of the Oklahoma City bombing of 1995, they observed that other Oklahomans "carried within their hearts the painful memories of an equally dark, though long ignored, day in our past." Occurring during the pervasive racial violence of the Jim Crow era, it was an event, they declared, "perhaps unequaled in the peacetime history of the United States," an event in which Greenwood, the African American commercial center of Tulsa, was destroyed, "some forty-square blocks in all—had been laid to waste, leaving nearly nine-thousand people homeless." The death toll remains uncertain, but, Franklin and Ellsworth write, "considerable evidence exists to suggest that at least seventy-five to one hundred people, both black and white, were killed during the riot."[9]

It was very moving to be in the presence of survivors, our last living links to this event. I remember stepping outside the Greenwood Cultural Center, trying in vain to visualize the area as it had been. Where was the site of this hotel or business that I had read about? Where had African Americans been marched down the street, hands held high? Even though James Hirsch observed in *Riot and Remembrance* that "the scars of the riot were still visible in abandoned concrete driveways and ghostly sidewalks, the exposed foundations of long-gone houses and large expanses of empty space," it seemed to me that even the landscape had forgotten the event.[10]

Consequently, what first impressed me mightily—along with my admiration for the number of people, black and white, with the moral courage to confront this important story—was the loving work of reconstruction done by the Tulsa Race Riot Memorial Commission. If even the physical traces were gone, only the hard work of public history could reconstruct the area. The final report informs us that "Commission members identified 118 survivors and 176 descendants of riot victims. Master-maps, both of the community on the eve of the riot and of the post-riot residue, identified every single piece of property. For each parcel, a map displayed any structure present, its owner, and its use. If commercial, what firms were there, who owned them, what businesses they were in. If residential, whether it was rented or owned. If the former, the landlord's name. If the latter, whether it was mortgaged (if so, to whom and encumbered by what debt). For both, lists identified each of its occupants by name."

Researchers from the Oklahoma Historical Society examined "every warranty deed recorded, every property appraisal ordered, every damage claim filed, every death certificate issued, every burial record maintained . . . every form registering every survivor bears notes recording information taken from every one of 118 persons." They gathered "sets of municipal records, files from state agencies, reports kept by social services, press clippings carefully bound, privately owned photographs never publicly seen . . . files from National Guard records . . . affidavits filed with the state Supreme Court." This is a profound act of memorialization in its own right, bringing to life, even just on paper, a destroyed community.[11]

There are so many vexing issues. Would a physical memorial in the Greenwood area ghettoize remembrance, saying, in effect, "this is only important for the African American community?" Would a memorial downtown say something quite different about the need for community-wide engagement with this event? Would rituals of reconciliation and remembrance serve this wider purpose just as well? And what of the issue of reparations that remains central and divisive in Tulsa?

Beyond commemorative interest in such sites of racist violence, the historic landscape is now being enriched by the commemoration of sites of "spectacle" lynchings, fairly regular occurrences in Jim Crow America. They were often advertised in entertainment sections of newspapers; sometimes special excursion trains would bring people to take part in the spectacle. Often the most respectable citizens took part. In 1909, for example, the United States senator W. V. Sullivan of Mississippi proudly spoke of his leadership of a lynch mob in Oxford. Torture, burning, the removal of body parts as relics were often part of spectacle lynchings. Historian Leon Litwack brings us to the horror of the lynching of Sam Hose on April 23, 1899, in Newman, Georgia. "Before Hose's body had even cooled, his heart and liver were removed and cut into several pieces and his bones were crushed into small particles. The crowd fought over these souvenirs. Shortly after the lynching, one of the participants reportedly left for the state capitol, hoping to deliver a slice of Sam Hose's heart to the governor of Georgia," an enthusiastic supporter of lynching.[12]

Why would we want to remember such events? Aren't sites of lynching places best forgotten? Aren't they stories best left untold, ghosts best left ignored? I used the term "enriched" to characterize the recognition and placement of such sites and stories on the historic landscape. A strange term, perhaps, for sites that confront us with racist violence almost beyond imagination. Such sites of horror make laughable the enduring presence of narratives of American innocence in the face of mass violence. (How often we heard, after the bombing of the Murrah Building in Oklahoma City in 1995, "How could this happen in America? How could Americans do this to one another?" That such questions could still be asked at the end of the twentieth century is revealing of an insidious innocence, feigned or not, that does not prepare us well to confront, for example, the reality of lynching.) However, such sites will remind American publics—if they will listen—that we, like all other peoples, are capable of mass sadism, ecstatic spasms of violence, carried out often, in these cases, by civilized, Christianized, "good" people. After all, what's good for the goose is good for the gander. We take great umbrage lest Germans trivialize or dare to forget the Holocaust. They *must* remember! So, then must we. These sites enrich our historical understanding because they confront us with what we have been, and still are, capable of.[13]

Audiences in New York City and Atlanta have encountered a museum exhibition entitled "Without Sanctuary: Lynching Photographs in America." The exhibition and its companion book are as difficult to engage as the killing fields of Poland. Lynching photographs often became postcards in the early twentieth century. A minister in New York who had condemned lynching in these years found in his mailbox a lynching postcard with a message, "this is the way we do them down here. The last lynching has not been put on the card yet. Will put you on our regular mailing list. Expect one a month on the average." A son sent a photograph of the burned body of Jesse Washington, lynched on May 16, 1916, in Robinson, Texas, to his mother, writing, "this is the barbecue we had last night. My picture is to the left with a cross over it. Your son Joe."[14]

This was not just a southern phenomenon, of course. We recall a famous photograph by Lawrence Beitler of the lynching of Thomas Shipp and Abram Smith in Marion, Indiana, on August 7, 1930. What is most revealing in this photograph—and so many others—is not the horrific image of the murdered, but the smiling faces in the crowd, the two pregnant women, the woman in the fur coat. This infamous photograph is often used as *the* lynching photograph, and this violence almost took the life of another African American, James Cameron, who eventually opened the Black Holocaust Museum in Milwaukee, Wisconsin. In 1978, he practiced his own ritual of remembrance, returning to Marion. Historian James Madison describes the scene. "Cameron walked the courthouse square with a local reporter to find the place where the lynching tree once stood. He climbed to the second floor of the Grant County jail and stood next to his cell as the local newspaper photographer snapped his camera." Cameron tried to have the jail listed as a national historic landmark, but residents were not enthusiastic. It has since been renovated and transformed into apartments.

Despite its consignment to oblivion, the event still festers. Madison informs us that "whites recalled the lynching with embarrassment and regret . . . for African American citizens the events of 1930 remained an 'open wound,' that still needed 'healing' . . . there were still white people who had in a desk drawer or attic box a copy of the Beitler photograph." Certainly, one significant transformation of consciousness took place in 1998, when Grant County elected a black sheriff.[15]

It is also the case that one episode of lynching gave rise to an important milestone in the American legal system. On March 6, 1906, Ed Johnson, an African American in his early twenties, was arrested on suspicion of the rape of a white woman in Chattanooga, Tennessee. He was convicted and sentenced to death. At enormous risk to their lives, two African American lawyers in the city, appalled at the kangaroo court that had passed for his trial, took their appeal for a stay of execution to the Supreme Court. On March 17, 1906, Noah Parden became the first African American to argue a case before a Supreme Court justice. Outraged over what they perceived as federal interference, local authorities made no attempt to stop Johnson from being lynched in spite of the Supreme Court's stay of execution. The court decided to make an example of the sheriff and others who were complicit in the lynching. Never before, note Mark Curriden and Leroy Phillips in *Contempt of Court*, "had a criminal trial taken place before the nation's highest court. Never before had the justices been asked to sit as a jury in determining the fate of an individual. And never before had the federal government attempted to prosecute a person involved in a lynching." Six defendants were found guilty of contempt of the Supreme Court. The longest sentence was ninety days, not all of which was served, because defendants were released early for good behavior. The city of Chattanooga remained defiant, erecting a monument to the sheriff. This case, Curriden and Phillips observe, offered the "first glimpse of the federal-court system's exercising its power to protect an individual's rights from wayward state authorities." Former Supreme Court justice Thurgood Marshall recalled it as "perhaps the first instance in which the court demonstrated that the Fourteenth Amendment and the equal-protection clause have any substantive meaning to people of the African American race."[16]

While the citizens of Chattanooga graced their city with the monument to a sheriff complicit in the lynching of Ed Johnson, there is no statue to the African American attorneys who sacrificed their career as lawyers and had to leave Tennessee. Ed Johnson was buried in an African American cemetery vandalized and ignored for many years. In 1999, however, volunteers sought to restore the site, and fearful of further vandalism, removed Johnson's tombstone—which reads, "God bless you all, I am an innocent man," his words as he was being lynched—to the city's African American museum. In 2000,

Curriden and Phillips's research led a successful mission to set aside John-son's conviction.

Those who work so diligently to excavate these sites and stories work out of the conviction that remembrance enriches in many ways. The Tulsa Race Riot Commission brings to life through archival research a destroyed community. At least some people in Marion confront the still festering wound of their lynching. Two authors work to overturn an unjust convic-tion. Interracial groups gather to clean forgotten graves of those murdered, or engrave a forgotten name on a grave, or preserve a tombstone in a mu-seum. These rituals of inclusion restore the forgotten dead to the human community. They announce, "these dead also count and must be remem-bered." Interracial rituals of reconciliation take place at several sites of lynch-ing, calling forth the spirit of a healthy community doing commemorative battle with toxic sites of our past.[17]

There is, of course, another haunted site in Oklahoma burdened with the moral imperative to remember, the Oklahoma City National Memorial. Lawrence Hart, whom we met in our reflection on Washita, participated in the first anniversary service of the bombing, recalling, "that morning, as the families of the victims were gathering for the special service, I went on the ac-tual site, knelt on the ground and touched the earth four times. When the service began, I read the first 42 of the 168 names . . . I sensed that the Mur-rah Federal Office Building site and the Washita site . . . have similarities . . . first, the site in Oklahoma City is hallowed ground just as the site where the village stood at Washita. It too is a holy place for our ancestors died there. Second, both events were highly traumatic."[18]

I would add a third similarity between Washita, Tulsa, and Oklahoma City: all three sites can be not only sites of remembrance and mourning, but dynamic sites for education, reconciliation, and expanding our appreciation of the complex nature of our history. We have noticed programs of Native American cultural renewal at Washita, careful reconstruction of the historic record in Tulsa, and ongoing intense argument about appropriate forms of memorialization.

I wrote the following words months before September 11, 2001, in the conclusion to *The Unfinished Bombing*. "Will the prominence of the Okla-homa City bombing be ensured by its location in the nation's official mem-ory? Will it become an enduring part of the nation's landscape, a site as important as Monticello, Gettysburg, or the Vietnam Veterans Memorial? Will a future terrorist act that inflicts even more death consign Oklahoma City to a less prestigious location in the landscape of violence? Or might such an act increase its prestige as the first event in a continuing body count of domestic terrorism?"[19]

In New York City, as in Oklahoma City, many turned immediately to a narrative of rebuilding and civic renewal as an act of protest against terrorism. Too soon we heard in both places the simplistic language of pop psychology, words of "healing process" and "closure," as if the enduring impact of violent loss can be regularized into coherent stages and put behind one. Such language tells us a good deal about the congenital incapacity of Americans to struggle with the dark reality of enduring trauma. Unsolicited memorial ideas flooded both cities, signs of mourning and yearning for human connection. Bereavement, perhaps, is one of the only ways Americans can imagine themselves as one. It trumps, for a time anyway, the many ways we are divided. (Certainly, the obscene words of Jerry Falwell on September 13, appearing on *The 700 Club*, blaming "the pagans and the abortionists and the feminists and the gays and the lesbians," called into immediate question the notion of a seamless bereaved community.) Perhaps such events both bring communities together and tear them apart simultaneously, as bonds of community affection competed with the fear that this event was what Hannah Arendt once characterized as an "unbearable sequence of sheer happenings."[20]

There were many differences, of course, between Oklahoma City and New York City, among them the scale of death and the complex nature of the World Trade Center site. Unlike the Murrah site, where all human remains were removed after implosion in late May 1995, cremated remains of thousands of people remain in New York, including those of the perpetrators. Oklahoma City has much to offer those struggling with the sites of September 11. Already, family members and survivors and rescuers have visited with New Yorkers in person and through video conferences, offering words of consolation and perspective from those who have been there.

I believe the Oklahoma City experience is an appropriate roadmap for the alien landscape of mourning and remembrance that is to come. In mid-December 2001 I traveled to Shanksville, Pennsylvania, where passengers fought against the terrorist-hijackers and brought down United Flight 93 in a field near this small community. There I joined Bob Johnson, who chaired the memorial task force in Oklahoma City for many years, and Phillip Thompson, who now lives in Tulsa and whose mother's remains were in the Murrah Building until its implosion five weeks after the bombing. Before they arrived, I had the opportunity to go to the site and was not prepared for its power. People still leave devotional offerings at a memorial fence that has been erected on a nearby rise, but that did not move me. It seemed a bit like memorial cliché, as if everywhere now memorial fences are the way things are supposed to be done. But the natural site was stunning. The plane crashed in a field near a beautiful grove of trees, in which stand a number of rustic residences. The remains of the plane and the people were scattered throughout the grove, and it has become another site transformed forever by the events of September 11. Estimates are that 92 percent of the human remains are still in the soil. Certainly, as the Flight 93 Memorial Task Force and a federal commission join with others to create a new unit of the National Park Service, this most intimate of places demands the most sensitive treatment. Should it be treated as a grave site, only for family members? Should the particular site where human remains transform the ground ever be accessible to the general public?

So that Sunday evening in mid-December 2001, Bob Johnson, Phillip Thompson, and I all shared thoughts about the Oklahoma City memorial process in a town meeting attended by more than two hundred people in Shanksville high school. The intensity of the meeting was incredible. There was at least one bereaved family who had traveled a long distance to be there, and a videotape of the meeting was sent to all families. Bob Johnson and Phillip Thompson spoke about the importance of an inclusive process, and how in Oklahoma City individual desires for certain kinds of memorials gave way to a larger vision of the civic function of memorialization. It was moving to listen to these friends share with a community groping for direction. It gave me a sense of just how alive the Oklahoma City memorial is and how important it can be to so many in the coming months and years. Even more than the unbearable eloquence of the empty chairs, or the intense memorial center narrative of the events of April 19, the way Oklahomans share their experiences with others seared by violence make this story and site come alive. For example, several years ago family members and others involved in the Flight 93 memorial process spent three days at the Oklahoma City National Memorial, and there is no question that the memorial process in Shanksville has been enriched by this interchange.

Paul Fussell, author of *The Great War and Modern Memory* and combat veteran of the European theater in World War II, also wrote about the cultural legacy of that war. "The damage the war visited upon bodies and buildings, planes and tanks and ships, is obvious. Less obvious is the damage it did to intellect, discrimination, honesty, individuality, complexity, ambiguity, and irony, not to mention privacy and wit."[21] These compelling words speak well to the cultural aftermath of September 11. Given the inevitable coarsening of public life in times of war, the constriction of unpopular voices, how will we repair the damage to the culture? I was as guilty as anyone in taking refuge in the rhetoric of the unprecedented in reacting to September 11, failing for the moment to realize that we bring recognizable resources to it, and it seems to me that our historic sites, perhaps particularly the nation's haunted landscape, so rich in potential as sites of reflection, education, refuge, and more recently sites of civic conversation, provide some orientation especially in this troubling time. They remind us of past challenges, some met well and others not, of courageous visions in the midst of despairing times, and they remind us that we are not the first generation to struggle with murderous forces that seem larger than life. Places like Washita, Tulsa, and Oklahoma City are part of the cultural fabric that will help us all shape the "new normal" in what seems to be a dark and foreboding future.

Chapter 3
Public Sentiments and the American Remembrance of World War II

John Bodnar

Victory in World War II did not mean that all Americans saw this cataclysmic event in the same way. Some people spent the war years helping to build bombers or partying in crowded nightclubs. Some slogged through jungles fighting enemies, and others mourned in the privacy of their homes. Americans have often referred to the experience as the "good war," but no one epithet could capture the full range of personal and national experiences that citizens encountered in the early 1940s. To be sure the war created winners and losers and transformed the lives and politics of individuals and nations. Less noticed, however, was the fact that the war engendered a vast public debate over its significance that outlived the time of battles, bombs, and killings. Because the war was global and war experiences innumerable, cultural discussions over the meaning of the war and its remembrance after 1945 were widespread and reflected an ongoing struggle to organize knowledge about the implications of all that had taken place in the early forties and beyond. And because the meaning of the war cut so close to the sense Americans had of who they were as a nation, the discussion and contest over meaning was heavily implicated in the continuous need to restate American national identity. Nations that fought wars could not escape the problem of remembering them nor the civic need to cast a war effort into the larger story of the nation itself.

The public debate over the war involved not only competing interpretations of the larger experience but fundamental epistemological issues of how to frame all of the bits of information about the event that circulated in public and private space. For the sake of discussion, this essay intends to stress the tension that existed between ways of knowing that can be labeled traditional or sentimental, on the one hand, and ironic or modern on the other. In his penetrating study of the "form and content of mourning" after World

War I, historian Jay Winter revealed how Europeans—in a general response to widespread grief and death—turned to "traditional motifs" in order to understand and accept all the dying and suffering that had just occurred. He found in public commemoration of the war—in monuments, poetry, and rituals—the widespread use of ideas grounded in what he termed "sentimentality" and "traditionalism." Specifically they included representations of the war centering on "patriotic certainties," "honor," religion, and masculinity. For Winter this language of "traditionalism" helped to explain why so many had to die and served what he felt was a universal or human need of people in several nations to mourn and put the war behind them. Winter's arguments put him in opposition to the classic work of Paul Fussell, who felt the Great War was recalled and understood in terms that were more "modern" than traditional. That is to say that conventional values seemed discredited after the war and that for many the scale of loss and destruction prevented the ready acceptance of rational descriptions of the war or consolation after all of the carnage. Traditional interpretations of the war promised to bring to individuals and groups honor, moral clarity, and comprehension. At the heart of modern memory were tropes of tragedy and trauma and the sense of "utter powerlessness" war brought to some individuals. How to establish the former over the latter was at the heart of the public discussion over the war in the first place.[1]

This essay seeks to examine this problem of remembering World War II in the United States. Clearly, America did not suffer the sort of homeland devastation that Europe saw in either World War I or World War II. Yet, nearly 400,000 Americans died in the conflict and nearly one million came home with physical wounds. The number with emotional scars has never been counted. The contributions Americans made to the defeat of evil regimes in Germany and Japan certainly contributed to a generally positive view of the war and of the nation that helped to win it. But efforts to understand how Americans might have reacted to both the significant number of casualties from their own country and the reality of all the killing and trauma around them have not often been made. Perhaps, in the glow of victory and the return of prosperity, Americans simply failed to take notice of all the suffering that had just taken place. This essay makes another assumption, however. It infers that the losses here and abroad were substantial enough to initiate cultural and political arguments even in the United States that sought to explain and even forget some of the suffering and the dying and, by implication, set the terms of a long-term debate over the American remembrance of the war that has not been fully appreciated.

Victory did not mean that all Americans remained unscathed by the war years. Archibald MacLeish, a writer who had backed Franklin Roosevelt's efforts at intervention in World War II and worked for the Office of War Information, publicly lamented all that was lost in the conflict. MacLeish's poetry in 1948 described a postwar world littered with "broken bodies" and "shriveled hearts." For him the late 1940s was a "rotting age" with "death camp cities" and even continued racial prejudice in the United States itself. In his poem "Young Dead Soldiers" (1948) this veteran of World War I expressed grave reservations that so many men from all nations had to die. In the images of death and suffering around him he could find no noble achievement or reason to celebrate victory or bravery. To him there was little reason for fanfare and any larger meaning of the conflict was unclear. "Whether our lives and our deaths were for peace and a new hope or for nothing we cannot say," he wrote. In the mind of this poet it still remained for the living to invest the war and the deaths of all the young soldiers with whatever significance they could.[2]

MacLeish was not alone in his refusal to be consoled. The writer Lewis Mumford, who lost a son fighting in Italy, "wept uncontrollably" at the news of his son's death and remembered it as the most "emotionally devastating" moment of his life. An Iowa farmer who recalled the war for oral historian Studs Terkel concluded that the cost of losing a son in the pursuit of victory was simply "too much of a price to pay." Another soldier told Terkel that the only lesson he drew from the event was that war was "madness." The father of the five Sullivan brothers from Waterloo, Iowa, who died together when their ship went down in the Pacific drank more heavily after the war than he did before. Anyone who has watched many of the films issued by Hollywood in the late 1940s knows that there was a pronounced tendency in many movies to present a sobering portrait of the war, from the depiction of the suffering of ordinary soldiers in *G.I. Joe* (1945), to the representation of veteran trauma in *Home of the Brave* (1949), to the critique of men who placed their loyalty to the military ahead of their loyalty to their families in *The Sands of Iwo Jima* (1949).[3]

Scholars have also documented a cultural debate in postwar America centered on the violent potential of human nature in general and the returning American veteran in particular that found its way into films, novels, and magazines. Sometimes this anxiety over the future was manifested in various forms of science fiction. Many postwar films presented stories in which conflict was resolved through acts of violence. Certainly this preoccupation with violence was at the center of two of the most powerful works of fiction of the postwar war era written by Norman Mailer and James Jones. Mailer's classic *The Naked and the Dead* (1948) had little to say about an American victory or the loyalty and virtue of the American soldiers who waged the battles. Rather, this veteran of the war offered a sober account of how American men exhibited an unlimited capacity for violence during the war and linked this tendency to the competitive nature of traditional American economic life and its proclivity to foster aggressive attitudes. James Jones offered a story as well that was critical of American society and of a military establishment that fostered aggressive and domineering attitudes.[4]

Romantic Visions

In our times images of remorse over all the carnage and critical appraisals of the brutality are harder to see when Americans recall World War II. Views of the war as a time of sadness and revulsion over its destructiveness have been relegated to the background—and at times erased completely—in favor of images that are considerably more heroic or triumphal. It is well known that this trope of a "good war" has been driven in part by a reaction to the more problematic memory of Vietnam. In American culture, however, it is not only the war that is praised but the ordinary citizens who fought it. Whether one calls them "the greatest generation" or a "band of brothers" they are now held to be people who were steeped in traditional notions of moral virtue and patriotic honor. Their sense of loyalty to nation is seen as innate. They are the opposite of Mailer's violent men and are imagined to possess inherent devotion to conventional ideas of love, marriage, and hard work. The experience of World War II and the temperament of the American generation that fought it have become almost mythical—symbols of what customary moral and patriotic behavior should be about in both its public and private dimensions. And as such, they tend to reinforce Winter's findings for post–World War I Europe of the universal power of traditional symbols to heal the scars of war. Yet, these images have been expressed by many not part of the wartime generation and seem to emerge largely out of a sense of nostalgia and romance rather than out of feelings of bereavement.

Romantic visions—and certainly romantic forms of nationalism—can lift people from the frustrations of everyday life and from a host of social and emotional realities. They offer hope and a sense of collective and individual empowerment. In the past such visions have been put to both good and harmful purposes but one cannot deny their power to persuade and to reestablish a sense of moral certainty. Tom Brokaw's book *The Greatest Generation* (1998), with its portraits of men and women who actually benefited from the war experience, stands as a powerful expression of both the romance of the individual in contemporary America and the mythical view of World War II. War is neither disillusioning nor destructive in this best seller but somehow empowering. The book suggests that the experience of self-sacrifice and military discipline gave men and women in the 1940s the tools they needed to build stable marriages, prosperous businesses, and successful careers. And in winning the war this generation bequeathed to the one that followed gifts such as economic prosperity, scientific progress, and even civil rights. The political dreams of this generation were even imagined to center more on individual agency rather than collective political movements. These people were mythical because they were able to manage the project of classic liberal individualism in America and still remain ethical and patriotic citizens at the same time. They are in this formulation models for all who follow and a reaffirmation of political values that are highly traditional and conservative. It is no wonder today that Americans are everywhere busily collecting oral histories of these exemplary people.[5]

While all citizens of the wartime generation can serve the purposes of this highly sentimental view of the war, it is the veterans of the conflict that stand above all others. Their deeds have been celebrated time and time again but nowhere more powerfully than in Stephen Ambrose's *Band of Brothers* (1992). In this history of the 101st Airborne from basic training to the final defeat of Hitler, Ambrose, who was impressed with seeing the troops come home from war when he was a young boy in Wisconsin, claims that his subjects were men who were "special in their values." A highly elite outfit, Ambrose tells his readers that they were "idealists eager to merge themselves into a group fighting for a cause, actively seeking an outfit with which they could identify." Unlike James Jones, he actually sees these men profiting from the Great Depression where he claims they acquired traits like self-reliance, hard work, and the ability to take orders. He also claims they gained a sense of self-worth through manly activities such as hunting and sports. Loyal to their country and to each other, to this author they were simply America's "finest youth."[6]

Mourning the dead—a key to seeing war in its most tragic dimensions—is not a concern for Ambrose and Brokaw. Both writers note the extraordinary adaptation to civilian life after the war for the survivors and note that they were remarkably successful—in Ambrose's words—because of their "determination, ambition, and hard work." For the men of the 101st, the army gave them self-confidence and the idea that they could endure more than they thought possible, a view that casts aside the highly critical view of military life offered by Mailer, Jones, and many other World War II vets. When Ambrose describes the various encounters with the enemy these men had, he merely offers without emotion or comment a list of individuals who died in a particular operation. There is triumph in Ambrose's story—on both a national and personal level—but no room for thinking that the loss of the men who did not come home was in any way a tragedy or "madness."[7]

A reading of best sellers by Brokaw and Ambrose might give the mistaken impression that trauma and death are completely absent from the current American version of World War II. This is certainly not the case. Glimpses of the calamity that befell some of the soldiers are certainly evident in our contemporary recollections. American soldiers die brutal deaths in recent films such as *Saving Private Ryan* (1998) and *Pearl Harbor* (2001). The story of James Bradley, one of the men who raised the American flag on Iwo Jima, revealed that this veteran suppressed a tremendous amount of horror and pain, which he would never forget throughout his postwar life. William Manchester, in his 1979 memoir of his fighting in the Pacific theater, expressed much the same admiration for the soldiers that Ambrose did but stressed as well the horror and anguish of battles like Okinawa. He noted the close sense of camaraderie the men felt for each other and their desire to "fight for their country." Unlike Ambrose and Brokaw, however, this member of the wartime generation articulated grief and sorrow over the loss of the men who were his comrades. He had shared the sense of vulnerability that men in war encountered (and later generations do not feel) and criticized war memorials he saw in the Pacific that failed to recall their agony and struggle.[8]

Sentimental celebrations of the wartime generation not only minimize the trauma of war within stories that are essentially triumphal but present both patriotism and human nature in terms that are both narrow and fanciful. This tendency to minimize the pain or loss connected to war is evident in the new World War II Memorial on the Mall in Washington, D.C. This site of remembrance, positioned strategically between the Lincoln Memorial and the Washington Monument, celebrates both the nation and the war in terms that are highly virtuous. Two memorial arches commemorate the idea of triumph on land, sea, and air. Four large eagles pay tribute to "triumphant warriors" coming home. Death is acknowledged but not in graphic terms. Rather a shield of four thousand gold stars represents the Americans who died in the conflict. This proclivity to dismiss the anguish of the war was already evident in 1995 when veterans and their supporters reacted angrily to a planned exhibit at the Smithsonian that had intended to depict not only the American victory over the Japanese but the suffering of many Japanese citizens after the dropping of two atomic bombs. Veterans objected strenuously to any compassionate view toward an enemy many of them had despised in the 1940s and to any hint that they were less than honorable themselves and culpable for the killing of innocent civilians. They saw the bomb as most of their contemporaries did in 1945 as something that saved American lives by removing the need to invade Japan and not as something essentially destructive. Thus, it is not surprising to read in Bob Greene's book, *Duty: A Father, His Son, and the Man Who Won the War,* that the pilot of the plane that dropped the first atomic bomb felt no sadness for the people in Hiroshima as he viewed the city from his plane after the attack. In much of the best-selling literature on the war in our times we find an aversion to seeing fully not only the suffering of the Americans but the pain and anguish of our former enemies as well.[9]

Romantic myths and traditional motifs refuse to recall war on its own terms. They prefer to use a past whose meanings are fixed and immortal. Yet, tradition like any idea has to be fashioned in a particular time and place and, as such, is subject to the influence of political actors. Thus, even if a sense of timeless tradition comes from a war—more than a sense of cynicism and despair—it still has to be fabricated. Understanding the nature of this political process helps to explain in this case not only why tradition was reasserted but why it tended to erase both the catastrophic aspects of war and the broad democratic idealism of the thirties and the forties. Public commemorations have been punctuated by calls to honor and emulate the good behavior of the wartime generation with its presumed commitment to patriotism and conventional values such as marriage and capitalism. Little is said in all of this about the idealism of the forties that was tied to the dream of the "four freedoms" and some of the aspirations of the New Deal. Patriotism is almost always demonstrated in military terms and almost never within an older (progressive) frame of citizen engagement in genuine civic or social reform. Certainly contemporary views of the war offer democratic overtones when they celebrate the defeat of totalitarianism. And more emphasis is directed toward the accomplishments and sacrifices of ordinary citizens than of great leaders or generals. Omer Bartov has called this process—visible in other nations as well—"a glorification of the rank and file." He argues that it has been necessary to see the qualities of the people who fought as exemplary in order to ennoble both the sacrifice of the dead and the achievement of the survivors as a way of making the entire national effort seem beyond reproach.

Thus, the move toward the "glorification" of ordinary people from the wartime generation is not as democratic as it may appear and does not directly sustain the idealistic hopes of many citizens in the 1940s that the war would lead to the spread of a New Deal-type democracy throughout society and throughout the world. In our times much of the progressive rhetoric of the forties has been effaced along with much of the traumatic experiences of the war itself. In its place have risen patriotic allegories of duty, honor, and individual character.[10]

The central problem for both individuals and nations in recalling war is grounded in the nightmarish aspects of war itself. Nations are not eager to proclaim responsibility for mass death. The individual encounter with widespread trauma, as Judith Herman has explained, can also lead to strong feelings of disempowerment and disconnection. The traumatized victim feels cut off from both a past and a future and left with strong feelings of vulnerability. Some relief can be gained, according to Herman and others, when individuals come to terms with the nature of their devastating experience, acknowledge all that was lost, and forgive those responsible for perpetrating the trauma in the first place. Yet, scholars have suggested that the presumed "healing" nature of coming to terms with such an event may never be fully achieved and a desire to grieve or even feel vulnerable and hopeless can return at any time.[11]

Nations are not individuals, of course, and we could not expect to explain their reaction to trauma in the same way we would for human beings. A quick glance at the landscape of public remembrance in the nations that fought World War II does suggest, however, a widespread effort to forget the sordid details of the war in one way or another. Nations were influenced on this issue less by psychological imperatives and more by political ones. No nation was anxious to assume responsibility for mass killings of any kind. In the war's aftermath victorious nations were preoccupied with affirming their virtue; nations encountering defeat moved to hide their crimes and assert their victimization. After the disruptions of wartime nearly all nations attempted to construct unified versions of the war that moderated the disparate experiences of various individuals and groups. Consequently some images and stories were promoted over others. Thus, in the Soviet Union after 1945 a "Myth of the Great Patriotic War" was used to sustain the centrality of the state; it praised the heroic defense of the "motherland" and led to the building of huge monuments that represented patriotism and strength but not images of the millions of Soviet dead or public controversies over Stalin's war policies that may have resulted in unnecessary slaughter of citizens. This would not change until the fall of the Communist regime. Germans were more likely to imagine themselves as victims of the Nazis rather than perpetrators of the Holocaust, although public talk about the massacre of the Jews could be heard in the immediate postwar period. The postwar decades in France focused commemoration more on the heroic actions of the French resistance and not nearly so much on the role of French citizens who collaborated in killing of the Jews, although females who consorted with German soldiers were ostracized. It was primarily the rise of "Jewish memory" after the trial of Adolf Eichmann in 1961 and the claims of victims that altered the tone of public memory—and the presentation of national identity—in many of these nations. In Japan it was more common to erect monuments to peace or to see the Japanese themselves as victims of the atomic bombs than it was to talk about the perpetration of atrocities in China. Rising anger in the rest of Asia among Japanese victims eventually ruptured the cultural lid on Japanese culpability. In Poland scholars have described a process of "psychic numbing" when it came to Polish memory of the war. The death of Polish Christians was generally lamented and marked. Jewish dead from the same society often remained invisible. Eventually the recognition of the Holocaust helped to erase some of this "numbing" in Poland as well, but the imperative on the part of both individuals and nations to forget the trauma is striking.[12]

There was some public debate over the issue of trauma in the 1940s in the United States despite its relative distance from most of the killing. Government censorship that covered up the true suffering of American men came under greater criticism over the course of the war as public demand for a more realistic accounting of the dying increased. And there was a modest amount of questioning of the decision to drop the atomic bomb in the late forties—before the Soviet Union acquired a bomb of its own. Yet, as in other nations, trauma and death were not central to public remembrance. Just why this was so has never been extensively analyzed except for some scholarship regarding the substantial public approval of the decision to drop the atomic bomb. One of the contentions of this essay, however, is that the issue was, indeed, troublesome for many and that efforts to justify, explain, and dismiss the killing and the dying everywhere were as extensive as they were because they challenged the project to unify and sanctify the nation itself. Even support for the "bomb" was based largely in a perception that it saved many Americans from death. It is crucial, moreover, to note that this effort to forget the complete horrors of the war began during the war itself in a public debate in America over exactly what World War II was about. This struggle to interpret and organize knowledge about the conflict, moreover, was fundamental not only for the formation of public opinion during the forties but for setting the terms of the remembrance of World War II over the next five decades. Especially crucial in terms of propelling wartime unity and moderating personal fears of war were noticeable strains of sentimentality that permeated the culture that tended to idealize both the war effort and the citizen-soldiers themselves. It is this highly patriotic and, for that matter, narrow identity ascribed to the nation and its citizens in wartime that I wish to probe in seeking to ultimately explain how myth triumphed over misery.[13]

Wartime

The dominant version of the why we were fighting in the early years of the conflict came from the Roosevelt administration's proclamation of the "four essential human freedoms." New Deal Democrats believed that victory would lead to a postwar world based upon freedom from the fear of totalitarianism, freedom from want or economic deprivation, freedom of speech, and freedom of religion. Soon after America entered the war Roosevelt presented to Congress a report from the National Resource Planning Board, which included designs for the overall war effort and a reaffirmation of many of his New Deal policies, including a right to a job, fair pay, medical care, and some form of assistance for the elderly. Eventually the political implications of the "four freedoms" became global in their impact and rallied people to human rights causes for decades to come.[14]

The New Deal thrust of this early attempt to define the war was taken up with enthusiasm by the Office of War Information (OWI), an agency charged with crafting a public meaning of war and winning support for the entire endeavor at home and abroad. In 1942 the OWI informed Hollywood, for instance, that its products should focus on the overriding theme of democracy as a rationale for the war—and, we can infer, for the trauma to come. The Roosevelt administration wanted to depict the struggle as a "people's war," showing loyal citizens of all races and religions making sacrifices willingly and stressing the dangers posed by dictators to the eventual realization of the four freedoms. To this end, staunch supporters of the president such as MacLeish and Robert Sherwood joined the OWI to articulate war aims. And Roosevelt's secretary of agriculture, Henry Wallace, proclaimed in a celebrated speech in 1943 that the war would lead to a "century of the common man" in which people everywhere would escape hard times, hunger, and social injustice. Wallace felt that such goals were enough for Americans "to fight with all that is in us."[15]

Conservatives in Congress reacted quickly and angrily to the idea of a "people's war." Ignoring the human costs of war itself, they complained that the OWI was more interested in promoting the president than the war. Southern congressmen were particularly upset with OWI publications that advocated equal rights for black citizens. In 1943 anti-New Dealers in Congress were able to emasculate most of the domestic budget for the OWI, allowing it to continue much of its work overseas while reducing funding for many New Deal programs from the 1930s. Conservatives even passed, over the president's veto, the Smith-Connally War Labor Disputes Act in an effort to reverse some of the gains made by organized labor over the past decade.[16]

Conservatives feared not only the egalitarian impulses of New Deal democracy when it came to investing the war with significance but the growing power of the state necessary to mobilize individuals and resources to fight the contest. They hated totalitarianism to be sure but worried that the American state itself, with its expanded economic and military role, now threatened the traditional ideal of individual freedom in America. The war, in fact, was very much a part of the beginnings of modern conservatism in the United States with its inclination to see the state (but not the nation) as an obstacle to personal freedom and power rather than as an agent of progress and a defender of human rights for all. Robert Westbrook has astutely noted that the private goals of individuals were never really eliminated from American political life during the war despite all the calls for sacrifice. Thus, he argued that the four freedoms were expressed not only to promote democratic idealism, but also to reassure citizens that some of their private rights as individuals still mattered. As he and others have suggested, the liberal state had a particular difficulty—asking citizens to make sacrifices and, perhaps, give up their lives during wartime for the existence of such a state was based on the idea of the protection of individual rights in the first place. Theoretically, citizens relinquished the right to dominate or fight one another by accepting the sovereignty of the state and its power "to command obedience for the sake of peace, justice and prosperity." Liberal states always had the capacity to inflict violence (rather than protect rights) domestically and internationally but they could not do so without raising serious concerns from some of their subjects. As some scholars have argued, "violence haunts liberal political thought."[17]

Writing at the end of World War II, Eric Sevareid reinforced Westbrook's contention that private interest remained strong and had to be acknowledged in order to win popular approval. The noted journalist did not think that the war had furthered the dream of a cooperative and just society for which many longed. Sevareid recalled his boyhood in the village of Velva, South Dakota, and the communitarian and egalitarian values that dominated this farming region in which people helped each other to plant and to harvest. He felt that the death and sacrifice of the world war would be for naught "unless the image of society that Americans showed the world was that of the little Velvas" that resided in his memory. With an air of dejection he felt strongly that this was not the case, however. He reported that during the war the nightclubs of New York were crowded and "gasoline and rubber bootleggers became our richest citizens." He also noted that Congress did its best to destroy the OWI and avoid price and income limits. And he argued that most Americans "sneered" at the vision of the war as a crusade to establish the "century of the common man," often calling such an idea "globaloney." For many Americans the war, according to Sevareid, was simply about making money and getting it over so they could return to "baseball and a full tank of gas." Westbrook would not say that private interests were necessarily selfish. One could fight simply for the survival of one's family. But both Westbrook and Sevareid suggest what Ambrose and Brokaw deny: that private and public goals were not always congruent.[18]

Sevareid's lament over the lack of ethical behavior and democratic idealism did not permeate the most powerful forms of cultural representation of the nation or its citizens and soldiers during the war for it was grounded too much in the political debates of the thirties, which were prone to reveal fundamental flaws within American traditions and practices. Although the political controversies of the thirties did not go away, the thrust of pubic discussions was already becoming romantic and sentimental during the war. This move toward a softer look at America and Americans originated in part early in the war from a political effort of the state to foster unity and acceptance of the suffering to come. The OWI, for instance, reviewed movie scripts with this in mind. Films like *Human Comedy* (1943) or *Since You Went Away* (1944) both offered a romantic view of Americans and muted the sort of social realism that permeated the political language of the previous decade. Popular songs of the period, such as "White Christmas," "You'd Be So Nice to Come Home To," and "God Bless America," idealized relations between men and women, the American home as a place free of discord and turmoil, and the relationship between citizens and the nation. Good people who loved each other and their country replaced Depression-era images of anger and discontent; the promotion of the conservative image of the "good war" was under way.

Private feelings of nostalgia, however, also drove this public expression of sentimentality as much as (and maybe more than) official propaganda. And to the extent that they did, the widespread expression of affectionate images represented a distinct denunciation of the state promotion of war itself. Historian Peter Fritzche has argued well that nostalgia is much more than a simple escape from the present. Its emergence in the modern world of the nineteenth and twentieth centuries is very much a sign of a general dissatisfaction with the increased sense of change and the ongoing experience with rupture and discontinuity. Thus, nostalgia (and we can add traditionalism) is really an insightful critique of the present—grounded very much in an individual's sense of loss—and a belief that the past was somehow better than the present. Nostalgia was sentimental because it tended to avoid the political "realism" of the present and moved intently toward the realm of private emotional life. As such its expression had the potential to reorder the "structure of feeling" that permeated a given time and place. In the 1850s such public emotions could be mobilized around the sympathy white mothers could express toward their black counterparts whose children were mistreated by the owners of slaves. The result of this public sentiment was that the traditional ideal of motherhood was deployed in way that supported the promotion of democratic equality through the agency of the American state in the Civil War. The historical context of the 1940s was different, however. It was the state itself—both in the United States and elsewhere—that administered the evil of war. People could believe on one level that a war was necessary but that did not mean that its costs could be readily assimilated into everyday life; it was, in fact, a massive rupture of that life. And now public sentiments revealed shared feelings not for the reform of society but the re-creation of a past life—before the war and the depression—filled with loving people and happy homes. It was no wonder that "White Christmas," with its longing for a family holiday in a former time, was so popular. And it was no wonder that GIs flocked to see Bob Hope wherever he appeared.[19]

Most expressions of sentimentality were directed toward the American fighting man, and because they were, his experience came to exercise a powerful influence over the entire way the war was recalled. Military mobilizations and wartime migrations strained many relationships and often threatened prevailing standards of moral behavior and conduct. Men and women came to distrust each other after long months apart; communities feared and experienced a rise in sexual permissiveness as women entered factories and newcomers moved into established towns. Racial tensions were exacerbated in many industrial cities from an increase in the migrations of

African Americans from the South. The sentimental image of the average GI and ordinary Americans in general, however, sugarcoated these problems and came to stand at the center of countless stories in the press and in fiction.

Leading the movement to fashion this highly emotional perspective was Ernie Pyle, one of the most popular war correspondents of the time. In his dispatches and his books, Pyle made an admirable effort to sympathize with the plight of the common soldier and tell the truth about the experience of combat. There was a sense of democracy in Pyle in the way he supported these ordinary men. But it was not the politics of the New Deal with its push for a restoration of the workingman and his family as much as it was a compassionate or affective politics that articulated a sense of concern for the trauma and suffering of others. It was empathetic without being hopeful or programmatic. Pyle recoiled from the horrors of war that he saw firsthand and reported on the intense feeling the men he knew had to get out of the war and return to a traditional home. He offered some of what Brokaw and Ambrose did when he described the men in rather narrow (or mythical) terms but was too close to the war itself to ignore the suffering and the need to mourn. At his most romantic, he always identified his subjects as ordinary guys from some typical American hometown. They were fully integrated into families and communities, in his view, and not alienated or domineering as they were on the pages of Mailer or Jones. Pyle affirmed over and over again that these men actually disliked war and, for that matter were not all that interested in a rugged sense of economic competition or the pursuit of power. He did admit that some of them had acquired "animal-like ways of self-preservation" in order to survive war but suggested that such violent impulses were only temporary. To him they were neither heroic nor individualistic, but certainly they were nearly unreal in the way he depicted them as devoid of immoral and dangerous traits. Some of this was due to censorship, but this sentimental view was too powerful to be the result of simple thought control. "I'm a rabid one-man movement bent on tracking-down and stamping out everybody who doesn't fully appreciate the common front-line soldier," he proudly proclaimed. Few would deny that Pyle's thoughts here were more his own than those of censors.[20]

Novelist John Hersey offered another romantic portrait of American fighting men in his 1944 novel *A Bell for Adano*, which made a hero out of a fictional American officer named Victor Joppolo. This Italian-American figure was appointed to administer a Sicilian town that had just been liberated from the Germans. He brought not a harsh militaristic spirit, however, but a true sense of democracy, telling the townsfolk that under him officials "are no longer the masters of the people." In the book Joppolo attended Catholic mass regularly, resisted any inclination to cheat on his wife, and talked frequently about his desire to return home. A true believer in the dream of creating a "century for the common man," he introduced New Deal-type reforms including a system of public assistance in which the distribution of aid was determined by a local committee of citizens. He also defended the rule of law by stopping a mob from attacking a former mayor who had sympathized with the Nazis. When an American general in the story—whom most readers probably saw as George Patton—forbade local Italians from bringing their food carts into town because they slowed the passage of military vehicles on the roads, Joppolo defied the general's edict and took the side of "the people" so that they could get the food and water that they needed. And in an effort to get the Italians to remember that the war was ultimately a struggle for democracy, Joppolo found another bell to hang in the town square to replace the one that had called the people to work each morning for generations but had been melted down by the Germans to make guns.[21]

The Soldier's Story

Neither nostalgic longing for home, nor democratic leanings were all that evident in stories told about the war by many of the men who actually fought it. Soldiers' narratives were lacking in the "big abstractions," according to Samuel Hynes, such as "a century of the common man," and more intent upon "bearing witness" to the horror and destruction around them. Hynes concluded after reading accounts from World War II battlefields that there may have been less criticism of the conflict than in other wars, but it was not "idealized" either. Historian Gerald Linderman, after looking at the way American men from the war explained their experience, concluded that there was a general absence of any discussion of politics—either democratic or conservative—and no extended account of home or family life. Linderman found that men talked mostly about the brutal reality of war, the bloodthirsty attitudes of some combatants and the camaraderie of those who fought.[22]

Men in combat tended to feel cut off from their past and their futures (much as with victims of traumatic episodes) and thus imagined their ties to home and to political life severely weakened. Feelings of vulnerability, cynicism, and demoralization were common and many became fatalistic, an attitude often expressed in the idea that there was a bullet somewhere with their name on it. Vulnerability bred extravagant searches for actions and ideas that restored a sense of order to their lives. Private dreams suddenly became more about the need to feel invincible—a drive that drove soldiers to bond closely with their comrades—and less about ties to home or to nation. William Manchester, who fought in the Pacific, recalled that he felt closer to his buddies in combat than to any friend he met during the remainder of his life. And these men began to talk about their military roles as mere "jobs" that needed to be done, an attitude that naturalized the killing and fighting process and allowed them to retain a sense of personal agency in an environment where they really had very little of it.[23]

Sensations of vulnerability could also be minimized in other ways. There were moments when men in battle took delight from the sheer spectacle of war such as the "dazzling lights of a firefight at night" or the sight of "tracer bullets" darting through the sky. A rush of elation would often follow the downing of an enemy plane. Sometimes a sense of weakness was overcome by engaging in acts of atrocity. Men collected gold teeth or skulls from Japanese bodies or at least tolerated such practices on the part of their colleagues. Consider this account from E. B. Sledge, who fought with the American forces against the Japanese at Peleliu in 1944. He recalled how he saw a fellow marine attempt to dislodge a large gold crown tooth from an enemy soldier. When the marine put his knife on the base of the tooth and hit the handle with the palm of his hand while the man was still alive, the victim began to kick his feet and thrash about. This movement caused the knife to sink deeper into the man's mouth, which upset the marine so much that he cursed the suffering soldier and cut his cheeks open to each ear. He then put his foot on the victim's lower jaw and tried again to get the prize tooth. Sledge wrote that he was amazed by "the incredible cruelty that decent men could commit when reduced to a brutish existence in their fight for survival amid violent death, terror, tension, fatigue, and filth that was the infantryman's war."[24]

American soldiers not only wrote about their experience in World War II but spoke with social scientists, who were constantly seeking their opinions in the 1940s. Their responses—like the soldier's own story—reinforced a picture of the men that tended to undermine the traditionalism and sentimentality of Pyle and Hersey. Most soldiers seemed "disgruntled," especially if they were forced to remain overseas for a long period of time. They also expressed resentment toward officers (as do many of the men in Mailer's novel) who enjoyed greater access to warm beds, women and whiskey. Many were consumed by private attitudes and also unsure as to why they were fighting in the first place. Ordinary GIs were not inclined to see the war primarily in terms of a battle for the four freedoms, which is not to say they did not support those basic concepts. In 1943 only about 15 percent of the men interviewed in one study said they were fighting for "idealistic concepts" like ending Fascism or making the world better. Most, in fact, had no response to the question of why they fought. The men also seemed dubious about excessive displays of "flag-waving" or patriotism because they felt such practices tended to obscure the harsh reality and terror of the battlefield. Surveys did detect a general sense that the war was, indeed, worth waging, although this support appeared to wane over the course of the conflict. Most men stated clearly that what really motivated them to fight was a compelling need to protect their comrades in arms. Three decades after the war was over Manchester confirmed in his memoir of the war in the Pacific that he and his fellow marines fought not for the flag or country but for each other.[25]

The Veteran's Perspective

Soldiers became veterans once the war was over and when they did their interpretations of the wartime experience began to change. The sense of weakness and demoralization that many of them felt from the experience of military life or the battlefield gave way. Cynicism toward political slogans and war itself were replaced by strong displays of male potency and faith in conventional political ideas. Once home and reconnected to the society and to the nation, many of these men joined organizations that vigorously defended flag, nation, and the traditional family, with its esteemed place for men, and solemnized the role they played in the war. In the way veterans defended the nation, the idea of patriotic sacrifice, and the traditional home or family, they sustained some of the sentimental ideas that had been ascribed to these men during wartime and helped to create the myth that public and private interests were aligned. The presumed aversion that many of them were thought to have to warfare, however, was now overturned by the assertions that many of them made of the need for the nation and its people to be ready for war again. They now acted less like vulnerable soldiers and more like strong men ready at a moment's notice to defend home and country. They were now also avowedly political, but their politics was not so much tied to New Deal–type reforms but aligned more with a kind of traditionalism and conservatism that felt the nation's future could best be assured if it were put into the hands of potent and honorable men in a world growing more and more threatening and not in grassroots political movements.

This is not to say that democratic ideals did not live after World War II and that some veterans did not support them. Even a conservative organization such as the American Legion would proclaim in 1945 that the "common good" should count for more than "individual interests." Black and white veterans fought for racial integration in the South after 1945. New Deal visions for the spread of justice and economic welfare for all human beings were encoded in documents like the United Nations Declaration of Human Rights (1948), which used the experience of mass killing to reassert the "inherent dignity" and equality of "all members of the human family" more than the ideal of a society defended by men who were strong, patriotic, and capable fighters. Eschewing calls for special compensation for veterans or victims, the U.N. declaration called for a "spirit of brotherhood" and the need to guarantee every human being the right to life, liberty, and the security of person. "Barbarous acts" of all kinds were condemned; New Deal programs like Social Security, the right to join unions, "equal pay for equal work," and health care were affirmed. This declaration, in fact, revealed a special sensitivity to the entire human suffering that had just taken place in the world—a feeling that had prompted MacLeish's poetry as well. The politics of veterans tended to move away from the liberal humanism of the U.N. declaration, however, to ideas about the need to secure the defense of the nation and importance of recognizing the special needs and innate patriotism of one particular group.[26]

Veterans stressed not only their particular medical and economic needs, but also the fact that they had exhibited exceptional levels of valor and loyalty. Their war experience was remembered more as an individual achievement of honor than one marked by feelings of weakness or dreams of remaking the world for the benefit of all common men. Scholars who have studied the idea of honor do not denigrate it in any way; it can serve to preserve one's integrity and ability to stand against unjust authority in various times and places. Yet, it is clear that honor is something that is mostly earned or pursued on an individual basis. Sharon Krause has argued that "one abides by an honor code not primarily for the sake of others but for one's own sake. One owes it to oneself to take the test fairly, to meet the challenge and to master it." It leads ultimately less to the pursuit of the common good and more to the celebration of personal achievements. Honorable men were not necessarily opposed to democracy, but they had other things on their mind, including the maintenance of national power and the needs and status of those who served.[27]

The veneration of honor and the ordinary GI allowed veteran organizations such as the Legion to recall the war in terms that were more heroic than when it was actually experienced and in terms that were less democratic than the rhetoric of the Roosevelt administration. If war was about honor, character, and national security, it was less about democratic crusades, dying, or feelings of vulnerability. And because it was more about the men who served, it stood to reason that the veterans merited not only respect but also some form of a reward. Interviews with soldiers coming home in 1945 strongly indicated that they felt they deserved special compensation, especially the right to have the first choice of available jobs. Thus, the Legion focused its postwar politics not only on the need to recognize and help the men who fought but on a continued need to preserve our military strength through the promotion of universal military training in the face of threats to the nation in the future. New Deal democracy and soldier vulnerability gave way to the celebration of men and of a nation who were honorable and powerful. And when it did, the sentimental view of the men nurtured in wartime culture was left alone to flourish in patterns of remembrance that coursed through the culture over the next half-century.[28]

This retreat from both the political idealism of wartime and the realities of the soldier's experience was also fueled by a sense of triumph and power that followed the American victory. Thus, death and vulnerability were not evident in postwar commemorations that focused on the image of the flag raising on Iwo Jima or the countless local efforts to save a tank, plane, or ship for public view. Indeed, Kurt Piehler has shown that popular sentiment was so favorably disposed toward the Iwo Jima photograph by Joe Rosenthal that those who wanted a marine memorial along more classical and allegorical lines were overruled. This same sense of savoring the victory was evident in countless pageants that were held in the late 1940s that simulated aspects of the war such as one in Los Angeles in 1945 that included mock carrier attacks, the marines landing at Iwo Jima, and the Japanese surrender. Veterans took it upon themselves now to continue the honorable defense of the nation in some cases by moving into the streets. Some marched in Legion parades with jets flying overhead. Others organized demonstrations in several towns in the early days of the Cold War to show citizens what it would be like if Communists took over America and denied its citizens their civil liberties. In Peekskill, New York, in 1949 men from the local chapters of the American Legion, Veterans of Foreign Wars, and Catholic War Veterans attacked people who were attending a concert by the African American activist and singer Paul Robeson on two different occasions because they saw Robeson and his radical democratic views as a threat to their community and their place in it. They now saw themselves as militant defenders of home and family.[29]

In some ways that were highly ironic the thrust of veterans' politics, despite its subjective attachments to notions of strong and honorable warriors, represented a desire to forget the actual experience of the war and trauma and vulnerability it brought to many of the soldiers. This was driven by the pursuit of patriotic honor and benefits, but also by a larger trend on the part of the entire population to push private interests and desires to the forefront and put aside the realities of war itself and the promotion of larger political crusades. Thus, in a study of a Midwestern town in the late 1940s, Robert Havighurst reported that most veterans were largely intent upon reestablishing their personal careers. In the local halls of the Legion and the VFW he found little interest in national or international politics and basic approval for the politics of national veteran organizations. In the larger society many parents wrote President Harry Truman, asking him to demobilize as soon as possible and bring the men home. Over the next decade, in fact, there was considerable opposition to the American Legion's calls for universal military training because it was simply too expensive. And the military itself had to improve its pay and become more tolerant of minorities and sensitive to the needs of enlisted men in order to recruit the men it needed.[30]

Conclusion

According to historian Phil Melling, a remembrance of war centered on the actions and people who are seen as "beyond reproach" only drains the past of all its complexity and responsibility and prevents it from being used to imagine both alternative pasts and futures. In short such a remembrance is sacred; it resists ironic depictions of war and critical analysis of its subjects—both in the past and the present. It does not even allow for the type of mourning Winter saw in Europe after World War I for it does not come to terms fully with the brutal realities of armed conflict itself. The heavily sentimental memory of World War II that dominates American culture and politics in our times and the images of the good people who waged the battles comes close to Melling's description. Yet, the version of the war that dominates our remembrance was not a simple invention of a subsequent generation or a political response to the criticism of America that emanated from the experience of Vietnam. Rather, it emerged during World War II itself from both the actions and thoughts of officials who desired to mobilize and unify the American population and from a nostalgic response among the population to the disruption and fear that war brought. The news of state mobilizations, calls to arms, extended separations, and killing produced in many citizens a counterresponse that fostered a withdrawal from large-scale politics, an idealized self-image, and an accentuated retreat into a political world that was highly emotional. This sentimental view of the war simultaneously fused people to the war effort by making the nation and its citizens seem much more virtuous than their enemies, but in the forties it also represented a form of resistance to war mobilizations themselves and a subtle way of mourning all that would be lost.[31]

Once the war ended, the politics of veteran organizations in particular seemed to recast the experience of war in ways that erased much of the nostalgia for a prewar past but not necessarily the sentimental view of America and its citizens. America and its citizens continued to be seen as essentially virtuous; preparations for another war were now seen as an ongoing necessity. No doubt this public face of the veterans was driven in part by Cold War realities, but they were also propelled by desires to forget much of what had just transpired. Veterans mourned their comrades but they also seemed ready to fight again. Sentimentality was now militarized and attached to the idea of the next war rather than a desire to escape to an idealized home or past; and that war would best be fought by brave men who were honorable and patriotic individuals. Faith in the future was based more upon the character of these men and their abilities than it was in democratic political movements and state-sponsored reforms. Thus, when Americans began to reconsider World War II in the 1990s on the occasion of the fiftieth anniversary of the war, they inherited a way of seeing the war that was both highly sentimental and less attached to both the nostalgia and the democratic dreams of the early 1940s. Combined with the rise of conservative outlooks in the aftermath of the 1960s and the rise of a new generation removed from some of the war's traumatic episodes, it was not hard for Brokaw and Ambrose to think of World War II and the generation that fought it in terms that mythologized both the experience of the conflict and the people who waged it.[32]

PART II

Public Image

Chapter 4
Sponsorship and Snake Oil: Medicine Shows and Contemporary Public Culture

Susan Strasser

Although we are surrounded by so many commercial messages that they work without our even noticing most of them, advertising keeps showing up in new places. Ads printed on the back of a cookie fortune or pasted onto an airplane tray table suggest that contemporary consumer culture abhors a blank space; a company's name on trail markers in a public park hints at the ways that public institutions must pander to private ones in order to flourish, and sometimes to survive (Figure 4.1). American culture, at home and across the globe, is corporate culture. The public is defined by and represented in cultural products designed for profit-making, and the corporations that manufacture and market those products shape our understanding of the possibilities for a public culture. Our news and our experience of human creativity are largely paid for by legal entities established to make money for investors while limiting the liability of the principals. Our largest public gatherings are contests of physical skill and musical entertainments that are as much about megabucks as about what happens on the field or the stage; they take place in arenas named for corporations that deliver packages and facilitate phone calls. In newspapers and magazines, on radio and television, we put up with advertising whether or not we like it, or look at it. We grumble about the commercials on NPR, now well beyond simple sponsor identification, but we understand that somebody has to pay the piper.

When it first appeared, advertising at the movies rankled in a special way. You'd paid serious money for your ticket, there was no channel changer or mute button, and even young people could remember when the time before the film was used to promote things that theaters actually sold, like other films and Coca-Cola. But from the time of the first automobile ad—or, for

Figure 4.1. Mile marker, Platte River Parkway, Casper, Wyoming, 2003. Collection of the author.

that matter, the first Coke ad—we knew we'd get used to it because we are completely accustomed to the fundamental fact of sponsorship. To use an image from the medicine shows that played American towns during the decades around the turn of the last century, you have to sit through the pitch if you want to hear the banjo player.

It took several years for the system that eventually became naturalized in radio and television—businesses buying time during broadcasts for commercial messages—to establish itself. Like today's movie patrons, many early radio listeners and communications policy makers opposed advertising on the air.[1] But even though they did not take sponsorship for granted, people then, too, were accustomed to the fundamental fact. They had learned it from the medicine shows, which brought sponsored live entertainment to American cities and towns of all sizes.

The medicine sold at these shows, although attacked by contemporary critics and never taken seriously by historians, was generally made from the same ingredients as that prescribed by legitimate physicians. Combinations of those ingredients, marketed as "patent" or proprietary medicines, achieved considerable commercial success in an unregulated market, manufactured by entrepreneurs who are now celebrated as innovators in the history of advertising and marketing. Some historians have taken these companies' advertisements and the success of their products to indicate the public's tolerance and even eagerness for persuasion, and for putting their faith in cures not substantiated by modern scientific medicine. Proprietary medicine was ridiculed and attacked by muckrakers and reformers; indeed, writes Nancy Tomes, the industry "helped bring into existence the modern conception of consumer protection."[2]

Americans who wanted to make decisions about treating their maladies without consulting professionals had to find their way in a marketplace defined and framed by the manufacturers, and by the irrational powers of imagery. Yet turn-of-the-century consumers—increasingly sophisticated media receivers rather than ignorant or superstitious dupes—interpreted the commercial messages they received, and acted on those interpretations, not necessarily on the intentions of the advertisers. As marketing methods developed, American audiences and consumers acquired a worldliness about the realm of advertising, a borderland where the distinction between truth and fiction is slippery. Medicine shows offered a superb introduction to that realm.

Pitchmen and Tent Shows

The term "medicine show" was applied to several kinds of entertainments, but usually referred to more than a solo act. Small, marginal shows performed on the street, while larger ones set up tents or rented halls, depending on the season. The "doctor," the central and necessary character, delivered the sales pitch (Figure 4.2). Like politicians and preachers, medicine showmen exposed nineteenth- and early-twentieth-century Americans to accomplished oratorical skills. As "Doc Foster," who was still playing the South during the Great Depression, reminisced, "it would be unthinkable simply to say, 'It's a clean show.' Rather it would be 'There will be nothing seen, heard, said, or done that will

Figure 4.2. Cover, "The Kickapoo Doctor," *Kickapoo Indian Medicine Co.*, thirty-two-page illustrated pamphlet, published by the Kickapoo Indian Medicine Company, New Haven, Connecticut, circa 1890. Reproduced by permission of the William H. Helfand Collection, New York.

mar the impunity or injure the propriety, in any way, shape, form, or manner, of the most fastidious little lady in the community.'"[3]

Some show doctors offered medical consultations before or after the show; some sang or played musical instruments when they were not delivering the pitch. They shared the stage with sword swallowers, magicians and musicians of all kinds, and stock characters like Sambo and Jake, borrowed from the blackface minstrel shows. The pitch was neither an interruption nor an interval to be endured; like Super Bowl commercials, it was itself entertainment, intended as much as the juggler to help hold the crowd. Some big shows sold tickets; some companies charged for children (who were not likely to purchase medicine) or for a special "double show," which featured shorter lectures and longer entertainment segments. But most medicine shows were free, and those that did charge cost less than comparable entertainments without commercial segments—independent circuses, and vaudeville, Wild West, and minstrel shows.[4]

The biggest medicine shows, which toured throughout the country but especially the Midwest and the South, featured dozens of performers, playing to audiences of thousands. Troupes advertising and selling John Hamlin's Wizard Oil, a liniment for sore muscles and rheumatism, operated in the open air, from wagons used as stages (Figure 4.3). Wizard Oil performances featured community singing; the company distributed songbooks at the shows and through the drugstores that performers stocked during runs as long as six weeks in a town. The shows of the Kickapoo Indian Medicine Company sold a similar liniment, Kickapoo Indian Oil, as well as the renowned Kickapoo Sagwa—"Nature's Remedy. Made from Roots, Herbs and Barks." Founded in 1881 in Boston, the Kickapoo company eventually moved to New Haven, Connecticut, where it manufactured medicine, published promotional magazines and almanacs, and managed numerous simultaneously touring shows, from a Barnumesque building displaying Indian curios and much else. The Kickapoo shows offered a medicinal version of Buffalo Bill's Wild West, hiring many Native Americans, mostly from New York and Canadian Iroquois tribes. Like the Wizard Oil troupes, Kickapoo companies spent several weeks in a town, ten to twenty performers operating out of teepees and tents, or, in winter, playing local halls and small-town opera houses. The shows featured Indian entertainment—mock powwows and authentic chants and dances—as well as standard vaudeville and circus acts, fireworks, music, and free medical consultations at the teepee village during the day (Figure 4.4).[5]

As an early career track for entertainers including Harry Houdini and many stars of twentieth-century bluegrass and country music, the medicine

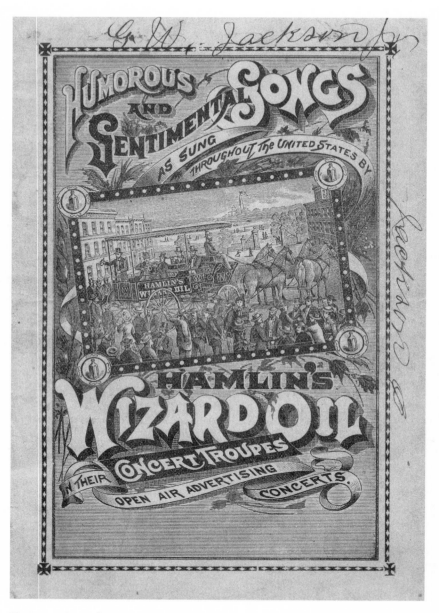

Figure 4.3. Cover, "Humorous and Sentimental Songs as Sung throughout the United States by Hamlin's Wizard Oil in Their Concert Troupes Open Air Advertising Concerts." From *Wizard Oil Humorous and Sentimental Songs*, a thirty-two-page pamphlet published by Hamlin's Wizard Oil Company, Chicago, circa 1900. Reproduced by permission of the William H. Helfand Collection, New York.

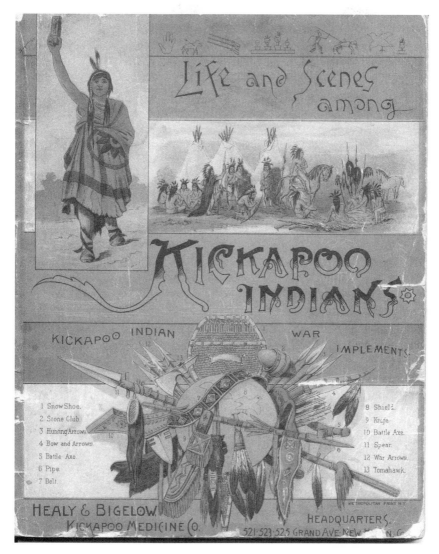

Figure 4.4. Cover, *Life and Scenes among the Kickapoo Indians*, an illustrated 176-page book published by the Kickapoo Indian Medicine Company, New Haven, Connecticut, circa 1900. Reproduced by permission of the William H. Helfand Collection, New York.

show can be understood as a chapter in the history of performance and entertainment. Selling medicine made money for the promoters in much the same way that selling popcorn does for movie theater owners. Some independent medicine showmen bottled their brews in hotel bathtubs before the show, but most acted as agents for commercial products, which they bought directly from manufacturers or from wholesale druggists. Manufacturers supported the shows with free posters, tickets, and flyers, which reduced the costs of production; some sold showmen cases of laxatives and salves for considerably less than they charged wholesalers, far enough under the retail price to undercut retail druggists on these branded goods (Figure 4.5). Medicines sold at the big shows were marked up for retail sale: an 1898 Kickapoo show in Chicago, for example, advertised Sagwa for sixty-nine cents, but it cost a dollar in the stores. Because most doctors dispensed their own prescriptions, drugstores depended on sales of self-dosage products, and pharmacists were understandably threatened; their organizations opposed medicine shows and supported legislation to regulate them.[6]

Understood not as show business but as advertising for self-dosage medicines, the shows used the strategy inherent in all manufacturer-sponsored advertising: courting consumers directly rather than relying on wholesale and retail druggists to promote goods. Medicine companies were leaders and innovators in originating and developing all kinds of promotional schemes, including the most significant, print advertising in newspapers and magazines.[7] The companies that sponsored big shows and supported smaller ones with premiums depended on drugstore sales after the show left town; they aimed not for a quick buck but for repeat sales to satisfied customers. Milton Bartok, hawking his Bardex ("The World's Medicine") well into the twentieth century, told audiences he didn't care whether they purchased it at the show or not. "You know the few bottles we sell here don't pay for this show," he insisted. "But I know the medicine's so good that when we leave here you're going to buy it ten years from now."[8] With numerous remedies competing on drugstore shelves, these manufacturers, like other marketers, aspired to brand loyalty.

Patent Medicine and Family Medical Practice

"Patent medicine," the phrase commonly used to describe these products, was almost always a misnomer; "proprietary medicine" is the more accurate term. Patent applications required inventors to explain the details of their inventions—in the case of medicines, to reveal the ingredients, which competitors

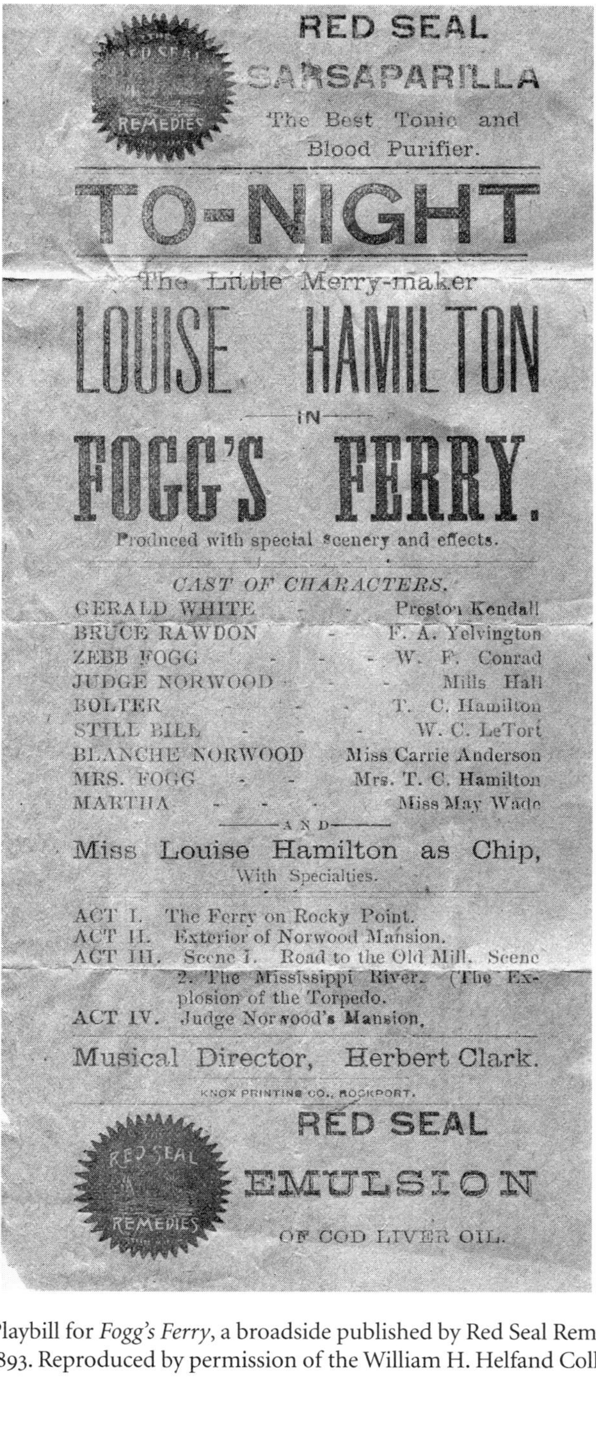

Figure 4.5. Playbill for *Fogg's Ferry*, a broadside published by Red Seal Remedies, Rockport, circa 1893. Reproduced by permission of the William H. Helfand Collection, New York.

might imitate. As James Harvey Young explains in *The Toadstool Millionaires* (1961), still the most frequently cited treatment of the topic, only "simple-minded folk unused to the clever ways of the commercial world" actually patented their remedies. "The shrewd could secure other forms of governmental protection"—trademarks, patents on containers, and copyrights on labels and promotional materials—while keeping their formulas secret. The secret formula was the essence of a successful product, since these medicines were easy to produce and easy to imitate.[9]

Young describes patent medicine and advertising as associated phenomena of "the commercial and printing revolutions."[10] Historians of advertising, too, emphasize the singular importance of the proprietary medicine industry to advertising's development: in the early years, the patent medicine and advertising industries were inseparable. Thanks to entrepreneurial energy, competition, and the development of transcontinental and international markets, proprietary medicine makers became the largest group of advertisers by the 1870s. Jackson Lears points out that they were the "chief clients" of nineteenth-century advertising agencies "and, indeed, the very basis of many agencies' success."[11] Pamela Laird portrays these manufacturers as the originators of branding: entrepreneurs motivated by intense competition, who sold their goods in consumer-sized packaging for which traditional generic, bulk merchandising methods were inadequate. Medicine makers had to argue for the unique merits of their remedies, and they associated their products with their claims in consumers' minds by means of trade names, emblems, and symbols for reassurance or potency.[12] In patent medicine, writes Daniel Pope, "whatever art and science there was in advertising could operate. Indeed, medical advertising of the era was the proving ground for persuasive techniques like testimonials, story-form ads, and vivid illustrations."[13]

In considering the products the medicine firms sold, most historians have relied almost exclusively on James Harvey Young, who—both in *Toadstool Millionaires* and his many subsequent works on the topic—has never made a secret of his contempt for these remedies. "The author," he writes in his 1961 introduction, "votes against patent medicines," and he describes them there as "quackery," as "an anti-rational approach to one of the key problems of life," and as "hazardous," while conceding that some sincere and ignorant purveyors of nostrums may have meant well.[14] Historians relying on Young tend to describe the ingredients in patent medicine either as utterly harmless or incredibly harmful or sometimes both, much like critics of contemporary herbal medicine. Most dismiss purchasers' motives with considerably less nuance than Young himself. In the only scholarly book about medicine shows,

Brooks McNamara writes, "the appeal of supposed miracle cures was strong among the ignorant, the superstitious, and those on whom regular physicians had given up hope." Lears proposes that the products be understood only in terms of their advertising (about which he makes complex and elegant arguments) and declares that "the appeal of patent medicines depended on the persistence of magical thinking among the American population."[15]

The arguments against proprietary medicines are well known and often repeated, echoing both Young and such turn-of-the-century reform voices as *Ladies' Home Journal* editor Edward Bok, a leader of the campaign against patent medicine, and muckraker Samuel Hopkins Adams, whose "Great American Fraud" series in *Collier's* was the drug counterpart to Upton Sinclair's *The Jungle*. Some of those arguments charge medicine makers with outright fraud, selling nostrums by making therapeutic claims they knew to be untrue. Others acknowledge that the use of patent medicines may have had therapeutic results, but they attribute those results only to alcohol, addictive drugs, or the placebo effect.

There must have been some truth to the placebo charge for some patients, but patent medicines were not placebos as they are now understood. Knowing that many complaints resolve without treatment, physicians had prescribed placebos for centuries; they used the word for prescriptions intended to please or cheer patients rather than to cure them.[16] But doctors did not begin to analyze the placebo effect until the mid-twentieth century, when scientific medicine demanded explanations for cures attributable to what had always been understood as the art of healing, and when the testing of new remedies in clinical drug trials required inert comparisons. One early discussion, published in the *American Journal of Pharmacology* in 1945, described three essential qualities for placebos and their prescribers. First, the placebo had to be totally inert. But unlike sugar pills, patent medicine formulas incorporated plants and minerals that had long been understood to affect the human body. Secondly, a placebo should have a "latin and polysyllabic name" that would befuddle even intelligent patients, certainly not true of Wizard Oil or Lydia Pinkham's Vegetable Compound. Finally, the prescription should be given with "some assurance and emphasis for psychotherapeutic effect."[17] Here, of course, patent medicine advertising and the "doctors" who pitched at medicine shows excelled.

Many medicines were indeed formulated with alcohol, a solvent of considerable value for extracting the active medicinal constituents from plants and for preserving the solution. Alcoholic solutions of plant materials do not ferment, as water-based preparations do, and alcohol extraction excludes such potentially undesirable properties of roots as gums, mucilage, and mineral salts. John Uri Lloyd, a pharmacist and prolific writer whose drug manufacturing company supplied botanical physicians, described alcohol as "indispensable and irreplaceable" in pharmacy, equaling water in importance among solvents.[18] Some people surely drank alcoholic tonics as substitutes for whiskey, especially in dry states and counties. But those who took alcohol-based preparations as the labels directed ingested dropperfuls or spoonfuls, quantities too small to create the purported boozy pleasures that generate sneers from so many commentators.

Even temperance activists, who were central to pure food and drug agitation, were by no means united against patent medicine, in part because many medicine companies promoted temperance.[19] Kickapoo company publications included doggerel suggesting that the Chief of the Kickapoos did not imbibe "brandy, nor whiskey . . . Nor the Chinaman's poisonous tea," but often took Indian Sagwa.[20] The Lydia E. Pinkham Medicine Company sought a good relationship with the Women's Christian Temperance Union. Lydia Pinkham's son Charles invited his local chapter to hold its annual lawn party at his house in 1899; the quid pro quo was a testimonial on WCTU letterhead, which the company published.[21] In 1904, Edward Bok charged that many members of the organization were "regular buyers and partakers," and that WCTU members had learned of the alcoholic content of proprietary medicines not from the organization's "Department of Non-Alcoholic Medication," but in the pages of his *Ladies' Home Journal.*[22]

Although many of the most popular patent medicines did not contain habit-forming drugs, the critics' charge that some did was true. Coca derivatives and opiates were not illegal even after the passage of the first Pure Food and Drug Act in 1906, which made it illegal to adulterate drugs, to sell them under false names, or to fail to print alcohol and narcotic contents on the label. One historian of drug regulation points out that this statute "was known universally—even in the margins of the United States *Statutes at Large*—as the Pure Food Act," and that the first Food and Drug Administration commissioner, Harvey Wiley, "neglected drugs" because he was primarily concerned about food.[23] The 1914 Harrison Narcotic Act limited the quantity of addictive substances that proprietary medicines could contain, but still did not completely outlaw the over-the-counter purchase of medicines containing cocaine or morphine.[24] In practice the provisions of the Harrison Act that effectively banned narcotic patent medicine were those calling for manufacturers and sellers of coca and opium products to register with the Treasury Department and to keep records of their transactions.[25] In an age when small retailers did little record-keeping, this demand was prohibitive to druggists, who now had to keep track of physician-prescribed narcotics, and would not want to do so for over-the-counter remedies as well. It is even harder to imagine medicine showmen performing such tasks—and, operating in public, they could not hide.[26]

Conventional arguments about alcohol, opiates, and placebos have some merit, then, but they do not account for the popularity of proprietary remedies. Most historians' understanding is further confounded by inadequate attention to purchasers' lifestyles and medical options. Nineteenth- and early twentieth-century Americans diagnosed and dosed themselves for minor afflictions in many of the same ways we do today. They cleaned and bandaged small wounds, and they treated themselves for upper respiratory symptoms, and for aches and pains. But they also suffered from some different ailments. People doing hard physical labor on farms, in factories, or in homes with open fires might seek expensive medical assistance when they broke bones or took sick with serious diseases, but bruises, muscle strains, and burns were everyday events that called for liniments and salves. People with no access to fresh vegetables through the long winter addressed digestive problems with tonics. And many diseases that can now be cured might reasonably have been countered with painkillers.

Most people depended on a kind of care that has largely disappeared. Women whose primary work was in their homes tended to the sick, employing plants from the garden, homemade remedies, and the bland recipes for invalids that may be found in most nineteenth-century cookbooks, in addition to whatever proprietary medicines they might purchase. Some women took to nursing more than others—as some did to sewing, cooking, or cleaning—but for most women, these chores were an essential part of housekeeping.[27] Caregivers sought written instruction in the many self-help manuals that went through dozens of editions throughout the nineteenth century, including William Buchan's *Domestic Medicine*, John C. Gunn's book of the same title, and A. W. Chase's *Dr. Chase's Family Physician*. As medical historian Charles Rosenberg suggests, "their very popularity tells us something significant about the medical system that produced them."[28] (The Lynds found an 1890 edition of Chase's book "still treasure[d]" by a business-class family in Middletown in the 1920s; they ridiculed its contents, and asserted that the kinds of remedies it prescribed were "largely confined to the working class.")[29] In addition to books issued by independent doctors and publishing companies, many were put out by proprietary medicine makers. One scholar who examined hundreds of nineteenth-century domestic medical manuals maintains that a fifth were "in part or primarily vehicles for selling drugs."[30] Patent medicine companies also issued countless pamphlets with instructions for treating specific ailments.

Some Americans relied on domestic medicine instead of on doctors because of geographical isolation; some regarded physicians with skepticism, thanks at least in part to such practices as bloodletting and the use of mercury. Many more considered physicians prohibitively expensive. " 'No use going to a doctor,' " Edward Bok portrayed patent medicine buyers arguing; " 'we can save that money,' and instead of paying one or two dollars for honest, intelligent medical advice they invest from twenty-five to seventy-five cents for a bottle of this, or a box of that."[31] But the difference between a quarter and two dollars meant more to most people than it did to a successful magazine editor, and one or two dollars then is equivalent to hundreds now.[32] When family members took sick, caregivers had to calculate their options. "I am giving both children Scoville's Blood and Liver Syrup now," one Kansas woman wrote to her mother in New York some decades before Bok wrote. "It may take a dozen bottles—but that is a comparatively small doctor's bill—and it may be the means of saving their lives, for Scrofula is a terrible malady."[33] Many other caregivers and patients used patent medicines not as lifesavers but to alleviate suffering in illnesses they understood as incurable. Consumers were not necessarily fooled by exaggerated claims; perhaps nothing they could buy would actually cure tuberculosis, but some proprietary might make a patient more comfortable at far less expense than a doctor's visit, and nationally advertised medicines might well be regarded as more modern than folk remedies. Yet the distinction between proprietaries and folk remedies was not so clear; people with face-to-face knowledge of the physicians, druggists, herbalists, and housewife-nurses who made much of their medicine probably also perceived the connections between proprietaries and these traditions of medicine-making.

Similarly, the distinction between physician-prescribed medicine and patent medicine was blurry, since many physicians prescribed patent medicines. Although the American Medical Association adopted resolutions against secret formulas at nearly every annual convention, proprietary medicines were advertised in medical journals, and by means of circulars and samples sent to doctors. In 1899, one university professor of medicine received 424 proprietary medicine circulars in the mail; a 1906 study in the *Journal of the American Medical Association* showed that most medical journals not only carried ads for patent medicines, but also published their public relations material as editorial matter.[34] Indeed, the *Journal of the American Medical Association* itself failed to keep its 1900 promise to ban nostrum ads from its pages; by 1905 it had published so many that it had to resolve to ban them again.[35]

From the consumer's standpoint, the line between proprietary and physician-prescribed drugs was also blurred because both were formulated with the same alcohol, narcotics, plants, and minerals. James Harvey Young maintains that, in an age of unscientific medicine, "patent medicines contained the same ingredients that physicians were prescribing, and physicians too were fooled into believing their drugs wrought cures."[36] But neither doctors nor patients were fools to believe that opiates ease pain, and for a long time, empirical success with the traditional plants and minerals, and chemicals synthesized from them, was the best that anybody knew, with or without a degree from a medical school. *Merck's 1901 Manual of the Materia Medica*, which lists "all those . . . drugs and chemicals . . . which are in current and well-established use in the medical practice of this country," includes plant materials now generally considered cooking ingredients (such as cardamom and ginger) and the materia medica of modern herbalists (including black cohosh, golden seal, and valerian), as well as herbs and chemical derivatives now considered street drugs (like marijuana, cocaine, and heroin).[37] Most of these had long histories of effective use in clinical practice, though few (at least in the first two categories) were as fast-acting or as powerful as the synthetics, antibiotics, and sulfa drugs that eventually supplanted them. Physicians prescribed opiates for a long list of conditions until World War II, despite increased concerns about addiction.[38]

At least some patent medicines, then, should be taken seriously as medications. Like purchasers of Nyquil and vitamin C, many people who bought Indian Sagwa and Lydia Pinkham's were looking for relief from everyday ailments that they did not consider consequential enough to merit a doctor's attention. And like people looking for relief today, they may have bought a first bottle because they bought the advertising, but if they came back for a second, they probably thought it had done some good.

Charlatans, Counterfeits, Con Men, and Tricksters

Notwithstanding the many good reasons why consumers might choose proprietary medicines, they were vulnerable to fraud. Medicine-making and remedy-selling attracted rogues as well as dedicated and talented healers. It offered many inspiring examples of successful firms, huge potential markets of suffering customers, and low barriers to entry, a business that did not require much capital investment. Lydia Pinkham began in her kitchen, and remedies could, in fact, be produced in a hotel bathroom.[39] Henry Helmbold, who ran palatial retail pharmacies in New York and Philadelphia and got rich on proprietary medicines including his well-known Extract of Buchu, claimed to have begun production with fifty cents.[40] Whether or not they sold effective medicine, the biggest of these firms were, as both muckrakers and historians have charged, making fortunes off people's ailments and, in some cases, their desperation.

This coexistence of the quack and the healer brings us into a realm where the distinction between "true" and "false" is murky—the realm where advertising resides, as Daniel Boorstin pointed out decades ago. "Advertising befuddles our experience, not because advertisers are liars, but precisely because they are not," he writes. "Advertising fogs our daily lives less from its peculiar lies than from its peculiar truths. . . . [T]he simple question, 'Is it true?' [is] as obsolete as the horse and buggy."[41] "Doc Foster" recalled that establishing credibility was a central goal for the medicine show doctor. "One method was to undersell rather than oversell. For example, people expecting to hear us insist that we had a cure for every disease . . . were much more impressed to hear us say, 'We don't have a cure-all. Our product is good for three things and three things only: the stomach, the liver, and the kidneys' . . . Similarly, they were receptive when I told them, 'Even though you will be hearing people call me "doctor," I am really not a doctor. I am not licensed, even though I did attend Northwestern Medical School for two years.' "[42]

"Doctor" was a title used by many unlicensed people during the medicine show years. Physicians trained in the medical schools of the Eclectics and homeopaths considered themselves fully qualified for the honorific. During the many decades of controversy over these groups' legal rights, Americans simply were not in accord about who was entitled to call himself (and sometimes herself) a doctor, and the victory of allopathic medicine did not put an end to long-time practitioners' use of the title. Moreover, "Doc" was a common sobriquet for pharmacists. The successful New York and Philadelphia druggist Henry Helmbold was known as "Dr. Helmbold" or "the Doctor," though he held neither a medical nor a pharmacy degree.[43]

Even without the slightest legitimate claim to the title of doctor, and even if they regarded themselves primarily as performers, medicine show players found some medical knowledge extremely useful. Those who offered consultations before and after the show needed something to say to suffering patients even though they were pushing bottled remedies. Show doctors who prepared their own medicines needed formulas. "Little Doc" Roberts, who operated a permanent tent show in Oklahoma City during the Depression, relied on recipes inherited from his uncle, a real doctor.[44] The unpublished booklets of Harry Helms, a magician and juggler who traveled with both the Kickapoo and Wizard Oil shows, suggest how genuine interest in and knowledge about domestic medicine might coexist with unapologetic duplicity.

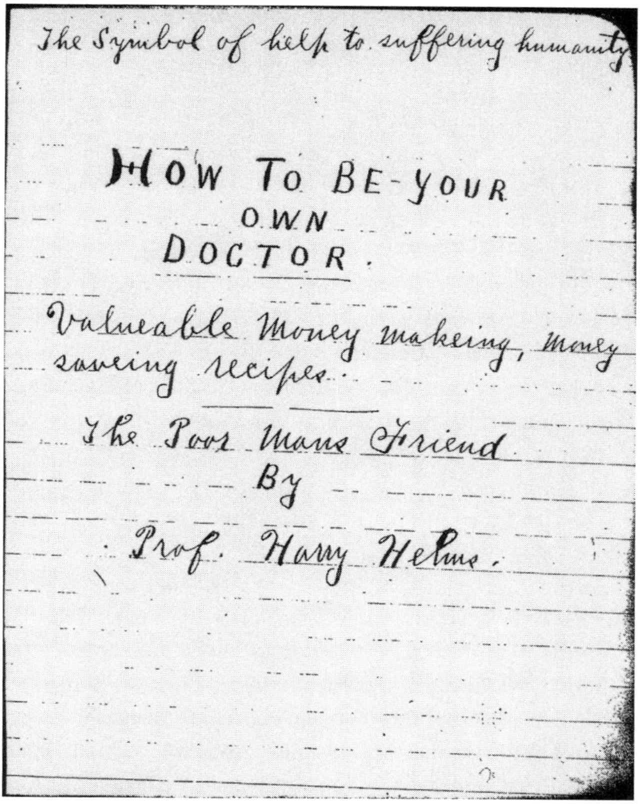
The Symbol of help to suffering humanity

HOW TO BE-YOUR OWN DOCTOR.

Valueable Money makeing, money saveing recipes.

The Poor Mans Friend
By
Prof. Harry Helms.

Figure 4.6. "How to Be Your Own Doctor." From Harry Helms's pamphlet in the Harry Houdini scrapbook collection, Library of Congress, Scrapbook 96, microfilm reel 21.

Helms was primarily a showman and his motives were hardly altruistic; he included directions for "How to Run a Medicine Show Successfull" [*sic*] among many other scams in his booklet "Schemes and Tricks."[45] But in "How to Be Your Own Doctor" (containing "Valueable Money Makeing, Money saveing recipes" [*sic*]), he compiled five pages of formulas for cough and asthma cures; five of liniments, oils, and salves; eight of remedies for worms; and numerous eye washes, tooth ache drops, inhalers, and remedies for female troubles, pimples, and other ailments (Figure 4.6). Although he did reveal a formula for Ayers Cherry Pectoral, he explained that he could not publish the recipes for famous proprietary medicines using their trademarks, and gave directions for making "Indian Sagwah" rather than Sagwa, and "H——s Buchu" rather than Helmbold's.[46]

Some writers have described medicine showmen like Helms as con men, exemplars of the frauds and swindlers who populated an industrializing and urbanizing society. Jackson Lears points us toward Herman Melville's *The Confidence-Man* (1857), an extraordinary novel whose "dense and circling prose, its self-canceling sentences, ultimately deconstruct language as a medium of communication, ridiculing all claims of social transparency and calling all fixed meanings into question." One of the confidence-man's many guises or manifestations is the "Herb-Doctor," selling "Omni-Balsamic Reinvigorator" and "Samaritan Pain Dissuader." "Entire pages of his conversations," writes Lears, "could have been lifted directly from mid-nineteenth-century advertising copy"; indeed, except for antiquated diction, they could have been lifted from twenty-first-century copy.[47] The Herb-Doctor invokes Nature, a realm without sponsors. He insists that his remedy is "nature's own. . . . Trust me, nature is health; for health is good, and nature cannot work ill. As little can she work error. Get nature, and you get well."[48]

But showmanship and sponsorship are not in themselves con games. Neither Melville's Herb-Doctor nor the nonfictional patent medicine salesman corresponds to historian Karen Halttunen's nineteenth-century urban confidence man, who seduced and corrupted innocent young rubes. Nor are they quite the same as the other types she describes: the gambler, the political demagogue, and the criminal imposter who swindled people out of money, posed as a businessman to steal unguarded cash, or cheated at cards.[49]

At least some medicine show "doctors" are better understood as trickster figures than as con-men. As Lears suggests, the faith of the medicine-show audience "was no doubt bracketed by a healthy skepticism"—they "expected to be tricked,"[50] for this was both show business and an utterly blatant example of somebody out to make a buck. Like other tricksters, the show doctor was a traveler, here today and gone tomorrow, and he took advantage of that; like others, he invited belief and disbelief at the same time. In an analysis that encompasses Hermes, Krishna, Coyote, and various contemporary cultural figures, critic Lewis Hyde describes tricksters on the one hand as liars and cheaters, and on the other as an inventive and creative cultural force—"trickster makes this world," he writes. There may be plenty to disparage, but the trickster is "*a*moral, not *im*moral," Hyde insists; he is not wicked, nor should he be mistaken for the Devil.[51] Patent medicine manufacturers and medicine showmen originated many advertising methods and the very idea of sponsorship; their creativity and inventiveness in the realm of marketing knew no

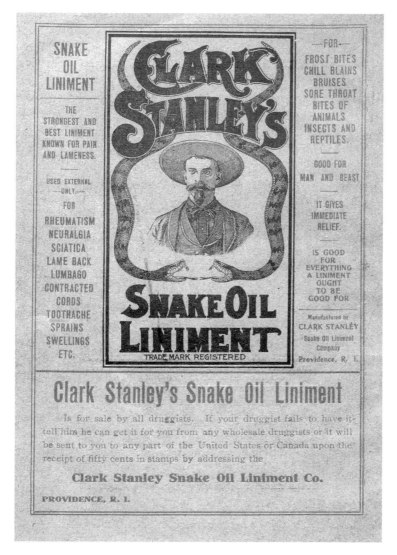

Figure 4.7. Cover, Clark Stanley's Snake Oil Liniment, *True Life in the Far West*, an illustrated two-hundred-page pamphlet, published circa 1905. Reproduced by permission of the William H. Helfand Collection, New York.

bounds (Figure 4.7). They did make the world that puts advertising on the cookie fortunes and in the public parks, the world where medicine is sold by actors pointing out that they are not doctors though they play them on TV, the world in which truth and falsehood are so difficult to ascertain.

Other performers in the medicine show were tricksters, too. The "blacks" were in blackface, even if they were actually African Americans. The Indians were advertised as "full-blooded," even if they spoke with German accents. They played contradictory roles: on the one hand attacking wagon trains in skits and on the other, dispensing "natural" Indian healing. The fact that many were real Native Americans only heightened the contradictions and complications. In 1897, the *New York Times* reported that one of the major employments for Indians who came to New York City was playing braves and squaws in the shows. The reporter was especially taken with White Moon (Louis Smith), a twenty-three-year-old Mohawk "with a touch of German blood," who had arrived in Manhattan as "the chief attraction of a traveling medicine show" and became a social success in "New York parlors [where he] charmed all. No picture can give any idea of his physical beauty and magnetism, which are most marked."[52]

Such magnetism could be dangerous. Three years earlier, the *Times* told the tale of Stella Brightman, the eighteen-year-old daughter of a Long Island businessman who went to a Kickapoo show with friends "as one would go 'slumming.'" Attracted to Deerfoot, "a fervid performer" and the leader of the "war dances and ridiculous incantations," she became a regular during the ten days the show was in Rockville Centre, and attempted to elope with the "wily redskin" when the performers moved to Hempstead. "[T]hese Indian shows," warned the *Times*, "are becoming a dangerous fad among rural maidens."[53] By the mid-1930s, the Kickapoo Company was history, but many imitators were still touring.[54] With real Indians, actors of mixed ancestry, or total fakes, the promoters of these shows, in Philip Deloria's words, "used Indian play to encounter the authentic amidst the anxiety of urban industrial . . . life."[55]

"Real medicine" was as slippery a category as "real doctor" or "real Indian." Numerous patent medicines were marketed as tonics—taken not so much to cure disease as to invigorate the constitution or restore health, much as Americans now take vitamins. Early soft drinks were first sold as tonics or remedies at drugstore soda fountains. Coca-Cola advertising before the turn of the century touted both its flavor and its healing qualities. As the advertising trade journal *Printers' Ink* told the story decades later, Atlanta druggist Asa Candler, who bought a headache recipe, reasoned that "the chronic sufferer from headaches may have but one a week," but everybody suffered from thirst every day.[56] Charles E. Hires, a Philadelphia pharmacist, first packaged

Hires Root Tea; he introduced his root beer at the 1876 Philadelphia Centennial Exposition as "the Greatest Health-Giving Beverage in the World."[57] The relationship between Dr Pepper and a Virginia pharmacist of that name is more a matter of myth than history, but that drink, too, was formulated in a drug store, in Waco, Texas.[58] Soft drinks are still called "tonics" in parts of the country, at least by older people, and sarsaparilla is still a flavor of soft drink offered by small specialty companies.

It was particularly difficult to define real medicine because patent medicine, like paper money, was frequently counterfeited. The New York dealer for a London medicine-maker wrote merchants in 1857 that one William Leith had been arrested for counterfeiting "to an enormous extent my Pills and Ointment, his order for Pill books alone being for 500,000!" The *New York Times*, which gave the number as 50,000, reported that Leith was selling the preparation in the West at half its normal price. "The case is a curious one," the *Times* commented.[59] But such cases became more common as the patent medicine industry grew. As the proprietors of Wistar's Balsam of Wild Cherry commented in a public notice warning consumers about imitators, "Unprincipled scoundrels can always be found ready to counterfeit anything by which they can put money in their pockets," and unscrupulous medicine dealers would purchase the stuff because it cost half the price of the real thing. "Avoid such a man as you would a dealer in counterfeit money, for he is the greater scamp of the two."[60]

Indeed, sometimes dealers in counterfeit medicines and medicine labels and dealers in counterfeit money were one and the same. The one-time proprietor of Mexican Mustang Liniment, a well-known proprietary, was arrested in 1873, in possession of a trunkful of counterfeit federal bonds, as well as plates "made in imitation of Treasury note plates, patent medicine and other labels."[61] Genuine patent medicine labels were often made by the same companies that printed bank notes; the labels for Henry Helmbold's Buchu, for example, were engraved by the National Bank Note Company of New York.[62] Similarly, counterfeits of drug labels were sometimes created by the same printers who counterfeited money. Both kinds of counterfeit depended on people's belief in the genuine articles: why bother to counterfeit something that people did not value?[63]

There was counterfeiting at all levels in the medicine business. Crude drugs were regularly forged, with cheap, common plants substituting for rare and expensive ones. John Uri Lloyd, the botanical drug manufacturer, suggested that sometimes this was a mistake of the ignorant collector and the unsuspecting merchant who "accepts in confidence the collector's stock of crude material." But in cases such as golden seal (*Hydrastis Canadensis*), which Lloyd described as endangered in the wild as early as 1884, adulteration was usually intentional.[64] When crude drugs were formulated into the counterfeits of well-known patent medicines, there was no telling what was in the bottle. In 1897 a Chicago physician was arrested as part of a gang counterfeiting a French medicine and its labels; at least twenty druggists were implicated, and scores of people were said to have died from taking the medicine.[65] "Many Counterfeits Worthless and Even Fatal," ran a subheadline in the *New York Times* seven years later, over a front-page article about a different gang, "the most daring and dangerous combination of drug swindlers and patent medicine counterfeiters that ever operated in this country."[66] Patent medicine companies with the resources to sue counterfeiters went to court; in 1898 the manufacturers of the popular Castoria, for example, won an injunction against firms from Chicago and Duluth that manufactured imitation Castoria and packaged it in imitation Castoria packages.[67]

One con man not only counterfeited Wizard Oil, but its marketing concept. He toured the Middle West in the 1880s with fake Wizard Oil shows, peddling fake Wizard Oil and claiming to be John Hamlin, although his show had a different format than those put on by genuine Hamlin troupes.[68] Another Wizard Oil trickster—the employer of poet James Whitcomb Riley, who wrote about his youthful experiences in the show—was Doc C. M. Townsend, who sold his own Magic Oil and some other remedies with his own name on them, but called his troupe the Wizard Oil Company.[69]

Final Acts

Townsend, Hamlin, and their colleagues—the "real" and the fake, selling useful medicines or spurious concoctions from the stage—were on their way out after the turn of the century. In 1911, George Jean Nathan declared the era of the medicine show over. "Here and there may still be found a lingering trace," he wrote in *Harper's Weekly*, "but the great, spectacular caravan of yesterday's medicinemen is gone, routed by the forward-marching force of science and education that has ended the credulities and superstitions of the people on the farms, in the villages and little towns and in the smaller, interior cities."[70] Over the next twenty years, the shows were weakened further, not only by the continuing advance of scientific medicine, but by other formidable forces and tendencies: drug legislation, licensing requirements, the shrunken consumer market of the Depression, and the triumph of radio and film over live entertainment.

As fading memories so often are, the big medicine shows were commemorated, romanticized, and ridiculed in the new popular culture. In the movie *Dangerous Nan McGrew* (1930), the show doctor was a pickpocket and one of the performers a bank robber. Jack Benny played a straight role in *The Medicine Man* (1930), a show doctor who falls in love with the abused daughter of a small-town merchant; here the con men were his associates. In *The Phantom President*, (1932) George M. Cohan played both a medicine show doctor and his double, a banker running for President; Claudette Colbert and Jimmy Durante co-starred. Later films memorializing the shows included *The Old-Fashioned Way* with W. C. Fields (1934) and *Medicine Show Santa Fe Marshal* with William Boyd (1940).[71]

By the time the medicine show was portrayed in the movies, "patent medicine" was becoming an old-fashioned phrase, and popular over-the-counter drugs—many manufactured by large pharmaceutical companies—were under attack by a new generation of consumer activists.[72] Radio sponsors were the new tricksters, conspicuously out to separate consumers from their money and clearly makers of the next new world of sponsored public culture. Like the medicine show doctors, they traded on intimacy with their audiences, and they achieved it by moving into domestic space.

The medicine shows and their sponsors had provided the template. Americans were not only habituated to sponsorship as a central feature of public entertainment, but they had learned a good deal about negotiating the contradictory realm of advertising, which, as Jackson Lears writes of Melville's prose, calls "all fixed meaning into question."[73] In the sponsored realm, things were neither true nor false—or they might be both. Here was a crucible for the techniques of modern political persuasion, and a domain where Americans seemed tolerant of being persuaded, perhaps even eager to fall for the con. At the same time, they learned to interpret commercial messages in this realm, sorting out the medium from the message, and differentiating between context and content.

Despite the condemnation of muckrakers and historians, people continued to self-dose, and to seek cures outside of scientific medicine and from healers other than licensed doctors. Sponsorship framed public discourse about illness as it walked the line between fact and fiction, creating new meanings, new realities, new shared ideas of what it meant to be sick and healthy. Commercial products linked audiences and consumers through images and language, and through the goods themselves. Eventually drug companies would seek to seduce doctors as well as patients, and to apply the direct-to-consumer advertising techniques that the patent medicine companies perfected to prescription remedies like Ambien and Lipitor. But that's another story.[74]

Chapter 5

Entertainment Wars:
Television Culture after 9/11

Lynn Spigel

After the attacks of September 11, 2001, traditional forms of entertainment had to reinvent their place in U.S. life and culture. The de
rigueur violence of mass media—both news and fiction—no longer seemed
business as usual. While Hollywood usually defends its mass-destruction
ethos with claims to "free speech," constitutional rights, and industry-wide
discretion (à la ratings systems), in the weeks following September 11 the industry exhibited (whether for sincere or cynical reasons) a new will toward
"tastefulness" as potentially trauma-inducing films like Warner Bros.' *Collat-
eral Damage* were pulled from release. On television, violent movies also
came under network scrutiny. USA canceled its prime-time run of *The Siege*
(which deals with Arab terrorists who plot to bomb New York). At TBS
violence-packed films like *Lethal Weapon* were replaced with family fare like
Look Who's Talking. TNT replaced its 1970s retro lineup of *Superman, King
Kong,* and *Carrie* with *Close Encounters of the Third Kind, Grease,* and *Jaws*
(although exactly why the bloodsucking shark in *Jaws* seemed less disturbing
than the menstruating teen in *Carrie* already begs questions about exactly
what constitutes terror in the minds of Hollywood executives).[1]

But it wasn't just the "hard" realities of violence that came under self-
imposed censorship. Light entertainment and "diversions" of all kinds also
didn't feel right. Humorists Dave Letterman, Jay Leno, Craig Kilborn, Conan
O'Brien, and Jon Stewart met the late-night audience with dead seriousness.
While *Saturday Night Live* did return to humor, its jokes were officially sanctioned by an opening act that included a somber performance by Paul
Simon, the entire New York Fire Department, and Mayor Rudy Giuliani himself. When producer Lorne Michaels asked the mayor if it was okay to be
funny, Giuliani joked, "Why start now?" (implicitly informing viewers that it
was, in fact, okay to laugh). In the midst of the new sincerity, numerous crit-

ics summarily declared that the attacks on the Pentagon and World Trade Center had brought about the "end of irony."[2]

Despite such bombastic declarations, however, many industry leaders were actually in a profound state of confusion about just what it was that the public wanted. Even while industry leaders were eager to censor trauma-inducing images of any kind, video outlets reported that, when left to their own discretion, consumers were eagerly purchasing terrorist flicks like *The Siege* and *The Towering Inferno*. One video retailer noted an "uneasy" feeling about consumer desire for films like *The Towering Inferno*, and one store owner even "moved such videos so they were arranged with only the spines showing, obscuring the covers."[3] Meanwhile, Internet companies worried about the hundreds of vulgar domain names for which people applied in the hopes of setting up Web sites. One major domain name reseller halted auctions for several names it considered tasteless, including "NewYorkCarnage.com."[4] As these cases suggest, the media industries had to balance their own public image as discriminating custodians of culture with the vagaries of public taste.

Given its historical status as a regulated private industry ideally meant to operate in the "public interest," television was the medium hardest hit by this conflict between maintaining the image of "public servant" and the need to cater to the public taste (or at least to what advertisers think the public likes). Getting back to the normal balance between its public service and entertainment/commercial functions posed problems for broadcasters and cablers alike.[5] In the midst of the turmoil, the Academy of Television Arts and Sciences and CBS postponed the Emmy Awards ceremonies twice.

To be sure, television executives' nervous confusion was rooted in the broader havoc that 9/11 wreaked on television—not just as an industry but also as "a whole way of life."[6] Most fundamentally, on September 11, the everydayness of television itself was suddenly disrupted by news of something completely "alien" to the usual patterns of domestic TV viewing.[7] The nonstop commercial-free coverage, which lasted for a full week on major broadcast networks and cable news networks, contributed to a sense of estrangement from ordinary life, not simply because of the unexpected nature of the attack itself but also because television's normal routines—its everyday schedule and ritualized flow—had been disordered. As Mary Ann Doane has argued about television catastrophes more generally, not only television's temporal flow, but also its central narrational agency breaks down in moments of catastrophe.[8] We are in a world where narrative comes undone and where the "real" seems to have no sense of meaning beyond repetition of the horrifying event itself. This, she claims, in turn threatens to expose the underlying catastrophe of all TV catastrophes—the breakdown of capitalism, the end of the cash flow, the end of the logic of consumption on which U.S. television is predicated.

By the weekend of September 15, television news anchors began to tell us that it was their national duty to return to the "normal" everyday schedule of television entertainment, a return meant to coincide with Washington's call for a return to normalcy (and, hopefully, normal levels of consumerism). Of course, for the television industry, resuming the normal TV schedule also meant a return to commercial breaks and, therefore, TV's very sustenance. Already besieged by declining ad revenues before the attacks, the television industry lost an estimated $320 million in advertising revenue in the week following the attacks.[9] So, even while the media industries initially positioned entertainment and commercials as being "in bad taste," just one week after the attacks the television networks discursively realigned commercial entertainment with the patriotic goals of the nation.[10] In short—and most paradoxically—entertainment and commercialism were rearticulated as television's "public service."

By September 27, Jack Valenti, president and CEO of the Motion Picture Association of America, gave this "commercialism as patriotism" ethos an official stamp of approval. In a column for *Variety*, he wrote: "Here in Hollywood we must continue making our movies and our TV programs. For a time, during this mourning period, we need to be sensitive to how we tell a story. But in time—and that time will surely come—life will go on, must go on. We in Hollywood have to get on with doing our creative work. . . . The country needs what we create."[11] Valenti's message was part of a much older myth of show business—a myth that ran through countless Depression-era and World War II musicals—a myth of transcendence in which showbiz folks put aside their petty differences and join together in patriotic song. If in the 1940s this myth of transcendence emboldened audiences for wartime sacrifice, now, in the twenty-first century, this transcendent myth of show business is oddly conjoined with national mandates for a return to "normal" consumer pleasures. In a bizarrely Baudrillardian moment, President Bush addressed the nation, begging us to return to normal life by getting on planes and taking our families to Disneyland.[12]

In fact, despite the initial tremors, American consumer culture and television in particular did return to normal (or at least a semblance of it) in a remarkably short span of time. Yet, while many people have noted this, the process by which this happened and the extent to which it was achieved beg further consideration. Media scholarship on 9/11 and the U.S. attacks in Afghanistan has focused primarily on print and television news coverage. This important scholarship focuses on the narrative and mythic "framing" of the events; the nationalistic jingoism (for example, the use of flag graphics on news shows); the relative paucity of alternative views in mainstream venues—at least in the immediate weeks following the attacks; the role of alternative news platforms, especially the Internet; competing global news outlets, particularly Al Jazeera; and the institutional and commercial pressure that has led to "infotainment."[13] Despite its significant achievements, however, the scholarly focus on news underestimates (indeed, it barely considers) the way the "reality" of 9/11 was communicated across the flow of television's genres, including its so-called entertainment genres.[14] The almost singular focus on news fails to capture the way television worked to process fear (even fear trumped up by the media) and return the public to "ordinary" life (including routine ways of watching TV). The return to normal has to be seen from this wider view, for it was enacted not just through the narrative frames of news stories but also through the repositioning of audiences back into television's fictive time and places—its familiar series, well-known stars, favorite characters, and ritualized annual events (such as the Emmy Awards).

In the following pages, I explore how an assortment of television genres—dramatic series, talk shows, documentaries, special "event" TV, and even cartoons—channeled the nation back to normalcy—or at least to the normal flows of television and consumer culture. I am particularly interested in how these genres relied on nationalist myths of the American past and the enemy/"Orient." But I also question the degree to which nationalist myths can sustain the "narrowcast" logic of today's multichannel television systems (and the more general movement of audiences across multiple media platforms). In other words, I want to interrogate the limits of nationalist myths in the postnetwork, multichannel, and increasingly global media systems. Admittedly, the fate of nationalism in contemporary media systems is a huge question that requires perspectives from more than one field of inquiry. (For example, we would need to explore the impact of deregulation and media conglomeration, the dispersal of audiences across media platforms, competition among global media news/entertainment outlets, relations between local and global media flows, audience and interpretive reception contexts, and larger issues of national identity and subjectivity.) My goal here is not to provide exhaustive answers to all of these questions (obviously no one essay could do so), but rather to open up some points of interrogation by looking at post-9/11 media industry strategies, the discourses of the entertainment trade journals, and especially at the textual and narrative logic of television programs that channeled the nation back to commercial TV "as usual."

History Lessons after 9/11

Numerous critics have commented on the way that the attacks of 9/11 were perceived as an event completely outside of and alien to any other horror that ever happened anywhere. As James Der Derian notes, as a consequence of this rhetoric of American exceptionalism, "9/11 quickly took on an *exceptional ahistoricity*" as even many of the most astute critics refused to place the events in a political or social context from which they might be understood. Der Derian argues that when history was evoked in nonstop news coverage of destruction and loss, it appeared as nostalgia and analogue, "mainly in the sepia tones of the Second World War—to prepare America for the sacrifice and suffering that lay ahead."[15] But, at least after the initial news coverage of which Der Derian speaks, history was actually marshaled in a much more contradictory field of statements and images that filled the airwaves and ushered audiences back—not just toward nostalgic memories of World War II sacrifice—but also toward the mandates of contemporary consumer culture. On television these "contradictory" statements and images revolved around the paradox of the medium's twin roles as advertiser and public servant.

In the week following 9/11, television's transition back to normal consumer entertainment was enacted largely through recourse to historical pedagogy that ran through a number of television genres, from news to documentaries to daytime talk shows to prime-time drama. The histories evoked were both familiar and familiarizing tales of the "American experience" as newscasters provided a stream of references to classroom histories, including, for example, the history of U.S. immigration, Pearl Harbor, and Vietnam.[16] They mixed these analogies to historical events with allusions to the history of popular culture, recalling scenes from disaster film blockbusters, sciencefiction movies, and war films and even referencing previous media events, from the assassination of JFK to the death of Princess Diana. Following 24/7 "real time" news strategies that CNN developed in 1991's Gulf War, major news networks provided a host of "infotainment" techniques that have over the past decade become common to war reporting (that is, fast-paced "MTV" editing, computerized/game-style images, slick graphics, digitized sound effects, banter among "experts," and catchy slogans).[17] On September 12, CNN titled its coverage "The Day After" (which was also the title of the well-known 1980s made-for-

TV nuclear disaster movie). NBC sported the slogan "America Strikes Back"—
based, of course, on the *Star Wars* trilogy. Meanwhile the FBI enlisted the television show *America's Most Wanted* to help in the hunt for terrorists.[18] As we
searched for familiar scripts, the difference between real wars and "made-
for-TV" wars hardly mattered. History had become, to use Michel de Certeau's
formulation, a heterology of science and fiction.[19]

But what did this turn to familiar historical narratives provide? Why the
sudden appeal of history? Numerous scholars, from Roland Barthes to
Marita Sturken, have analyzed the ways in which history and memory serve
to produce narratives of the nation. This work has shown how media (from
advertising to film to television to music) play a central role in conjuring up
a sense of national belonging and community.[20] Certainly, after 9/11, the
media's will to remember was connected to the resuscitation of national culture in a country heretofore divided by culture wars and extreme political
partisanship. For the culture industries, however, the turn to history was not
only connected to the resuscitation of nationalism; history was also connected to the parallel urge to restore the business routines and marketing
practices of contemporary consumer media culture.

At the most basic level, for television executives who were nervous about
offending audiences, history was a solution to a programming dilemma. History, after all, occupies that most sought-after realm of "good taste." It is the
stuff of PBS, the Discovery Channel, the History Channel—it signifies a
"habitus" of educated populations, of "quality" TV, of public service generally.
History's "quality" appeal was especially important in the context of numerous critical attacks on television's lack of integrity that ran through industry
trade journals and the popular press after 9/11. For example, Louis Chunovic,
a reporter for the trade journal *TelevisionWeek*, wrote: "In the wake of the terrorist attack on the United States, it's hard to believe Americans once cared
who would win *Big Brother 2* or whether Anne Heche is crazy. And it's hard to
believe that as recently as two weeks ago, that's exactly the kind of pabulum,
along with the latest celebrity/politician sex/murder/kidnapping scandal, that
dominated television news." Chunovic therefore argued, "We cannot afford to
return to the way things were."[21] Ironically, however, the industry's post-9/11
upgrade to quality genres—especially historical documentaries—actually
facilitated the return to the way things were. Historical documentaries served
a strategic role in the patriotic transition back to "normalcy"—that is, to
commercial entertainment and consumer culture.

Let's take, for example, ABC's programming strategy on Saturday, September 15. On that day, ABC became the first major network to return to a

semblance of normal televisual flow. Newscaster Peter Jennings presented a children's forum, which was followed by an afternoon lineup of historical documentaries about great moments of the twentieth century. The lineup included episodes on Charles Lindbergh, the Apollo crew and the moon landing, and a documentary on the U.S. press in Hitler's Europe. Interestingly, given the breakdown in surveillance, aviation, and communication technologies that enabled the attacks, all of the chosen histories were about great achievements of great men using great technologies, especially transportation and communications technologies.[22]

Meanwhile, from an economic point of view, these historical documentaries were first and foremost part of the contemporary network business strategy that industry people refer to as "repurposing." The documentaries were reruns repackaged from a previous ABC series narrated by Jennings and now "repurposed" for patriotism. This is not to say that Jennings or anyone else at ABC was intentionally trying to profit from disaster. Certainly, Jennings's forum for children provided a public service. But, as anyone who studies the history of U.S. television knows, the logic of capitalism always means that public service and public relations are flip sides of the same coin. In this case, the public service gesture of running historical documentaries also served to transition audiences from TV news discourse and live reportage back into prerecorded narrative series. Similarly, with an even more bizarre resonance, on the evening of September 15 NBC ran a special news report on *Dateline* followed by a rerun of the made-for-TV movie *Growing Up Brady*.

More generally, history was integral to the transition back to entertainment series programs. On October 3, 2001, NBC's *The West Wing*, one of television's leading quality series, preempted its scheduled season premiere to air a quickly drafted episode titled "Isaac and Ishmael." On the one hand, the episode (which teaches audiences about the situation in the Middle East) was clearly an earnest attempt by the cast and creator/executive producer Aaron Sorkin (who wrote the script) to use television as a form of political and historical pedagogy.[23] On the other hand, the episode was also entirely consistent with contemporary business promotional strategies. Like the ABC strategy of repurposing, the NBC network followed the business strategy of "stunting"—or creating a stand-alone episode that attracts viewers by straying from the series architecture (the live *ER* is a classic example of the technique). In this case, *The West Wing* was in a particularly difficult position—for perhaps more than any other network series, it derives its "quality" appeal from its "timely relevance" and deep, if melodramatic, realism. (The series presents itself as a kind of parallel White House universe that runs simultaneously with everyday goings-on in Washington.)[24]

Figure 5.1. High school students trapped in the White House, *The West Wing*, October 3, 2001.

The credit sequence begins with successive headshots of cast members speaking to the audience in direct address (and in their celebrity personae). Martin Sheen welcomes viewers and announces that this episode is not the previously scheduled season premiere. In a subsequent headshot, another cast member even refers to the episode as "a storytelling aberration," signaling its utter discontinuity from the now routinely serialized/cumulative narrative structure of contemporary prime-time "quality" genres. Meanwhile, other cast members variously thank the New York fire and police departments, while still others direct our attention to a phone number at the bottom of the screen that viewers can call to donate money to disaster relief and victim funds. In this sense, the episode immediately asks audiences to imagine themselves foremost as citizens engaged in an interactive public/media sphere. Nevertheless, this "public service" ethos is embroiled in the televisual logic of publicity. The opening credit sequence ends with cast members promoting the new fall season by telling audiences what kinds of plots to expect on upcoming episodes. The final "teaser" comes from a female cast member, Janel Moloney, who hypes the fall season by promising that her character will have a love interest in future shows.

Figure 5.2. Josh teaches students about Islamic fundamentalism, *The West Wing*, October 3, 2001.

After this promise of titillating White House sex, the episode transitions back to its public service discourse. Essentially structured as a teach-in, the script follows a group of high school students touring the White House and caught in the west wing after a terrorist bomb threat (Figure 5.1.). Attempting to calm the nerves of the students, various cast members lecture this imaginary high school class about the history of U.S.-Middle East relations. In an early segment, Josh Lyman, a White House "spin doctor," teaches the frightened students about terrorism and Middle East animosity toward the West. After a wide-eyed female student asks, "Why is everyone trying to kill us?" Josh moves to the blackboard, where he begins his history lesson (Figure 5.2.). While he admits that the United States is somewhat to blame (he mentions economic sanctions, occupation of Arab lands, and the U.S. abandonment of Afghanistan), he says all of this at such rapid-fire speed that there is no in-depth consideration of the issues. Instead, the scene derails itself from its "teaching" mission by resorting to the colonialist rhetoric of "curiosities." The scene ends with Josh telling the students of his outrage at the cultural customs of Islamic fundamentalists. The familiar list of horrors— from the fact that women are made to wear a veil to the fact that men can't cheer freely at soccer games—redirects the episode away from ethics toward an ethnocentric celebration of American cultural superiority.[25] Josh concludes by reminding the students that, unlike Islamic fundamentalists, Americans are free to cheer anything they like at football games, and American women can even be astronauts.

In this regard, the episode uses historical pedagogy to solidify American national unity *against* the "enemy" rather than to encourage any real engagement with Islam, the ethics of U.S. international policy, or the consequences of the then-impending U.S. bomb strikes. Moreover, because the episode's teach-in lectures are encompassed within a more overarching melodramatic rescue narrative (the terrorist bomb threat in the White House), all of the lessons the students (and by proxy, the audience) learn are contained within a narrative about U.S. public safety. In other words, according to the logic of this rescue narrative, we learn about the "other" only for instrumental reasons—our own national security.

In all of these ways, *The West Wing* performs some of the fundamental precepts of contemporary Orientalism. As Edward Said argues, in the United States—and in particular after World War II—Orientalism retains the racist histories of othering from the earlier European context but becomes increasingly less philological and more concerned with social-scientific policy and administration that is formulated in federal agencies, think tanks, and universities that want to "know" and thus police the Middle East. In this configuration, the production of knowledge about the Middle East is aimed at the maintenance of U.S. hegemony and national security, and it winds up producing an image of the Arab as "other"—the antithesis of Western humanity and progress.[26] Indeed, when Josh details the cultural wasteland of Islamic fundamentalism, he enacts one of the central rhetorical principles of Orientalism, for, as Said argues, the "net effect" of contemporary Orientalism is to erase any American awareness of the Arab world's culture and humanity (its poets, its novelists, its means of self-representation), replacing these with a dehumanizing social-scientific index of "attitudes, trends, statistics."[27]

The West Wing's fictional schoolroom performs this kind of social-scientific Orientalism in the name of liberal humanism. And it does so through a pedagogical form of enunciation that places viewers in the position of high school students—and particularly naive ones at that. The program speaks to viewers as if they were children or, at best, the innocent objects of historical events beyond their control. The "why does everyone want to kill us?" mantra espoused by *The West Wing*'s fictional students, becomes, to use Lauren Berlant's phrase, a form of "infantile citizenship"[28] that allows adult viewers comfortably to confront the horrors and guilt of war by donning the cloak of childhood innocence (epitomized, of course, by the wide-eyed figure of President Bush himself, who, in his first televised speech to Congress after the attacks, asked, "Why do they hate us?").

In the days following the attacks, the Bush administration spoke often of the eternal and "essential goodness" of the American people, creating a through-line for the American past that flattered a despairing public by making them the moral victims of a pure outside evil.[29] In a similar instance of denial, commentators spoke of "the end of innocence"[30] that the attacks ushered in as if America had been completely without knowledge and guilt before this day.[31] Not surprisingly, in this respect, the histories mobilized by the media after 9/11 were radically selective and simplified versions of the past that produced a kind of moral battlefield for "why we fight." As Justin Lewis shows in his survey of four leading U.S. newspapers, print journalists writing about 9/11 tended to evoke World War II and Nazi Germany while "other histories were, regardless of relevance, distinctly less prominent." Lewis claims that "the more significant absences [were] those histories that signify the West's disregard for democracy and human rights [such as] the U.S. government's support for the Saudi Arabian Theocracy."[32] He argues that the history of World War II and Nazi Germany was mobilized because of its compelling narrative dimensions—especially its good versus evil binary. While this creation of heroes and villains was also a primary aspect of television coverage, it seems likely that many viewers weren't really looking for "objective truth" so much as narrative itself. In the face of shock and uncertainty that seemed to make time stand still, these narratives offered people a sense of historical continuity with a shared and, above all, moral past.[33]

The need to make American audiences feel that they were in the moral position ran through a number of television's "reality" genres. One of the central ways that this moral position was promoted was through the depiction of women victims. According to Jayne Rodgers, journalists tended to frame news stories in "myths of gender," and, she claims, one of the central trajectories of these myths was a reversal of the gendered nature of heroism and victimization. Rodgers points out that even while "male deaths from the attacks outnumbered female deaths by a ratio of three to one," news narratives typically portrayed men as heroes (firemen, policemen, Giuliani) and women as victims (suffering and often pregnant widows). Despite the fact that there were thirty-three women firefighters and rescue workers on duty on September 11, the media portraits of heroism were mainly of men, which, as Rodgers aptly argues, worked to "restore gender, as well as social and political order."[34]

On television, these myths of gender were often connected to age-old Western fantasies of the East in which "Oriental" men assault (and even rape) Western women and, more symbolically, the West itself. (Cecil B. DeMille's *The Cheat* [1915] or Valentino in *The Sheik* [1921] demonstrate the longevity of this orientalized "rape" fantasy.) In the case of 9/11, the United States took its figural place as innocent victim in stories that interwove myths of gender and the Orient. Both daytime talk shows and nighttime news were filled with melodramatic tales of women's suffering that depicted women as the moral victims of Islamic extremism. And "women" here meant both the women of Afghanistan and American survivors (the widows) who lost their husbands during the attack. While of course these women are at one level real women who really suffered, on television they were fictionally rendered through melodramatic conventions that tended to elide the complexity of the historical causes of the tragic circumstances the women faced.

For example, in the weeks following the attacks, *The Oprah Winfrey Show* (aka *Oprah*) ran episodes featuring pregnant survivors who had lost their husbands. These episodes intertwined personal memories (via home videos of the deceased) with therapy sessions featuring the traumatized women. In these episodes, the "talking cure" narrative logic of the talk show format was itself strangely derailed by the magnitude of events; the female guest was so traumatized that she was literally unable to speak. In one episode, for example, a young pregnant woman sits rigidly on stage while popular therapist Dr. Phil tells her about the twelve steps of trauma (and Oprah interjects with inspirational wisdom). The episode presents this woman as having lost not only her husband but also her voice and, with that, her ability to narrate her own story. In the process the program implicitly asks viewers to identify with this woman as the moral and innocent victim of *chance*. In other words, any causal agent (or any sense that her suffering is actually the result of complex political histories) is reduced to the "twist of fate" narrative fortunes of the daytime soap.

Writing about the history of American melodramas, Linda Williams demonstrates that this theme of the "suffering" moral victim (particularly women and African Americans) can be traced through cinematic and televisual media representations (including depictions of American historical events). Williams claims that victim characters elicit our identification through sentiment (not only with them but also, allegorically, with historical injustices they face). Following Lauren Berlant and Ann Douglas, she cautions that sentiment and vicarious identification with suffering—in both media texts and politics more generally—are often a stand-in for actual

social justice, but, importantly, sentiment is not the same as justice. By offering audiences a structure of feeling (the identification with victims, their revealed goodness, and their pain), melodrama compensates for tragic
injustices and human sacrifice. Or, as Williams puts it, "melodramatic cli-
maxes that end in the death of a good person—Uncle Tom, Princess Charlotte, Jack Dawson (in *Titanic*) offer paroxysms of pathos and recognitions of
virtue compensating for the loss of life."[35] In political melodramas (like the
stories told of 9/11's female victims), pathos can often be an end in itself; the
spectator emerges feeling a sense of righteousness even while justice has not
been achieved in reality and even while many people feel completely alienated
from and overwhelmed by the actual political sphere.

Addressing the public with the same kind of sentimental/compensatory
citizenship, President Bush used the image of female suffering in his first televised address before Congress after the attacks. Harking back to Cold War
paranoia films like Warner Bros.' *Red Nightmare* (which was made with the
Defense Department and showed what a typical American town would look
like if it were taken over by "commies"), President Bush painted a picture of
the threat that terrorism posed to our freedom. "In Afghanistan," he claimed,
"we see al Qaeda's vision of the world," after which he listed a string of daily
oppressions people might be forced to face should al Qaeda's vision prevail.
First on his list was the fact that "women are not allowed to go to school." The
rhetorical construction here is important because by suggesting that al
Qaeda had a vision for the world, President Bush asked TV audiences literally to imagine themselves taken over by al Qaeda and in the women's
place—the place of suffering. Having thereby stirred up viewers' moral indignation and pathos, he then went on to justify his own plan for aggression,
giving the Taliban a series of ultimatums. Whatever one thinks about Bush's
speech, it is clear that the image of suffering female victims was a powerful
emotional ploy through which he connected his own war plan to a sense of
moral righteousness and virtue (and it is also clear that we had never heard
him speak of these women in Afghanistan before that day).

A more complicated example is CNN's airing of the documentary *Beneath the Veil*, which depicts the abuses that women of Afghanistan suffered
under the Taliban. Originally made in the spring of 2001 for Britain's Channel 4, *Beneath the Veil* was produced "undercover" by Saira Shah (who grew
up in Britain but whose father is from Afghanistan) and with considerable
risk to the filmmaker (photography was outlawed by the Taliban, and the fact
that Shah is a woman made the whole process doubly dangerous). *Beneath
the Veil* outlines not only the Taliban's oppression and cruelty but also the

history of global neglect of Afghan women, as well as the need for political action now. Shah is careful to reflect on her own Western assumptions about women, feminism, and Islam, and she shows that it is the Afghan women themselves—a group known as the Revolutionary Association of the Women of Afghanistan (RAWA)—who were the first to fight against the Taliban.

Beneath the Veil opens with footage shot (via hidden cameras) by RAWA. There are images of women huddled in a pickup truck and being brought to a football field turned public execution arena. They are killed for alleged adultery. Interspersed throughout the film are images of and dialogues about the women's oppression, RAWA's own efforts to liberate women, and Shah's documentary witnessing of the events. An accompanying Web site provided numerous links to information and zones of action and participation. The program and its Web site constitute an important political use of electronic media. While there are images of female suffering, the pathos elicited by the pictures is organized around the desire for action (which Williams reminds us can also be part of melodrama) rather than just sentiment as an end in itself.

When *Beneath the Veil* was rerun and repurposed by CNN in the context of the post-9/11 news coverage, however, its politics were significantly altered. In the two months following the attacks, CNN reran *Beneath the Veil* so many times that it became a kind of daily documentary ritual. Although it was certainly important for audiences to learn about this human rights disaster, we should nevertheless wonder why Western eyes were willing to look at this documentary with such fascination after 9/11 (as opposed to, say, on September 10). First, it should be noted that in the wake of 9/11 documentaries of all sorts (but especially ones about terrorism) were, according to *Variety*, a "hot property."[36] Second, whatever the original achievements of the program, in this new context audiences were led to make easy equivocations between the kind of oppression the women of Afghanistan faced and the loss of innocent life on American soil on September 11. In the context of CNN's programming flow, we saw *Beneath the Veil* adjacent to news footage depicting Ground Zero, stories of American victims and heroes, anthrax attacks, public safety warnings, mug shots of the FBI's most-wanted terrorists, and war footage depicting a bizarre mix of bombs and humanitarian aid being dropped on Afghanistan.[37] In this programming context, *Beneath the Veil* could easily be read as a cautionary tale (like *Red Nightmare*) and a justification for the U.S. bombings in Afghanistan. In other words, it might well have conjured up national unity for war as a moral position.

In the midst of the U.S. bombings, Shah produced a follow-up film,

The Unholy War, which aired on CNN in mid-November 2001. This film documented the lives of women (especially three young Afghan girls) in the midst of the U.S. war against the Taliban. The film showed the destruction caused by bombings, the problems entailed in building a post-Taliban regime, and Shah's own failures in trying to help the three girls (she attempts to get them an education), whose father rejected her humanitarian efforts. *The Unholy War* disrupted the "flow" of CNN's rotation of *Beneath the Veil*. It also punctured President Bush's melodramatic rescue/war narrative and questioned (the usually unquestionable) ideologies of "humanitarianism" that legitimated the U.S. bombings. As Shah said in an interview with *Salon*: "I couldn't believe that we couldn't help them and that money wouldn't solve their problems. . . . That was a real revelation for me. I rather arrogantly, in a very Western way, assumed that I could solve their problems because I had good will and money. It taught me that their problems are more complex. It also taught me a lot about what's needed in Afghanistan, and how frustrating it is rebuilding a country that's been destroyed to the extent that Afghanistan has."[38]

Event TV and Celebrity Citizenship

While Shah's *Unholy War* suggests that there were indeed counterhistories and antiwar messages to be found on the airwaves and on Web sites like Salon.com, the news images of unfathomable destruction that aired on 9/11 resulted in industry attempts to match that spectacle with reparative images on a scale as great as the falling towers. In this respect, "event TV" (or television programs designed to take on the status and audience shares of media events) flourished after 9/11, allowing for another staging of national unity after the attacks. These staged events created a "meta-universe" of Hollywood stars enacting the role of patriotic publics.

The first of these events was the celebrity telethon *America: A Tribute to Heroes*. Telecast live from New York, Los Angeles, and London on September 21, 2001, the two-hour program was simulcast on more than 320 national broadcast and cable networks. According to the Nielsen ratings, the telethon garnered a 65 percent share of U.S. households, making it one of the most-watched programs of the year, behind only the Super Bowl.[39]

America: A Tribute to Heroes featured an overwhelming community of stars recounting the stories of those who died or risked their lives in the struggle. These eulogies were interspersed with musical performances of popular hits from the baby-boom to post-boomer past (the assumed gener-ations of donors). Like all televised funerals, this one deployed television's aesthetics of liveness to stave off the fear of death. In other words, not only the "live" feed but also the sense of unrehearsed spontaneity and intimate revelations gave viewers a way to feel that life goes on in the present. The rit-ualistic and funereal atmosphere resurrected the recently dead for the living, restoring faith not only in spiritual terms but also in terms of the medium it-self (in other words, it was that most "degraded" of media—television—that brought us this powerful sense of healing and community).[40]

While certainly designed to be a global media event, this was a deliber-ately understated spectacle, achieved through a deliberate display of "star capital" minus the visual glitz and ego. Staged with "zero degree" style (just candles burning on an otherwise unadorned set), the program appealed to a desire to see Hollywood stars, singers, and sports heroes reduced to "real" people, unadorned, unrehearsed (or at least underrehearsed), and literally unnamed and unannounced (there was no variety host presiding over the entertainment, no identification of the stars, and no studio audience). This absence of style signified the authenticity of the staged event, thereby giving stars the authority to speak for the dead. So, too, the actual mix of stars (for example, Muhammad Ali, Clint Eastwood, Paul Simon, Julia Roberts, En-rique Iglesias, Bruce Springsteen, Celine Dion, Chris Rock, Sylvester Stal-lone) combined what might otherwise have been a battle-of-star semiotics (given their often at-odds personas and historical associations) into a com-pelling and, for many people, moving site of mourning. The program's "in-teractive" aspect further strengthened the telethon's aura of community, as on-demand celebrity phone operators, from Goldie Hawn to Jack Nicholson, promised to reach out and touch us. In all of these ways, *America: A Tribute to Heroes* is a stunning example of how post-9/11 television has created not a public sphere per se, but rather a self-referential Hollywood public sphere of celebrities who stand in for real citizens and who somehow make us feel con-nected to a wider social fabric.

The Fifty-third Annual Emmy Awards ceremony, which was twice de-layed because of the attacks, is another example. Jack Valenti's "show must go on" ethos was everywhere in the publicity leading up to and culminating in this yearly television event. Somehow the industry was convinced that the airing of the Emmys was so important to America that any sign of celebrity resistance to gather (whether for fear of being attacked or for fear of looking crassly self-absorbed) would somehow be tantamount to "letting the terror-ists win." As the Academy of Television Arts and Sciences chairman Bryce

Zabel told viewers, canceling the Emmys "would have been an admission of defeat. Like baseball and Broadway, we are an American tradition."[41]

It seems just as probable, however, that the Academy and CBS were also worrying about their own commercial viability in the post-9/11 climate. In other words, canceling the Emmys would not just be an admission of the defeat of the nation; it would also be an admission that the consumer logics of TV—its annual ceremonies and self-congratulations—had been defeated. In the wake of 9/11, the Emmys came to signify the degree to which the televisual and marketing scene could be revitalized. The broadcast, which took place on November 4 at Los Angeles's Shubert Theatre (almost two months after the originally scheduled broadcast), was carefully orchestrated in this regard. Although there were more "no-shows" than usual, and while the area outside the theater was reportedly a "surreal" scene of rooftop sharpshooters, the Emmy producers encouraged the stars to perform their roles in the usual fashion. Before the broadcast, executive producer Gary Smith coached the stars: "Don't be afraid to be excited. . . . That's what people are looking for."[42]

The Emmy Awards program was another self-referential celebrity public sphere, this time constructed through appeals to television and Hollywood history. The opening sequence begins with Christian trumpet player/singer Phil Driscoll doing a bluesy rendition of "America the Beautiful" with a backup choir of students from different colleges across the country. The national unity theme is underscored by a large screen display of video images (everything from images of the flag and the Statue of Liberty to historical footage of Charles Lindbergh's liftoff and civil rights protests to landscape images of prairies and cities, all spliced together in a seamless quilt of meaning). This is followed by a female voiceover that announces: "Tonight television speaks to a global audience as we show the world images of an annual celebration. Our presence here tonight does more than honor an industry, it honors those cherished freedoms that set us apart as a nation and a people." After this, the scene cuts to veteran newscaster Walter Cronkite, who appears via satellite from Toronto. Cronkite directly addresses the camera and narrates a history of television's importance to American politics and culture. Evoking the words of the World War II broadcaster Edward R. Murrow, Cronkite says, "Television, the great common denominator, has lifted our common vision as never before, and television also reminds us that entertainment can help us heal."

The Driscoll performance, the video backdrop, the female voiceover, and finally the widely respected Cronkite provide a prelude to what will be the night's apologetic theme: the ritualistic honoring of stars is not narcissistic, commercialized self-indulgence, but instead a public service to America and its image in the world.[43] The opening sequence then transitions to host Ellen DeGeneres, who delivers her monologue as the cameras cut back and forth to a bevy of Hollywood stars seated in the audience. Significantly, among those singled out are stars associated with Hollywood liberalism, including the cast of *The West Wing* and Bill Maher (who had already been in trouble with his sponsors for what they perceived to be unpatriotic comments). In other words, like the telethon, the Emmy ceremony was not simply "right-wing" in its approach to patriotism; it presented well-known Hollywood liberals (including a grand finale by Barbra Streisand and, of course, DeGeneres herself) as part of a national community who leave their identity politics home to join together and defend the larger American cause. Drawing attention to the patriotic mission of this liberal constituency, DeGeneres humorously asks the audience, "What would bug the Taliban more than seeing a gay woman in a suit surrounded by Jews?"

While the opening act establishes television as its own historical reference and television stars as their own public, a sequence near the end of the broadcast is even more blatant in its self-referential memories of Hollywood nationalism and celebrity citizenship. And while the first act uses network-era "hard" newsman Cronkite (who is in Toronto and far removed from the pomp and pageantry), this later segment features the ultimate postnetwork celebrity journalist, Larry King (who is dressed in a tuxedo and obviously part of the Hollywood community). King introduces a montage of vintage footage portraying Hollywood's efforts in wartime (for example, the Andrews Sisters; Betty Grable's legs; Bugs Bunny; Bob Hope and the USO; Marilyn Monroe posing for the boys and kissing a wounded GI; Frank Sinatra signing an autograph; Harpo Marx clowning on stage; Bob Hope and a bevy of sexy starlets in Vietnam; Bob Hope, Steve Martin, and Jay Leno in the Gulf interspersed with Vietnam footage of Hope and Phyllis Diller as well as black-and-white images of Nat King Cole and Milton Berle performing for the troops). The rapid, decontextualized series of star fetish icons and the musical accompaniment (from the Andrews Sisters' World War II hit "Boogie Woogie Bugle Boy," to a standard rock riff, to Lee Greenwood singing "I'm Proud to Be an American") establish a "commonsense" and highly sentimental history of Hollywood patriotism (or as Larry King put it while introducing the montage, "Over the years the beat of the music changes, but the heart beneath it never wavers"). This nostalgic display of stars, with its thesis of unchanging Hollywood sentiment, obscures the different historical contexts in which World War II, Korea, Vietnam, and the Gulf War were fought (and obviously also the very different levels of popular support these wars had).

The montage sequence ends with an overhead traveling shot picturing a vast audience of GIs applauding Bob Hope during the Gulf War. The sequence then dissolves back to an overhead traveling shot of the celebrity audience applauding in the Shubert Theatre. This dissolve from the GIs to the Emmy audience—and the fact that the shots are perfectly matched—establishes a visual rhetoric that asks viewers to imagine that soldiers and celebrities are contiguous publics, and perhaps even comparable public servants. Immediately after the dissolve, the show cuts back to Larry King (live) on stage, where he speaks into the camera: "Once again we're in a time when America's armed forces are being sent to defend our freedom, and once again the entertainment industry is giving what it can." The entire segment legitimates future wars through a sentimental journey through Hollywood's wartime past.

The segment is capped off by yet another invocation of Hollywood's self-referential public sphere. Larry King speaks directly into the camera but not, as is usually the case, in order to address the home audience. Instead, he addresses an ailing Bob Hope at home: "We know that Bob Hope is watching at home tonight. And you should know, dear Robert, that we are thinking of you. . . . From all of us here, thanks for the memories." King's direct address to Hope—intercut with stars applauding in the studio audience—creates a completely enclosed universe of citizen celebrities, orchestrating a set of complex relays between popular memories of vintage Hollywood, military history since World War II, and the present-day meanings of nationalism and war. In this televised display of celebrity patriotism, public service and publicity find their ideal meeting ground.

Osama bin Laden Meets the *South Park* Kids

In the introductory pages of his essay "The Uncanny," Sigmund Freud discusses the intellectual uncertainty he faced during World War I when he found it impossible to keep up with the flow of international publications.[44] In the world of electronic "instant" histories, these problems of intellectual uncertainty are compounded in ways that Freud could never have imagined. The "uncanny" seems an especially appropriate trope for the current situation, as nothing seems to be what it was and everything is what it wasn't just minutes before it happened. In this context, the literate pursuit of history writing seems slow to the point of uselessness. This is, of course, compounded by the fact that the publishing industry is painfully behind the speed of both war and electronic media. So rather than partake of either historical "conclusions" or future "predictions," I want to open up some questions about television and nationalism vis-à-vis the changing economies of industrially produced culture.

Given the political divisions that have resurfaced since 2001, it seems likely that the grand narratives of national unity that sprang up after 9/11 were for many people more performative than sincere. In other words, it is likely that many viewers really did know that all the newfound patriotism was really just a public performance staged by cameras. Still, after 9/11 many people found it important to "perform" the role of citizen, which included the performance of belief in national myths of unity. And if you didn't perform this role, then somehow you were a bad American. In this respect, no matter what they thought of the situation, in the wake of 9/11 stars had to perform the role of "love it or leave it" citizen to remain popular (a lesson that Bill Maher learned with a vengeance when his TV show *Politically Incorrect* was canceled).[45]

But did the performance really work? Just days after the attacks, the limits of performative nationalism were revealed in the televised celebrity telethon *America: A Tribute to Heroes* when, in the final sequence, everyone gathered 'round Willie Nelson to sing "America the Beautiful" (Figures 5.3 and 5.4). Now, this was certainly a bad performance. Most of the celebrities were either too embarrassed to sing, or else they just didn't know the words to this show tune turned national anthem.[46] Some stars were visibly squinting at teleprompters with consternation, hoping to sing a verse. Yet, because the telethon was foremost aimed at baby boom and post-baby boom generations, most audiences would have known the popular ballads that were directly aimed at these niche generations. Clearly, pop songs like John Lennon's "Imagine" (sung by Neil Young), Bob Marley's "Redemption Song" (sung by Wyclef Jean), or Paul Simon's "Bridge over Troubled Waters" have more historical meaning to these taste publics than any national anthem does.

More generally, I think the post-9/11 performance of nationalism will fail because it really does not fit with the economic and cultural practices of twenty-first-century U.S. media society. The fact that there is no longer a three-network broadcast system means that citizens are not collected as aggregate audiences for national culture. As we all know, what we watch on TV no longer really is what other people watch—unless they happen to be in our demographic taste culture. The postnetwork system is precisely about fragmentation and narrowcasting. While the new five-hundred-channel cable

Figure 5.3. Willie Nelson leads a celebrity sing-along on *America: A Tribute to Heroes*, September 21, 2001.

systems may not provide true diversity in the sense of political or cultural pluralism, the postnetwork system does assume a culture that is deeply divided by taste, not one that is unified through national narratives.[47] In a multinational consumer culture it becomes difficult for media to do business without addressing the niche politics of style, taste, and especially youth subcultures that have become central to global capitalism. In the end, the new media environment does not lend itself to unifying narratives of patriotism, if only because these older forms of nationalism have nothing to do with the "return to normalcy" and normal levels of consumption. While nationalist popular culture does, of course, exist (and obviously rose in popularity after 9/11), it appears more as another niche market (those people who hang flags on their cars) than as a unifying cultural dominant.[48]

The actual cultural styles in these new narrowcast media markets are increasingly based on irony, parody, skepticism, and "TV-literate" critical reading protocols. For people who grew up watching *The Simpsons'* hilarious parodies of mass culture and national politics; for people who fell asleep to Dave Letterman or Conan O'Brien; and for viewers who regularly watched *Saturday Night*

Figure 5.4. The celebrity anthem on *America: A Tribute to Heroes*, September 21, 2001.

Live, In Living Color, The Daily Show, and *Mad TV*'s political/news parodies, a sudden return to blind patriotism (and blind consumerism) is probably not really likely.

In the first week after the September 11 attacks, the cable operators and networks all did cover the same story—and for a moment the nation returned to something very much like the old three-network system.[49] Yet, the case of 9/11 also demonstrates that in the current media landscape it is hard to sustain the fantasy of utopian collectivity that had been so central to previous media events. Comparing media coverage of 9/11 with the coverage of the Kennedy assassination, Fredric Jameson argues that back in 1963 a utopian fantasy of collectivity was in part constructed through news reporters' "clumsiness [and] the technological naiveté in which they sought to rise to the occasion." But, he claims, the media are now so full of orchestrated spectacle and public violence on a daily basis that many people had a hard time seeing media coverage of 9/11 as documents of anything sincere, much less as any kind of intersubjective, utopian communication. As Jameson puts it, despite the many claims that America lost its innocence on 9/11,

Figure 5.5. *South Park*, "Osama Bin Laden Has Farty Pants," November 7, 2001.

it was "not America, but rather its media [that had] . . . definitively lost its innocence."[50]

Certainly, for industry executives who work in the competitive environment of narrowcasting, sentiments of national belonging and utopian collectivity quickly gave way to the "bottom line." In fact, even in the "good will" climate of September 2001, the industry was still widely aware of the competitive realities of the postnetwork marketplace. CNN, which then had an exclusive deal with the Al Jazeera network, tried to block other news outlets from broadcasting its satellite transmissions of bin Laden's video address.[51] Even the celebrity telethon was a source of industry dispute. Worried that cable telecasts would undercut audience shares for broadcasters, some network affiliates and network-owned-and-operated stations tried to stop a number of cable channels from simulcasting *America: A Tribute to Heroes*. According to *Variety*, upon hearing of possible cable competition, "some of the vocal managers at the Big Four TV stations . . . went bananas and threatened to cancel the telethon and schedule their own local programming."[52] So much for humanitarianism in the postnetwork age!

Given this competitive media marketplace, it comes as no surprise that industry insiders quickly revised their initial predictions about the fate of

Figure 5.6. Osama "Le Pew," lovesick for a camel, *South Park*, November 7, 2001.

American popular culture. By October 4, the front page of the *New York Times* proclaimed, "In Little Time Pop Culture Is Back to Normal," stating that the industry was backtracking on its initial predictions that the events of September 11 would completely change culture. David Kissinger, then president of the USA Television Production Group, told the *Times* that the industry's initial reaction to the attacks may have been overstated and that because most industry people were "terror stricken" on September 11, "we shouldn't be held accountable for much of what we said that week."[53]

In fact, within a month, even irony was back in vogue, especially on late-night TV, but increasingly also on entertainment programs. By early November, Comedy Central's *South Park*—a cartoon famous for its irreverence—ran an episode in which the *South Park* kids visit Afghanistan. Once there, Cartman (*South Park*'s leading bad boy) meets bin Laden (Figure 5.5), and the two engage in an extended homage to Warner Bros. cartoons. Bin Laden takes the roles of the wacky Daffy Duck, the dull-headed Elmer Fudd, and even the lovesick Pepé Le Pew (he is shown romancing a camel much as Pepé romances a cat that he thinks is a skunk, Figure 5.6). Meanwhile, Cartman plays the ever-obnoxious Bugs Bunny (like Bugs, he even does a drag performance as a harem girl wooing a lovesick bin Laden, whose eyes, in classic Tex Avery cartoon style, pop out of his head).

Although the episode was the usual "libertarian" hodgepodge of mixed political messages (some seemingly critical of U.S. air strikes, others entirely Orientalist), its blank ironic sensibility did at least provide for some unexpected TV moments. In one scene, when the *South Park* kids meet Afghan children in a war-torn village, American claims of childish innocence (promoted, for example, in *The West Wing*'s fictional classroom) are opened up for comic interrogation. Dodging a U.S. bomb attack, the Afghan children tell the *South Park* kids, "Over a third of the world hates America." "But why?" ask the *South Park* kids, "Why does a third of the world hate us?" And the Afghan kids reply, "Because you don't realize that a third of the world hates you." While the episode ends with an over-the-top cartoon killing of bin Laden and an American flag waving to the tune of "America the Beautiful," the program establishes such a high degree of pastiche, blank irony, and recombinant imagery that it would be difficult to say that it encourages any particular "dominant" reading of the war. The laughter seems directed more at semiotic breakdowns, perhaps mimicking the way in which news coverage of the war seems to make people increasingly incapable of knowing what's going on—a point that one of the *South Park* characters underscores at the end of the show, when he says, "I'm confused."

To be sure, programs like *South Park* and the niche cable channels on which they appear might not translate into the old enlightenment dream of "public service" TV with a moral imperative for its national public. Television studies is, of course, riddled with debates over the question of whether these new forms of narrowcasting and multichannel media outlets will destroy what some critics call common culture. In response to the increasing commercialization and fragmentation of European electronic media, scholars like Jostein Gripsrud, Graham Murdock, and James Curran champion European public service broadcast models, and even while they do not advocate a simplistic return to paternalistic models of "cultivation" and taste, they seek a way to reformulate the ideal of an electronic democratic culture.[54] In the United States the situation is somewhat different. The "public interest" policy rhetoric on which the national broadcast system was founded has been woefully underachieved; broadcasters did not engage a democratic culture of diverse interests, but rather for the most part catered to the cultural tastes of their target consumers (which for many years meant white middle-class audiences). Moreover, the networks often interpreted public service requirements within the context of public relations and the strengthening of their own oligopoly power.[55] Meanwhile, the underfunded Public Broadcasting System grew increasingly dependent on corporate funding. And, as Laurie Ouellette argues, by relying on paternalistic notions of "cultivation" and catering to narrow-minded taste hierarchies, the network has alienated audiences.[56]

Still, I am not saying that the new multichannel and multiplatform system of niche culture is necessarily better. Instead, we need to ask exactly what the new fragmented niche networks, as well as the proliferation of Internet sites, provide. What do the new forms of multinational media outlets offer beyond the proliferation of products and styles? The question is even more complex when we consider the fact that cable and broadcast networks, Internet sites, search engines, television producers/distributors, movie studios, radio stations, newspapers, and publishing companies are increasingly part of global conglomerate media structures (Disney, Rupert Murdoch's News Corp., Viacom, Time-Warner, and so on).[57] In the media industries, as in other postindustrial modes of capitalism, there is both fragmentation and centralization at the same time. Any attempt to consider the political effects of the multiplication of channels (and fragmentation of audiences) still has to be considered within the overall patterns of consolidation at the level of ownership.[58]

Perhaps I am a bit overly optimistic, but I do want to end by suggesting some alternative possibilities within the highly consolidated, yet also fragmented, global mediasphere. As Daniel Dayan and Elihu Katz argue, although media events may be hegemonically sponsored and often function to restore consensual values, they always also "invite reexamination of the status quo." Following Victor Turner, Dayan and Katz claim that media events put audiences in a "liminal" context, outside the norms of the everyday. Even if media events do not institutionalize new norms, they do "provoke . . . mental appraisal of alternative possibilities."[59] In this sense, although I have focused primarily on media myths of reunification and nationalism, it is also true that 9/11 provoked counternarratives and political dialogues. In particular, 9/11 made people aware of new prospects for communication in a rapidly changing media environment.

Certainly, the Internet allowed for a collective interrogation of mainstream media and discussions among various marginalized groups. According to Bruce A. Williams, while "mainstream media reiterated themes of national unity, the chat rooms allowed different groups of Americans to debate what the impact of the attacks was for them specifically."[60] Internet sites like Salon.com—as well as access to a host of international news outlets—

provided alternative views and global discussions. Convergence platforms opened up venues for expression. For example, after 9/11 a chat room hosted by the Black Entertainment Television network included conversations about whether it was possible to reconcile black beliefs about racist police and fire departments with the heroic images of police and firefighters after 9/11. Resistance groups from around the globe used the Internet as a forum for anti-war e-mails, virtual marches, and group organizing. The Social Science Research Council's Web site allowed scholars to weigh in on the events at Internet speed. The "low-tech" medium of radio (especially National Public Radio) likewise provided alternative voices.

That said, my point here is not that "new" media or "alternative media" are categorically "better" than TV. Certainly, many Internet sites and talk radio stations were filled with right-wing war fever. As Williams suggests, because the Internet allows for insular conversations, some message boards (such as "Crosstar") discussed ways to draw clear ideological boundaries and to keep "dissident voices" (that is, liberals) off the board.[61] In this respect, we should not embrace the Internet in some essentialist sense as a pure space of pluralism which is always already more democratic than "old" media. Instead, it seems more accurate to say that the presence of multiple media platforms holds out hopeful possibilities for increased expression, but what this will amount to in terms of democracy and citizenship remains a complex historical question.

In addition to the Internet, the presence of the Al Jazeera news network had a destabilizing effect on the status of information itself. Al Jazeera officials defy the democratic legacy of the "free press" that had been so crucial to U.S. Cold War politics. Whereas the United States used to claim that its so-called free press was a reigning example of "free world" democracy, Al Jazeera now has taken up the same public pose, claiming that it will present all sides of the story from a Middle Eastern vantage point. In their book on Al Jazeera, Mohammed El-Nawawy and Adel Iskandar discuss how the network's post-9/11 coverage—especially its graphic coverage of the U.S. bombings in Afghanistan and the circulation of bin Laden's videotapes—quickly became a public relations crisis for the Bush administration.[62] Troubled by the bad PR, the Bush administration formed a Hollywood summit to discuss the role the industry might play in the war on terrorism. The military also met with Hollywood talent at the University of Southern California's Institute for Creative Technologies, a military/Hollywood alliance that Jonathan Burston aptly terms "militainment."[63] By late November 2001 President Bush had signed an initiative to start the Middle East Radio Network (which strives to counterbalance anti-Americanism in the Arab world and is aimed especially at youth audiences).[64] As such federally sponsored efforts suggest, the proliferation of news outlets, entertainment networks, and Internet sites, as well as the mounting synergy between Hollywood and the military, has changed the nature of semiotic warfare, and the United States is certainly keen to play by the new rules of the game.[65]

Back to Normal?

On the one hand, as I have suggested, much of the TV landscape looks like a continuation of the same kinds of programs that aired prior to 9/11, and for this reason it is tempting to say that television's "return to normal" transcended the events of 9/11 and that everything is as it was before. On the other hand, 9/11 haunts U.S. commercial television.[66] The memory of 9/11 now circulates in ways that disrupt the kind of historical narratives and nationalist logic that had been so central to the initial return to the normal TV schedule.

Since 2001 the history and memory of 9/11 have in fact become a national battleground—not only in the notorious fights over Ground Zero's reconstruction but also in the electronic spaces of television. By March of 2002 major networks had begun to feature commemorative documentaries that told the story of 9/11.[67] By March of 2004 President Bush launched a presidential campaign with TV ads that show historical footage of the firefighters, implicitly equating their heroism with his presidency. But whereas nationalist historical pedagogy initially served to solidify consent for the Bush administration, now the history and memory of 9/11 are not so simply marshaled. On March 5, 2004, just one day after the ads began to circulate, CNN interviewed a woman who had lost her husband on 9/11. Unlike the speechless pregnant widows on *Oprah* back in 2001, this woman had regained her voice and spoke quite articulately of her disgust for the president's use of 9/11 footage for political ends.

In the end, I suspect that the current situation is ripe for new visions of apocalyptic techno-futures, with satellites, guided missiles, surveillance cameras, and communication media of all kinds at the core of an ongoing genre of techno-warfare criticism waged by Jean Baudrillard, Paul Virilio, and many others.[68] But it seems to me that, as forceful and perceptive as this kind of work has been, this is really just the easy way out. Instead of engaging in yet another stream of doom-and-gloom technological disaster criticism, it seems more useful to think about how cultural studies and media studies in particular might hold on to a politics of hope. What I have in mind is in no way the same as utopian claims to transcendence and unity (whether local, national, or global) through new media technologies. Rather, this politics of hope is situated in a confrontation with the actually existing historical divisions around us. This materialist politics of hope should embrace the new global media environment as an opportunity to listen to "the third of the world that hates us" rather than (to use Bush's formulation) clutter the globe with messages about "how good we are." The world has heard enough about America. Time now to tune in elsewhere.

Chapter 6
Screening Pornography

Wendy Hui Kyong Chun

In the 1990s, the Internet was sold as *the* marketplace of ideas, as democracy, come true. Al Gore contended that a global information infrastructure heralded "a new Athenian Age of democracy" because it gave citizens free access to information and thus the power to control their lives.[1] The U.S. judiciary declared the Internet "the most participatory form of mass speech yet developed . . . [and thus deserving of] the highest protection from governmental intrusion."[2] It was so deserving not only because there were extremely low barriers to speech, but also because it allegedly eradicated inequalities that belied the public sphere as a marketplace of ideas. As MCI's *Anthem* commercial announced, on the Internet "there is no race; there are no genders; there is no age; there are no infirmities; only minds," or as Bill Gates put it, "we are all created equal in the virtual world."[3] According to this logic, erasing one's physical body erased the discrimination that *stemmed from* it and ensured a marketplace of ideas in which the best could finally emerge triumphant. There were, of course, dissenting voices: many argued that the Internet created new inequalities, a new digital divide. This argument, however, still largely buttressed claims that Internet access was key to the democratization of countries and economies, which is why the same companies pushing the Internet as utopia were hosting roundtables on the digital divide.[4] The issue that galvanized debate over the inherent worth of the Internet and its democratization of public speech was pornography.

Cyberporn became a pressing public danger in 1995. *Time* and *Newsweek* published special features on cyberporn with the respective titles "On a Screen Near You, Cyberporn—A New Study Shows How Pervasive and Wild It Really Is" and "No Place for Kids, the Internet: The Frontier of Cyberspace Unregulated and Uncensored?" Philip Elmer-Dewitt's "On a Screen Near You" launched a heated on- and off-line debate over pornography's pervasiveness on the so-called information superhighway and was accused of launching the

"Great Internet Sex Panic of 1995."[5] The Telecommunications Act of 1996, which contained within it the Communications Decency Act (CDA), both deregulated the telecommunications industry—signaling an end to government ownership of the Internet backbone—and regulated online indecency. Prior to the Internet going public (by being sold to private corporations), legislators showed no concern for minors who accessed the alt.sex hierarchy, or signed onto "adult" bulletin board systems (BBSs); pornography's online presence was so wellknown among users it was not even an open secret. "Discovering" the obvious, the media and politicians launched a debate about "free" speech focused on assessing, defining, and cataloging pornography.

Intriguingly, although pro- and anti-CDA forces did spar over competing notions of the Internet as a marketplace, the discussions about cyberporn also facilitated conversations in which electronic interchanges were acknowledged as contagious and exposed. That is, they were discussed in terms that engaged the dangers and freedoms of democracy, albeit in terms that made vulnerability contingent rather than constituent. This essay examines cyberporn's role in addressing and negotiating the public as guardians of underage users (and thus "our future"), as well as possible users. Debates over cyberporn revealed underlying changes in disciplinary and regulatory structures: the remapping of private versus public; the waning of the panoptic model of discipline; the increasing move of governments to regulate through commercialization.

Exposed, or the Walls of the Home That Cannot Hold

The public furor over cyberporn, as Philip Elmer-Dewitt, author of the extraordinarily controversial and influential *Time* article, noted, exposed a peculiar paradox: "sex is everywhere," and yet "something about the combination of sex and computers seems to make otherwise worldly-wise adults a little crazy."[6] Specifically, "most Americans have become so inured to the open display of eroticism—and the arguments for why it enjoys special status under the First Amendment—that they hardly notice it's there," yet online pornography, which most Americans had never viewed in July 1995, had become hypervisible.[7] Indeed, secondhand viewings of cyberporn were sufficient to pass legislation and to raise public concern. According to a 1995 survey run by Princeton Survey Research Associates, 85 percent of people polled were concerned about children seeing pornography on the Internet.[8] The key difference, Elmer-Dewitt argues, lies in context:

Pornography is different on the computer networks. You can obtain it in the privacy of your own home—without having to walk into a seedy bookstore or movie house. You can download only those things that turn you on, rather than buy an entire magazine or video. You can explore different aspects of your sexuality without exposing yourself to communicable diseases or public ridicule. (Unless, of course, someone gets hold of the computer files tracking your online activities, as happened earlier this year to a couple dozen crimson-faced Harvard students.)[9]

Hence the "truth" revealed by cyberporn is that in private, without fear of contamination or exposure, sexuality veers toward the deviant; technology brings to the surface the perversity lying within us all, which is why materials available on the Internet "can't be found in the average magazine rack: pedophilia (nude pictures of children), hebephilia (youths) and what the researchers call paraphilia—a grab bag of 'deviant' material that includes images of bondage, sadomasochism, urination, defecation, and sex acts with a barnyard full of animals."[10]

The importance of context rather than content, however, means the supposed perversity particular to electronic pornography spreads to all online material, for all materials—pornographic or not—can be read with the same belief that alone before our personal computers, we temporarily evade public norms. Indeed, this whole discussion, framed as a personal interaction between an individual and his or her monitor, reveals the computer industry's success in reconceiving computers as personal belongings rather than institutional assets. The networked computer as personal or private is deceptive, though, since the possibility of someone getting "hold of the computer files tracking your online activities" is constitutive of, rather than accidental to, this medium. The fact that surfing the Web has been heralded as an act cloaked in secrecy that needs to be publicly illuminated is simply bizarre, a fact acknowledged by the many users whose behavior does change in front of a personal computer, albeit not in the terms Elmer-Dewitt describes. Those aware of and concerned with tracking treat possibility as fact and assume that all their electronic data transfers are recorded and analyzed, an assumption that flies in the face of their everyday experience with crashing computers, undelivered e-mail messages, and inaccessible Web sites. They therefore encrypt their messages, guaranteeing that their messages will be recorded.[11] Those who know of, but are not concerned with, tracking believe they can "survive the light" because either they consider the likelihood of exposure negligible, think the standards for public interactions online are different, or want their misdemeanors to be spectacular. Regardless, visibility fails to produce automatically disciplined subjects (if it ever did).[12]

Visibility's failure to ensure discipline underscores the differences between the Internet and the panopticon, which Michel Foucault has called the diagram of disciplinary power. The panopticon, as formulated by Jeremy Bentham, was a humane and cost-effective solution to dark, festering prisons, unsanitary hospitals, and inefficient schools and workhouses. It comprised a central guard tower and a shorter outer annular structure with windows on the outer circumference and iron gating on the inner in which the prisoners/workers/patients were individually housed. Thus, the inhabitants could always be viewed by the central tower, but, since the windows of the central tower were to be covered by blinds (except during chapel service), they could never be certain when they were being watched. Further, the central tower was to be designed in such a manner that the guards themselves could not know when they were being watched from above by other guards. As a final precaution, the panopticon was to be open to the public—the doors never closed—so that the franchise owner of the panopticon could be inspected at any time. Constant publicity, then, was to keep things orderly and the point, as Thomas Keenan argues, was "to induce in the inmate a state of conscious and permanent visibility that assures the automatic functioning of power."[13] Panoptic discipline worked by causing the inmate/worker/student to re-create his or her world, to internalize the light and become light.[14]

The Internet may enable surveillance, or dataveillance, but it is not a panopticon. First, computer networks "time shift" the panoptic gaze; second, users are not adequately isolated. According to Bentham, the inmate had to "conceive himself to be [inspected at all times]" in order for the panopticon to work.[15] The inspector's quick reaction to misbehavior early in the inmate's incarceration and the central tower's design, which made it impossible for the inmate to verify the inspector's presence, were to make the inmate internalize the gaze and reform. Contrary to Hollywood blockbusters, real-time spying is the exception rather than the norm on computer networks—and arguably all media frustrate real-time discipline. Digital trails and local memory caching, inevitably produced by online interactions, do make prosecution easier, though.[16] Thus, it is not that someone could be looking but that—at any point in the future—someone *could* look. In front of one's "personal computer," one does not immediately feel the repercussions of one's online activities, but one is never structurally outside the gaze (yet, to be precise, there is no gaze, since the function of seeing has been usurped by nonphonetic reading and writing—seeing has become increasingly metaphoric in the age of fiber optics). Whether or not someone will or can access your files, however, is fundamentally uncertain and depends on software. Glossing over this uncertainty and this dependence screens information's ephemerality and software's impact.

Significantly, computer network-aided interactions validate so-called deviant behavior, tempering the effect of time-shifted visibility. Although Bentham, to offset solitary confinement's detrimental effects, revised his plan so that two or three quiet inmates could work together, his system depended on isolating the inmate. In contrast, the Internet physically separates, but virtually connects. The Department of Justice in its portable guide to law enforcement officers, *Use of Computers in the Sexual Exploitation of Children*, argues, "communicating with other people who have similar interests validates the offender's interests and behavior. This is actually the most important and compelling reason that preferential sex offenders are drawn to the online computer."[17] On the Internet, others mirror one's perversities; one recognizes in others one's personal idiosyncrasies. On the Internet, one becomes a statistic, but through this reduction, one's "personality" is reinforced (statistical analysis is itself predicated on individual deviation—prediction is necessary only when the exact result is uncertain).

This validation of so-called private desires, also described as community, leads to broader questions of computer networks and crises of discipline—questions foreclosed by the emphasis on children. This myth of the agentless child victimized by cyberporn "simplifies" issues (just as focusing on pornographic materials simplifies the issue of electronic exposure); it enables adults to address issues of vulnerability without acknowledging their own, and enables parents to admit their deficiencies as disciplinary agents without fear of condemnation. As Congressman Pete Geren put it, "for many of us our children's knowledge of the computer, just—to say it dwarfs ours is not really an exaggeration at all."[18] In hearings and articles about cyberporn, lawmakers and others transform their own anxieties into concern over their children's (and thus our future generation's) sexual safety, whether or not they actually have said (computer-savvy) children. Online pornography intrudes into the home, circumventing the normal family disciplinary structure, subjecting children and threatening to create deviant subjects. As Elmer-Dewitt asserts, "this [exposure to cyberporn] is the flip side of Vice President Al Gore's vision of an information superhighway linking every school and library in the land. When kids are plugged in, will they be exposed to the seamiest sides of human sexuality? Will they fall prey to child molesters hanging out in electronic chat rooms?"[19] Similarly moving without explanation from online pornography to child molestation, CDA proponents

Figure 6.1. Cover, "Cyberporn," *Time*, July 3, 1995. *Time* Magazine © 1995 Time Inc. Reprinted by permission.

proffered "high-profile cases" of child abduction/seduction to support their demand that Internet content be regulated in the same manner as television.[20]

Although Elmer-Dewitt's article ends by endorsing family discipline rather than legislation, its accompanying illustrations undercut this resolution by emphasizing the computer connection as breach.[21] These illustrations do not reproduce online pornography but rather play with the tension between exposure and enlightenment, between licit and illicit knowledge. They reveal that the fear of too much light, of too much exposure and uncontrollable contact, is what drives worldly-wise adults a little crazy if not paranoid. The cover of *Time*'s cyberporn special issue (Figure 6.1) enacts first contact. The glare of the computer screen, in stark contrast to the darkened room, simultaneously lights up and casts shadows over the startled blond boy's face, literalizing his enlightenment/overexposure. His eyes and mouth are open and his tiny hands are lifted off the keyboard in horror or surprise: the images emanating from his monitor open and immobilize his facial orifices. The roundness of his open

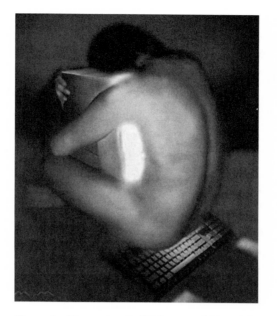

Figure 6.2. Illustration for "Cyberporn," *Time*, July 3, 1995 by Matt Mahurin. Reproduced by permission of Matt Mahurin.

mouth evokes images of vagina-mouthed inflatable dolls. Further, the screen's glare exposes wrinkles under the little boy's eyes, signs of a premature aging, of a loss of innocence that belie his tiny hands and two front teeth. His solitude in front of the computer screen and the room's dim lighting suggest secrecy. Instead of basking in the cozy light of his family home, he is immobilized by *us* watching him, since we—the readers—are in the position of the intruding pornographic image. Or else he serves as our mirror image, his surprise and invasion mirroring our own. This image evidences—through a mass-circulated print representation—the spectacularity of Internet pornography and, by implication, the Internet as a whole.

The full-page illustration (Figure 6.2) that introduces this article features the screen's glare more prominently. An anonymous, presumably male figure wraps his arms and legs tightly around the bright computer monitor, his bottom resting gingerly atop a lighted keyboard. Again, the computer screen serves as the room's only source of light, and this bright light shines through his translucent body. If the cover emphasized the innocence of the little boy, this image represents the possible ramifications of first contact: the desire to be touched and penetrate/be penetrated. In a logic akin to Catharine MacKinnon's in *Only Words*, the progression of these images implies that pornography creates a pornographic culture by inciting desires/ erections in its viewers rather than revealing the perversity lurking within us.[22] As opposed to MacKinnon, however, these images seem to support pro-CDA arguments that pornography's danger stems not from its abuse of women, but rather from its violation of viewers, specifically its underage viewers, who are unable to reason against its temptations. Also, rather than desiring the images on the screen, or more properly the objects represented by these images, this anonymous man appears to desire the computer itself, highlighting another "perversity" or "obscenity" associated with online pornography. This image mirrors Jean Baudrillard's complaint that "the obscenity of our culture resides in the confusion of desire and its equivalent materialized in the image; not only for sexual desire, but in desire for knowledge and its equivalent materialized in 'information.'"[23] Paul Virilio, in *Open Sky*, similarly argues that cybersex is a form of prophylaxis that threatens the health of the human species. Cyberporn seems to amplify pornographic images' tendencies to "usurp their referent."[24] Desire detours through the transportation medium, posing the following questions: does the viewer of cyberporn desire the computer, the image, or the image's referent, if such a referent exists? Can these objects of desire be separated? These illustrations allege that violation leads to contagious and perverse desire, that pornography starts a wildfire that overwhelms and engulfs enlightenment and reality, so that content cannot be separated from medium.

These images portray pornography as unsupervised enlightenment, as information that perverts rather than advances; the 105th U.S. Congress, quoting Dr. Gary Brooks, also advanced this claim in its report on the Child Online Protection Act (COPA), or CDA II: "The type of information provided by pornography . . . does not provide children with a normal sexual perspective. Unlike learning provided in an educational or home setting, exposure to pornography is counterproductive to the goal of healthy and appropriate sexual development in children. It teaches without supervision or guidance, inundating children's minds with graphic messages about their bodies, their sexuality, and those of adults and children around them."[25] Pornography, and by extension the Internet, inundates and overwhelms. According to those arguing for the CDA, *the message is the medium*: it (the Internet as pornography) threatens the future health of society by enabling unsupervised enlightenment, a situation that Brooks associates with learning

Figure 6.3. Illustration for "Cyberporn," *Time*, July 3, 1995 by Matt Mahurin. Reproduced by permission of Matt Mahurin.

outside normal disciplinary settings. And so the solution is to change the message and thus the medium.

Further complicating this "obscene" and risky scenario, the illustration on *Time*'s table of contents page reverses the gaze (Figure 6.3). Although the caption reads "People are looking at pictures of *what* on the Internet?" an eye peers from the monitor at the viewer. Analogous to Elmer-Dewitt's use of "you," this image places *Time*'s reader in front of the monitor, suggesting that everyone is at risk. Once more, the screen provides the only light source and the eye appears wrinkled, indicating an aged other, prematurely so or not. The computer screen becomes a window through which this other looks at and exposes us. Rather than an interface, the screen becomes an *intra*face: a moment of face-to-face contact with this mature eye. The monitor monitors: someone could be watching.

Building on this ambiguity between watcher/watched, *Time*'s other illustrations make explicit Internet pornography's "deviance." In the one illustration that is clearly an "artist's conception," a man, hiding behind a computer screen, lures a little child with a bright red lollipop (Figure 6.4).

Figure 6.4. Illustration for "Cyberporn," *Time*, July 3, 1995 by Matt Mahurin. Reproduced by permission of Matt Mahurin.

This image alludes to oral sex or homosexual contact, but more important, it illustrates one of society's hypervisible fears: young boys being lured by older men (presumably, this scenario is so dangerous that it could only be rendered as a drawing rather than a digitally altered photograph). This picture of a vulnerable prepubescent child clashes with empirical evidence: most online seduction/abduction cases involve adolescents rather than young children hanging out in AOL tree houses. As the Department of Justice explains, "investigators must recognize that children who have been lured from their homes after online computer conversations were not simply duped while doing homework. Most are curious, rebellious, or troubled adolescents seeking sexual information or contact."[26] The group "at risk" for statutory rape are "adolescent boys who spend many hours 'hacking' on their computers," adolescents who have wills and desires that others are constantly trying to deny them (unless, of course, they commit a serious crime, at which point the same cultural conservatives who argue that "children" are victimized by cyberporn, contend that minors should be tried as adults).[27] The myth of the agentless child is precisely that and, through this myth, risks endemic to all online interactions are refigured as catastrophic risks to children, and homosexuality is rewritten as a form of child abduction.

As mentioned earlier, law enforcement and other psychological "experts" link the Internet to pedophilia because it enables "community," not because it enables greater access to children (indeed, many articles insist that real-life access to children is much easier—pedophiles tend to be schoolteachers, coaches, priests).[28] It also facilitates the circulation of child pornography, which some view as a "precursor" to, and others a substitute for, the actual pedophilic act.[29] Regardless, proactive police units use the hypervisible pedophile to validate their methods, which arguably—although ostensibly not illegal—entrap: police officers pose as curious young boys and actively seek, and perhaps create, pedophiles.[30] The so-called "Innocent Images" initiative, which simultaneously seeks to make images innocent and declares no image innocent, foreshadows the proactive police methods implemented more broadly after September 11, 2001. These techniques that entrap, but are not legally considered entrapment, that lead to the routine arrest and conviction of people for crimes they have not actually committed, reveal the difference between discipline and control. To be clear, I am not arguing for child pornography or pedophilia but rather seeking to understand how, through the Internet, pedophilia has been established as *the* most hypervisible deviant sexuality useful to methods of control. Significantly, the popular conception of the Internet as aiding and abetting pedophiles does not reflect networking protocols but rather propaganda about the Internet as "empowering" and anonymous. Given its constitutive tracking ability, the Internet could easily have been heralded as facilitating the *prosecution* of pedophiles (that is, now we can catch those people who, before the Internet, circulated their images in a less accessible manner). The fact it was not so heralded reveals assumptions about technology as *inducing* perversity.

To return to the *Time* images, they illustrate the dangers lurking behind cyberporn: overexposure, intrusion, surveillance, and the birth of perverse desires. Anxieties over cyberporn exceed the simple worry over present conditions. In order to understand cyberporn's ramifications, we are told to imagine a catastrophic future of unbearable and uncontrollable contact.[31] This call assumes that catastrophe could be avoided if pornography were simply purged from this medium. By focusing on pornographic images as the source of vulnerability, those hyping cyberporn perpetuate two "competing" visions of the Internet that are really the obverse of each other: the sunny information

superhighway and the "smut expressway." For those hyping the information superhighway, self- or corporate-censorship is key and a rudimentary marketplace
of ideas already in place; for those behind the smut expressway, government intervention is needed to create an orderly marketplace. Regardless of these differences, both adhere to a notion of electronic interchange that portrays the ideal
user/consumer as fully in control—bathed in the soft light of rationality rather
than in the glare of publicity or the relentless light of surveillance. Both seek to
quarantine the good from the bad, the empowering from the intrusive, the rational from the illogical in order to preserve their vision of communication
without noise—communication that proceeds in an orderly fashion, with little
or no misunderstanding, with no harassment or irrationality.

The excessive accounts of the Internet's intrusiveness also express anxiety over being in public not quieted by marketplace analogies. Online, one is
not simply a spectator-citizen-commodity-owner. Even when "just viewing"
or "lurking," one actively sends and receives data (all spectators are still visible—the degree of their visibility, or more properly traceability is the issue).
Dreams of vision from afar coexist with the media's relentless drive toward
circulation. Fiber-optic networks threaten to break the glass so that nothing
screens the subject from the circulation of images. Instead of only celebrities
being caught in the glare of publicity, average citizens find themselves
blinded and harassed. Others' words, transported as light—indeed translated
into light and shooting through glass tubes—invade us. And the computer
window does not seem to come with dimming controls. Instead, it engages
all acts enlightening—all types of light streaming from a window—from the
relentless light of surveillance, to the blinding light of harassment, to the ar-
tificial light needed for self-contemplation or self-reflection. Rather than
marking an end of the enlightenment in either sense of the word "end," the
Internet asks us to rethink enlightenment so that the act of enlightening is
not limited to rational discourse or to soft light. Fiber-optic networks, then,
physically instantiate and thus explode enlightenment. To contain it, legislators had to create new laws, adding another twist to the intertwinings of
power and pleasure coating fiber-optic networks.

Pornocracy

Responding to cyberporn's "dangers," the U.S. legislature enacted two laws,
the CDA (1996) and COPA (1998), that restricted minors' access to "unsuit-
able materials." Leaning on a series of court decisions that have placed the

protection of minors above the First Amendment rights of adults, the government cited the need to shield minors as compelling interest.[32] These acts, unlike other laws designed to regulate media content, sought to protect speakers by commercializing pornography and indecency, by creating a soft and fuzzy public sphere in which people literally "buy and sell" ideas.

In the United States, twentieth-century battles over the limits of mass media centered on pornography and obscenity. Each U.S. Supreme Court decision offers a different relationship between regulatory and disciplinary power, a different way of understanding the relationship between allowable and forbidden speech, while at the same time always giving the Court power to decide the limits of the "speakable."[33] According to *Kovacs v. Cooper* (1949), "the moving picture, the radio, the newspaper, the handbill, the sound truck and the street corner orator have differing natures, values, abuses and dangers. Each . . . is a law unto itself."[34] Because broadcast "invades" the home and because children can hear and see before they can read, broadcast receives the least First Amendment protection, while cable and the telephone receive more.[35] These decisions reveal the intimate relationship between pornography legislation and mass media: without mass commodification, transmission, and production, there would be no pornography legislation (if not pornography itself).[36] These decisions also explain why the debate over Internet regulation was centered on analogies: was the Internet like broadcast, or was it like the telephone or print? Was the Internet mainly filled with images or text?

Faced with the privatization of the Internet backbone in 1996, the U.S. government passed the CDA, an act key to understanding the Internet as both a threat to and enabler of democracy. The CDA threatened with fines (up to $100,000), imprisonment (up to two years), or both, "anyone who makes, creates, solicits, and/or initiates the transmission of any communication that is obscene or indecent, knowing that the recipient is under eighteen years of age, regardless of who placed the call." It also threatened to do the same to "anyone who displays, in a manner available to anyone under eighteen years of age, any communication that, in context, depicts or describes, in terms patently offensive as measured by contemporary community standards, sexual or excretory activities or organs, regardless of who placed the call."[37] Lastly, it threatened to fine and/or imprison anyone who knowingly permits any telecommunications facility under his or her control to be used for such communications. The government would offer safe harbor to those who have, in good faith, taken reasonable, effective, and appropriate actions to restrict or prevent access by minors. Verified credit cards, debit accounts, adult access codes, or adult personal identification numbers—all methods employed by commercial pornography sites in 1996—were named as adequate restrictions.

Although the CDA revised provisions initially aimed at regulating telephony, the crux of the CDA was an analogy between cyberspace and broadcast: the Internet, like broadcast, "invades the home." Further, the Department of Justice in its brief to the Supreme Court argued that the Internet is worse than broadcast, "because millions of people disseminate information on the Internet without the intervention of editors, network censors, or market disincentives, the indecency problem on the Internet is much more pronounced than it is on broadcast stations."[38] Because of this lack of intervention, while the Internet has "incredible potential as an education and information resource,"[39] "that same technology . . . allows sexually explicit materials, including 'the worst, most vile, [and] most perverse pornography,'" to be "only a few click-click-clicks away from any child."[40]

This click-click-click proximity of net porn compromises the efficacy of zoning laws. As Senator Daniel R. Coats put it during congressional debate over the CDA, "perfunctory onscreen warnings which inform minors they are on their honor not to look at this [are] like taking a porn shop and putting it in the bedroom of your children and then saying 'Do not look.'"[41] The government moved toward zoning partly because "cyberspace" lends itself to questions of spatial segregation and partly because the CDA leaned on previously upheld zoning laws to prohibit the display of obscene and indecent materials. According to the Department of Justice, "the display provision operates an adult 'cyberzoning' restriction, very much like the adult theater zoning ordinance upheld in Renton and Young."[42] Through this move, the geography of the physical world and cyberspace are correlated; thus, concerns over pornography are "directly analogous to the concerns about crime, reduced property value, and the quality of urban life." Since the porn shop resides in the bedroom rather than the street, zoning becomes a more pressing and intimate issue.

Zoning regulations, which restrict the display of "indecent" materials to certain commercial zones, combined with credit card verification as safe harbor, seek to protect access to sexual content by commercializing all sexual content. This effectively moves regulation from the auspices of the government to the market, while at the same time enormously expanding the materials to be regulated (COPA makes this strategy more explicit). The government thus protects free speech by making it no longer free. The CDA, with its "safe harbor" of credit-card-based age verification, effectively forces all obscene or indecent content providers to become commercial; as the non-commercial plaintiffs such as Stop Prisoner Rape argued, the costs of employing such a system are prohibitive. This "negligence standard," as the legal scholar and activist Amy Kapczynski argues, in contrast to a strict liability standard, enables the relatively free flow of commercial pornography and the discretion to self-regulate.[43] The "problem" the CDA attacks is not commercial pornographers but rather entities that provide pornography—or more properly "indecent materials"—for free. Residing outside market forces, without the pressures of having to sell programming to advertisers and the general public, these entities make the "vilest" materials readily available, seemingly out of the goodness of their own heart. The Senate justified the forced commercial regulation of "indecency" by maintaining that providers, rather than parents, should shoulder the monetary burden.[44]

For the future of our children, then, the CDA sacrificed the *free* circulation of some ideas. Or to spin it more attractively—as the Department of Justice did in response to the Eastern District Court's decision to grant a preliminary injunction against the enforcement of the CDA—Congress decided that it must stop the free circulation of some obscene ideas in order to ensure the free flow of others, in order to make cyberspace truly public, where public means free from pornography. According to the Department of Justice Supreme Court brief, the inadequate segregation of pornography from the rest of the Internet effectively violated the rights of adults, since "the easy accessibility of pornographic material on the Internet was deterring its use by parents who did not wish to risk exposing their children to such material."[45] Through this argument, the Department of Justice sidestepped the relationship between access and infrastructure/income/education, while also appearing to support access.[46]

This reasoning however, failed to persuade the judiciary of the CDA's constitutionality.[47] In response to the attorney general's argument that the CDA follows precedents set for broadcast regulation, the Supreme Court decided, "the special factors recognized in some of the Court's cases as justifying regulation of the broadcast media—the history of extensive Government regulation of broadcasting . . . the scarcity of available frequencies at its inception . . . are not present in cyberspace. Thus, these cases provide no basis for qualifying the level of First Amendment scrutiny that should be applied to the Internet."[48] Given that cyberspace, unlike broadcasting media, receives "full" First Amendment protection, the vagueness of the terms "indecent" and "patently offensive" become key: without *FCC v. Pacifica* to rely on (because *Pacifica* was restricted to broadcast), "indecent" does not have a judicial history; Congress's definition of "patently offensive" leaves open the question of whose community standard is pertinent and is without the usual clauses about artistic merit and parental support.[49] The vagueness of these words— the lack of a bright line—causes individuals to steer clear of constitutionally protected speech and deprives the medium of its richness in content.

Thus, according to the decisions of the Supreme and District Courts, Congress did not adequately tailor the CDA to the medium. Whereas broadcast is marked by scarcity, pervasiveness, and intrusiveness (thereby enjoying the least First Amendment protection), the Internet is distinguished by plenitude and user participation. Specifically, "four related characteristics of Internet communication have a transcendent importance to our shared holding that the CDA is unconstitutional on its face. . . . First, the Internet presents very low barriers to entry. Second, these barriers to entry are identical for both speakers and listeners. Third, as a result of these low barriers, astoundingly diverse content is available on the Internet. Fourth, the Internet provides significant access to all who wish to speak in the medium, and even creates a relative parity among speakers.[50] These four characteristics make the Internet "the most participatory form of mass speech yet developed . . . [and thus it] deserves the highest protection from governmental intrusion."[51] This characterization highlights the act of posting (most surfers do not post to newsgroups, listservs or the Web) and ignores the nonvolitional "speech" driving Internet protocol. Regardless, it was decided that the government, rather than pornography, intrudes.

Judge Stewart Dalzell, one of three District judges on the panel that granted a temporary injunction against the CDA, quotes from Justice Oliver Wendell Holmes's famous dissent: "[W]hen men have realized that time has upset many fighting faiths, they may come to believe even more than they believe the very foundations of their own conduct that the ultimate good desired is better reached by free trade in ideas—that the best test of truth is the power of the thought to get itself accepted in the competition of the market."[52] Prior to the Internet, this theory seemed "inconsistent with economic and practical reality." Economic realities have skewed the marketplaces of mass speech in favor of "a few wealthy voices . . . [that] dominate—and to some extent, create—the national debate. . . . Because most people lack the money and time to buy a broadcast station or create a newspaper, they are limited to the role of listeners, i.e., as watchers of television or subscribers to newspapers."[53] To worsen the situation, economic realities have forced competing newspapers to consolidate or leave the marketplace, effectively leaving most Americans with no local competing sources of print media. Lastly, cable has not delivered on its promise to open the realm of television. "Nevertheless, the Supreme Court has resisted governmental efforts to alleviate these market dysfunctions [since] . . . the Supreme Court held that market failure simply could not justify the regulation of print."[54] With the advent of the Internet, however, the judiciary can go on the offensive, by simply preserving indecency.

According to Dalzell's decision, the presence of indecency proves the diversity of the medium, "speech on the Internet can be unfiltered, unpolished, and unconventional, even emotionally charged, sexually explicit, and vulgar—in a word, 'indecent' in many communities. But we should expect such speech to occur in a medium in which citizens from all walks of life have a voice. We should also protect the autonomy that such a medium confers to ordinary people as well as media magnates."[55] Thus, diversity of content stands as evidence of the diversity of people, whether or not such economic or, perhaps more specifically, occupational diversity exists. Without indecency, "the Internet would ultimately come to mirror broadcasting and print, with messages tailored to a mainstream society from speakers who could be sure that their message was likely decent in every community in the country."[56] Indecency thus moves from an evil that must be accepted to proof of democracy, to establishing the "much-maligned 'marketplace' theory of First Amendment Jurisprudence."[57] Albeit in very different terms, Dalzell like Foucault sees pornographic resistance or blasphemous knowledge as supporting, rather than destroying, power.

Judge Dalzell is openly outspoken and enthusiastic in his defense of the Internet, but even Justice John Paul Stevens, in writing the majority opinion in *Reno v. ACLU*, ends by celebrating the phenomenal growth of the Internet, declaring, "the interest in encouraging freedom of expression in a democratic society outweighs any theoretical but unproven benefit of censorship."[58] He also argues that the CDA's breadth is "wholly unprecedented. Unlike the regulations upheld in *Ginsberg* and *Pacifica*, the scope of the CDA is not limited to commercial speech or commercial entities. Its open-ended prohibitions embrace all nonprofit entities and individuals posting indecent messages or displaying them on their own computers in the presence of minors."[59] The Supreme Court—which has repeatedly decided in favor of media monopolies and against antitrust laws, effectively reducing consumer choice—thus stands up for individual citizens in a decision, applauded by all telecommunications companies, that completely ignores the larger implications of the Telecommunications Act of 1996, such as the privatization of the backbone. This privatization and the policy-based routing it enabled would profoundly change the Internet.

These decisions hinge on user control. Concentrating on the act of searching and surfing, both the Eastern District and Supreme Court agree with the plaintiffs that "although such [sexually explicit] material is widely available, users seldom encounter such content accidentally. . . . The receipt of information requires a series of affirmative steps more deliberate and directed than merely turning a dial. A child requires some sophistication and some ability to read to retrieve material and thereby to use the Internet unattended."[60] Rather than being passively attacked by images or speech, a child must deliberately choose indecency. The Internet is not like broadcast, but telephony:

In any event, the evidence and our Findings of Fact based thereon show that Internet communication, while unique, is more akin to telephone communication, at issue in Sable, than to broadcasting, at issue in Pacifica, because, as with the telephone, an Internet user must act affirmatively and deliberately to retrieve specific information online. Even if a broad search will, on occasion, retrieve unwanted materials, the user virtually always receives some warning of its content, significantly reducing the element of surprise or "assault" involved in broadcasting. Therefore, it is highly unlikely that a very young child will be randomly "surfing" the Web and come across "indecent" or "patently offensive" material.[61]

Internet pornography—and by extension its content in general—does not assault the viewer, because the user must click and read. Because one usually receives textual descriptions before one receives an image, the random retrieval of indecent or pornographic materials is "highly unlikely." In fact, the question of the random retrieval of smut becomes absorbed into the larger problem of imprecise searches since the technology makes no distinction between decent and indecent materials: "Sexually explicit material is created, named, and posted in the same manner that is not sexually explicit. It is possible that a search engine can accidentally retrieve material of a sexual nature through an imprecise search, as demonstrated at the hearing. Imprecise searches may also retrieve irrelevant material that is not of a sexual nature. The accidental retrieval of sexually explicit material is one manifestation of the larger phenomenon of irrelevant search results."[62] By emphasizing "imprecise searches," the judiciary further highlights user control. The "facts" presume that precise searches do not uncover uninvited and extraneous sites. The Internet is not a porn shop in the bedroom but rather a library or mall with secret exits to porn shops that one accidentally finds by looking too far afield (much like the video store with the pornography section visually cordoned off).

The Supreme Court's ruling did not end the legislature's attempts to regulate Internet content. Instead, Congress intensified its efforts to make Internet content commercial through COPA. At face value, COPA would seem to be a more restricted law, since it only prosecutes "whoever knowingly and with knowledge of the character of the material, in interstate or foreign commerce by means of the World Wide Web, makes any communication for commercial purposes that is available to any minor and that includes any material that is harmful to minors." This law takes out the display condition and seems to follow the standard Miller test, by requiring that the text, "taken as a whole, lacks serious literary, artistic, political, or scientific value for minors."

COPA may be limited to commercial speech but, by its definition, most speech on the Web is commercial. In its definition of "commercial purposes," the act states: "A person shall be considered to make a communication for commercial purposes only if such person is engaged in the business of making such communications." It goes on to state:

The term "engaged in the business" means that the person who makes a communication, or offers to make a communication, by means of the World Wide Web, that includes any material that is harmful to minors, devotes time, attention, or labor to such activities, as a regular course of such person's trade or business, with the objective of earning a profit as a result of such activities (although it is not necessary that the person make a profit or that the making or offering to make such communications be the person's sole or principal business or source of income). A person may be considered to be engaged in the business of making, by means of the World Wide Web, communications for commercial purposes that include material that is harmful to minors, only if the person knowingly causes the material that is harmful to minors to be posted on the World Wide Web or knowingly solicits such material to be posted on the World Wide Web.

According to this definition, "free" sites—sites that consumers do not pay to access, but that receive money from advertisers, qualify as commercial speech. That is, the government treats as commercial many We sites that are "free" or whose print versions are not regulated as commercial speech, such as the *New York Times* (in print, since such regulations apply to advertisements, not to entire periodicals because they carry advertisements). Thus, COPA's definition of commercial speech exceeds the current definitions of print commercial speech, which COPA uses as its precedent. As Third Circuit U.S. Court of Appeals judge Leonard J. Garth argues, "although COPA regulates the commercial content of the Web, it amounts to neither a restriction on commercial advertising, nor a regulation of activity occurring 'in the ordinary commercial context.'"[63] Although the Third Circuit Court upheld the preliminary injunction on the grounds that "community standards" are inapplicable in cyber-space, Garth also stated the court's "firm conviction that developing technology will soon render the 'community standards' challenge moot, thereby making congressional regulation to protect minors from harmful materials on the Web constitutionally practicable."[64] Garth is probably referring to digital certificates, electronic identification papers that will reveal the age and the location of the user, among other things. Digital certificates, produced in re-action to the CDA, but also useful to e-business, reveal that passing legislation—whether or not it is ever enforced—has a profound impact on the technological and cultural development of the Web, and that the U.S. government seeks to legislate as "the invisible hand of the market."

These "failed" efforts to commercialize speech, to use commerce as a means to govern, have helped transform the Internet from an research/military system to a mass medium/marketplace. Both the CDA and COPA of-fered credit card verification as a "safe harbor" against prosecution, even though many minors legitimately own credit cards. The year 1996 marked the transition of online porn from "amateur swapping . . . to commercial ventures" because many noncommercial Web sites ceased operating or adopted credit card verification out of fear of prosecution (or desire for money).[65] The government's listing of credit card verification essentially validated com-mercial porn sites by making porn sites that charged for access seem respon-sible, rather than greedy (for charging for something that was freely accessible elsewhere, for information that, as the hacker adage insists, "should be free"). As such, the threat of government regulation—however unlikely its enforcement—gave Web site developers the necessary "reason" to access their visitors' credit cards and to acclimate them to "paying" for some information.

The impact of the CDA thus reveals that laws, in order to be effective, do not need to be enforced or constitutional—laws are not only a form of sover-eign power.[66] The government, especially in the age of "small" government, seeks to impact the public and private corporations "indirectly," through measures that respect the market and corporate self-regulation. Corporate self-regulation, endorsed by some of the plaintiffs for the CDA, has had a "chilling" effect on Internet speech. For instance, AOL decided in 2003 to re-ject all e-mail coming from residential DSL servers in order to reduce spam and regularly ejects users who do not follow AOL's etiquette rules. Most of the larger news Web sites carefully filter their content. And all commercial media organizations constrain content in order to boost ratings or click-throughs.[67]

Crucially, independent noncommercial pornographic or erotic sites still thrive, using the "click here if you are 18" to enter portal in order to remain legal—although the Justice Department in 2005 seemed likely to launch an offensive against Internet pornography. Doubtless, small noncommercial sites exploring nonnormative sexuality will be the department's first targets. But given increasing corporate self-regulation and changes to the fundamental structure of the Internet, what do individuals now do? Do they, based on the so-called privacy of the Internet, engage in public acts of nonregulation? And how do acts of nonregulation, and the freedom that stems from them relate to questions of agency?

In Public

> *The public is the experience, if we can call it that, of the interruption or the intrusion of all that is radically irreducible to the order of the individual human subject, the unavoidable entrance of alterity into the everyday life of the "one" who would be human.*
> —Thomas Keenan, "Windows: Of Vulnerability"

The CDA court decisions privilege agency over contact, empowerment over disruptions, text over images. The Supreme Court's description of the web summarizes this conviction nicely:

The Web is thus comparable, from the readers' viewpoint, to both a vast library including millions of readily available and indexed publications and a sprawling mall offering goods and services.

From the publisher's point of view, it constitutes a vast platform from which to address and hear from a world wide audience of millions of readers, viewers, researchers, and buyers. Any person or organization with a computer connected to the Internet can "publish" information.[68]

According to the Supreme Court, all users—whether readers, publishers, or both—deliberately act. They read, consume, publish, research, address, listen or view. They may accidentally retrieve the wrong information and they may, through slips of the keyboard, expose their gender, race, age, and/or physical fitness, but, in general, they control what information they receive and send. This deliberateness stems from the textual nature of online communication. Literacy proves a thinking subject. Textual exchange guarantees fair exchange. The Internet, by resuscitating and expanding "print" publishing, restores eighteenth-century optimism.

This conclusion relies on a dangerously naive understanding of language, one that rivals "they wouldn't print it if it wasn't true." It erases the constant involuntary data exchange crucial to any user-controlled exchange of human-readable information, and disastrous to any analogy between print and the Internet. It also assumes an intimate and immediate relation between the written word and the mind, bypassing the unconscious and the ways in which language is beyond the individual. Further, it perpetuates an extremely safe notion of contact between readers and publishers: users do not interrupt each other, stalk each other, or really engage each other at all. Instead, they offer their statements, wait for replies, and perhaps reply back again in an orderly fashion. It assumes that texts can be reduced to ideas, and that people merely consume ideas. Lastly, it assumes that users are always the authors of texts and never their objects: again, the major objection against online pornography was not that it objectified women, as MacKinnon would have it, but rather that it assaulted its viewers. It considers pornographic—and indeed all electronic—intrusion accidental.

This decision also reveals popular belief in the "danger" of images. As mentioned previously, pornographic images are dangerous because they usurp their referent, unless the issue is child pornography—then, the danger stems from their indexicality. U.S. child pornography laws regulate image-based, and not text-based, pornography. The 1977 Sexual Exploitation of Children Act, the first U.S. law to outlaw the production, sale, circulation, and receipt of child pornography, stated that image-based child pornography was a "form of sexual abuse which can result in physical or psychological harm, or both, to the children involved."[69] It also stated that children were especially vulnerable to these images, for seeing them could make unwilling victims willing. Although pornographic images do "move" their viewer, like all images, they are read, and reading predates writing. As Laura Kipnis puts it, "pornography grabs us and doesn't let go. Whether you're revolted or enticed, shocked or titillated, these are flip sides of the same response: an intense, visceral engagement with what pornography has to say. And pornography has quite a lot to say. . . . It's not just friction and naked bodies. . . . It has meaning, it has ideas."[70] Kipnis's insistence on pornography as having meaning is missing in all analyses of pornography around CDA and COPA. This insistence of pornography as having meaning also enables a discussion of different kinds of pornography. Just as all books or films are not the same, all pornography is not the same.

In addition, the Supreme Court's conclusion that the accidental retrieval of pornography results from "imprecise searches" drastically simplifies language. Although adding qualifiers, in proper Boolean fashion, usually pares down the number of unwanted sites, the unexpected, the antithetical, and the pornographic do not only emerge when a search is imprecise. For one, those producing and consuming information are not cooperating together. Metatags—the tags that determine the site's keywords for which search engines scan—expose this noncooperation (for instance, Coca-Cola's metatag at one point contained "Pepsi"), as do pornographic sites that take advantage of typos, such as the former porn site whitehouse.com (versus whitehouse.gov). Marketers, at least, have not discounted the importance of slips of the keyboard, of serendipity; they have reinserted serendipitous "shopping" by taking advantage of various cracks in the subject's conscious control. The government, in filing COPA, also showed the inadequacies of the "imprecise search" argument through searches on "toys" and "girls" that produced pornographic sites (also inadvertently complicating simple notions of pedophilia by revealing the widespread sexualization of childhood). As well, a search on "Asian + woman" on Google produces more pornographic sites within the first ten hits than one using "pornography."

Exploring what the Supreme Court renders accidental and what high-speed telecommunications networks have made metaphoric—such as archive and vision—reveals the differences the Internet makes. Internet pornography calls into question visual knowledge. Using cinematic pornography as their basis, critics assume that pornography has an all-engrossing visual impact. Fredric Jameson, for instance, asserts in *Signatures of the Visible* that pornographic films are "only the potentiation of films in general, which ask us to stare at the world as though it were a naked body." To Jameson, "the visual is *essentially* pornographic, which is to say that it has its end in rapt, mindless fascination; thinking about its attributes becomes an adjunct of that . . . all the fights about power and desire have to take place here, between the mastery of the gaze and the illimitable richness of the visual object; it is ironic that the highest stage of civilization (thus far) has transformed human nature into this single protean sense."[71] This understanding of the visual as essentially pornographic, Jameson admits, stems from cinema and is perhaps not applicable to other media. Regardless, by discussing the Internet within the rubric of pornography, the 1995–97 debates sought to understand—if not create—the Internet as fascinating through a fundamentally visual paradigm. Fiber-optic networks, however, both enable and frustrate this all-pervasive visuality: visuality, the camera, and the gaze are *effects*, often deliberately employed to make "jacking-in" sexy. Although Internet pornography is visual, its invisible workings are more significant and its visual impact less than cinematic pornography.

Pornographic sites notoriously rewrite the basic functions of Web browsers, revealing the ways in which "user choice" is a software construction. By rewriting the "back" button, once an easy and readily available JavaScript, these sites push the user onto another Web site, precisely when he or she wishes to leave. By opening another window when the user seeks to close it, another easy and readily available JavaScript, they box in the user. The user usually gets stuck in a web ring and is forwarded from one member site to another, which, if the user follows for any length of time, belies notions of endless pornography/information. Porn sites were the first to use the now standard pop-up window to push images at viewers. These tactics often create panic, since the user has lost "control" over his/her browser. Users also panic when they receive pornographic e-mail messages after visiting certain sites (taking advantage of this panic, porn sites now feature pop-ups by "security companies" that warn you of the porn on your hard drive. By listing the contents of your C: drive, they make you believe (mistakenly) that everyone can access your entire hard drive). During the heyday of Netscape 3.0, porn sites used JavaScripts that culled a person's e-mail address. Although e-mail address capture is more difficult, even the most nonintrusive seeming sites, such as penisbot.com, collect statistics about the user usage (for example, what site the user last visited, or whether or not penisbot is bookmarked). Stileproject.com keeps track of which links have been clicked.

Porn sites take advantage of the many default variables provided by the hypertext protocol and use the latest "trapping" JavaScripts, while also offering content that reifies users' control. Taking advantage of "live" technology, they offer you models who respond to your commands, who interact with you in the manner that the Supreme Court understands interactivity—your mouse-click does seem an affirmative action. They offer you "tours" and give you samples based on your preferences. They enable you to keep a window open for hours, so that while you work, these images patiently wait for you. Online pornography seems less pornographic—less fascinating, less demanding. Pornographic Web sites reveal the tension between and synthesis of individualization and mass interest in their many intro sites, which pick up on porn key words such as "oriental" and then push you into larger sites, in which oriental may or may not be a category. They also pick up on the fantasy of amateur knowledge, of "do-it-yourself" webbing, through sites, supposedly produced by entrepreneurial women models. Thus, the content and structure of pornography sites expose the tension between freedom and control that underlies the Internet as a new mass medium: on the one hand it enables greater freedom of expression; on the other hand, it facilitates greater control. Porn site models are amateurs liberating their sexuality, or they are dupes you control. Porn sites enable you to investigate your sexuality without fear of exposure, or they track your every move. This opposition of control/freedom erases the constitutive vulnerability that enables communications. It is not either subject or object but both (metaphorically) at once. Publicity stems the breach between seeing and being seen, between representing and being represented. Publicity is an enabling violence—but not all publicity is the same. The key is to rethink time, space, and language in order to intervene in this public and to understand how this public intervenes in us, in order to understand how the Internet both perpetuates and alters publicity.

The dangers described by the pro-CDA forces are real: there exists information on the Web that can play a role in serious tragedies such as the Columbine shootings. Yet, democracy has always been about dangerous freedoms, to which the many revolutions to date testify. This is not to say that one must take a libertarian view; this is to say that these "dangers" can also be the most fruitful products of the Internet, that the disruption the Internet brings about can be utilized to formulate a more rigorous understanding of democracy. The key is to refuse hasty leaps between speech and "minds," and between diversity of content and diversity of people.

In short, the Internet is public *because* it allows individuals to speak in a space that is fundamentally indeterminate and pornographic, if we understand pornography to be as Judith Butler argues, "precisely what circulates without our consent, but not for that reason against it."[72] As Keenan remarks,

The public—in which we encounter what we are not—belongs by rights to others, and to no one in particular. (That it can in fact belong to specific individuals or corporations is another question, to which we will return.) Publicity tears us from ourselves, exposes us to and involves us with others, denies us the security of that window behind which we might install ourselves to gaze. And it does this "prior to" the empirical encounter between constituted subjects; publicity does not befall what is properly private, contaminating or opening up an otherwise sealed interiority. Rather, what we call interiority is itself the mark or the trace of this breach, of a violence that in turn makes possible the violence or the love we experience as intersubjectivity. We would have no relation to others, no terror and no peace, certainly no politics, without this (de)constitutive interruption.[73]

In this sense, we are the child—vulnerable to pornography and not yet a discrete private individual. And this position can be terrifying, yet without this we could have no democracy. This essay, through an examination of cyberporn, has outlined the necessity of this position, the necessity to deal with questions of democracy in terms of questions of vulnerability and fear. Resisting this vulnerability leads to the twinning of control and freedom, a twinning that depends on the conflation of information with knowledge and democracy with security.

We are now facing a turn in what Claude Lefort called the "democratic adventure," and these questions are pressing precisely because it is too easy to accept the Internet as the great equalizer: diversity of content easily becomes an alibi for ignoring questions of access; the Internet as the second coming of the bourgeois public sphere easily closes questions of publicity.[74] By questioning the position of the consumer—and its counterpart of the user—we can begin to expose the objectification and virtualization of others that underlie this myth of supreme agency and begin to understand how the Internet can enable something like democracy. By examining the privatization of language, we can begin to understand the ways in which power and knowledge are changing.

PART III

Public Space

Chapter 7
The Billboard War:
Gender, Commerce, and Public Space

Catherine Gudis

*The highway has become the buyway. There is a highway greater than
Broadway, Fifth Avenue or Main Street. It includes them all. It is the road
the public travels. It is millions of miles long. And billions of dollars are
spent because of what the public sees when it travels this buyway.
This is the Rue de la Pay.*

—*Advertisement,* The Poster, *December 1923*

As the urban environment decentralized in the 1920s and 1930s
with the adoption of the car as a routine part of American life, the highway
became more than merely a route to be traveled. It became the site of a new
kind of public landscape and conception of public culture. To some, including the outdoor advertisers who are the main subject of this essay, the highway had become the "buyway," a boundless marketplace bursting out of its
traditional confinement within town and city centers that was "millions of
miles long" and, thanks to the throngs it carried, "billions of dollars" strong
(Figure 7.1). No greater sense of "the public" could be imagined by those
wishing to commercially develop the roadside—including advertisers, entrepreneurs, real estate developers, town boosters, and automobile-related industries—than the seemingly endless stream of mobile consumers
populating the highways of the automobile age. Other observers, however,
held a different vision of the highway as public space. They imagined that the
view from the road, as well as the road itself, belonged to all citizens, had aesthetic and civic value, and was subject to public oversight and debate. As
rural and ex-urban areas became colonized by highways and buyways, and
the public landscape sold as advertising space, civic activists asserted their
beliefs that markets ought not mix with Mother Nature and that private

Rue De La Pay

THE HIGHWAY
and THE BUYWAY

The highway has become the buyway. There is a highway greater than Broadway, Fifth Avenue or Main Street. It includes them all. It is the road that the public travels. It is millions of miles long. And billions of dollars are spent because of what the public sees when it travels this buyway.

This is the Rue de la *Pay*.

Here outdoor advertising pays and pays and pays.

O-double-A is a useful institution to advertisers because, among other reasons it understands the geography and the psychology and the buyology of this Rue de la Pay.

OUTDOOR ADVERTISING AGENCY
OF AMERICA, INCORPORATED
Successors to Ivan B. Nordhem Co.

*Poster
Advertising*

8 WEST FORTIETH STREET, NEW YORK
CHICAGO   PITTSBURGH   DETROIT

*Painted
Displays*

Figure 7.1. Advertisement for outdoor advertising. From *The Poster* 14 (December 1923): 34. Outdoor Advertising Association of America Archives, John W. Hartman Center for Sales, Advertising, and Marketing History, Rare Book, Manuscript, and Special Collections Library, Duke University, Durham, N.C.

Highways, or

Buy-ways?

Nature Magazine,
Washington, D. C.

Figure 7.2. Anti-billboard cartoon. From *American Civic Annual* (Washington, D.C.:
American Civic Association, 1929), 140.

interests ought not to prevail in shaping the roadside environment (Figure 7.2).
The debates between these factions thus concerned the very nature of public
space—what constituted it, how it should be used, and who had the right to
determine its use and appearance.

This essay focuses on the deeply gender-divided "billboard war" that
pitted the beauty of nature against the beast of commerce, and usually
women against men. Roadside reformers, drawn from the ranks of women's
clubs, garden clubs, and other civic associations, set out to rid the public
highway of the signs of commerce. Outdoor advertisers constituted their foe,
men who asserted their commercial right to broadcast across public space.
Both the warring women, named "scenic sisters" by scornful outdoor advertisers, and their billboard "brethren" (also called "boys" and oftentimes
"barons") were cultural producers and arbiters of the road and the roadside
environment.[1] Their battle was over aesthetics, access, economics, and the
physical location of markets, and as much about class ideals as about cultural

conflict. The example of the billboard war reveals the ways in which all land-scapes are negotiated spaces, a layered composite of historically changing and culturally contested conceptions of nature, commerce, and aesthetics. It also reveals the permeability of what are often considered separate realms of public and private, nature and the market.

Scenic Sisters

Opposition to outdoor advertising began in the late nineteenth-century urban arena and then stretched into the countryside along with cars, high-ways, and national advertising campaigns.[2] By the 1920s and 1930s, resistance to outdoor advertising became a national battle that lasted more than forty years. Many women's civic groups, including art and garden clubs, banded together in defense of the roadside, rural, and natural environments and in opposition to roadside advertising, much as their predecessors in the municipal housekeeping and City Beautiful movements had fought on behalf of urban reform in previous decades.[3] Later, when the Depression halted urban development and construction everywhere except along the highways, the women followed with broom and dustpan—not to clean up behind the Civilian Conservation Corps building the rural roads, but to sweep aside the advertisers, merchants, farmers, and others who wished to follow the paved paths to profit.

By 1924, the General Federation of Women's Clubs (GFWC), represent-ing more than three million members, voted to support a coalition called the National Committee for Restriction of Outdoor Advertising (later renamed the National Roadside Council, or NRC). The NRC was to serve as a clear-inghouse for anti-billboard organizations, including the various state mem-bers of the GFWC (and the 3,500 women's clubs they represented), the Garden Club of America (organized in 1912 and committed to conservation), the American Scenic and Historic Preservation Society (founded in 1895), and even groups with membership dominated by men, including the Na-tional Highway Association, the American Society of Landscape Architects, the American Civic Association, and the Nature Association. Initially the NRC claimed forty such affiliates. Five years later it had one hundred. With a membership representing over forty states, from rural areas and small towns to big cities, the NRC was well positioned to have a national impact.[4]

The NRC was the brainchild of Elizabeth Boyd Lawton, who dedicated her life to obliterating "billboard blight" and would dominate the arena of roadside reform until her death in 1952. Her epiphany was as sudden as it was visceral. One summer, while driving upstate to escape New York City's heat and disarray, Lawton became appalled by the signs that marred her view. Billboards had ruined the journey to her Lake George retreat. With the help of the Woman's Civic Club of Glens Falls, in 1920 she surveyed the highways in her area, noted who the advertisers were, and conducted a letter-writing campaign to convince them to remove their signs. She also petitioned for restrictive legislation.[5] After some success, Lawton proposed to the New York State Federation of Women's Clubs that her local strategies be applied on the state and national levels. The GFWC promptly responded by condemning billboards "as preventing the full enjoyment of outdoor beauty" and dedicating its national art committee to the issue.[6] Naturally, these efforts were presided over by Lawton.[7]

As a volunteer working on behalf of the NRC, Lawton wrote for a great variety of planning and general interest magazines, lectured nationally, and lobbied widely for roadside regulations and nature conservation. She also conducted extensive state-by-state surveys documenting roadside conditions and then distributed the results in the publications of the NRC and its affiliates.[8] She recognized the new strength that lay in women's voting rights. She also saw that women's clubs had an "old-girl network" with access to the "old-boy network," which could be harnessed to persuade the men with whom they were affiliated. The outdoor advertising industry recognized these strengths and also understood the threat that the NRC posed when it inspired both women's and men's organizations devoted to nature conservation, urban planning, and architecture.[9] Rightly, they tended to see Lawton as the primary troublemaker. Her campaigns were so effective that when she died, leaders of the Outdoor Advertising Association of America (OAAA), which represented billboard businesses nationwide, circulated her obituary with a handwritten eulogy, "File: Nuisances Abated."[10] Within several years of her death, the NRC dissolved.[11]

With the slogan "Save the Beauty of America: The Landscape Is No Place for Advertising," Lawton claimed that the NRC wished simply "to arouse and express public opinions" that the billboard "desecrates scenic and civic beauty."[12] While explaining the NRC's purpose to the federation, she benignly averred that "it consists solely in telling the advertiser how we feel about these rural boards; calling his attention to the fact that the scenic beauty of our country will soon be ruined if the rapid increase of signboards goes unchecked."[13] But politically savvy plans lay beneath her gracious words. While she established a base of grassroots consumer activism and welded "a chain of community interest," as one colleague said, the real core of her activity was aimed toward another realm—the legislature. Her true purpose was to induce zoning restrictions, taxation, and other regulations that limited outdoor advertising.[14]

For decades, however, the courts had ruled that aesthetic concerns were an inappropriate application of the police power's regulation of private property, which could only restrict land use to serve the public safety and welfare. "Aesthetic considerations are a matter of luxury and indulgence rather than of necessity," a New Jersey court ruled in 1905, "and it is necessity alone which justifies the exercise of the police power to take private property without compensation."[15] Even when courts upheld billboard regulations, as one did in St. Louis in 1911, the judicial decision veiled all aesthetic concerns by making linkages to the ways that billboards jeopardized public safety and welfare. Billboards were fire hazards; blew over in high winds; obstructed light, air, and sun. The grounds behind them were used as privies, places of prostitution, trash receptacles, and retreats for "criminals and all classes of miscreants." A Chicago court in 1917 also ruled that billboards could be forbidden in residential areas, and for similar reasons of public well-being. These cases provided important precedents for restricting billboards, but courts did not utilize aesthetics to justify restrictions, nor would they until the 1950s and 1960s.[16]

Lawton and her organization thus faced a serious obstacle. One of her main arguments for the limitation of billboards was aesthetic. It was also the argument that most inspired the women who joined her organization, since many roadside reform groups grew out of art clubs. Yet the courts would not recognize aesthetics as legally significant. Fortunately for Lawton, there was arising in the 1920s the recognition of an equally important arena, that of public opinion. "We believe that a public opinion campaign will pave the way for successful legislation later," Lawton decided, "that, club women, is our job."[17]

Despite the slighting expectations of gender, the clubwomen often organized their publicity campaigns with the precision of a pyramid scheme. A case in point was Philadelphia's Congress of Art, an active member of the NRC. The congress represented forty-five civic associations, each of which appointed four members to write weekly letters to advertisers who were contributing to "Billboard Boulevards" such as South Broad Street and Roosevelt Boulevard. Then, each month, all congress members targeted four national advertisers for additional canvassing.[18] The congress was just one supporter of the NRC's platform, and it was a local, not a statewide, representative. Multiplied nationally, the NRC became more than just an annoyance.

Fingure 7.3. Typical "billboard alley," photographed to accompany a survey of Illinois by Elizabeth Lawton. From *American Civic Annual* (Washington, D.C.: American Civic Association, 1932), 164.

Lawton and her scenic sisters engaged the mass media carefully. In addition to its own quarterly magazine, the NRC published pamphlets, circulars, and postcards as well as game books and other materials for schoolchildren that used billboard reform as civics lessons. Members regularly wrote letters to the editor and articles for newspapers and national magazines such as *Reader's Digest, Ladies' Home Journal*, and the *Saturday Evening Post*, and worked hard to publicize their events.[19] Meanwhile, Lawton kept a rigorous speaking schedule in which she showed slides of billboard alleys that had been tunneled through the countryside and barns, trees, and posts slathered with tin, paint, and paper signs (Figures 7.3–7.4).

Though the reformers took their cues from corporate public relations professionals, their efforts were often described in feminizing terms. The *Philadelphia Record* stressed the NRC's "dignified, courteous and kindly manner," while other papers suggested what they were up to was a form of "moral suasion." Charmingly impotent rather than politically challenging, the clubwomen, according to another publication, were "priestesses of hospitality," "hostesses" of their towns, and "debutantes in public affairs." They were not meddlers in business, but rather keepers of public morality and aesthetic guardians, helping to nourish the corporate soul and to preserve public rights. They were doing their womanly civic duty.[20]

Since the most straightforward approach—seeking policy change by

Figure 7.4. "Snipe" signs covering trees on the west side of Los Angeles, circa 1930. Automobile Club of Southern California Archives.

going directly to the legislature—had met with such limited success, reform groups took yet another tack, aligning their power as consumers with their obligations as citizens. They engaged their civic duty through consumer boycotts, following a tradition of women's activism that accessed power by pulling the strings of the family purse.[21] "Women are the buyers," Lawton explained. "When our merchants, local and national, realize that the women are determined to wipe out the rural billboard, the boards will fall."[22] Although Lawton could not convince the GFWC to endorse a nationwide boycott of manufacturers that all their clubs would abide by, she did succeed in urging some local organizations to do so and suggested that clubwomen everywhere exercise their commercial "rights of selection" (ably combining social Darwinism and consumerism) (Figure 7.5).[23] "I favor products not advertised along the roads!" was the slogan of a national campaign, imprinted on stamps and stickers.[24] Throughout the 1930s, the NRC distributed a "White List" of manufacturers that clubwomen (and men) were urged to patronize.[25]

The "old-girl network" was partially responsible for the NRC's success with this campaign. For instance, one of the influential names on the White List from the start was Standard Oil.[26] As it happened, roadside betterment was a pet project of Mrs. John D. Rockefeller, the wife of Standard Oil's president, whose donations also supported the American Civic Association's roadside improvement campaigns.[27] Other companies that used national billboard advertising soon fell into line under the threat of negative publicity, including Pillsbury Flour, Kelly Springfield Tire Company, and Gulf Oil, which all agreed that though they would continue to use billboards, they would limit them to commercial areas only. (In fact, this was Standard Oil's policy, too, though one would never guess at this limitation from the publicity the company produced.) Though the Outdoor Advertising Association of America publicly smirked at these results, their members hastily checked and repaired relations with national manufacturers.[28]

Some local organizations found economic retribution to be a more direct tool, Honolulu's Outdoor Circle achieving perhaps the most success. The Outdoor Circle was formed in 1912 to protect Hawaii's panoramic vistas, recently marred by such commercial detritus as soap ads at Punchbowl, Bull Durham billboards on Diamond Head, and an immense pickle sign on the road to Waikiki. Members effected little change until about 1923, when they began boycotting stores and products that used billboards; they also refused to frequent stores merely carrying products advertised on billboards. Four years later they hit the streets, tearing out the last billboards of the sole remaining local billboard firm in Honolulu. Each clubwoman paid $150 for the

Figure 7.5. As part of the anti-billboard movement's consumer activism, this motorist vowed to "make a list of advertisers I'm never going to patronize." From *American Civic Annual* (Washington, D.C.: American Civic Association, 1929), 136.

honor, and for partial ownership of the Pioneer Advertising Company, which the Outdoor Circle purchased (and then dissolved). The Hawaiian legislature even came to pass restrictions in 1927, limiting outdoor advertising to commercial areas and imposing a high licensing fee.[29] Still, it was the vigilance of the women that kept their landscape free of advertising. In the 1950s, when airplanes trailing advertisements for whiskey cast unsavory shadows on Hawaiian beaches, the Outdoor Circle again sprang into action, using boycotts to convince businesses to refrain voluntarily from outdoor advertising. Today the Outdoor Circle still works on environmental issues and has branches on four islands. Hawaii is one of four states that ban outdoor advertising entirely.[30] While the Outdoor Circle used their purchasing power, as consumers, to effect political change, it is notable that the policies they desired were enacted only after private industry folded to their request rather than the other way around.

The Outdoor Circle was unusual, however, among women's groups, which were largely unwilling to threaten free enterprise in like manner. The group's personal approach of visiting each shopkeeper, its very defined and local geographical focus, and its persistent willingness to exert economic pressure formed the Outdoor Circle's winning combination. Perhaps the Honolulu women were also better able to defend their activities given the dependence of the Hawaiian economy on natural resources and the tourist trade. As the Outdoor Circle claimed, "we are [just] a tiny Paradise in the Pacific."[31] But Hawaii could not serve as a useful example for every locality in the United States since, unlike elsewhere, it had no problems determining what qualified as scenic beauty (all of Hawaii) and in demonstrating why beauty was deserving of preservation (tourism). Elsewhere, things were not as obvious.

The Pastoral View

Could one justify protecting areas in Illinois, Nebraska, and Oklahoma as easily as California's redwood forests or Hawaii's tropical foliage and beachfronts? What about the myriad other landscapes that composed the American terrain that highways were making accessible? What sorts of environments were the reformers aiming to conserve? Whose nature counted? And, since aesthetic arguments alone seemed to get nowhere, what were the expected benefits that these scenes would provide? In other words, how did one justify protecting landscapes opened to view by the automobile?

Despite their embrace of modern methods of publicity and networking, the clubwomen looked back to previous centuries of American and European ideas about nature and long-held literary and artistic traditions concerning the landscape in order to answer these questions. They did not, however, merely mimic the visions of their predecessors. They fastened gender to these visions, and thereby transformed the roadside into a domestic enclave where one learned, through nature and beauty, moral rectitude and civility. They asserted that "outdoor beauty . . . is one of the greatest character-molding influences of the nation," a "public heritage" and a "spiritual resource," thereby assigning good republican motherhood to Nature herself.[32] Extending the idea of the sanctity of the home to the landscape at large, women reformers claimed "a landscape free from unnecessary commercialism; a landscape where, escaping from the ugliness, the rush and the turmoil of our cities, we may find for both body and soul, the soothing calm and the re-creation which the beauty of nature brings."[33] The separation of spheres that had long been used to characterize the relationship between women and men, home and workplace, reformers now applied to the landscape at large, where nature became the domestic realm, necessarily separated from commerce and signs of the city, while women became upholders of its purity. As such, their ideal for the landscape was consistent with other domestic, middle-class, suburban, and arcadian ideals.

To be scenic and appropriately uplifting, reformers thought a landscape had to be picturesque and sublime.[34] It can be no coincidence that reformers' outlines of the necessary aspects of a worthwhile landscape—mountains, waterfalls, cliffs, canyons, and forests—adhered to principles of landscape painting articulated in the eighteenth century by such theorists as Edmund Burke and William Gilpin, and were widely employed by nineteenth-century American artists and writers such as William Cullen Bryant, Thomas Cole, and Washington Irving.[35] Serving as paeans to nature and to good taste, quotes from Bryant, Burke, John Greenleaf Whittier, and others who poeticize nature and the spiritual uplift it offers were liberally sprinkled through their anti-billboard materials. Reform materials also employed a stock of images that fell into two categories of landscape scenes, which, if not for billboards, should have been seen by passing motorists: ruggedly sublime images of untouched nature, and pastoral scenes of rural peace and beauty, usually displaying rolling hills, orchards, and patchwork plots of farmland (Figures 7.6 and 7.7).[36]

The categories of picturesque and sublime also referred to established assumptions about nature and its importance to society. Associations ranged

Figure 7.6. "Go Prepared If You Wish to Enjoy American Scenery," 1925. Albert Sprague Bard Papers, Box 21, Manuscripts and Archives Division, New York Public Library, Astor, Lenox, and Tilden Foundations.

Figure 7.7. Sublime views are displaced by commerce in this cartoon lampooning Massachusetts highways, circa 1928. Albert Sprague Bard Papers, Box 21, Manuscripts and Archives Division, New York Public Library, Astor, Lenox, and Tilden Foundations.

from the garden in Genesis to the yeomen farmer and Jeffersonian agrarianism to James Fenimore Cooper, Frederick Jackson Turner, and Theodore Roosevelt. The rhetoric of reformers especially acknowledged the importance of nature in helping to mold the American national character of individualism and self-reliance. They reiterated ideas about nature's powers to inspire, civilize, and rejuvenate, notions that gained popularity as America and Europe industrialized.[37] Thus armed with such a readily understandable and unquestioned cache of tropes about nature, reformers could laud the road as serving public rather than merely private, commercial purposes. The road brought people into contact with the natural world (or could, if the reformers' suggestions were followed), and offered an optimistic promise of prosperity in spiritual, cultural, and even nationalistic terms. As Grace Poole, president of the GFWC, said, "beauty is not simply a money value to the United States of America." Lawton completed the thought, explaining that landscape beauty "is a spiritual asset, a power for uplift," and "one of the great character-building forces of our nation."[38]

Roadside reformers often extolled the potential democratizing power of highway travel for its ability to bring the masses of motorists in contact with America's natural resources, beauty, and agrarian past. They went so far as to imagine not just the road, but the roadside too as public space. They claimed a public right to the view. Their conjuring of nineteenth-century painterly images, and their desire to landscape that which was not naturally picturesque, indicates that this view from the road was not of the simple roadside as it existed. Rather the public had a right to an imagined panorama, a landscape of the mind's eye that allowed viewers to ignore the brutal facts of commercial and industrial development and property division. In his 1836 essay "Nature," Ralph Waldo Emerson described this ideal view: "The charming landscape which I saw this morning, is indubitably made up of some twenty or thirty farms. Miller owns this field, Locke that, and Manning the woodland beyond. But none of them owns the landscape. There is a property in the horizon which no man has but he whose eye can integrate all the parts, that is, the poet."[39] Conceptual ownership of the landscape fell to the eye of the beholder. Roadside reformers wished the same and, on those grounds, argued that when farmers Miller, Locke, and Manning erected signs on their property, they were invading that which should belong to "no man" and to all: the view.

In the twentieth century, the roadside reformers repeated Emerson's question and again asked, "Who owns the scenery?" Charlotte Rumbold from Cleveland wondered, "The real estate developer or the farmer owns the land," but "does he own the landscape?"[40] The road itself was public since taxpayers paid for it. Reformers desired more, however, and claimed that the roadside was also public because it was within the surveying, or scopic, field of spectatorial vision of the taxpayer. The act of viewing was acquisitive, appropriative, itself an act of consumption. Reformers considered the public part of the roadside to be all that one could gaze upon magisterially. The imperial eye of individuals determined its ownership by conceiving it, much as Emerson's poetic eye had conceived his landscape and thereby come to own it.[41]

If the roadside vista was public space and thereby open to democratic access, then billboards constituted both a physical and a conceptual blight. They blocked the view from the road, that was obvious enough, but they also blocked the notion that the American landscape was held commonly, without property borders and free to all. By placing images of commodities in the midst of this landscape, advertising interrupted the ideal conception of the imperial eye that this landscape was somehow owned by all and reminded motorists that not they, the people, but rather the market was in possession of even the most remote American vista. Billboard alleys lining the highways endlessly repeated that commercial fact. Billboards were "an invasion of common rights," an abominable "expression of private gain and public loss."[42] As Lawton put it, natural beauty "belongs to the people, and no individual, no corporation has a right to commercialize it for their own private gain."[43] Reformers contended, rather boldly, that unlimited signs of business in the form of billboards that impeded the spectacle of the landscape foreclosed another foundation of the American way, namely democratic access, not just to the view, but to all it represented—the very notions of individualism, independence, freedom, and self-realization.

Billboard Barons

While roadside reformers articulated their visions of public space, the organized outdoor advertising industry fought back. To the reformer's amazement, the outdoor advertising industry began to suggest that it, too, was guardian of the landscape, and moreover that billboards comprised the business of beauty. In printed materials circulated to clients and through efforts of specially organized groups of industry representatives, advertisers conducted a comprehensive public relations campaign. Typically the industry appropriated select elements of the rhetoric of aesthetics expressed by the roadside reformers and civic beautifiers and used these to its own advantage.

Figure 7.8. Billboards frequently depicted the natural wonders one might experience through the car windshield. From *The Poster* 20 (1929): 11. Outdoor Advertising Association of America Archives, John W. Hartman Center for Sales, Advertising, and Marketing History, Rare Book, Manuscript, and Special Collections Library, Duke University, Durham, N.C.

Why concede to detractors when one could potentially win them over? As is so often the case with public relations campaigns, in time the outdoor advertising industry engaged and propagated the very same idealized view of the landscape as its detractors.

Billboard businessmen most apparently engaged the arguments of their detractors in their common construction of a national myth of the American road. Advertisers utilized this myth to promote automobility and consumption on, alongside, and beyond the road. Advertisements, particularly for automobile-related goods and services, stressed the same ideals of pastoralism and scenic beauty accessed through auto-tourism that clubwomen promoted (Figure 7.8).[44] Both women reformers and admen stressed history, national heritage, and civic identity as part of America's uniquely pastoral landscape, and both commonly depicted this landscape as a rural idyll. This ideal view differed, of course, from the actual one seen from the road, even when billboards were absent. The commodious scenes of which the women dreamed were the very commodities that admen wished to sell.

Outdoor advertisers understood the advantage of a rural pastoral ideal. One billboard salesman explained that the benefit of his medium was that it stood outdoors, where nature "puts people in a friendly, cheerful, optimistic frame of mind. The poster is kith and kin to Nature herself. When the buying public is motoring, in the hills, it is out from under the dead weight of much materialism, of worry, of self-analysis."[45] His language compares with that of clubwomen who described the allure of "smiling landscapes" in Illinois and the "mantle of beauty" of Washington.[46] Outdoor admen also agreed about the appeal of tourism, and recognized their own role in creating the desire for it. When a weekend jaunt or a "gypsy" camping vacation brought a motorist to nature, these trips also commercialized the roadside environment.

When outdoor admen engaged criticisms of female foes, they carefully addressed gender dynamics. Advertisers focused on their manly responsibility to distinguish the use of nature and art for the sake of the economy from their detractors' less useful desires for scenic pleasures. They used masculine obligations, as providers and protectors, to justify the hard monetary benefits of outdoor advertising for full employment and a healthy economy. When admen defined their role in rationalizing the distribution of both goods and consumers they addressed long-standing economic fears of having overproduction accentuated by underconsumption.[47] Their rational, even scientific, self-justifications criticized their female foes for soft emotionalism and idyllic delusion. While outdoor advertisers might sympathize with clubwomen, as corporate caretakers of the American way and facilitators of the flow of commerce essential to the nation, their duty was to the economy first.

Besides, said the admen, billboards did not blight, they built. They were usually put on semi-commercial "marginal lands no longer desirable or saleable for residential purposes." They provided revenue to pay the taxes on that land and sowed the ground for additional commercial development. This, they claimed, was the way new towns rose between cities. Billboards aided the proper use of highways as commercial arteries that contributed to the well being of the country.[48] The question posed in a 1924 *Printers' Ink* article summed up the position: "Are private property rights, effective marketing of goods, and the rights of industry to be sacrificed to a question of good taste? Good taste is relative."[49]

In the Depression, their rhetoric sometimes grew downright ungentlemanly. The booklet *100 Reformers versus 25,000 Wage Earners*, which, according to its own title page, had been "approved by every labor group to which it has been submitted," attacked the "professional reformers" and uncharitably described them as "wealthy 'leisurables' who with nothing else to occupy themselves must espouse a 'cause.'"[50] A similar debate occurred in 1931 when the Maryland House of Delegates sought to pass a bill to restrict billboards. One side, represented by garden clubs, the League of Women Voters, and Chambers of Commerce, argued to "save the beauty of the Maryland countryside" while the billboard faction argued to "save the wives and children of working men from being starved to satisfy a group of idle women."[51] In the darkest days of the Depression, the outdoor advertising industry claimed to be a dependable source of employment for workers and rent paid to farmers—often their only source of income and means of survival.[52]

Outdoor advertisers also asserted the multiple ways in which they were safeguarding public culture. Billboards, they said, could provide a tremendous educational medium with civic welfare at heart. One adman asserted the value of the billboard in teaching thousands of people "a knowledge of letters," for which it "should win the blessing of every kind-hearted lady in this crusade for beauty."[53] Just as reformers sought to provide access to the arts through their clubs and exhibitions, advertisers claimed a role for the poster in democratizing art, reaching "the great masses of people, the illiterate, the uneducated, the foreigners, those who are not yet Americanized." In contrast to "art for art's sake," this was "art for life's sake."[54] Another publication argued, "We have our beautiful museums and Art Galleries, but the people will not go to them—at least, not in great numbers."[55] Another writer said, "This is an unpleasant but inescapable proof that art must be brought to the people."[56] There was no better medium than the billboard, which could "talk the vernacular . . . the language of the common people," to mediate between high and low.[57]

Outdoor advertisers claimed not only to educate and Americanize through posters but also to upgrade the neighborhood at large. The West Coast company, Foster and Kleiser, wished not to blend in, but to make a neoclassical statement in civic reform with architectural innovations and the creation of "sign parks," complete with drinking fountains and benches. With a staff of over forty professional horticulturalists, Foster and Kleiser landscaped their billboard parks with manicured lawns edged with beds of roses and begonias. "Nature's gorgeous colors are used to supplement the work of America's foremost poster artists," the company boasted, citing their maintenance costs as evidence that outdoor advertisers were essentially in the business of "good housekeeping" and could sympathize with women. It was a "real housekeeping job on a big scale . . . a never-ending fight against dirt, papers and all sorts of rubbish." Foster and Kleiser was exemplary and other companies, from St. Paul, Minnesota, to Ponca City, Oklahoma, followed suit with parks of their own.[58]

Examples of Foster and Kleiser billboards from Los Angeles, Seattle, Portland, and San Francisco in the 1920s also show illuminated, white pilaster, and latticed billboards sporting neoclassical nymphs they called "lizzies." A

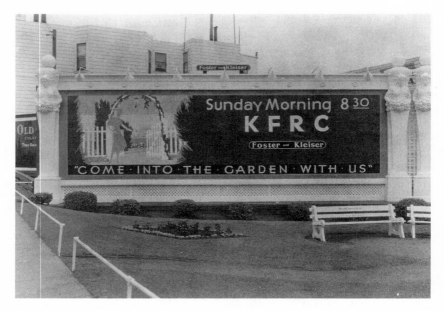

Figure 7.9. Foster and Kleiser outdoor advertising company publicized its radio show and offered gardening lessons on the sites of its "sign parks," which were also spruced up by white columned "lizzies." Clear Channel Outdoor, Los Angeles.

sarcastic rendering of the garden club gal? Perhaps. But even more explicit was Foster and Kleiser Company's nod to the clubwomen with their weekly radio program, "Garden Clubs of the Air," which provided tips on gardening as well as free cuttings from the plants on the billboard lots (Figure 7.9).[59] It was a clever strategy for diffusing the criticism of the clubwomen.

Dumps, vacant lots, parking lots, and garages were cleaned up and hidden by walls of white or green latticed, landscaped, and adorned billboards. Shrubs and flowers were planted along the roadways, surrounding the billboard structure. Children's sandboxes and educational flower and vegetable gardens utilized the grounds behind the billboard structures, and during World War II that space was turned over to communities for victory gardens, with outdoor advertising companies distributing manuals for raising crops.[60] In California, Foster and Kleiser Company even bought up "special sites of land" that "have rare scenic beauty."[61] In this case the purpose was not so innocent, since it kept valuable advertising space from their competition. Taken together, these strategies aimed to beautify business and to mitigate, if not outright co-opt, the scenic sisters' opposition.

The industry did not just plant shrubs, flowers, and crops. It also planted spies. In 1920, the industry undertook special public relations efforts in response both to the passage of the Nineteenth Amendment granting women the vote and to the formation of special art and billboard committees of the General Federation of Women's Clubs (GFWC).[62] Women previously perceived as merely annoying were now an organized, political threat to the billboard industry. In response, poster association leaders delegated "the best women plant owners in our Association" and any other "capable" women staff members to attend the GFWC conventions and to speak on the industry's behalf. Their mission was "to learn first hand what's going on and how it is being 'cooked up.'"[63]

Orchestrating these industry women's activities and keeping an educated eye on Elizabeth Boyd Lawton and her roadside reformers was a special public relations committee headed by Lillian Lilly. With her Fifth Avenue, New York, address and her experience doing public relations work on censorship issues for the Motion Picture Association of America, Lilly managed an infiltration of the women's clubs with industry-friendly plants. She herself was a prominent figure on the club scene, an active leader in the GFWC, and frequent speaker, tea hostess, and slide presenter. She kept her influential club friends friendly to the industry. Lilly also recruited the female relatives of industry members to join clubs, to attend meetings, and to put a "pretty face" on the outdoor advertising industry.[64] Lilly's activities lasted for decades as she continued to shepherd the industry in its development of a comprehensive public relations division.[65]

Lilly and her female "infiltrators" arranged teas and lectures to promote outdoor advertising to clubwomen. As both club members themselves and as industry representatives they acted as double agents, circulating back and forth across the battle lines, representing each side to the other, able to speak both the language of business and that of reform. Their circulation in both worlds neutralized the threat posed by the clubwomen to the billboard men in the political arena, and perhaps it also neutralized the clubwomen's distaste for billboard blight.[66] What stands out about the formation of Lilly's group is the similarity of interests and class positions held by both clubwomen and billboard men. These activities also suggest that the industry recognized women were part of their public, had political clout, and could potentially turn the highway as "buyway" back into just a highway. The industry also viewed women as the primary market of consumers whose attention and goodwill they needed to court.

Perhaps unwittingly, clubwomen even joined the organized OAAA in finding a common enemy in the small-time itinerant billposter who painted or tacked "snipe" signs to trees, rocks, and buildings, and who generally was not a member of the organized trade association (see Figure 7.4).[67] The industry had long sought to overcome its reputation of circus ballyhoo conducted by immigrant journeymen and mom-and-pop shops, and the women aided its cause. When reformers agitated for laws that kept advertisers off public land such as parks and highway easements, the OAAA stood at their side. When the women pushed for enforcement of those laws, advertisers were again with them. And when the women struggled to assure that ads posted on private property had permission, were properly leased, or paid requisite license and permit fees, they actually provided a free service for the standardized outdoor advertising industry.[68] They helped the companies consolidate nationally by removing the small, independent, and ad hoc competition that was otherwise difficult for the industry to combat.

The outdoor advertising industry consolidated its services throughout the 1920s and 1930s with and without the women. The industry standardized its prices and the quality of its services nationwide during these decades. It offered national distribution through one service, which doled out advertising campaigns to only those billboard companies who were members. The industry effectively closed out the small, family-run shops characteristic of the industry in the nineteenth century. By the mid-1920s, many of the smaller billposting firms were already subsumed by larger companies. As that happened, more territory came under the control of fewer companies, with several large firms dominating each sector of the East Coast, Midwest, and western states, despite antitrust suits aimed to combat such industry monopolies.[69]

What emerges, then, is that the scenic sisters and their billboard brethren ultimately shared a surprising amount. Though at times reform groups seemed aimed against big business—"the vandalism of the rich corporations that sell gasoline" and advertising space, as they put it—a closer look shows the contrary. By decrying the desecration of the landscape by the hand of "the ignorant vendor of hot dogs"[70] and by campaigning to remove small signs, for instance, they helped liquidate the smallest roadside businesses and billposting services and thereby belied their rhetoric promoting the rights of the individual citizen over the corporate conglomerate. Reformers were far from anti-commercial in their sentiments—they were, after all, promoting automobility and tourism as they sought to protect the landscape view—while the billboard brethren were far from being against the enjoyment of aesthetics, or even of the open road. It was the myth of an open American road, promising all kinds of utopian mobility—either commercial or idyllic, but always bourgeois—that locked the contenders together in the first place.

Zoning and the Road to Federal Legislation

From the time she founded the NRC, Lawton asked the fundamental question: "Why commercialize the entire countryside?" "Why not keep business where business belongs?"[71] As Struthers Burt explained, "Nobody objects to anyone taking a bath in a bathroom, but there would be a great deal of objection if our highways were lined with people taking baths."[72] Legally, the means of keeping everything in its proper place was zoning. By the mid-1920s, Lawton realized that while the law might not be willing to regulate based on aesthetics, the growing application of zoning to cities and towns could serve just as well. Zoning divided building and land use into separate residential, commercial, and industrial districts. It aimed to protect public health, safety, morals, and welfare, and presumably property values. Areas that passed zoning ordinances might bar outdoor advertising from residential areas, since these areas excluded commercial and industrial uses. Though this worked for cities and towns that employed zoning, could the vast expanses of state and interstate highways that passed through rural areas also be regulated?

Throughout the 1930s, and originally in the face of strong opposition from professional planners and highway officials, the National Roadside Council supported highway zoning as a promising approach for controlling the encroachment of billboards, junkyards, roadside businesses, and other signs of commerce along rural roadways. The NRC defined and publicized a program for regulation that took its cues from zoning, and sought to separate natural and commercial uses of the highways by consolidating commercial development into regularly spaced intervals along the highways. By making business areas compact and centrally located, they hoped to maximize trading value yet minimize sprawl. Such an organization and separation of purposes, Lawton wrote, "would build up better towns, preserve the rural character of our arterial highways, and protect the beauty of the countryside."[73]

In the 1910s and 1920s, zoning plans were usually promoted by residents, property owners, merchants, and real estate interests. In contrast, roadside reform groups advocated zoning as a national solution to national needs. They claimed to represent the interests of all mobile audiences, a traveling public from widespread parts of the country whose interests in the roads stemmed from their investment in them as taxpayers, citizens, and consumers. This mobile audience constituted the citizenry that roadside reformers sought to represent. Though they may have been property owners while at home, their national political power derived from their mobility.

Like urban planners, roadside reformers sought to regulate the environment in which their constituents—the traveling public—had vested interests. They advocated for them based on their fundamental beliefs in mobility, moral aesthetics, and environmental purity as a national heritage. Under dispute, though, were the interests of the mobile public versus those of the property holders who actually owned the roadside. Reformers recognized that not everyone felt as kindly toward zoning as they did, acknowledging that "the communities and the rural sections that most need it are slowest to use it, and it is not rare to see, even in a zoned community, the entire length of the through road given up to business."[74] The rural and agricultural regions that roadside reformers were most intent to protect generally were the most resistant to controls. Farmers usually saw the land as a site of work, and not simply a pretty landscape picture to behold. Frequently this meant that farmers and other rural proprietors were pitted against roadside reformers, whom they saw as effete leisure seekers for whom nature was recreation, not work.[75]

Not all clubwomen could bear the limitations of free enterprise that were implicit in some of the National Roadside Council's plans, including their zoning proposals. For instance, the New York City Federation of Women's Clubs, many of whose members were represented in NRC publications and in discussions of roadside reform, voted against NRC proposals that they believed limited property rights and the spirit of entrepreneurialism.[76] Perhaps the location of this group, in the advertising capital of the nation, meant they were more closely connected to the industry, too. Indeed, Elizabeth Lawton distrusted the leadership of the New York City Federation, believing it to be a pawn of the outdoor advertising industry.[77] But their views cannot be so easily discounted as kowtowing or compliant. Though the heart of the message sent by the New York women was the defense of private interests, they justified their activity on behalf of the collective rights of those private entities. They stressed that the public was not just mobile; it included property owners and business interests as well. Accordingly, they decided that private property rights came first; and beauty came second. This, too, was a bourgeois value, perhaps equal to that of the landscape.

By 1940, the role of outdoor advertising in creating ribbon developments and helping to decentralize the city had become more apparent to groups with greater political clout than the National Roadside Council.[78]

However, national attempts to regulate outdoor advertising diminished as the country began mobilizing for war. After World War II, when highway construction and, importantly, plans for a national system of interstate and defense highways resumed, reform efforts also returned.[79]

The battles of the 1950s and 1960s continued along the lines established in the previous half century of activity. The weapons each side used also remained consistent. It was the billboard barons against the scenic sisters, dollars versus aesthetic sense, professional lobbyists and lawyers versus letter-writing, flower-sniffing crusaders. Though roadside reform had become a national cause and the subject of congressional debate and extensive coverage in the popular press, when the issues and sides boiled down to essentials the old stereotypes still reigned. Now, instead of Elizabeth Lawton being pilloried by her opponents, there was Hilda Fox of the Pennsylvania Roadside Council, Mrs. Vance Hood, of the New Jersey Roadside Council, and Helen Reynolds, of the California Roadside Council, state chapters that continued strongly on even after the National Roadside Council dissolved, in an untimely way, just at the start of the postwar round of the billboard war. Although the Garden Club of America, the American Planning and Civic Association, and the American Automobile Association continued to fight for billboard reform, without the NRC or some other group orchestrating the activities, the movement lacked a center.[80]

But at this moment the roadside reform movement was given new life from an unlikely corner, the White House, and from the very man who had opposed stringent billboard restrictions in 1958 and had used billboards for his own campaigning in 1960 and again in 1964. For Lyndon Johnson, the decision to fight for highway beautification was not sympathy for the cause, but love for his wife, Lady Bird.[81] Though the most powerful man in the nation led this new round in the billboard war, the struggle was again cast in gendered terms.[82] Attention to beauty, no matter what the burly Texan in the White House said, was woman's work and the Highway Beautification Act was "Lady Bird's Bill," "a frivolous frill, and a woman's whim," as some senators took to calling it.[83]

Journalists loved to report, often sarcastically, on Lady Bird's affection for flowers and her belief in the power of beauty to uplift even the economically depressed, as if she was the leader of the garden club armies that were championing beautification.[84] However, the women of the roadside councils and garden clubs, despite their field experience, were offered no role in helping to shape legislation and had scant contact with members of the administration.[85] The roadside reformers were never invited into the inner sanctum of the

White House, and for good reason. The seats there were already filled by their competition, the lawyers and lobbyists of the billboard industry. The outdoor advertising industry had been working its political connections behind the scenes. Early on it supported the Highway Beautification Act, knowing well from meetings with White House officials that the bill included the provisions it desired.[86] What finally passed as the Highway Beautification Act of 1965 could hardly be called a victory for the roadside beautifiers. The act called for controls on federally funded primary and interstate highways, restricting billboards within 660 feet of highways but permitting them in areas zoned commercial and industrial and in unzoned areas used for commerce or industry.[87] The billboard industry even succeeded in having an amendment passed that assured "just compensation" to be paid to all billboard or property owners whose billboards were removed as a result of the Highway Beautification Act. For roadside reformers this was humiliating, as it meant the defilers of the landscape were now paid to keep from polluting, rather than being fined for having done so all these years.

Neither the actions of these states nor the Highway Beautification Act crippled the billboard industry. Far from it, the act actually recognized the outdoor advertising industry as "a legitimate business use of land."[88] It also helped put the outdoor advertising industry in the hands of fewer and bigger companies, sounding a death knell for the small-scale, rural billposting businesses and sign companies. As John Primrose, the owner of a Kentucky outdoor advertising business bluntly interpreted the act, "it will work very little hardship on the big Metropolitan plants but it will practically put the small rural plants, like mine, out of business."[89] In this sense, the Highway Beautification Act actually smoothed the process of incorporation and consolidation that the outdoor industry had begun three-quarters of a century earlier.

Losers and Winners

Billboards, of course, have come to wrap themselves around us so thoroughly that it would seem the scenic sisters failed. Actually they succeeded in many ways. They took early and necessary first steps to employ zoning and planning outside of urban centers; they recognized the value of preserving in-between places and defending the rights of the mobile public, on a national basis; and they had tremendous foresight in addressing the areas and issues that would ultimately draw resources, development, and people away from cities and lead to commercial and residential sprawl. In all of these ways, they

articulated their role as civic leaders and defined highways as important public spaces, where the economic functions of the marketplace were supported
by an interlacing cultural ideology. They shared more with their opponents
than they were willing to acknowledge, though, admittedly, their differences
are not easily effaced. To the billboard industry, highways were also important public spaces, as the mobile marketplace of the twentieth century, whose
value was determined entirely by its ability to reach the consuming public. To
the reformers, the very value of the automobile and the road would be de-
flated if signs of commerce were to be found everywhere the car could go.
Some spaces had to be saved as bucolic and scenic. That is to say, while outdoor advertisers had an utterly commercial ideal of the roadside's value as
public space, reformers thought the roadside had inestimable aesthetic and
civic value as well, worth preserving.

Yet as much as the values of the two groups could sometimes differ, and
as much as their worldviews seemed to share, they shared nothing quite as
strongly as their common promotion of the myth of the open road and the
different sorts of mobility it promised. Both sides idealized and promoted a
pastoral view through the windshield of the automobile, saw the landscape
and the road as commodities with value (aesthetic and pecuniary, respec-
tively), and used the rhetoric of democracy, national identity, individual
rights, and civic pride to express their visions.

This is not to say that the billboard war is over, far from it. Conflicts persist, and in even more arenas. For in the twenty-first century, new electronic
telecommunications technologies, which often use the metaphor of the highway to suggest a new public thoroughfare of cyber-audience mobility, take
the challenges of the scenic sisters to new extremes. Today, the lines between
private and public space blur along with what constitutes public discourse,
while issues of speed, decentralization, and mobility intensify along the new
virtual buyway of the Internet. What outdoor advertisers defined in the 1920s
as the mobility of the market is now axiomatic. Few are the places that do not
bear the literal and conceptual signs of the market. Advertising and marketing follow us, the consumer, wherever we go, actually and virtually. In the
public bathroom we meet Flush media, while on the street we look up to
buildings, buses, and taxicabs shrink-wrapped with advertisements. Cruising
online, we are bombarded by pop-up billboards, find informational and
commercial messages intertwined, and are tracked in our every move, while
billboards on highways now have the ability to talk back to us (via shortwave
radio links and MP3s), to change as we pass them (through motion detectors,
digital ink, and electronic modems), and even to follow us around town

(thanks to GPS-aided billboards and vehicle ads).[90] It does indeed seem that advertising is not just omnipresent but that it is also omniscient, the market and the marketer everywhere present, attuned to our every move, and sometimes more aware of our next step than we are. The signs of commerce have so proliferated that now they all but engulf us as they line the greatest expanses of our communities and landscapes.

What does this say about public space and public culture? According to the perspective of the advertisers I have discussed, we are indeed well-endowed if the ever-expanding mobile market constitutes public space. Though, if public space is that which is exempt from commerce, as roadside reformers would have it, then it would seem we are bereft. Yet neither view seems quite right. For if the battles of the billboard war offer any lessons at all, they are that, first, highway spaces are socially as well as physically constructed. They are the result of negotiation between multiple publics, whose access to power has been unequal but whose struggles have nevertheless had an impact on the built and natural environment and resulted in new relations between people and places. Second, highways are spaces of consumption, whether products are consumed or simply a good view, and whether or not the physical signs of commerce are present. Perhaps if roadside reformers had more fully acknowledged this, they would have waged stronger economic and environmental arguments on behalf of the landscapes they wished to spare from development. Third, and related to the previous point, the billboard war suggests that the categories of public and private, nature and commerce are not mutually exclusive; they are neither discrete nor impermeable, and their sites are multiple. To think otherwise would dismiss a century of conflict over the road and roadside environment.

However, suggesting that public space has been privatized (and vice versa) and nature commercialized offers an answer of sorts to the question of who won the billboard war. Although billboard brawn has not won out over beauty (after all, the most green and ad-free landscapes seem to be in areas that are wealthy, enfranchised, or a draw to those two groups), power and access remain dominant issues. Americans still seem to be fascinated with the idea of mobility and to find hope in the idea of the open road. In the mind's eye if not in physical fact, we might find our reprieve from commerce, search out a good view, and imagine that it is indeed open to all. But translating this work of imagination into reality will require another generation of activists more successful at intercepting the forces of commerce and consumption than the last.

Chapter 8

The Social Space of Shopping: Mobilizing Dreams for Public Culture

Sharon Zukin

I lined up a set of copper pans, every size in order, just out of reach, so the customer would have to get together with the person in the store. It was the beginnings of a conversation, a way of shopping that disappeared during the [second World W]ar, unfortunately.
—*Chuck Williams, founder of Williams-Sonoma*[1]

Nostalgia for older forms of community and the public space in which they were enacted stirs us to appreciate the places where we have shopped in the past. Partly this reflects their technological and social obsolescence—as my grandparents recalled "the delights of corner-shops, gas lamps, horsecabs, trams, pisstalls: all gone, it seems, in successive generations," so I regret the passing of friendly chats with shop clerks and greengrocers and their replacement by the soulless autonomy of Internet shopping.[2] But the feeling of attachment to, or alienation from, shopping places is not all a matter of structural change. It also varies with the distance we ourselves have branched out from our social roots. Despite the daily experience of shopping in Manhattan, where I have lived for many years, I still have dreamlike memories of carrying out errands for my mother on the neighborhood shopping street in Philadelphia where I grew up. The butcher, baker, and owner of the dairy store knew me well, at least by face; I greeted most of them by name; and I became an awkward adolescent at my mother's side while she chatted with them about small events and even smaller purchases. These conversations weren't only economic exchanges, they were a means of cultural reproduction. My family tacitly understood that the shopkeepers were, in a larger sense, *like us*. From the smoked fish that was displayed in the front half of the delicatessen to the concentration camp inmate's number that was tattooed in blue on the wrists of the couple that bought the dairy store from Mrs. Fox, when she grew too old to stand on her feet behind the counter, and the jokes my mom made with Meyer the butcher or Ethel his wife, who doubled as the cashier, we knew that we were members of the same ethnic community—although we never met outside the store.[3]

My memories linger on this shopping street because I left it many years ago and because the place that I remember so vividly is gone. Half the block was razed after a subterranean pocket of natural gas that no one had known about exploded, and the remaining houses were judged too dangerous for anyone to live in. Most of the children I grew up with had already left the neighborhood, spreading out to farther regions of the city, like my parents, or to another city, like me. Today, only the shells of half a dozen small stores with apartments on the second floor cling sadly together at one end of the block. All that remains of Meyer's butcher shop is a hand-scrawled sign—"chicken 39 cents a pound"—taped to the plate-glass window. On a weekday morning, the shop is closed, the bare white enamel refrigerator cases gleaming like ghosts in the darkness. My memories return to this shopping street because of the public space that we took for granted, but which is so hard to re-create around shopping today. This was a walking street, surrounded not by parking lots but by blocks of houses, a place of intimate encounters among people who were otherwise strangers.

Not everyone has such romantic feelings about the neighborhood shops of their childhood. Alfred Kazin, the famous "walker in the city," was repulsed when he returned to Brownsville, the mostly Jewish, working-class area of Brooklyn where he grew up in the 1920s. Climbing the subway stairs to the street, he sensed an acrid smell, read the aging signs, and remembered the dingy store interiors with their second-rate selection of goods. I think he would have preferred to grow up among the secondhand bookshops of Lower Manhattan. Or maybe he liked the big department stores that we see in old black-and-white photos, illuminating Gotham with the bright lights of their seasonal window displays. These windows drew novelists like Theodore Dreiser, who strolled along Fifth Avenue in the early 1900s, gazing at the windows; tourists, eager to take part in a big city ritual; and elegant, perfumed shoppers who were loyal to the same stores year after year and to the saleswomen who greeted them by name and brought the very best new dresses to the fitting room.

Alfred Kazin is not the only American to have unpleasant memories of shopping in his youth, for the social space of stores, regardless of how plentiful their stock, can expose the wounds of social inequality. African Americans were shortchanged for many years by local merchants of a different ethnic hue. After the Civil War, they were shunned by the elderly white men sitting around the stove in the country store and insulted by racist images of black people as mammies and buffoons on advertising posters on the wall. In the 1980s, during the early years of the current wave of immigration, misunderstandings coupled with a lack of empathy between Asian shopkeepers and black shoppers smoldered in rude encounters and sometimes sparked arrests, boycotts, and wider community protests in New York and Los Angeles. For large groups of people, then, the experience of shopping may stir unforgiving memories.[4]

The very same shopping place can arouse feelings of both conflict and comfort. Older Americans who were raised in small towns and big cities can recall the thrill of fingering makeup, stationery, and toys in the separate compartments of counters at Woolworth's Five and Ten Cent Store—but they also remember how shoddy the merchandise eventually became before the variety chain went out of business. Elderly Southerners fondly remember the old Woolworth's lunch counter—a local hangout before McDonald's—as a place where they carried out the friendly routines of a small-town community. But Northerners recall newspaper photographs of Southern whites heaping abuse and pouring ketchup on the heads of college students holding sit-ins at the lunch counter to protest racial segregation in public places during the 1960s. Feelings of conflict are not always racial. For everyone, close relations with shopkeepers on a small town's Main Street could be confining, compared to the liberation of shopping in a brand-new, more anonymous, and infinitely more varied shopping mall. And teenagers can't wait to move beyond their mother's Sears or small department store to the brighter, youth-centered world of Abercrombie, Virgin Megastore, or Jimmy Jazz, depending on what's temporarily cool.

As these brief notes suggest, the places where we shop are organizational grids of social life. Not only brick and mortar boxes built along streets and highways, stores are social spaces where people enact community and build a public culture. This is not a civic culture based on mutual obligation, rights, and duties, but a set of internalized rituals anchored in the routines of daily, weekly, and seasonal provisioning, as well as in modern values: a creative desire for novelty, the hard work of identity construction, and the burdensome freedom of individual choice. From a strictly economic point of view, stores are nodes in markets that organize the distribution of consumer goods. But stores are also nodes of sociability and centers of information, where shoppers do "research" on new products, prices, and styles, and check out what it means to be modern in the continuous now. It is true that the excessive exuberance of consumer culture has given shopping a bad reputation. "Shop 'til you drop," shopping as a form of leisure entertainment, and stores that are open 24/7 imply moral weakness rather than public good. If Americans "bowl alone," they are probably out together shopping. But shopping is a purposeful way of being alone together with others. Stores are where people go to be "in public" *without* feeling obligation.[5]

Stores organize publics across different scales of space and time. On a neighborhood shopping street of small, locally owned stores, where shoppers get to know the merchants from frequent visits, stores are still places of face-to-face social interaction. In a large supermarket, shoppers may not know each other's faces, but they chat with the cashiers. In a regional supercenter, owned by a distant corporation, shoppers develop a relationship with the products, internalizing their locations in the store by the repeated ritual of wheeling a cart through the aisles, filling it with merchandise taken from the shelves or pallets, unloading items onto a conveyor belt, watching them disappear into large paper bags, and bringing these bags home. Because of the patterns shoppers develop—where they shop, whom they talk to, and which products they look for, stores are also very specific places of identity formation. Teens learn to be Goth by hanging out at Hot Topic. They pass from one age status to another when they stop shopping with their moms and go shopping with their friends. Women learn a central part of their gender identity by shopping for clothes, for gifts, and for their children—while men, who hand these routine tasks to women, eagerly shop for hardware, music, and electronics. In the most direct way, stores organize publics around sensual desire. The diamond ring in the display case, the red stiletto heels in the plate-glass window, and the racks of CDs enclosed in plastic boxes embody dreams of possession, perfection, and self-improvement. Stores provide a public space for pursuing these private dreams, while offering a common experience of public culture.[6]

Shopping has become such a pervasive part of public culture that we are hardly aware of how much it defines what we do and who we are. "Let's Shop!" the cover of *O* magazine, with a smiling Oprah Winfrey, calls out to us. "Grab This Fall Check List and Go!" Oprah's invitation confirms the importance of consumption to women's sense of efficacy and self-esteem, but shopping is no less important to the economy at large. Since the 1930s, the federal government has made the right, if not the ability, to buy consumer goods a central promise of citizenship, a sign of national prosperity and a key to voters' well-being.[7] It is this dual public function—both objective, in terms of the economy, and subjective, in terms of a sense of living well—that makes shopping so important today. This is what drove the mayor of New York City

and the president of the United States to press Americans to go shopping
after the terrorist attack on the World Trade Center and the Pentagon, on
September 11, 2001: Go shopping to restore our sense of normalcy and help
the national economy recover from the blow.

Especially for women, who are still the most frequent shoppers, stores
are where modern public culture is born. In the act of shopping women learn
to develop a "choosing self," consciously putting their identities together by
selecting commodities they find in stores.[8] The freely choosing individual is
equally adaptable to voting, when she chooses between candidates, moving,
when she chooses where to live, and schooling her children, when she goes to
"look at" a school and chooses the best alternative. The choosing self is ideally suited to a market economy, for supermarkets, malls, and Internet retail
sites all naturalize the magic formulas by which markets work, matching sup-
ply and demand, price and quality, need and want. When these equations
work out right—when shoppers find items in the right size, in the right color,
at the right price—the public culture of the market economy seems to be coherent. When they don't work, the processes of choice, surrounded by an
abundance of alternatives and the apparent satisfaction of other shoppers,
suggest the individual rather than the system is at fault.

In fact individual choices are bounded by a complex system of institutions aimed at making and marketing consumer goods. From e-mail that sends
designs overseas to jet planes that bring overnight deliveries of finished goods,
global networks carry out production and distribution. Market research firms
and advertising agencies analyze products' intangible appeal and figure out
how to persuade consumers to choose them. While product designers create
better, cheaper, and newer items, display directors design store environments to
heighten their appeal. Magazines dedicated to every kind of product join the
game: entice, seduce, persuade. The point is to mobilize dreams that *everyone*
has and direct consumers toward a sense of *individual* fulfillment. Whether
they are strictly functional like Wal-Mart and Home Depot or aesthetically
spare like the Japanese designer boutique Comme des Garçons, eerily museum-
like in their luxurious displays like Prada or matter-of-factly expensive like
Tiffany, shopping spaces are launching pads for this sort of mobilization.

Mobilizing Dreams

Shopping spaces have always been a strategic site for mobilizing dreams of
beauty.[9] Even at the dawn of industrial society, in the early 1800s, stores in

Figure 8.1. Civic and public culture in the Cleveland, Ohio, Arcade. Photograph by Dennis Adams, Federal Highway Administration.

the city center used the most advanced building methods and new construction materials like steel and glass to create awe-inspiring visions of luxury goods. Urban arcades were forerunners of today's shopping malls, from the light streaming through the glass dome of the atrium to the hermetic sense of being enclosed with the merchandise. Built in European and North American cities, from Paris, Milan, and Manchester to Cleveland, Ohio, throughout the nineteenth century, the arcade's concentration of small boutiques drew shoppers from the broad public streets into a narrow passage, or gallery, carved out of the middle of a city block. It was both an interior and an outdoor space, and it privatized the experience of walking and gazing while reducing the flow of pedestrians and compelling each passerby to become a speculator. I mean "speculator" in all senses, for strolling through the arcades and gazing into their shop windows involved shoppers in projecting an inner dream image of the self onto the products displayed, and imagining how these commodities might effect fantastic transformations of both body and spirit. Each walk through the arcades called for an investment of the self. But shopping for pleasure also implies a financial speculation. For the price, each purchase may return beauty, or social acceptance, or sensual pleasure to the investor. Not only through the circulation of goods, but also through the circulation of images, the arcades brought urban shoppers into the core of capital and money at the heart of the modern economy (Figure 8.1).[10]

I have felt a little of this, myself. The arcades that remain in Paris today are clustered around the Palais Royal, a park that was, in earlier times, a vibrant marketplace and staging ground for street artists, charlatans, and dandies.[11] Its gardens are now well planted and sedate. On a sunny summer day, solitary readers sit on benches in the shade, while children play on the gravel under their minders' eyes. To one side is the building that used to house the Bibliothèque Nationale, to another is the Ministry of Culture, and the stock market, or Bourse, is nearby. You stroll past the fancy toy store and jewelry shop at the northern entrance to the gardens and walk on through the park; crossing the street, you enter the Galerie Colbert, which, like some of the other arcades and older shopping streets in other cities, has been modernized and revitalized in recent years. Shops press close upon you on each side, their large plate-glass windows allowing you a full view of their wares, which spill from the small interiors into the narrow space in front of the store. The arcade retains the sense of the past and the exoticism that Walter Benjamin appreciated as both a historian and a connoisseur. You can't help browsing at an antiquarian bookstore with racks of books in front and the address of its Web site painted on the window; at the fine wine shop and chocolatier; in a few inexpensive dress shops, the good stationery store, the shoe stores, and even the fabric stores and sewing shops that evoke the city's history of "little" seamstresses and tailors. Maintaining the arcades' tradition of introducing new foreign goods, the Galerie Colbert today includes a bagel shop—the only one I have ever seen in Paris.

Just as in the past, the arcade still induces the pleasing vertigo of modern shopping. There is so much to see and often too many choices. But there are also implicit rules to obey and ambiguities to accept. Under the transparent glass roof, you are both inside and outside—protected from bad weather, cosseted with warmth, inhaling pleasant smells, and thinking you should just sit down and drink a cup of coffee (doesn't this remind you of today's gallerias and enclosed malls?), but you are wearing your coat, you haven't broken your stride, and you are able to walk away quickly from a salesperson's siren song: "Just looking." The privilege of the eye adapts to the impermeable transparency of the plate-glass window: look but don't touch. The procession of walking, stopping, gazing, evaluating, and moving on—

and endless repetitions of this sequence—recalls the bodily discipline of visiting a museum. This exercise in limited mobility suggests both the freedom of a *flâneur* or *flâneuse* to enjoy the city and the alienation of an individual who dreams alone.[12]

Department stores, which enjoyed a long century of retail dominance after the arcades declined, took the "dream world" of shopping to a higher level by building on a larger scale and framing consumer goods in designs for living. Twentieth-century materials replaced the iron and glass construction and gaslight of the arcades with more color, more extensive use of glass, and electric light. Borrowing techniques from theatrical décor, department stores created dramatic spaces like model rooms that enveloped shoppers, stimulated all their senses, and entertained them in new ways. It is astonishing even in today's consumer society to consider the array of goods, colors, and sensations that shoppers encountered in the great department stores a century ago. In 1915, when you entered the main floor of B. Altman & Co., a twelve-story department store on Fifth Avenue in New York (which several years ago was converted to classrooms and offices for the City University Graduate Center, where I teach), you would see "silks and velvets; laces, embroideries and trimmings; veilings; women's neckware; ribbons; gloves and hosiery; millinery; black, colored, and white fabrics for making dresses; linings and notions, also for sewing; umbrellas; handkerchiefs; jewelry and silverware; toilet articles; leather goods; stationery and engraving; cameras; men's clothing and underwear (the boys' department was on the second floor); men's hats, coats, and shoes." Aside from the presence of cameras and a few obsolete items, and the absence of cosmetics, this collection of commodities looks a lot like the main floor of department stores today. How compelling it must have been, then, especially for women who rarely worked outside the home, to browse among these goods—midway between the self-sufficiency of an old-fashioned household where women sewed all the clothes and the factory power of industrial mass production. How profitable it must have been for the merchant to arrange this scene, when today's department stores estimate that 40 percent of their profits derive from main floor sales.[13]

Department stores needed to move shoppers upward and deeper into their dream world. They installed elevators and, better still, escalators to bring them face to face with an enormous variety of products imported from all parts of the globe, highlighted in stylish displays, and abundantly piled on counters and in drawers. B. Altman brought solidly middle-class women shoppers up to the second floor for underwear, both "French and American-made," children's clothing, and "maids' dresses." On the next floor, shoppers could search privately for mourning clothes in a special department or look next door for elaborate gowns. Luxurious furs shared a department with smaller fur pieces for "women of moderate resources," and shoppers on both income levels were courted by the annual fur sale, which was said to attract "eager purchasers from nearly every State in the Union."

The department store was an enticing bureaucracy. Like its less seductive but equally functional contemporaries, the professional military and modern state, it treated everyone alike while selectively promoting some recruits upward through a hierarchy of specialized rituals and experiences. Gowns were separated from readymade dresses and servants' clothes; the bargain basement (although not found at better stores like B. Altman!) occupied a different, and certainly lower, realm from the heavenly precinct of luxury furs. Less affluent shoppers were welcome to ride the elevators and escalators to the upper floors. But when they went upstairs, they also rose several degrees on the social ladder. Passing through the more expensive departments, they could glimpse the high-price items they could not afford to buy. Like the big plate-glass windows on the street, and somewhat like the social geography of today's multilevel malls, the escalators made luxury visible. The dream world of the department store "democratized desire" while separating the public by income and price.[14]

In contrast to the military and state where men ruled, the department store moved women through an organizational grid of desire. It offered pleasure and safety—not just on the shopping floors, but also in the restrooms and tearooms where women could socialize without fear of harassment. In return, women made a loyal public: loyal to specific stores and to the act of shopping itself.

But the ease of using a department store hid cause for embarrassment. The stores offered easy access to credit for middle- and upper-class shoppers, and, as a result, many of them overbought. This was especially painful for women who legally depended on their nearest male relatives—fathers or husbands—to pay the bills. Yet department stores encouraged shoppers to spend. Seasonal sales created a special calendar for repeated spending, and any sale, especially in the bargain basement, brought an exhilaration that shoppers could get "something for nothing" by spending more.

A tsunami wave of corporate mergers and acquisitions during the 1980s shut venerable department stores like Hudson's in Detroit, drove Bloomingdale's and Macy's close to bankruptcy and then into common corporate ownership, and shifted the discourse of commercial civility promoted by many local department stores toward a frenzy of cutthroat, brand-name competition. But the golden age of the department store had already ended. As early as the 1920s, the downtowns of many U.S. cities where department stores were located began to lose their appeal when middle-class shoppers bought cars, moved to the suburbs, and demanded parking lots instead of crowded streets. Central business districts that had looked modern in 1900 needed renovation. The building of wider highways and larger shopping malls after World War II made it easy for families to escape the downtown— and separate themselves from the city's increasingly poor, ethnically diverse population.[15]

Faced with the loss of more prosperous shoppers, department stores branched out into the suburbs. They starved their mother stores of investment capital for modernization and retrenched their downtown work force, especially if it was unionized. Within a few years, the department store chains were crushed between the low prices of discount stores like Wal-Mart and the specialized styles of new boutiques.

Obituaries for department stores that closed during the 1980s voiced regret for a dream world that was really lost during the 1960s. Women and men alike mourned the loss of spectacles that the department stores had mounted, including the organ recitals that were held in John Wanamaker's central court in Philadelphia from the early 1900s and the fashion shows that were first developed by Neiman Marcus in Dallas in the 1920s. Despite shopping malls' efforts to program special events, they could not meet the expectations of shoppers who had grown up with the department store's creation of spectacle. The physical isolation of a suburban mall and the smaller scale of stores there did not prevent consumers from accumulating goods, but the less formal, more amorphous space of a mall did not inspire monumental dreams.[16]

The dreaming that people do in stores has a rational economic function. Daydreaming, or fantasizing about self-improvement, stimulates the desire for new products that maintains consumer demand.[17] Whether we call this daydreaming fantasy, hedonism, or the fetishization of commodities, it arguably sparks much of the innovation in technology and organization that, through the mass production and consumption of commodities, keeps capitalism afloat. And storeowners know it. Though the local stores where we make our daily or weekly rounds cannot afford to cater to illusions, the spectacular, capital-intensive places where we also shop provide a setting for our dreams. Because they try to appeal to all of us—to some of us more than to others, of course—they speak to the archetypal dreams of our public culture. Low prices represent social equality. Brand names represent our search for a better life. And designer boutiques represent the dream of an ever-improving self.

Archetype 1: Low Prices as Social Equality

Although almost everyone today would name Wal-Mart as the temple of low-price shopping, the archetypal social space of bargain culture was Woolworth's Five and Ten Cent Store. Founded in the 1870s, in the small cities of Utica, New York, and Lancaster, Pennsylvania, the five-and-dime brought the novelty and abundance of mass production to consumers who weren't rich and didn't live in metropolitan commercial centers. Like Sam Walton, the founder of Wal-Mart, F. W. Woolworth believed that these consumers would most appreciate the variety of goods that he brought into their lives at affordable prices. Woolworth cannily set the prices for all goods at just a nickel—and the store only raised this price, during the Great Depression of the 1930s, to a dime. Because prices were fixed, there was no opportunity for shoppers to haggle over a bargain; yet shoppers believed they were getting one. From a business owner's point of view, the five-and-dime store was good because it did away with the need for periodic sales of unsold inventory, or markdowns: prices were always low. From the shopper's point of view, the availability and variety of factory-made tools, paper goods, cooking pots, thimbles, and decorative objects for the home was irresistible. The low prices invited everyone, regardless of social class, to enter public culture by shopping.

Unlike the hierarchically arranged department stores, the five-and-dime made all its merchandise visible on a single floor. Shoppers could touch the many items that were arrayed on counters, or they could ask the salesclerks, mainly young women, to show them items that were shelved behind. After 1909, shoppers could handle the merchandise themselves because Woolworth's moved all the items to countertops—anticipating, by a few years, the wave of self-service that would roll through the larger grocery stores. Self-service lowered labor costs for business owners, who passed these savings on to customers in the form of bargain prices. This arrangement brought shoppers of all social classes into the store on an equal basis: all the goods were equally visible and equally cheap. In this space, Americans began to have a new understanding of social equality—not as workers, but as consumers.

By welcoming everyone, stores like Woolworth's moderated shoppers' perception of differences based on social class. In the liberal view of the historian Daniel Boorstin, which recalls Tocqueville's much earlier observations,

Americans' "consumption communities" contrasted with the class cultures and divisive politics of Europe. These consumption communities were as "quick" to change as consumers' tastes: "they were nonideological; they were democratic; they were public, and vague, and rapidly shifting."[18] I would not say that mass consumption overcame the reality of social inequality, but the specific spatial arrangement of many stores built for mass consumption—like the five-and-dime—embodied the sense that all consumers are equal because they can all find something that they can afford.

This social equality did not extend to the workforce. Woolworth's was a traditionally hierarchical business organization, with the entirely male corps of store managers supervising a workforce of low-paid female clerks. Managers, moreover, received incentives in the form of stock in the company, an early form of profit sharing. During the Depression, before the federal government raised the minimum wage, the salesclerks worked between forty-eight and fifty-six hours a week, for an average salary of $11 ($13–14 in cities). On these wages, the mainly young, unmarried clerks had to buy lunch and pay for transportation, as well as purchase the smocks they wore in the store; they also contributed to household expenses. When business was slow, managers sent them home or reduced their salaries. Needless to say, Woolworth's stridently opposed labor unions.[19]

The organizational grid of social life set by Woolworth's bears a striking resemblance to what we see in Wal-Mart today. The slogan "Low Prices—Always" could have been the mantra of the five-and-dime, and the corporate emphasis on customer service without individual attention repeats Woolworth's practice. Wal-Mart also pays low wages, insists on limiting many employees to part-time jobs, and relies on managerial authority to keep workers in line. Expanding F. W. Woolworth's paternalistic model, Sam Walton introduced profit sharing in the form of stock ownership for all workers to persuade them not to join labor unions. Also like Woolworth's in its time, Wal-Mart scours the globe for low-price merchandise. A major difference between the stores is that Woolworth lured richer customers with small novelties like glass reindeer and tiny tubes of toothpaste; Wal-Mart, since the 1980s, has lured them with brand-name jeans, toys, and DVDs. Though Wal-Mart deliberately keeps prices low to appeal to middle-income shoppers, the store attracts more affluent men and women who pride themselves on being smart shoppers or just can't resist a bargain.[20]

Despite the windowless architecture of the big box store, Wal-Mart maintains the transparency of the earlier five-and-dime. Transparency is even helped by the change in building materials from wooden to vinyl floors, which offer a shiny, almost reflective surface, the extensive use of air-conditioning, and bright, fluorescent light. Like a supermarket, Wal-Mart openly displays a range of competing products at different "price points." Prices are prominently marked, with signs urging shoppers to save money by spending more. Wal-Mart submerges income differences in the presumption that everyone is happy to capture bargains. A working-class shopper gets up at dawn on the day after Thanksgiving to capture a DVD player for twenty-nine dollars, while a more affluent shopper buys one for each bedroom. But the incredibly low price speaks to the dream Wal-Mart urges them to share: pay less, buy more. The social space of Wal-Mart—so democratic and so rational—establishes bargain shopping as a universal norm for rich and poor alike.

Brand names play an important role at Wal-Mart and in the entire public culture of shopping. Until the 1980s, although brand name products were widely available in the United States, they were not universally affordable. Marketers applied the term "aspirational" to branded shopping precisely because, as commonplace as Tide laundry detergent or GE refrigerators might appear to be, they represented higher levels of disposable income and thus higher consumer status. Both manufacturers and stores charged premium prices for brand names because consumers believed these products were better than generic products—better made, more durable, or visibly more distinctive. Partly this premium reflected the selective promotions of manufacturers and stores, especially expensive national advertising on radio and TV, but it also reflected antitrust laws, which required stores to sell more expensive, branded products along with cheaper generic and house brands, and "fair trade" laws, which prevented stores from charging less than manufacturers' list prices. Fair trade laws gradually fell out of use during the 1950s, a decade before Wal-Mart and its sister discount chains, Target and Kmart, began. But it wasn't until the 1980s that Wal-Mart, competing with Kmart for second position among discount chains, devised the strategy of selling nationally advertised brands at discount prices. By doing so, Wal-Mart made aspirational shopping a reality for everyone who walked into the store. This confirmed the perception of Wal-Mart as a space of social equality while increasing the pressure on everyone to buy. It also brought brand names into the lingua franca of public culture.

Archetype 2: Brand Names and the Search for a Better Life

The ability of brand names to represent distinctive social traits was sharpened by manufacturers' efforts to capitalize on the "creative revolution" that spread through advertising in the 1960s and on the identity politics that followed in its wake.[21] Each social group, beginning with teens and youth, was encouraged to express its own needs and tastes by shopping for different products—in different stores. Social movements of hippies, feminists, Black Power advocates, and gay rights activists gave rise to entrepreneurs who provided commodities like clothing and music that served as identity markers. Their stores became social spaces for men and women who identified both actively and passively with these groups. In these spaces they could be together with others who appeared like-minded, without taking the risk of being arrested as at a political protest or ostracized by their families. These social spaces had no political platform or common ideology, but they enabled shoppers to experience both individuality and collective identity, to proclaim solidarity without taking risks. And yet, they were only retail stores.

The evolution of the Gap from a specialized clothing store for hippie youth to a worldwide sportswear chain offers a nice illustration of how stores capitalized on their new social role. Founded in the 1960s, the Gap gradually opened branches from the San Francisco area to the East Coast, selling cheap jeans and T-shirts under a variety of manufacturers' labels. Their popularity lasted about fifteen years and then, by the 1980s, sales fell. Gap stores were still decorated in a post-hippie aesthetic and lacked what marketers would call a clear image or personality. But after the Gap's founder hired a new CEO who had begun his career at Bloomingdale's and then revived the women's clothing chain Ann Taylor, the store developed a distinctive social space that was modeled on the special cachet of designer boutiques. Emphasizing the strategic importance of visual display, the Gap painted all its stores bright white and piled merchandise on counters, in neat stacks, by color. The logo was changed to echo the sleek lines of the clothes and the clean look of the stores. It figured prominently throughout the store, adorned all sizes of shopping bags, and, most important, became the only name on the label of all the clothing the Gap sold. This was the essence of branding. The strategy required all company personnel to wear Gap clothes, which reinforced the store's image. Through these methods of display, as well as catalogs and advertisements, the Gap transformed itself from a store that sold casual, cheap apparel into a space where people shopped because it was cool. That aura, in large part visual but also highly interactive, became a model of branding strategy—recently duplicated by the iPod.

Just as buying brand-name products represented upward social mobility for generations of consumers, so shopping at branded stores now suggests membership in status groups with higher degrees, and different kinds of cultural capital. Less crude than price, and less cruel than social class distinctions, branding allows everyone to have a "lifestyle." If we shop at a cool store, we are cool; if we shop at a preppy store, we are preppy; and if we shop at a number of stores, we can express different aspects of our personalities. Social class and income have nothing to do with lifestyle differences; they reflect, it is said, individual choices. Although lifestyle shopping does nothing to eliminate the social inequality of higher and lower standards of living, it does reorganize differences in a nonconflictual way. The idea of lifestyle is not only a marketers' but also a social panacea because it displaces upward social mobility from the measurable differences of incomes and wealth to the social space of the store. Consumers remain working class while progressing from Kmart generics to the Martha Stewart brand and from traditional Kmart to middle-class "contemporary" at Pottery Barn. All branded stores are equally branded, but some are more equal than others.[22]

Archetype 3: Designer Boutiques and the Perfection of Self

The great achievement of designer boutiques is that they control the social space of the store as their own private universe of identity and desire. By shopping in a designer boutique, a shopper—historically, women, but increasingly men, too—agrees to assume a role the designer wants her to play. This role varies from season to season, as the "look" of the collection changes. But the shopper always subordinates her self to the image of perfection created by the designer. Though a designer's artistic, as well as commercial, success depends on intuiting the consumers' momentary mood, both products and store ultimately tell a story of beauty and triumph. Whoever the designer is, the vision is simply Perfection. Who can reject this appeal? Buying into it instills self-confidence in the dating market or on the labor market. The authority of the designer's name makes the strategy, so popular in the 1980s, of "dressing for success" redundant, for anyone who shops in a designer boutique is bound to feel successful.

When the high fashion houses of Paris opened boutiques for ready-to-wear clothes in the 1960s, they did so to stave off bankruptcy. With too few clients for their extravagantly designed apparel, members of the haute couture decided to make products accessible at lower prices to a wider public without diluting their cultural authority. Licensing perfume, sunglasses, and eventually lingerie and jeans was one strategy of increasing sales without diluting the brand of the designer name. But another reason for introducing ready-to-wear was for the established designers to develop popular styles for the young, affluent shoppers whom they had lost to younger, newer, and edgier design-ers, many of them in London and New York as well as in Paris. In the United States, by contrast, most fashion designers worked for manufacturers instead of heading independent houses. Under these conditions, the idea of designer boutiques originated with department stores. Competing with small bou-tiques that offered the newest styles by unknown designers, department stores took the risk of luring shoppers by nurturing their own designers, and selling their fashions within the big store, but under the designers' names, in separate small departments, or boutiques. From the store's point of view, the risk of backing a new designer was minimized by the small size of the boutique's in-ventory. This is why Bloomingdale's subsidized the career of Ralph Lauren forty years ago, while Bonwit Teller helped Calvin Klein.[23]

Although these designers still sell the major portion of their collections in department stores, they have long since outgrown their early patrons. They have become the iconic heads of their own companies, celebrities in their own right, symbols of perfection. Yet we can enter their universe of meaning in many ways. We can buy expensive "Ralph Lauren" clothes in one of the freestanding Ralph Lauren stores. Or we can descend several price points and buy "Ralph" in a designer boutique at Macy's and "Lauren" in a designer boutique at Bloomingdale's. Regardless of which form we choose, we join our destiny, and relinquish our judgment, to Ralph's. If his taste is perfect, then so is ours. And if we just buy a piece of Ralph Lauren, by choos-ing Ralph Lauren perfume at the Sephora cosmetics chain or Ralph Lauren house paint at Home Depot, we still symbolically enter a social space under his control. The company's "real estate"—a shelf or a separate boutique—in a larger store is just a gateway to our dream of perfection.

Cautions and Contestations

Mass consumption plays an indisputably important role in public culture. But how can we grasp exactly what this role is—and through which institu-tions it affects our lives? We know that stores are cauldrons of globalization, that brand names exert a spellbinding power over many young lives, and that buying consumer goods makes Americans spend too much and save too lit-tle. We read polemics that criticize our tendency to shop for status items, to covet our neighbors' houses and cars, and to spend money that we don't really have. But we have paid less critical attention to the social space of shop-ping, ignoring how the organization of stores shapes us, as a society.

The social space of stores embodies both the most alienating features of modern life and the most closely held ideals of modern culture. Despite variations between types of stores, and differences between the immediacy of physical stores and the mediation of Internet shopping, a few general patterns hold true. Shopping has become less local and more abstract. It is more highly mediated by agents, brokers, and technology, yet more hermetically focused on products. Shopping adopts the liberation ideology of consumer choice yet reinforces the collective power of a small number of brands and companies.

Certainly, the archetypes of social space that I have discussed—low prices, brand names, and designer boutiques—are ideal types. Not all shoppers are motivated to buy by visual displays and promises of perfection. The more we know about corporate business strategies, and the more informed we are by product reviews and consumer guides, the more critical about shopping we learn to be. Most important, when we are awakened by the terribly disadvantaged situations of low-wage clerks and immigrant janitors at Wal-Mart, or by striking supermarket workers in California who are asked for givebacks on their health benefits because their employers anticipate a price-cutting bloodbath of competition with the discount chain, we begin to make connections between the family that shops for jeans at Wal-Mart in Antelope Valley and the men and women who make them in sweatshops half a planet away. The public culture of shopping is able to change.[24]

When employers resort to providing self-service with a small workforce of low-wage cashiers and salesclerks, outsourcing janitorial work to undocumented immigrants, and opening supercenters that drive smaller stores out of business while persuading us to buy more imports, we confront the concentrated power of a new institutional network that works against our national interest. Unlike in earlier times, when consumers strengthened the power of young industries, shoppers now undercut the basis of the national economy. This forces shopping to become less of a civic activity.

It is also, in many ways, a less social activity. Since the mid-twentieth century, the scale of stores has got larger while the density of stores in residential neighborhoods has decreased.[25] We drive longer to get to stores and, because we have large closets and refrigerators in our homes, we make less frequent shopping trips. Because "blue laws" that prohibited stores from opening on Sundays and other limits on working hours have disappeared, we are able to go shopping any day of the week—and, through Internet shopping, at any hour of the day, in our home or place of work. But many shoppers still feel that shopping is burdensome, especially since most shoppers spend a longer time in stores or on the Internet, and often report they cannot find what they truly need. Whom does this benefit? Storeowners, mall developers, and Web site designers all know the bitter truth: the more time we spend shopping, the more we buy. Just as the maze of supermarket aisles conditions us to proceed through a set sequence of grocery buying activities, so the arrangement of products in both stores and malls, and on retail Web sites, keeps our attention and prods us to stay longer. New combinations of bread and circuses—like "entertainment retail," "temporary" stores, and the "experience economy"—try to keep us involved. This is not a healthy public culture.

The Internet poses a special problem for it presents electronic shopping as a means of liberation—saving us time or money—while luring us to shop more.[26] The ease of setting up a Web site promises to democratize shopping choices—like information sources—by broadening the public sphere. Theoretically, the competition between many different sellers' Web sites "lets a hundred flowers bloom." But, despite this competition, shoppers tend to concentrate their purchases on a relatively small number of sites, leading to the emergence of a few brand names like Amazon and eBay. Paradoxically, the apparently democratic features of many retail sites—starting with consumers' ability to post reviews of products and sellers—reinforce their power. In contrast, moreover, to its ethos as a democratic consumption community, eBay has intensified the commodification of public culture. The opportunity to raise money by selling things in online auctions encourages people to offer things that would not have been put on sale before: a telephone number, the Division I swim team of Dartmouth College; the town of Bridgeville, California; the right to name a new Benedictine monastery in Philadelphia.[27] Because eBay has transformed shopping from just buying things to use them, to buying things in order to sell them—it reduces consciousness to mercantile calculations and economizes humans' social nature. EBay is a Web site for "economic man."

Yet as labor movements and electoral politics suggest, even Wal-Mart has become a contested space of public culture. The anti-sweatshop and antiglobalization movements, as well as studies by anthropologists and geographers, teach us to think about the connections between production at one end of the commodity chain and consumption at the other. Low prices, many Americans now see, are connected to low wages—both in this country and overseas. Consumers have always been skeptical of advertisements. Adbusters and culture jammers play a crucial role in forcing us to pay attention to the ways in which ads manipulate our minds. A very few companies and celebrities are willing to support products that speak to usefulness rather than social status—Stephon Marbury's new fifteen-dollar sneakers instead of Michael Jordan's two-hundred-dollar Nikes. These are still small efforts to reform a huge global system of mass production and consumption, but they are important steps nonetheless.[28]

Since the Diggers' "free stores" in the 1960s, alternative means of consumption have offered opportunities to opt out of this system. These days, many shoppers go to vintage stores or flea markets as an alternative to dominant institutions like Wal-Mart, Ralph Lauren, and Gap. While some of them are just disenchanted with the standardized offerings of mainstream stores, others are seriously rebelling against the whole institutional system. This point has been made explicit by the social movement for simpler, and less, consumption: buying only what you need instead of buying for conspicuous consumption, eating "slow food" instead of the fast food of agro-industry and McDonald's, "downshifting" from McMansions and SUVs to a less expensive, less environmentally explosive standard of living. There are also other collective strategies to make shopping a part of a more social, more democratic public sphere.

Buying local and shopping at small stores is important. This supports local farmers and manufacturers as well as local merchants—saving land from suburban sprawl as well as saving jobs.[29] Shoppers are not the only ones who should change their priorities. Property owners should also limit their rentals to chain stores and antilocal or antisocial uses—even if they have to forgo higher rents. Developers should build smaller stores closer together. Despite their problems and large scale, some new stores have been created that deliberately challenge the hegemony of branded and discount stores. The American Apparel stores, which sell sportswear made in U.S. factories that are said not to be sweatshops, establish a social space where shopping is explicitly an ethical choice and a political act. Costco, a discount chain, pays its employees better than Wal-Mart. My favorite form of store—the enormously popular urban farmers' markets—offers an alternative of locally produced foods to the supermarkets' chemically enhanced, plastic-wrapped imports, and also makes shopping a matter of politics and ethics. In farmers' markets, shoppers can often speak with the direct producers of their food, an encounter that encourages exchanges of opinions—even with other shoppers—about social issues like public health, environmental risks, and even war and peace. Farmers' markets create a public space for political as well as economic exchanges.

Shopping should be not only about buying things; ideally, it should be an opportunity for a conversation. Instead of surrounding us with endless choices of things to buy, the social space of stores should provide a place for practical yet intimate encounters. Small in scale, local in clientele, open to the street: this is the kind of shopping space I grew up with and the kind of shopping I still prefer. Ironically, to create such a store today requires government action. Local zoning laws against superstores have to be upheld by planning commissions and town councils. Commercial rent subsidies—which are unacceptable to most property owners—have to subsidize small stores. More than anything, however, shoppers have to rediscover their roots in the shopping spaces of the distant, pre-megamall and pre-Wal-Mart past. Only in local spaces like those can shopping be a less abstract and more social process. Only in those small spaces can the conversations of a public culture be heard.

Chapter 9
Gates, Barriers, and the Rise of Affinity: Parsing Public-Private Space in Postindustrial America

Hal Rothman

I pulled my car in front of the building, where a large sign welcomed me to "Home Courts," a combination gym and recreational center that sponsored youth and adult basketball and volleyball leagues and instruction. The sign advertised courts for rent, leagues for kids and adults, and space for parties of all sorts. A schedule offered a weekend volleyball tournament, advertising club teams from around the region.

As we entered, the sound of squeaking tennis shoes, dribbling basketballs, and excited young voices was music to my ears. It brought back memories of my own youth, of the endless games that dominated my afternoons and summers. The gym we entered was large and wonderful, with sixteen courts of various kinds. Three games were going on and what looked like volleyball practice for some kind of Amateur Athletic Union (AAU) team. My nine-year-old beamed, kicked off his flip-flops, laced up his game shoes, and ran to join his new team. I stood by the side, awestruck. Wow! What a great place for a kid to play some ball and make some friends.

Then it struck me: this was pay space, not play space; private, not public. There was nothing public about it; you had to belong to get in and for good reason. The investment in the operation had to be enormous, in the millions; they had a marketing department that encouraged and even urged parents to sign their kids up for leagues, and there were no scholarships for needy kids advertised. This was a business, where someone stood to make a significant profit off the decline in the concept of community and public space that has overtaken America.

As much as I liked it, I was also repelled. Home Courts was a far cry from my youth, when we went to the schoolyard and played against all comers, the winners keeping the court sometimes from early in the morning until it was too dark to see. In those days, there were no adults around, no bathrooms except the bushes, no parents wearing jerseys emblazoned with their kids' names, no electronic scoreboard, no coaching or skill work, no sense of hierarchy except that among the kids, and no one to solve the inevitable problems that occurred except the kids who wanted to knock off the nonsense and keep the game going.

This phenomenon is everywhere, where private space masquerades as public or at least community space. The motto over the waiting area at my daughter's dance studio reads: "this isn't a lobby, it's a neighborhood," but it is really a neighborhood from an earlier exclusionary America, not from the post-1960s world. Again, the only people there have paid; the only reason to be there is because your child is enrolled in a dance or gymnastics class. So admittance to the neighborhood costs and is driven by a new kind of relationship, based on affinity, not the proximity of old.

The world today is different: for the most part, my kids do the same things I did, play the same games during the same seasons—we have yet to succumb to the disease of specialization that runs rampant in youth sports today—and in the same ways. The difference is they do it in private space for which we pay; I played in public spaces that everyone shared and nobody had to shell out a few bucks to get in. Here is a metaphor for what has happened to the United States. What we once did in public we now do in private space; what was once free now has an admission charge.

Since 1980, the United States has undergone a transformation as great and dislocating as the Industrial Revolution itself, the shift from industrial society and economy to its postindustrial successor. The catalyst of this transformation came from a minuscule piece of silicon called the microchip. This little chunk of information-storing material caused the radical, inexorable, fundamental, and overnight transformation of the basis of the world economy; it created a divide across which people peered with great trepidation. The Microchip Revolution changed life as we knew it. Microchips created the Information Age, in which knowledge and the ability to manipulate it genuinely became power, and it dramatically increased the range and significance of the service economy.

In the end, this revolution changed life in the United States. Cyber transactions now move capital around the globe, creating what the noted thinker and cultural critic Christopher Lasch recognized as a transnational class of monied individuals who are essentially stateless, without an evident sense of national obligation. This boundary-free wealth has few obligations to people and places and its incredible mobility can be a threat to the stability of national economies. We don't work as we did even twenty years ago; personal computers, the Internet, cell phones, and wi-fi created easy access and information transfer that seemed to someone from the 1970s to be science fiction. I listen to the music of the 1960s through my computer and can take it with me on my iPod. Nor do we rely on the sources of capital that once drove the American economy. The junk bonds of the 1970s became the derivatives, a computer-generated sort of splitting and matching, of the 1990s. We don't do the same tasks in the same ways, and we barely experience the constraints that once placed limits on the way business was done.

The transformation has been powerful and comprehensive. It has diminished not only the market value of American resources but a significant piece of the national mythology as well. The United States was built on two premises: cheap labor, often provided by immigrants, their children, and other family members, and cheap natural resources. Labor hasn't been cheap in the United States since before World War II and the formerly cheap natural resources are both more expensive and less necessary in a global economy. The ways in which resources are organized, used, and the purposes to which they are put have dramatically changed—especially in the first world.

These changes, loosely defined as a shift from extraction and production to service and leisure, have fomented a progressively denser urbanism, often where urbanity barely before existed. Suburbs have become exurbs, which turned into "Edge Cities," which became posturban pods. San Jose, California, epitomizes this pattern. The megalopolis of San Francisco and the Bay Area has swallowed the once parochial town. The patterns of life, the ways of making a living have been overcome by space-based commuter culture, dependent on the proportionately outrageous number of telephone and fiber-optic lines and the cellular phones of the region.

The changes in economic basis have resulted in a redefinition of the space that was once American downtowns. Throughout the nation, downtowns have attempted to redo themselves to attract not new industry, but visitors. Throughout the country, distraught communities invested in downtown spaces, only to replicate one another. The pathetic efforts of Flint, Michigan, chronicled in Michael Moore's 1989 *Roger and Me*, served only as a bottom line. From the Farmers' Market and nightclub district of Wichita, Kansas to the renovated mills of Lowell, Massachusetts, an attempt to create public spaces with public dollars took shape. My own favorite is the fictitious Museum of Science and Trucking in HBO's *The Sopranos'* waterfront Newark, New Jersey, redevelopment.

In postindustrial America, the goods that we consume have ceased to be good enough. When anyone could get anything he or she wanted in virtual time and space, a new premium was added to real experience. In an age when anyone could wear a Rolex or lease a BMW, when you could ski the Alps from your home computer, actual experience, the commodity that differentiated travel and tourism from other activities, gained significance. The result was new importance for recreation and leisure and a new premium on the spaces used for that purpose. This further blurred already indistinct lines between public and private.

The battles over private and public space in American society have become the terrain on which the national definition of freedom is worked and reworked. In theory, "public" meant open to all, places where the state-sanctioned power embodied in the First Amendment held sway and where all people, regardless of economic status, caste, race, or any other marker, were welcome. Until the rights revolution of the 1960s, this openness was a fiction, an ideal that served as a code as much as did the word "freedom." "Private" evoked something different, the right to exclude based on the prerogative of ownership, derived from a long tradition in English common law. This exclusionary propriety protected a more personal interpretation of the meaning of American law, of rights as individual rather than communitarian in nature. The two visions, what the historian Robert Morse Crunden called a struggle between "self" and "society," collided with increasing frequency as the nation shifted to a postindustrial footing.

Americans have always contested the meaning of freedom, but in postmodern America, where the ideals, desires, and limitations of the baby boomers have come to dominate the horizons, the contestation is more fierce, more selfish, and more representative of the distance between liberal consumerism and neoliberalism. The 1960s gave Americans a new ideal of freedom as the right to do, in postmodern America, whatever we want, wherever we want, however we want, whenever we want, and with whomever we want. Paul Revere would have seen freedom as the right to do as you pleased within the boundaries established by the community, but the emphasis on the self would have been foreign to the man who was "ready to ride and spread the alarm; through every Middlesex village and farm."

This "freedom to" greatly contributed to the cultural revolution that has remade the nation as the epitome of individualism, an increasingly self-indulgent and even selfish place where the individual *über alles* seems to be the only value of any consequence. The ethos of the Three Musketeers, all for one and one for all, is as foreign to postmodern Americans as the sermons of eighteenth-century fire and brimstone preacher Jonathan Edwards. The collectivist visions of the student movement of the 1960s have morphed into fundamental individualism. In this latest America, people vote against libraries for their grandchildren, against public schools because they pay for private education, and against anything that smacks of all of us being in it together. We've become a nation of CAVEs—citizens against virtually everything.

There are advantages to this change. People now serve as their own moral compass. They've thrown out the old mores, the ones that collapsed under the weight of their own inconsistencies as upper-middle-class students of the 1960s tried to transform the largesse of their world into their stunningly skewed concept of justice. Now they, not their pastors or the PTA, establish their cues for what's good and bad. They choose among a broad but strangely narrow range of sources for their information, for even the vaunted Internet offers only a limited sweep of the possibilities. In the process they contributed to the liberation of the self and the rise of a new, seemingly value-free America. When what had once been a vice became a choice, the overarching pressure of generations of neo-Victorian morality lifted their weight from even the middle and upper-middle classes. In the process, they redefined the boundaries of freedom.

As a city built on this very personal prerogative, Las Vegas is a funny place to discover the next stage of this revolution: the transformation of the idea of "freedom to" into "freedom from," the ability to use the idea of individual freedom to regulate and otherwise limit the prerogatives of others when they are offensive or threatening. In this sense, "freedom from" is not freedom in the conventional American sense. It is its fearful descendant, when freedom means the right to have the world the way you want and everyone else's choices be damned. "Freedom to" bred "freedom from." One could only lead to the other as individual rights superseded community sanction and personal obligation. When anyone could see anything as a right, there had to be some way to exclude, even control. In a confessional culture, where readmittance to what passes for polite society hinges on the approval of a talk show audience after the transgressor confesses on air, the only way was to change the definition of space. After the end of legal segregation, the law no longer functioned as a tool to exclude. Only commerce and the American obsession with private property could draw such exclusive distinctions.

This construction, "freedom from," the right to be free of noxious and offensive behaviors, is not guaranteed in the U.S. Constitution, but it is a clear focus of social custom. As a solution to the woes of a society that demands experience and encourages personal expression, this idea crystallized in the new Las Vegas, the place where instinct replaced restraint as Wall Street threw billions of dollars into the development of the first wonder of the postmodern world. In the new Las Vegas, where the Strip itself has become the greatest investment of private money in public art anywhere on the planet, the codes of the future are already in play. In the process, it has become the harbinger of the future, for better and worse, in all kinds of ways.

As the nation's closest thing to a libertarian state, Nevada is a peculiar place to see the consequences of this change. In Nevada, your property is your property more than anywhere else in the nation; the old outcast among American states still clings to its historic condition. At the same time, Nevada's libertarianism is really freedom for business ahead of individuals, an unusual code for protecting commercial interests at the expense of the public. As a result, an ongoing battle about public space and the First Amendment has become a hallmark of Las Vegas. In a town where there is little public space for meetings or play, where government is weak on its best days, private entities fill the gaps left by authority to serve a useful function while appearing to have long-standing commitment to community. In Las Vegas more than anywhere else in the United States, the line between public and private space blurs and the boundaries become indistinct. You can stumble across them with the best of intentions. The accidents that follow provide a lesson in the future of democracy.

Well before the 1990s, downtown Las Vegas had a serious problem. The old Glitter Gulch, the place where people spilled from the train depot into the streets of Mammon under the waving hand of Vegas Vic, the neon cowboy in the sky, had been overshadowed by the Strip for nearly one-half century. After the construction of Caesars, the Aladdin, and Circus Circus in the mid-1960s, visitation tipped toward the Strip. By the 1980s, corporate money dominated the Strip, and local money, much less of it, resided downtown. The Mirage phase, the stunning eleven-year building spree that added 60,000 hotel rooms and took Las Vegas from gambling to gaming to tourism to entertainment, made the differences even more stark. Downtown couldn't compete. By 1990, downtown served a niche market of one kind or another. While the Strip built theme parks and attracted families, serious low-dollar gamblers, locals, and people who liked the old days, the looser slots, and the cheaper buffets and meals, came downtown.

Fremont Street, the heart of Glitter Gulch, was funky. It felt like a real city instead of a movie set, a relic of the past, with casinos that opened into the street. The million-dollar horseshoe in the entry to Binion's Horseshoe and the ever present ninety-nine-cent shrimp cocktail at the Golden Gate were its trademarks. Street people hung out, panhandlers sat with palms up, and streetwalkers in high boots and ridiculous get-ups paraded up and down. Fremont Street felt like a carnival, a boardwalk, a place of nighttime recreation in the American memory, except with slot machines and a little more sleaze than you'd want your kids to see.

As the city spread out, the area around Fremont Street deteriorated, and by the 1990s downtown certainly wasn't where locals went to take care of their daily business. Fremont Street catered almost exclusively to tourists. Gift shops and convenience stores dominated the space casinos and hotels didn't fill. Government was the only other industry downtown. Bail bond offices were close at hand. The housing that surrounded the area was mostly lower income. It wasn't quite the problem of most American downtowns, that you could fire a cannon after five o'clock and never hit a soul, but most people in downtown Las Vegas in the evening, excepting hookers and the homeless, weren't locals. Downtown was populated by tourists and by the people who preyed on them, not the image 1990s Las Vegas wanted to project.

Downtown suffered from the problems of similar public space around the country. As greater Las Vegas upscaled throughout the 1990s, the seediness of Fremont Street lost its appeal to the new constituency. The grittiness of the area intrigued some, but it was also threatening, hard to sell in a town that had been promising better than real for three decades. Panhandlers and streetwalkers increased, and downtown didn't seem like the new Las Vegas, sanitized to keep your fears away while encouraging your desires. Even the downtown restaurants, once among the most renowned in the city, were overshadowed by the nationally known chefs on the Strip. Hugo's in a cellar of the Four Queens, once the city's premier gourmet dining experience, could not compete with Aureole at Mandalay Bay or Picasso at the Bellagio. Only the Golden Nugget, the initial property in Steve Wynn's empire, could match the Strip for elegance, but it seemed out of a Graham Greene novel, a declining Saigon, a stultified Caribbean or perhaps from a V. S. Naipul novel about the detritus of colonialism somewhere in the third world.

Redevelopment of Las Vegas's core had been an ongoing theme since the 1960s. In the 1960s, downtown Las Vegas did not face urban renewal, but it was already in transition. After the opening of the Boulevard Mall in 1967, locals drifted away and did their business elsewhere. The parallel migration to new homes west of the interstate and behind the mall in the early 1970s accelerated the trend. Downtown became a place for visitors, and stores that stocked souvenirs and kitsch did better than those that sold groceries and sundries. The solution proposed was a typical 1960s response, a mall, in this case one block in length that permitted north-south traffic flow. Little happened. The idea of the mall didn't go away, resuscitated in 1975 and again in 1986. If either had been implemented, downtown would have been different. Without any action, by 1990, downtown's fall was obvious to anyone who looked.

After Benny Binion's death in 1989, most downtown properties had shifted from their founders, men like Binion and Sam Boyd, to the next generation. The younger men had been raised to be local aristocracy, privileged since early in life and accustomed to accommodation by government, the law, and even people on the street. They took their crowns with zest, only to find new kings just up the road, building enormous palaces that, from the point of view of the old-timers, blurred the town's vision of their own importance.

The downtown hotel owners had one entity that they could count on, the City of Las Vegas. Far less significant than the Clark County Commission, Las Vegas city government still had admirable access to resources. Unlike the Strip, located in the unincorporated county, downtown fell within the boundaries of the city. Saddled with debt, watching their share of the local market dwindle, and unable to secure the financing that Strip moguls found with ease, downtown casino owners followed the path of so many American oligarchs in decline in so many towns across the nation: they looked to an entity with taxing power that they could control. It was their last stab at retaining the power their parents wielded.

Discussions began in the mid-1980s, but no coherent redevelopment plan resulted until October 1993, when eight downtown casinos founded the Fremont Street Experience Company. With help from the Las Vegas Convention and Visitors Authority (LVCVA), the company created a public-private partnership with the City of Las Vegas to redesign downtown and return it to its historic vibrancy. To succeed, they had to make law accommodate their desires. In 1993, the state legislature increased the room tax at the downtown hotels that stood to benefit from the development and followed with a bill permitting a pedestrian mall on Fremont Street. A total of $70 million in capital improvement money was raised, $27.6 million from the City of Las Vegas and $8 million more from LVCVA, which designated the Fremont Street Experience a public recreational facility in order to make the allocation. The funds allowed the partnership to hire Jon Jerde, catalyst of Minneapolis's Mall of America, San Diego's Horton Plaza, Rotterdam's Beursplein, as well as Universal Studios CityWalk in Los Angeles, to transform five blocks of Fremont Street, from Main Street to Las Vegas Boulevard, into something, anything, with allure.

Famous for his ability to create livable urban environments and using "the communal experience is a designable event" as his motto, Jerde grappled with urban space that was more small town than big city. Downtown had once been the city center, but that time had long passed. Local observers such as the prescient Geoff Schumacher, long argued that "downtown" was a misnomer, a description of location alone. The city's real downtown was the Strip itself, the skyline that defined the city and the hub from which its economic activity emanated. An equally strong argument could be made that Las Vegas didn't have a downtown at all. The valley had become a series of interconnected and competitive commercials zones that grappled for dominance of geographical sectors of the valley, demarcated by the presence of the local chain Station Casinos. You knew you were in another sector when you saw the next Station property. In this view, Las Vegas was many cities masquerading under one name.

Jerde touted his ability to create attractive and livable space, and he designed and built another of the projects his detractors revile. The plan malled off five blocks of Fremont Street, destroyed the street level architecture, and converted a bona fide urban streetscape into a sidewalk with pushcarts. But this wasn't CityWalk in Los Angeles, with Universal Studios behind locked gates next door. This was Las Vegas, where every attraction had to compete with every other one. Jerde tried to rescue the endeavor with glitz. Ninety feet above the street, a five-foot-deep, forty-four-foot-wide canopied frame sported a light and sound show that covered four blocks: 7.8 megawatts of power lit 2.1 million light bulbs in a computer-generated light show of animated images; 540,000 watts of sound completed the show, filled with strobe lights and images. It sounded impressive. In daylight, the canopy looked like a great big circular chain link fence in the sky above the four blocks.

When I went to see the show, I came away underwhelmed. As soon as the lights went down, everyone stopped and looked up. Music blared. Images shot across the frame. All I remembered was a series of animated buffalo—I think—stampeding across the sky. When it ended, I looked at my friends and said: "That's all? For $70 million?" The project brought in almost 20,000 onlookers each day, but it didn't staunch the decline of casino revenues downtown. The show simply wasn't all it was cracked up to be. Jerde's planning made the Experience a B-grade attraction in a town where an A routinely fails.

The project had other important dimensions. When the Fremont Street Experience opened in December 1995, it already had in place one of the preeminent goals of its planners, a series of city ordinances that included prohibitions on solicitation and complete exclusion of panhandling within the four blocks under the screen. The company could charge admission to the area. With the complicity of government, a welfare project for downtown hotel owners also included a remarkable social ramification. It privatized public space with public money, permitting the exclusion of behaviors noxious to property owners that were endemic in the area. The city gave the keys to the property to the hotel owners, admitting that it abdicated responsibility for the streets. The project created a faux fortress inside a real and far more rugged space. While physically downtown, the Fremont Street Experience was no longer there. It was, like so many of Jerde's projects, a faux downtown that happened to be surrounded by the real downtown.

At the time, no one really noticed. The public-private blurring was so typical in Las Vegas, the idea of common good so remote, and the antipathy for government action so great that the Fremont Street Experience was routine. Since nobody's freedom was affected, at least no one who counted, few cared. "Freedom from" triumphed, and with the typical Nevada flourish, eyewash for the mind, the deal was done. People eagerly anticipated the revival of downtown.

The efforts to blur public and private were brazen. In 1995, the city council voted to let the Experience hire its own security force and restrict access for special events such as New Year's Eve. The city retained the right-of-way to Fremont Street, further confusing jurisdiction. No one really knew whether the Experience was public or private, but as was often the case, few cared. The change was greeted with ennui.

The cheers turned to boos on New Year's Eve, when the Experience charged admission to the area. The law permitted the charge, and it was just like paying to go to one of the hotels or a swank private party, spokesmen protested. Look at the benefits, they blared. You can walk on the streets and not be hassled. We'll have our security force protect you. All you have to do is pay the twenty bucks to get in. We'll even give you a glass of champagne. But the public disagreed, steaming about being charged to use public streets that they'd paid for—that the law had made private, or at least nonpublic—while no one noticed. The same vaunted Nevada individualism, the quasi-libertarianism endemic in the Silver State, that let people think that privatizing space wasn't a bad idea had the opposite effect when people found out that "private" could mean they had to pay to get in.

This battle brought the American Civil Liberties Union (ACLU) in a hurry. The ACLU had fought such battles since the 1960s, and in 1997 it sued the City of Las Vegas over the ordinance that prohibited solicitation on the public-private space. "We think the whole damn law is unconstitutional," thundered Gary Peck, ACLU's executive director in Nevada. "We will fight it all the way to the Supreme Court if we have to." Peck and the ACLU contended that the agreement between the city and the Fremont Street Experience Company restricted all First Amendment activity except company-sponsored events. This, the suit alleged, "attempted to redefine the Fremont Street Experience's essential character as a public forum." It made public space truly private, in Peck's view, illegally overriding the protections of the U.S. Constitution.

The ACLU's appearance spoke volumes about the changing vision of rights in American society. Closely associated with the Left, the ACLU became the champion of the second generation of the rights revolution, the libertarians, property-rights movement types, and others who embraced the doctrine of personal privilege. The political Right became heir to the left-leaning tradition of individual expression inherited from the 1960s. The constellation of changes of the 1960s offered the now hackneyed cliché "do your own thing." But doing your own thing in the terms of the 1960s young was really an interior exploration, an internal activity that took on outside traits. Especially in the West, the inheritors of that idea, many of whom were dismayed by the extension of rights to people they didn't much care for, took the soft edges of 1960s rights and made them absolute. Never mind that Paul Revere and the Founding Fathers would have recognized the right of the individual to be free only within the constraints of the community. In the late 1990s, freedom truly meant individual rights and little else. Those who embraced that interpretation of the First Amendment differed from the advocates of free speech during the heyday of the rights revolution. Instead of wanting to fix government as had most of the activists of the 1960s, these new rights activists feared government, blamed it for the chaos that they felt ruined their lives and their society, and wanted to dismantle it and live in a state of armed individuals, near anarchy. To them, the rights of the individual were the only ones of consequence.

The ACLU had another equally powerful rebuttal. Although it escaped notice in Las Vegas, the bastion of free-market capitalism, the city had given away $30 million to create not public, but private space. Recouping that from the tax revenues might happen, but it would take a long time. Questioning whether the city could give away taxpayer dollars and property rights together prompted more inquiry. The LVCVA money, the $8 million earmarked for a public park, complicated the city and the company's position even more. The LVCVA had to designate the Fremont Street Experience as "public recreational space" before it could give the project money. "It's parochial to think of a park as a field or a baseball diamond," observed Mark Paris, president of the Fremont Street Experience, in a self-serving assessment. But a public park meant that the space was open to the public and that the traditional rules of free speech in public places applied. "They want to call it a public park in order to pay for it," Peck observed, "but then they give authority to a private security force to regulate it."

The U.S. District Court did not see the issue in clear terms. In an April 1998 decision, Justice David Hagen decided that the Fremont Street Experience was not a traditional public forum, but it wasn't entirely private either. He deemed provisions banning leafleting and message-bearing merchandise unconstitutional. "The purpose and use of the mall today is revitalization of downtown business," Hagen wrote, "by promoting commercial activity in a safe convenient relaxing pedestrian environment." The decision allowed the city to make the distinction between what it regarded as good and bad public speech. The law allowed unions to leaflet, but no one else could. Las Vegas mayor Jan Jones gladly permitted unions, but she didn't want pornography. Both sides claimed victory: The provisions were unconstitutional, pleasing the ACLU. The city and the Fremont Street Experience were ecstatic; the development was not a traditional public forum.

The nexus of American law has always been the intersection between property rights and personal freedom. The Bill of Rights lays out individual freedom, but ever since the Constitutional Convention closed its eyes and held its nose about slavery in 1787, American law has been about property. When private property was pitted against individual rights, the right of the property owner proved paramount. This made the designation of the Fremont Street Experience as public or private crucial. If it was private, the owners enjoyed certain rights to restrict behavior. If it became public, the plethora of freedoms protected in American law prevailed.

Hagen's decision was based in economics. Since the Fremont Street Experience promoted a more vital downtown, the state could permit it to restrict activities even if they impinged on its public status. Hagen did not address the ways in which the transfer of public space to private hands with public money might constitute dereliction of duty, nor did he engage the dangers that resulted when a free society allowed "freedom from" to exceed "freedom to" in law and practice. The case followed from the Slaughterhouse cases of 1873, which ruled that while states could not discriminate on the basis of race, creed, or color, the court could not forbid individual property owners from doing so. The ACLU appealed.

Public and private space had blurred, tangling the First Amendment between them. Nevada and Las Vegas's libertarianism proved only skin deep. It protected business, but at the Fremont Street Experience, it protected individuals only when coerced by the courts or public opinion. The privatization of formerly public space proceeded, not only in Las Vegas, but around the country. People chose to abdicate their rights in favor of the perception of safety. Law leaned away from communal and community goals toward the enshrinement of local oligarchy. Economics and the marketplace trumped civil rights.

In this regard, Las Vegas pointed the country to a place that the nation might not want to go. In a state that never really grappled with the rights revolution—staunch Nevadans said they didn't need to because in Nevada you were freer than anywhere else in the nation—the new vision of American rights, as protection for liberal consumerism, creating safe, clean environments devoid of noxious behaviors, led to a cumulative trouncing of individual rights. In a series of incidents, the police exonerated officers who threatened, harassed, or otherwise impinged upon people passing out leaflets in downtown Las Vegas. It seemed Kafkaesque, the harbinger of a more tightly regulated state. The protection of liberal consumerist freedom over constitutionally enshrined rights of free expression in Las Vegas meant substantially less freedom, a circumstance that ran directly counter to the city's image of itself.

But if people didn't care, who was going to stop the curtailment of First Amendment rights? Most Las Vegans and indeed most Americans had become willing to sacrifice rights for individual safety and comfort. Nearly everyone in Las Vegas found the pornographic solicitation pamphlets disgusting, but the courts ruled in favor of dissemination. People wanted to be free of nuisance in the short term. Most just didn't think about the long run.

Noxious is in the eye of the beholder, and to Steve Wynn, whose empire in 1999 included the Bellagio and the Mirage, the smut peddlers who shoved graphically vivid images of outcall escorts into the hands of passersby in front of resort properties were truly obnoxious. At Wynn's newly opened Bellagio, on the beautiful promenade he'd built, Wynn didn't see why he should have to endure tawdry pornography handed to his visitors by sleazy people. In a city with more than a little sexual exploitation in its fabric, Wynn built the Bellagio to be the casino where women were comfortable, where the spaces and the amenities made them want to stay another day. But in front of the hotel, on the sidewalks he built, smut peddlers disseminated lurid pamphlets, making a mockery of Wynn's sanitized environs.

Wynn was outraged. Over a lavish breakfast at his exclusive $48 million

Shadow Creek Golf Course, he vented his anger at smut peddlers. They were tacky and indiscreet, an affront to the dignity of women. They held the city back, limited what the Bellagio and indeed Las Vegas could and should be. By 1999, he'd tried everything to stop them. His lawyers worked constantly for a solution, but none was forthcoming. The very freedom that made Las Vegas also made it possible for smut peddlers to disrupt Wynn's vision and cut into the future he planned. Las Vegas could overcome the stigma of gambling, but it couldn't forbid the exercise of even noxious First Amendment rights. The issue drove him to distraction.

It is impossible to think of Las Vegas without thinking of sex. The image of the city was purposefully risqué, an effort to enhance its status as the first city of sin at a time when Las Vegas served as an outlet for the nation's excesses and a scapegoat for its moral shortcomings. The combination of Mob roots, gambling, and distance from the norm made the city the place to be for people looking to get laid. Even though Las Vegas's legalized prostitution ended during World War II and a number of prostitution scandals brought down postwar local law enforcement officials, exploitative sex was part of what brought people to Sin City and what they bought into by coming. The Las Vegas Convention and Visitors Authority recognized as much when it turned the new city full circle toward sex with its amazingly successful "What happens in Vegas, stays in Vegas" advertising campaign that began in 2002.

As with every other commodity, sex is displayed more openly and less modestly in Las Vegas. If you believed that the idea of sin was meaningless in Las Vegas, its public displays of sexuality were respectable. After the girls in Minsky's Follies dropped their tops in 1957, the city's entertainment had an adult cast and the city capitalized on its position as a titillating place to bring in the many who sought relief from the button-down respectability of mid-century America. The big extravaganzas, the most public form of this pulling on the gonads of a society, came to be known as "Las Vegas shows," and everybody knew what that meant: topless. The last of them, Jubilee at Paris Las Vegas, struggled to survive in the new century.

Titillation was the norm in 1950s and early 1960s Las Vegas, and sex was even more widely available. The Mob world from which so many gamblers came was filled with available women, gun molls or dames in the popular literature, and sex became part of the appeal of Las Vegas, personal prerogative in a space outside of morality. Showgirls dated high rollers and an active and seemingly independent world of prostitution flourished. Individual women made fortunes as prostitutes, Ralph Pearl, the city's premier gossip columnist during the era, asserted. Ian Fleming, the creator of James Bond, so admired

Las Vegas that he included it in *Thrilling Cities*, his paean to the exotic. Fleming reveled in Las Vegas's openness, comparing it to other cities without the normative rules of disintegrating Victorian culture: Singapore before Lee Kuan Yew, Macao, Havana before Castro. Fleming glorified Las Vegas, stretched and changed it, but he recognized in it a social scapegoat, a place where Americans could distance themselves from the society they created. *The Green Felt Jungle*, the classic 1960s Las Vegas exposé, called Las Vegas "one huge whorehouse" and announced that 10 percent of the city's 65,000 people were involved in the sex trade. Although authors Ed Reid and Ovid Demaris sounded indignant, they did little more than whet the public's appetite for more salacious exposés. Even boosters like Ralph Pearl couldn't help but use sex to sell their stories. Before it was fashionable to explicitly market sex, Las Vegas excelled at its commodification.

The American cultural revolution, the constellation of behaviors and practices that hit conventional America with full force in the 1960s, transformed commercial sex in the United States. Once the "new morality" hit, selling the image of sex became easier. As Hugh Hefner's *Playboy* magazine and subsequent empire provided men with a model for sex without commitment and Helen Gurley Brown's *Sex and the Single Girl* and her revamped *Cosmopolitan* magazine gave women a similar message, Victorian morés finally collapsed. The birth control pill freed women from the constraints of historical morality. Without the threat of pregnancy, personal behavior really became a private choice. Properly managed, it did not have to have consequences, and after *Roe v. Wade* in 1973, it theoretically didn't even have to be managed. With the stigma removed, the American middle class exercised its desires. Young women no longer guarded their chastity with the supposed vigor of old, and as they became more amenable to the entreaties of young men, sexual transaction became social rather than commercial. Even more, communities soon set their own standards. Court cases established local standards for obscenity, which translated as grudging permission for public sexuality. After the *Miller v. California* decision in 1973 that established a three-part standard for pornography, a community's level of tolerance became the governing standard.

With liberalized law and technological innovation, the modern sex industry was born. The VCR was catalytic. Pornography on videotape became endemic. People could watch porn in the comfort of their homes and often could rent it nearby. Home camcorders meant that anybody with a little money could put their own kinkiness on tape and keep it for themselves or sell it as widely as the traffic would bear—as Pamela Anderson Lee and later Paris

Hilton found to their chagrin. The porn industry became massive. Wide exposure to pornography again softened community standards and further enhanced demand. The proliferation of gentlemen's clubs, a euphemism for high-dollar, upscale strip clubs, followed, and they became places to be seen as well as to see. In 1990, a national stripper's convention at the Sahara became an HBO special. By the late 1990s, Internet pornography services accumulated the highest numbers of hits from consumers and porn stars cavorted with Kid Rock on MTV videos. Slutty chic became high fashion. The sex industry had gone upscale and acquired pretensions of respectability.

By any American measure, Las Vegas was tolerant. Its public displays of sexuality and the way it accepted casual and commercial sex made it a natural for the sex industry. With adult superstores galore, the Yellow Pages featuring 105 pages of adult entertainers, the emergence of gentleman's clubs, the array of topless, nude, and other sex clubs throughout the valley, and in 1999, 46 of every 100 businesses Web-based, a trend observers believed reflected the predominance of cyberporn, Las Vegas offered a mature sex industry as public sex became more widely accepted.

When the sex industry discovered the Consumer Electronics Show (CES), it became even more visible. Since the 1970s, CES had been the most important trade show for electronics, drawing cutting-edge industry types as well as the usual hangers-on. Plenty of them were easy marks for adult entertainment, and adult entertainers flocked to town during the show. The porn industry added its own trade show and faux Academy Awards to coincide with the CES each January. In 1993, the organizers staged a free-speech fundraiser that was simultaneously a live sex show at an off-Strip adult bookstore. The place was packed and the audience ate it up, but the police didn't find it funny. They moved in and arrested the performers. The existence of the zone without sin did have limits. You could look, but you couldn't touch. If you did, the performers and the proprietor were arrested, not the audience.

By 1997, the porn industry found even more lucrative timing for its meeting. Comdex, the giant computer show, brought in 250,000 of the most puzzling conventioneers around. Unlike the cowboys who came for the National Finals Rodeo or the rappers and NBA stars who followed the heavyweight boxing circuit, the computer geeks had none of the obvious Las Vegas vices. They didn't drink much and they sure didn't gamble. The hotels adjusted to their profile. During Comdex, hotel rates in Las Vegas paralleled the rest of the nation. A room that could regularly be had for $89 was $250 or more. The hotels had to make their money some way.

But Las Vegas will find your weakness and the largely male entourage of computer geeks had a clearly evident one: sex. Saddled with the image of being pimply faced nerds with pocket protectors and desperately wanting to be suave, the male prototypes of the dot.com revolution wanted girls, girls, girls. AdultDex, what reporter Joe Schoenmann called "the illegitimate child of Comdex," emerged as a profitable outlet during the most unusual week in the city's year. In 1997, excitable computer types pressed into the third floor of the Imperial Palace for AdultDex '97. Among them were a number of undercover vice police, who issued nine citations during one of the shows. Seven were for "lewd and dissolute conduct," a misdemeanor that occurred when some of the vendors bared their breasts. The final two, for performing a live sex act, occurred when two women touched each other on stage. The citations came, Vice Sergeant Robert DuVall told the press, because AdultDex did not require entrants to prove they were of age, a bizarre explanation that sounded like it was produced for the TV news.

This conventional free-speech issue pushed the buttons of libertarian Las Vegas. AdultDex really was an exercise of constitutionally protected speech, loosely defined. It was also offensive to many. But Las Vegas's history and tradition of tolerance dictated that such behavior was acceptable. After all, the porn industry's trade association was called the Free Speech Coalition, a concept that defined the old Nevada. The *Las Vegas Review-Journal*, the antigovernment local daily, well to the right of the mainstream press but libertarian in its political outlook, defended AdultDex as free speech. It ran photos from the porn confab on page one, a decision that brought some criticism from the larger community already on the demographic road to normality. The new Nevada was prepared to look the other way in the best state tradition, but it didn't want to confront the adult industry on the front page of the paper. When local columnist John L. Smith defended the decision to run the photos, a barrage of letters to the editor hammered him. With all the in-migration, Nevada's tolerance had become something new.

There were other defenders of public morality out there in southern Nevada, not the least of which was the Clark County Commission, the governmental entity that benefited most from the growth of the valley. Late in 1996, a draft ordinance circulated that would have banned "off-premises canvassing," the practice of standing on a public sidewalk to hand out leaflets or flyers advertising a business transaction. Despite Nevada's hard-core tradition of personal freedom, most politicians and the LVCVA board enthusiastically supported the ordinance. Although the measure didn't specify adult entertainment, it did relieve the city of one major embarrassment during the transition to mainstream entertainment. As the city shed its past and reinvented itself once again, explicit material for outcall services in Las Vegas or legalized prostitution in nearby counties clashed with the veneer of respectable entertainment that the city sought for itself.

There was also a class dimension to the handbill issue. A lot of the people passing them out looked poor and many appeared to be immigrants. A significant number were Latinas or Asian women, often with young children in tow. They reflected the lack of choices of people at the economic bottom. In New York in 1910, they might have sewed shirts in sweatshops. In Las Vegas in the 1990s, they handed porn to upper-middle-class tourists, reprising the old class hierarchies of early twentieth-century America. The women Steve Wynn wished to protect came from far more comfortable circumstances.

The battle lines were clear, if a little confusing. On one side stood most of the power in Clark County: Glenn Schaeffer of Mandalay Resort Group told the county commissioners that his customers "have a right to feel safe" and "not be harassed" near hotel property. Public officials echoed Schaeffer's sentiment. "We need to make Las Vegas Boulevard a showplace, not a garbage dump," County Commissioner Lorraine Hunt, who went on to become lieutenant governor in 1998, said. "We want to make it an enjoyable experience, free of harassment and intimidation of people." In opposition stood a few handbill companies, an anonymous man referred to by his attorney, JoNell Thomas, as a "major smut peddler," and the ACLU. The scenario had all the makings of a David and Goliath–style showdown. Opponents asked for a temporary injunction, but when U.S. District Court Judge Lloyd George ruled, he followed local power as much as law. He denied the motion for an injunction in early March and the ban took effect. Stunned, opponents appealed George's decision to the Ninth Circuit Court of Appeals in San Francisco, which ordered an injunction and remanded the case to George. Even as litigation continued, the law did not achieve its social purpose. It failed to stop the handouts.

The county ordinance was questionable from its inception, proof that power brought inchoate arrogance that couldn't see beyond the county line. Clark County got creamed in every subsequent court hearing. In August 1998, the Ninth Circuit Court of Appeals overturned the ordinance. Early in 1999, the county wrote a new ordinance to circumvent the ruling in 1999. It didn't work. Chastened by the appeals court's reversal of his earlier decisions, Judge Lloyd George promptly declared the new ordinance "overbroad" and ordered the county to remove its anti-handbill notices from the Las Vegas Convention Center. "I don't consider it an obscenity case," the chastened judge said. "I consider it a First Amendment case." After George's decision, there wasn't really anything the county could do. The most powerful industry in Clark County had been defeated by a bunch of smut peddlers.

The handbill controversy really was about much more than distributing sleazy pamphlets. Because the entire debate focused on public spaces, off-premises canvassing became closely linked to the larger but more amorphous discussion about the sanctity of private space and the growing preference for it over conventional public spaces. In public spaces, even political heavy-weights couldn't exclude activity, and they well knew it. But casino owners couldn't get their patrons into their carefully designed private space without crossing public space, a First Amendment gauntlet where guests could be hassled and their experience disrupted. At its core, Las Vegas was a script that placed the visitor at the center of the story. Every major operator worked to fashion the script so that visitors left their concerns behind and found themselves center stage. The process had to be controlled from beginning to end, and people offering handbills at the entrance to imagined paradise intruded in a way that threatened every other dimension of the experience.

This measure of control was particularly important for Wynn, who was the master of this process as well as such a perfectionist that some thought him a bully. During the 1990s, Wynn's needs ran the state; nearly every politician kowtowed to him, and in most cases his vast power carried the day. Wynn was classic Las Vegas, a funny mix of benevolent captain of industry and sometime tyrant who bent the state to his will. No one invested more in the quality of visitor experience, in making private feel not only public, but friendly. Wynn's approach was born of a desire to transform experience, the key feature of the latest transformation of Las Vegas.

It was commonly assumed throughout the 1990s that what was good for Steve Wynn was good for Las Vegas, but even he couldn't get handbilling stopped. In a one-industry state, its primary industry's most important purveyor spent enormous political capital and millions on lawyers. Though Wynn told people he would do anything to solve this problem, even he could not get around the First Amendment. Despite efforts to curtail the First Amendment across the nation, exclusion remained an all-or-nothing proposition. You could exclude either everyone or no one. Public space is "still the place where some guy can stand on a soapbox, shout what he wants to, hand out what he wants to and if the tourists don't like it, that's the price we pay for freedom," observed Allen Lichtenstein, a First Amendment attorney for the ACLU. "It doesn't mean that harassment can't be stopped or littering can't be stopped." The alternative was insidious to conventional definitions of freedom. "If in order to prevent First Amendment activity, all government had to do was quitclaim the sidewalks to private enterprise," Lichtenstein insisted, "there'll be no place in the town, in the world, where people have the right to express themselves. That's a scary thought."

Wynn's problem was solved for him. In 2000, with his stock price low, MGM bought the Mirage group for a then record $6.4 billion. Afterward, Wynn bought the old Desert Inn and demolished it to make room for Wynn Las Vegas, his newest ultraswank hotel, which opened in 2005. With a mountain that faced the Strip and shielded what was within, and with what early reviews described as "intimate interior space," Wynn Las Vegas solved the problem. Wynn removed his hotel from the streetscape, requiring you to enter to experience it. He separated public and private space—so he could eliminate handbilling. The First Amendment reshaped the face of what is already one of Las Vegas's premier hotels.

One of the signal points of contention over space involves the rise of neighborhoods of affinity, the successors to the neighborhoods of American lore. Simply, a city that quadrupled in size in two decades had few of the conventional mechanisms that sustained older American communities and even more reasons for embracing new ways of organizing life, space, and social interaction. Transience was the crystal clear characteristic, the one feature that defined the social landscape. Everyone was new and the habits that bind had to be stitched together from the practices of dozens of communities. The result was disconcerting for people who arrived, expecting to find what they'd left behind.

Las Vegas's newest additions, the grafted upper middle class, were drawn to the town because of the opportunity it offers, and, when they arrived, they were shocked to find the signposts of cultural familiarity, both visual and cultural, absent. Las Vegas was truly a backyard culture, a place where everyone had a pool not only to keep cool but as a way to choose friends. Social life was driven not by geography or proximity but instead by affinity. Your neighbors were not the people who lived next door to you, but the ones you shared activities with, the parents who chatted as they watched their children during karate or gymnastics class or Little League games and practices, or who shared an interest in dancing and belonged to your church, synagogue, and more recently mosque.

The key to the difference was Las Vegas's transience. Most Las Vegas newcomers expected to find a town with formed institutions. Las Vegas had to build continuity even at the most basic level, the schoolyard. Hierarchies changed rapidly. Anyone who had gone to grade school and high school with the same people from first through twelfth grade found the fluidity disconcerting. If there had ever been a core in Las Vegas life, it had long been over-whelmed by the tidal wave of newcomers. Nowhere was that constant tide of new people more evident than in the suburbs that appeared almost like magic on the edges of the city.

The new suburbs have distinctive traits in the postmodern United States. They lack the dynamic core of the mid-twentieth century, the layered and tex-tured structure of space that characterized the United States into the 1970s, but instead spread out and contain row after row, mile after mile of the same restaurants, chain stores, ball fields, churches, and everything else that forms the basis of postmodern community. More decentralized than any urban area since industrialization, they revolve around a series of indistinguishable cen-ters, all providing the same commercial amenities. These fixtures mirror one of the problems of the future, the way in which private commercial space stands in for public space. Without such private space, the stores, coffeeshops, and restaurants, most suburbs would have no social space at all.

Most of these suburbs, from Overland Park, Kansas, by Kansas City, to Orange County, California, also have older cities nearby, long traditions of community and identity, ways of defining local reality that graft the new communities onto the limb of the existing regional tree. Such suburban areas are extensions of changes in the cities on whose edge they perch, creations of the perception that demographic change is decline. They hinge on the older cities and their psychic importance, extending older dominion in a new and different way. They exclude, commentators such as NPR's Ray Suarez say, on the basis of race, but if he's right, the new suburbs do an outstanding job of using class differences to mask race. There's more, much more at stake in this remarkable transition.

Once upon a time, sages like Robert Putnam and James Howard Kunstler insist, the United States was a front-yard culture, where people knew and em-braced their neighbors, had block parties, and shared the glue that bound com-munities in American memory. This was an ideal world, where social control stemmed from power relationships, where kin, culture, and caste defined boundaries that were understood by all. Everyone knew where he or she be-longed and, even more important, where he or she could go. They also knew how they were supposed to behave, and the mythic cop with Irish brogue tap-ping his nightstick on his palm was there to enforce the law of the land. That world was all white, exclusionary as hell, and it may even have existed for a few short moments somewhere. But like much of what we think we know about the past, the idea of an idyllic American past is one more example of the only good thing about the good old days being bad memory.

This vision of community was simultaneously a reflection of romanticized experience and a creation of television. Intimacy, goodwill, and interaction in community, called by some "social capital," may once have been commonplace in the United States. The tales of Nathaniel Hawthorne illustrated its power and, more telling, its oppression. Sinclair Lewis showed its limits. Sherwood Anderson, Thornton Wilder, and the rest of a generation of writers exalted it. By the 1960s, urbanist Jane Jacobs still found its ingredients even in the modern metropolis. Then television took it over, with *Ozzie and Harriet, The Donna Reed Show, My Three Sons*, and even the hysterically dysfunctional *Bewitched*. The path from there to *The Sopranos* and now *Desperate Housewives* is clearly marked and probably even truer than the myth. Yet the memory of this faux connectedness has shaped American perceptions of what a neighborhood should be.

World War II precipitated the demise of small-town America and changed the fundamental basis of the relationship between people in neighborhoods. Suburbanization played a crucial role, for new communities replaced the glue of internal ties with the lubrication of external linkage. When the Southern California suburbs came together after World War II, they were populated by two groups of people: those who left tightly woven and often ethnic urban neighborhoods and those whom the war and its aftermath propelled from the equally tightly knit small towns of rural America. The adults who inhabited these new suburbs had grown up in a world of kinship, ethnic loyalty, and neighborhood fraternity. They made these new places as they remembered home. This time the difference was that instead of sharing religion, family, or ethnicity, they shared stage of life, aspiration, and even occupation. The aerospace suburbs of Southern California were populated by engineers and their families, people from all over; the nearby slightly less well-off ones were filled with firemen, policemen, and clerks. They made community from the memory of closer ties, foisting upon their children the never-ending round of barbecues and touch football games, of block parties and drive-in movies. "We were blithe conquerors, my tribe," David Beers remembered in *Blue Sky Dream*, his memoir of this life. "When we chose a new homeland, invaded a place, settled it, and made it over in our image, we did so with a smiling sense of our own inevitability."

But those neighborhoods could be oppressive too, constraining, stultifying, trampling. For the ones who set the standards, who hosted the barbecues, who starred in the pickup games, who enjoyed the social games—the drunkenness, the flirting and its consequences, the increasing rate of divorce and the shattered lives of children that resulted—it was a joyous world. For those uncomfortable with closeness bred by proximity, who'd just as soon be left alone, or the children subjected to the taunts of bullies or whose home lives were wrecked by the affairs among parents, proximity seemed too close, a threat to their emotional security. The experience left an imprint. As adults, they felt reticence about their neighbors, wanting to know them enough to discern who belonged and who didn't, but not so well that they feel like they can stroll over and chat at any time. It was a fine line, between unfriendliness and the creation of structure in a community, designed to defend, but not to insist on participation. After all, they were only neighbors and you didn't choose your neighbors like you choose your friends.

This has led to the creation of neighborhoods of affinity, communities that are based on interest instead of proximity. Your neighbors aren't necessarily the people who live next door to you—although they can be. They are instead the ones who share interests and activities with you, the people who like what you like, be it kiteflying or model rocketry, dance, or Little League baseball. They are the ones you meet at church, synagogue, or mosque, who answer the same organizational flyers you do, or even the people who walk for exercise at the same time in the morning. This is a different formulation of community, friendships that are gendered male—that is, activity based— rather than female, or based upon intimacy. They can and often do become intimate. It is just that their basis—in a shared activity—is different from what we imagine for the genesis of such relationships in the American past.

Neighborhoods of affinity are a tricky business. In the transience that is postindustrial America, they become the foundation of community. They take on a frontline importance, replacing the relationships that date back to eighth grade. Such relationships embody communities of interest, not of space, and are accentuated by the reality that parents who let their preteen and young teenagers move about unsupervised court disaster. The "Soccer Mom" phenomenon reflected this change in another way. Instead of finding their own way to after-school activities and even to school, today's children are shepherded everywhere. The prevalence of carpools, play dates, and chaperoned children's activities show how communities of affinity have taken on new roles in neighborhoods across the nation. A life led on these terms is more structured than the childhood of the generation past, and for a long time, a parent is a more intimate part of it—if as nothing else, an eavesdropping transportation device.

Because affinity involves relationships that used to be second tier—the parents of the other kids on your son's Little League team—that achieve new primacy, they promote other kinds of markers of status and security. Gated communities, theoretically a sign of a perceived need for safety, really turned out to be markers of status. How secure could a gated community be when everyone has a landscaper, a pizza delivery guy, and countless friends who drop off kids and need the code so they won't bother you? Many of the gates can be accessed by typing 0000, the first numeric combination any crook would try. Even more are accessed by typing in the year, still others by the last four digits of zip codes.

Along with homeowners' associations, gates are consequences of the rise of communities of affinity. Especially in transient places without firm institutions or where larger, community-wide institutions are in decline—which is to say everywhere—homeowners' associations stand in lieu of the social fabric of the mythic America. With confidence in state and national government at an all-time low and local government regarded as the province of special interests, the homeowners' association becomes simultaneously a hedge against the decline of the centralized state, the closest thing to the grassroots democracy Tocqueville envisioned, and a way to assure the conformity of image that is at the heart of stability in a liberal consumerist society. In an age when people operate under the premise that government works for someone else, when they work twelve-hour days and only nod to their neighbors, homeowner's associations provide the vast majority with a security blanket. They yield smaller lots and yards and have lots of restrictions, but they keep purple houses and old cars off the block. Done properly, they seem to function in place of community relationships, in place of the shame of being the worst house or yard on the block, in place of sharing life with your neighbors.

But there's a cost in the nature of linkage among people and in the freedom to explore. The linkages are more fragile, for they are generally built around the activity that is the genesis and they require little more than a wave to the proximate people who used to provide de facto security. We see the same people from season to season, but the closeness of the relationship can be predicated on the assignments of players to a team. Even more, the investment remains shallow; these are still people you can easily walk away from if you choose and because of that, the maintenance that all relationships require can easily be subjected to a cost-benefit analysis. It seems somehow mercenary sometimes, an equation or a formula that follows closely the trajectory of the postindustrial world. For kids, it is even worse. Little of what they do occurs beyond the prying eyes of adults, for adults are ever present. And of course, you'd be an idiot to let your kids roam on their own in this day and age.

The weak institutions of Nevada and its libertarianism gave way to another problem of potentially great proportions, I thought as I sat in a police substation in the suburbs attending a organization's meeting. There wasn't much in the way of public space anywhere for any purpose, forcing community organizations and nonprofits to meet in unusual places. Most logical places for your sewing circle or book club didn't exist or were booked all the time, and a certain amount of creativity and cooperation from local businesses made the wheels of civic-mindedness turn. One organization in which I participated held its meetings in an eye doctor's office; later, we moved to the patio of a coffee shop that belonged to friendly business owner. Some car dealerships built community centers into their showrooms. They added playrooms for kids first, diners, and short-order-type restaurants that were designed to be fun—one suburban Ford dealership opened a "Mustang Sally's" diner on its premises—and some even advertised for non-profit and other civic groups to use their meeting rooms. Start-up churches routinely meet on the university campus or in public schools. I once gave a talk to a VFW post gathering in a hospital. On another occasion, I spoke to mid-career professionals in an assisted living center for seniors. Only on rare occasions were conventional public spaces, public libraries, churches, community or senior centers, available for such gatherings.

Even more, similar activities compete for public attention, one in public and the other in private space. One weekend the Renaissance Festival and the Elizabethan Festival competed, one in a county park, the other at the newly opened upscale urban village called the District. This forty-acre development had lofts, apartments, shops, and restaurants with ample parking and a faux street permanently closed to vehicle traffic—a fake malled street really—that drew enormous crowds. The Elizabethan players strolled and performed, with mini-stages scattered about. Throngs joined them, shopping, eating ice cream, and relaxing in private space. At the county park, with its older facilities and more diverse and considerably younger overall crowd, the tension was palpable. The Renaissance Festival was a minor attraction to the largely Spanish-speaking crowd, but the families in the park had a fine time anyway. The players worked largely among their own, the public space they had chosen occupied by a constituency not much interested in their efforts.

Such contrasts may seem unusual and benign, but they are indicative of a larger trend in American society of which Las Vegas is the most pronounced example. As government loses its luster, the services it once provided, essential to the concept of community, are being parceled out. In a liberal consumerist society, they're handed to people who can make money from them, commercial entities that seek to bring people through the doors. The creation of public private space attributed an ostensibly civic purpose to a commercial activity; before long the commercial motivations show through and take precedence. Without civic options, they fall de facto to people with economic goals that at least equal any civic objectives they possess. The result is a democracy of dollars: a place where commerce serves all of our needs in myriad ways, where the marketplace takes the place of civic space.

There's nothing inherently wrong with this scenario—except for its implications about who we've become. There isn't a common American culture any more, no dominant set of values that dictates norms. The ones we had we threw out in the 1960s after they collapsed under the weight of their own inconsistencies, but their replacement, a rampant and often malignant individualism, doesn't do much for knitting ties between individuals or communities. The decline of civic culture is everywhere, observers like Robert D. Putnam of *Bowling Alone* proclaim, and to a certain degree, they're correct. We're not really bowling alone, though. It's more like the parallel play of small children, nonintersecting dances with a glance out of the corner of our eyes to see who's watching.

There's little shared space left in American society. In postmodern America, we insult each other in traffic and think of it as communication. Public spaces are open to all, but in a society where we lack faith in government and the ability to talk across fences, that openness is inherently threatening. Polls show that Americans think the tolerance inherent in the First Amendment needs to be tempered. Too much sex and violence in the media, asserted Paul McMasters in *Media Studies Journal* in 2000, have prompted Americans to wonder whether the community's need to maintain order and set limits might supersede the right of individuals to express themselves. People have already announced that fear by voting with their feet. Scared of the world they created, they've abandoned the public for the semipublic and the private in droves. They've found what they feel is a better scenario: private space designated for public purposes, which seems a mild compromise if "freedom from" is your goal. This is the type of reasoning that enshrined segregation, that led to the privatization of sidewalks and the creation of private space with public money.

But it is very comfortable. Sunset Station, one of the ubiquitous Station Casino chain, contains a multiplex movie theater, an ice cream store, a supervised area for children to play, half a dozen restaurants ranging from a coffee shop to high-end dining, bars, and a nightclub, and an outdoor stage. It's fun and not at all threatening. There's no sense of being compelled to gamble, although a lot of people do. Instead it feels like a shopping mall. Devoid of civic space, Las Vegans use such private commercial space as public space, a style of use that casino executives and others who point to the value of gaming as an industry tout as an advantage. It costs the state nothing, they say, and in fact generates that paragon of Nevada revenue, sales tax. Station casinos are friendly to everyone and all kinds of people like them. They were the first chain to include an interracial couple in their television advertising. This subtle portrayal—Las Vegas's sense of freedom extends to personal relationships in ways that don't occur so easily in other places—deftly nodded toward a local reality that most advertisers avoid. What's wrong?

The use of private space as public space masks something insidious, a combination of the many flaws of government and the hidden pressures that are ripping American society apart. In public space, the postmodern definition of freedom—the right to do as you want, whenever you want, however you want, and with whomever you want—holds. All kinds of obnoxious behavior, from people handing you pamphlets for prostitutes and outcall services to pounding boomboxes with amplified bass, are legal and are widely tolerated. In private or controlled public space, whether it's a casino, an airport, or a mall, that isn't the case. The property owner retains the right to exclude as long as that exclusion occurs in an impartial manner. If they forbid by activity instead of by appearance or skin color, the law will uphold their decision. In a public park, you do have to worry about who is out there, who might impose upon you in all kinds of ways. You have to share space in a fashion that requires that you and others to regulate the space for yourselves. You have to trust the people around you to live by the same rules as you do. There's no arbitrator, no handy authority to march out and rule against someone who refuses to leave you alone. You have to sort it out yourself.

But in private space, especially in a casino through which millions of dollars float on a daily basis, there are rules and there are arbitrators. Make so much as a hard and fast motion toward someone else, and the eye in the sky will alert a number of the large, suit-coated men whose job it is to make sure everyone gets to play unmolested, and they'll pounce. The offender will be removed from the area and probably from the premises so quickly that whatever happened will be a brief interruption in the eternal quest for leisure. Private space permits security, a comfort we associate with a rose-colored past of shared values and avid citizenship. It was also a shared past because many were excluded, by race, ethnicity, religion, and on all kinds of other esoteric grounds, and because the people who determined the values of common culture could enforce that through media, with the law at their back, and if necessary with the force that only wealth could buy. After thirty years of the triumph of individual rights over community, in an era that has scrapped notions of common values, the public spaces have become maddening. It's the private spaces that now articulate privilege and prerogative, that offer privacy and security, that let people be free enough "from" to do as they please.

In this sense, the new organization of public/private and truly private space that Las Vegas has engendered is the equivalent of commercial gated communities. In Nevada, gaming space is open to anyone of legal age. You can enter, but you can stay only as long as you conform. There's a Big Brother-type atmosphere. The cameras, the eye in the sky, and the security officers abound, creating an illusion of safety along with that of the perceived danger that seems to insist upon their presence. You're safe from whatever lurks in or out here. Enjoy yourself, secure in the knowledge that you're protected by private security, which keeps you safer than the state can promise to do.

This division is a step on the road to a very different society. Turmoil in the American economy broke the middle class into two distinct groups, the large downwardly mobile cohort of the old middle class and the professionals and entrepreneurs who pushed upward. The 1990s restored prosperity, placing a premium on the trappings of privilege, on the ways people can make themselves distinctive. Even with the uniform crime index on the decline, Americans fear people unlike them. With immigration at an all-time high and local news featuring mayhem, the association is clear. Everyone knows their rights; few understand that they come with obligations. People widely perceive that the protections of the private sector are better than those of the public.

Even I have become comfortable at Home Courts; a year later, we know everyone there and they're our affinity friends. We socialize casually, transport kids too and fro, and generally keep an eye on what goes on. The life of the young is in view of their parents. We feel safer and maybe they do too. But if we do, it is because paying for space excludes those who can't, and American society today presumes that if you can't pay for space, there's something wrong with you. It's a very long way from Paul Revere.

PART IV

Public Identity

Chapter 10

To Serve the Living: The Public and Civic Identity of African American Funeral Directors

Suzanne Smith

[I]t dawned upon me with a certain suddenness that I was different from the others; or like, mayhap, in heart and life and longing, but shut out from their world by a vast veil. I had thereafter no desire to tear down that veil, to creep through; I held all beyond it in common contempt, and lived above it in a region of blue sky and wandering shadows.
—*W. E. B. Du Bois,* The Souls of Black Folk

I am an invisible man. No, I am not a spook like those who haunted Edgar Allan Poe; nor am I one of your Hollywood-movie ectoplasms. I am a man of substance, of flesh and bone, fiber and liquids—and I might even be said to possess a mind. I am invisible, understand, simply because people refuse to see me.
—*Ralph Ellison,* Invisible Man

The House of Diggs . . . the funeral home that does the most to serve the living.
—*Advertisement for the House of Diggs Funeral Home, Detroit, Michigan, 1965*

African Americans historically have had a fraught relationship with public culture and, consequently, with their public identity. W. E. B. Du Bois's metaphor of the veil, which captures both the envy and contempt black Americans have felt toward the white world, centers on the idea of the veil as visual barrier. The veil both obscures the wearer from being seen and empowers one's ability to survey others without being noticed. The portrayal of invisibility as depicted in Ralph Ellison's novel *Invisible Man* offers the more stark idea that African Americans do not have a public identity as they are completely ignored by those who, through their own racism, refuse to acknowledge their existence. The message of both of these seminal African American texts is clear: public culture has no place for those individuals who do not fit the dominant white ideal of American identity. For this reason, any examination of African Americans' attempts to participate in public culture must first begin with the acknowledgment that these ventures were rarely, if ever, welcomed by the larger American society.

How, then, do we begin to understand African Americans' place in American public culture? How has the African American fight for racial equality and full citizenship been shaped by this pattern of exclusion from the public sphere? One of the most useful ways to measure the public and political life of minority groups involves acknowledging that some of the most strategic activity occurs in covert and hidden ways—from "behind the veil." Political anthropologist James C. Scott argues that subordinate groups are always negotiating a type of "infrapolitics," which he describes as the "hidden transcripts" of resistance that oppressed groups use against the "public transcript" of the "dominant elites."[1] Scott argues that "[s]o long as we confine our conception of the political to activity that is openly declared we are driven to conclude that subordinate groups essentially lack a political life . . . [t]o do so is to miss the immense political terrain that lies between quiescence and revolt."[2] Consequently, it is essential to find ways to more closely examine how the "infrapolitics" of African Americans influences their relationship to public culture.

In order to understand this dynamic, I present here a brief case study of the history of African American funeral directing, which will provide an example of how one group of African Americans has sought to influence public culture and have a public identity. African American funeral directors hold a unique place in African American life. Often the most successful business people in their respective communities, African American funeral directors historically have used their prominence as local leaders to actively engage in public life. The advertisement copy from Charles C. Diggs's funeral home, the House of Diggs, quoted in the epigraph raises an intriguing question: how do African American funeral directors "serve the living" while burying the dead? Since the funeral industry began in the mid-nineteenth century, African American funeral directors have worked actively as civic leaders, politicians, and civil rights organizers. Moreover, these funeral directors sustained the cultural life of their local communities by acting as lay—and sometimes ordained—religious leaders, sponsoring radio stations, and promoting the arts and education through outreach programming. Yet relatively little historical research has been done to understand how funeral directing became such an influential, and public, profession within African American communities.

In this essay, I argue that African American funeral directors' relationship to the living was (and is) as important as their relationship to the dead. Specifically, I analyze how black funeral directors used their public role as community leaders in a variety of ways, most notably to combat racial discrimination. By exploring how these funeral directors served their communities, I demonstrate how black entrepreneurship created unique opportunities for African American funeral directors to construct a public identity and to engage in politics and infrapolitics that ultimately contributed to the broader fight for racial equality. African Americans' participation in the funeral industry offers a rich opportunity to understand some of the larger issues surrounding the involvement of any minority group in public culture.

For African Americans, the emergence of Jim Crow racial segregation after the Civil War completely truncated their ability to engage fully in public culture and, interestingly, paralleled the rise of the modern funeral industry. As soon as the war ended, the defeated Confederate states quickly tried to keep African Americans in a state of subservience by legislating "Black Codes" or laws. These codes sought to limit African Americans' ability to function as equal members of society and included legislation that prevented African Americans from owning property or firearms, testifying in court, and also threatened any unemployed African Americans with being criminally charged with vagrancy. The vagrancy legislation presaged the full implementation of Jim Crow segregation in the late nineteenth century in that it sought to monitor, control, and restrict African Americans' presence in the public sphere. Jim Crow segregation proliferated after the end of Reconstruction in 1877. Throughout the South, African Americans were prohibited from using public facilities such as trains, other forms of public transportation, and schools that were reserved for "whites only." After 1896, when the Supreme Court's *Plessy v. Ferguson* decision upheld the "separate but equal" doctrine of public accommodations, Jim Crow racial segregation became far more widespread and accepted. From this point on, African Americans' ability to participate in public culture was severely limited.

Against the backdrop of the rise of racial segregation, American death practices were also undergoing a significant transformation in the mid to late nineteenth century. Antebellum funeral rituals in the United States were primarily private, intimate affairs. When the funeral industry developed in the late nineteenth century, it created—as I will detail—a more public and commercialized concept of death and mourning. As the funeral business became more established and profitable, African Americans pursued the new field as an opportunity that was denied them in other trades and professions that more actively discriminated against them such as medicine. These funeral directors fought against some forms of discrimination from within the funeral industry, which sought to limit their participation in its professional organizations. Nevertheless, these same funeral directors also benefited from the Jim Crow racial segregation system as it provided them with a stable market of African American customers. In other words, as death became a public commodity in a segregated industrial America, capitalism created both new possibilities and limitations for African American funeral directors to influence public culture. For these reasons, the African American funeral director's role as a public figure was complex and often involved the sometimes-contradictory impulses to serve one's community and preserve the best interests of one's own business enterprise.

To best explore these complexities, I will look first at the shift in death practices from the early to the late nineteenth century, which witnessed the creation of the modern funeral industry. I analyze how African American funeral directors navigated discrimination within the industry and yet, at the same time, fought to maintain control over their portion of a very segregated marketplace. The degree to which many of these funeral directors were able to succeed in the business world largely determined how much they did or did not engage in traditional politics or infrapolitics to fight racial inequality. I conclude with some specific examples of African American funeral directors who engaged in infrapolitics to illustrate the complicated role black entrepreneurship played in the African American effort to participate in public culture and to attain full citizenship.

Death and Mourning in Nineteenth-Century America

Nineteenth-century America witnessed a remarkable transformation in funeral and mourning practices from private ceremony in the antebellum period to public ritual by the 1890s. Death, mourning, and burial all occurred at home in the rural funeral of the early nineteenth century. The dying person found comfort in the care of loved ones and perhaps the local physician or a member of the clergy. When death finally took place, close family members of the deceased performed the intimate tasks required to prepare the body for burial. These actions helped participants navigate their grief and strengthened family bonds during a time of loss. As soon as death was confirmed, survivors—usually the female members of the household—worked together to "lay out" the body. They washed and wrapped the corpse in a shroud or "winding sheet" and then placed it in a coffin. In warm weather, a large block of ice in a tub sat underneath the coffin to preserve the integrity of the corpse. The deceased was kept in the front room or parlor of the home from one to three days and was rarely, if ever, left alone. To represent the state of mourning, survivors often draped the room that held the deceased in black crepe, removed the furniture, and covered all mirrors.[3]

When they were ready to move the corpse to the place of burial, mourners gathered in the home of the deceased, said prayers over the body, and then began the funeral procession. Mourners, depending on their economic status, might then move to a meetinghouse or church for a more formal funeral service. After the religious ceremony, the family moved the body to its final resting place, which—in the early nineteenth century—was usually the grounds of the family farm. Respect for family ties, which allowed survivors to care so intimately for the deceased, was perhaps the most striking characteristic of antebellum funerals in rural America. By the end of the century, the intimacy of these early nineteenth-century funerals no longer existed and the change reflected how much urbanization and industrialization had completely altered American life. Funerals ultimately became a public ritual that occurred entirely outside of the domestic sphere.

The obvious shift in American funeral practices from a private family affair to a more commercialized and public ritual began at the time of the Civil War. The Civil War acted as a catalyst that would permanently alter Americans' relationship to death and mourning. The staggering carnage wrought by the war and the more than 600,000 deaths that resulted from the conflict created a cultural crisis of sorts that demanded new ways of managing death and burial. The massive casualties left many Americans struggling to reconcile their cherished beliefs about what constituted a dignified burial with the grim realities of sudden death on the battlefield. For logistical reasons, soldiers who died in battle were buried as soon as possible, often in makeshift graves near the site of combat. As death tolls rose over the course of the war, many families—especially of Union soldiers—demanded that the bodies of their dead be returned home for what was deemed a proper burial. Transporting these deceased soldiers home was not a simple task, however, especially in the heat of the summer months when decomposition occurred more rapidly.[4]

Consequently, embalming gained sudden and widespread popularity as an effective means to preserve the corpse for shipment home. Before the war, embalming had only limited use: for the preservation of cadavers for dissection in medical schools. The Civil War not only illustrated to the public that embalming could facilitate the grief process, but it also was critical to the early formation of the funeral industry.[5] Some embalmers went directly to the front lines of battle and advertised their ability to preserve the "honored dead." As embalming became a skilled trade, historical records from this time period clearly document evidence that African Americans were training as embalmers. In a personal journal, W. R. Cornelius, an established white embalmer, described his assistant, a man he refers to as Prince Greer. Cornelius wrote, "I undertook embalming myself with a colored assistant named Prince Greer, who appeared to enjoy embalming so much that he became himself an expert, kept on at work embalming through the balance of the war, and was very successful." Cornelius continued that Greer could "raise an artery as quickly as anyone, and was always careful," and only needed Cornelius's guidance when there was "a critical case," which indicates that he viewed Greer not simply as an assistant, but as a valued peer.[6]

While the popularity of embalming grew throughout the war, it became firmly established as an essential part of the mourning experience after the assassination and funeral of Abraham Lincoln. Lincoln's corpse, which traveled across the country on an extended funeral procession, dramatically advertised the marvel of embalming. Starting in Washington, D.C., Lincoln's funeral journey lasted a full twenty days before it reached its final destination in Springfield, Illinois. The cross-country cortege allowed American citizens—of all races—to pay their respects to the fallen leader. When the body finally arrived in Springfield, the embalmed corpse had begun to decompose. Nevertheless, the nation's ability to witness Lincoln's embalmed corpse for such an extended period of time taught the American public the important role embalming could play in the grieving process.[7]

Postbellum America witnessed the exponential growth of the funeral industry. A new era began in which death practices became commodities in the burgeoning industrial society and, as a result, funerals were envisioned as an important part of public culture and identity. The funeral industry fueled this trend toward the commercialization of death by offering a wider range of products and services to the buying public. Coffins, which had previously been made by cabinetmakers, evolved into the "casket" industry, which offered increasingly more ornate designs. Funeral directors began selling an array of products including burial robes and "mourning cards" that were given as mementos to grieving relatives and friends. The proliferation of these funeral products demonstrates how much the death experience in America had changed by the end of the nineteenth century into a very commercial enterprise.[8]

Within African American communities, the post–Civil War period witnessed the growth of burial societies, which were founded to assist individuals and families who could not afford all of the accoutrements of the modern funeral. Also known as "burial insurance," burial societies had members contribute money into a central fund that would then help pay or defray the costs of embalming and other funeral services when a member passed away. Many African American funeral directors founded burial societies of their own as a means to generate business. Before long, burial societies were questioned as a business practice. Opponents believed that they simply capitalized on people's fears of dying without a proper funeral, while proponents felt that they created a sense of communal responsibility to bury the dead with dignity. The popularity of burial societies proved how successful the funeral industry had become at selling the idea—especially to African Americans—that a respectable burial must include all of the requisite products and services.[9]

Funeral Directing as Profession

As the funeral industry became more commercially successful in the late nineteenth century, funeral directors sought to gain legitimacy with consumers by working to cultivate a public image as professionals. In the 1880s, two major developments revealed this shift toward professionalization: (1) the founding of embalming schools, and (2) the establishment of a national association of funeral directors. African American funeral directors participated in both of these trends, but not always on equal footing with their white counterparts.

In the case of the establishment of formal embalming schools, African American students surprisingly were allowed to enroll with white students. The most famous embalming school, which was founded by Dr. August Renouard, who is considered the first "dean" of embalming instruction, was the Rochester School of Embalming. Before these schools were created, training in embalming occurred only in medical schools or very informally as embalming chemical salesmen demonstrated their wares on the road. Embalming schools allowed funeral directors to get formal training and credentials as certified embalmers. By the turn of the century, African American students were among the graduates of the Rochester School of Embalming. Consequently, while the funeral business has been largely segregated by race, the training of embalmers has been—for the most part—racially integrated.[10]

The founding of the National Funeral Directors Association (NFDA) in 1882, which also sought to establish funeral directing as a legitimate profession, had a more complicated relationship to race. Membership in the association had many benefits, including: protection from unfair competition and fraud; increased credibility as a recognized professional rather than a mere tradesperson; and access to publications that disseminated trends in the industry. For example, one of the most prominent journals of the funeral business was *The Casket*, which reported on new embalming techniques, discussed marketing strategies for winning the patronage of middle and upper-class consumers, and advertised caskets and embalming fluids.

Given the advantages of membership in the NFDA and its founding during the height of Jim Crow segregation, it would be logical to assume that the organization was for whites only. Yet, for the first thirty years of its existence—from 1882 until 1912—the NFDA did *not* overtly discriminate against African American funeral directors. Since the organization was founded as a national group that oversaw state associations, each of which had individual constitutions and bylaws, it was difficult to monitor the practices of all state branches. There were, however, African American members of the NFDA, who were considered members primarily through their membership in state associations. In 1912, however, the constitution of the NFDA explicitly stated for the first time that, "no delegate . . . shall be admissible to membership in this association, however he may be accredited by a state or territorial association, who is not of the white race."[11]

Although it is not entirely clear why this discriminatory clause appeared in 1912, I speculate that the NFDA was motivated to restrict its membership by race at this time because funeral directing was becoming such a highly lucrative business venture. From the 1880s through the turn of the century, the number of American funeral directors grew rapidly and reflected general trends in population growth. In 1900, NFDA had a membership of 3,920 members; by 1910, this membership jumped to 9,281.[12] Moreover, the structure of the business also changed dramatically. Up through the turn of the century, most funeral directors maintained only a small office and did their embalming via house calls. By the second decade of the twentieth century, the funeral home, which acted as embalming clinic, business office, and chapel, had become the preferred venue for the business. This new multipurpose building gave funeral directors more credibility and control over the funeral service and an ability to increase their services and prices.[13] All of these developments, as well as the general racist tenor of the early twentieth century, which included pervasive Jim Crow segregation practices, increased lynching in the South, and race riots in the urban North, may have motivated the NFDA's more racially exclusive membership practices.

The Colored Embalmer: African American Funeral Directors Organize

Once they were barred from membership in the NFDA, African American funeral directors sought to establish their own professional organizations. The first association of African American funeral directors was a branch of Booker T. Washington's National Business League and was moderately successful at keeping members abreast of current developments in the field. In 1924, however, a group of funeral directors decided to break away from Booker T. Washington's organization and found their own group, the Independent National Funeral Directors Association. The leader of the new group was Robert R. Reed. Reed graduated in 1901 from Wilberforce University in Wilberforce, Ohio, with a bachelor of science degree. He worked for several years in the newspaper business before entering the funeral directing profession in West Virginia, and was one of the first African Americans to earn an embalming license from the West Virginia board. He eventually was hired as the first and only "colored reporter" for *Casket and Sunnyside*, the leading journal of the NFDA. In his work as a reporter for the journal, Reed became increasingly frustrated with the editors' unwillingness to let him report on stories relevant to black funeral directors. It was at this time that he was inspired to found the Independent National Funeral Directors Association and to publish the first trade journal for black funeral directors entitled *The Colored Embalmer*.

The Colored Embalmer became a critical tool of the Independent National Funeral Directors Association as it kept members abreast of industry trends, announced important meetings and conventions, offered advertising space to vendors and members, and actively discussed debates about the future of the profession from a "Negro" perspective. The editorial page also included a manifesto of the organization's broad goals including: (1) to support race manufacturers in the funeral industry; (2) to launch a finance company to protect the credit of Negro funeral directors; (3) to unite Negro funeral directors to elevate the standards of the profession; and finally, the most provocative goal, (4) "To use every instrument, argument within our realm *to induce White Funeral Directors to refuse to bury Negroes who seek their services*, when Negro Funeral Directors are equipped to bury their own dead" (italics mine).[14]

The goal of encouraging white funeral directors to, in essence, discriminate against Negro customers in the hopes of ultimately supporting the business of Negro funeral directors raises several important issues. First, it reveals how challenging it was for African American funeral directors to succeed in this burgeoning industry. Second, it indicates that some white funeral directors were offering their services to African American customers. Most important, it complicates the common assumption that racial segregation in the capitalist marketplace of the early twentieth century existed *only* as the result of racist practices on the part of white business owners. On the contrary, African American funeral directors clearly understood the benefits of a segregated market that would guarantee a steady customer base in an already competitive field. In fact, the competition between white and black funeral directors in the second decade of the twentieth century was so high that in 1918 black protesters in Jacksonville, Florida, blocked the funeral procession of a "prominent Colored family" because they had employed a white undertaker and overlooked "the race men in the same business."[15]

For these reasons, the Independent National Funeral Directors Association became one of the most influential African American business associations in the country. As is the case in many organizations, however, it was constantly challenged by internal politics among its members. Most notably, a faction of members began to question Robert Reed's leadership in the 1930s. They argued that Reed was not a practicing funeral director and, therefore, not the best person to head the organization. In 1938, the association changed its name to the Progressive National Funeral Directors Association and Reed assumed a less prominent role. By 1940, the group's name changed again to the National Negro Funeral Directors Association. Finally, in 1957, the organization dropped the word "Negro" from its title and settled on its current name, the National Funeral Directors and Morticians Association (NFDMA). These name changes alone reveal a fascinating, yet largely understudied, history of how African American funeral directors negotiated their public identity within the funeral industry.

The most dominant figure of the association in the postwar era was Robert Miller. Miller exemplifies the idea of the African American funeral director who "serves the living" as public servant, community leader, and entrepreneur. Miller began funeral directing in the 1920s and by the 1940s had established himself as one of the most prominent funeral directors in Chicago. In 1948, Miller became the general secretary of the National Negro Funeral Directors Association and, using his own finances, he began publishing *The National Funeral Director and Embalmer Magazine*, which served a function similar to *The Colored Embalmer*. One of Miller's most important contributions to the NFDMA was his outspoken support of the nascent civil rights movement. Through his leadership, the NFDMA was the first African American business association to donate $1,000 to the Southern Christian Leadership Conference and the Montgomery Bus Boycott in 1955.

In addition to donating funds to the civil rights struggle, African American funeral directors had another battle to fight to end the discriminatory practices of their own profession. By the late 1950s and early 1960s, several African American funeral directors began to directly protest the National Funeral Directors Association's "whites only" membership policies. By October 1963—a few months after the March on Washington—the NFDA officially dropped its white's only membership clause from its bylaws. Unfortunately, this gesture initially did not influence many state associations—particularly in the South—to end their restrictive membership practices. It was not until October 1970 that the NFDA took a hard line on racial discrimination and passed a new resolution that any state association that practiced racial discrimination would no longer be considered a part of the NFDA. Even today, the number of African American funeral directors who are members of the NFDA is relatively small.[16]

The Infrapolitics of African American Funeral Directing

While African American funeral directors worked collectively through professional associations such as the NFDMA to support themselves in an industry that was racially segregated, individual funeral directors also used their status as civic leaders to combat racial discrimination and segregation at the local level. In particular, I am interested in understanding how funeral directors in African American communities used their businesses and capital in unexpected and often surreptitious ways to further political goals. In other words, I define "political engagement" broadly to include activities that are not as overt as campaigning for public office or casting a ballot. In the case of African American funeral directors, individuals in the profession regularly engaged in infrapolitics, which encompasses a wide range of subversive and often hidden political acts of resistance.

The role of the funeral director as civil rights activist began as early as the landmark *Plessy v. Ferguson* decision of 1896, which established the concept of "separate but equal" segregation of public facilities. In 1890, New Orleans passed the Separate Car Act, one of the many Jim Crow laws passed in the post-Reconstruction South to keep African Americans segregated from whites in public places. The Separate Car Act ruled that "passenger trains shall have the power . . . to assign each passenger to the coach . . . used for the race to which such passenger belongs."[17] Soon after its passage, a group of influential black leaders in New Orleans founded the Citizens Committee for the Annulment of the Separate Car Act. Among the leaders of this organization were two prominent funeral directors, Alcée Labat and Myrthil J. Piron. Although Piron passed away soon after the Citizens Committee formed, Labat worked diligently to fight New Orleans's segregationist laws. Labat paid a price for his willingness to be a leader in the fight against racial segregation in New Orleans. In the midst of the *Plessy* case, Labat's funeral home was burned to the ground in an act of retaliation against the civil rights activist.[18] Although the Supreme Court ultimately ruled in favor of "separate but equal" facilities in the *Plessy* decision, Labat and others learned the value of using their clout as local business leaders to fight racial injustice.[19]

The activism of funeral directors such as Alcée Labat in the *Plessy* case was not an isolated occurrence. As the *Plessy* decision set the stage for the civil rights battles of the twentieth century, other African American funeral directors across the country took action to help their communities. In 1921, Charles C. Diggs Sr. opened his own funeral home, the House of Diggs, Inc., which became the largest black funeral home in Detroit and financially one of the most successful black businesses in the country.[20] Early on, Diggs used his business success to work with other prominent funeral directors to found the Detroit Memorial Park, which was the first cemetery in Michigan incorporated by African Americans. These funeral directors were responding to the overcharging and discrimination black customers experienced at white cemeteries in the city. The Detroit Memorial Park was located in Warren Township, north of the city of Detroit. When Diggs and his colleagues first purchased the land, there was not any resistance to the project. Yet, when local whites discovered the planned use of the real estate by black investors, a movement began to stop the project. In a move to secure the property for its designated use, Diggs and one of his fellow funeral directors quickly buried the body of a stillborn infant to insure that the land could not be reclaimed for other purposes.[21]

The Detroit Memorial Park not only provided African Americans with a dignified burial ground, but it also offered home loans to black Detroiters who were denied financial aid from white-owned banks. By using the funds from the Detroit Memorial Park to finance mortgages, the funeral directors who founded the cemetery created a viable means to private homeownership for African American Detroiters who were regularly discriminated against in the city's real estate market. Later in the postwar era, African American funeral directors in urban areas such as Detroit, Chicago, and Los Angeles would fight their own battles to maintain a foothold in the urban real-estate market as many urban renewal projects targeted their businesses for demolition.

Charles Diggs Sr.'s success in the funeral business motivated him to campaign for public office. In 1936, he became the first black Democrat to be elected to the Michigan State Senate. By the 1950s, his son, Charles C. Diggs Jr., followed his father's example when he took over management of the funeral home and was elected to Congress to serve in the House of Representatives. Representative Charles C. Diggs Jr. would also go on to be one of the key founders of the Congressional Black Caucus in 1969. Throughout the 1950s and 1960s, the House of Diggs Funeral Home was renowned in Detroit for serving its community and keeping African American citizens abreast of local and national political issues. For example, the funeral home sponsored a weekly *House of Diggs* radio show that announced who was buried each week, played gospel music, and publicized community events and political campaigns. The multifaceted quality of the House of Diggs Funeral Home illustrates a few ways in which African American funeral directors cultivated public and civic life within their respective communities.

While the Diggs family served in public office, other funeral directors facilitated the political life of their communities but in much less obvious ways. For instance, African American funeral directors have used and continue to use their hearses to drive people to the polls on election day.[22] Moreover, during early years of the nonviolent civil rights movement, certain funeral directors—particularly in the Deep South—used their caskets and hearses to assist civil rights activists, who were being threatened with violence. Hearses served as ambulances in rural areas and provided much-needed and less obtrusive means of transportation to civil rights workers. When some African Americans prepared to arm themselves in self-defense against those who threatened them with violence, local funeral directors were known to hide weapons in caskets.[23] Most poignantly, African American funeral directors have been asked to use their skills at embalming to make a political statement. When Emmett Till was lynched in Mississippi in 1955, his mother, Mamie Bradley, requested that his mutilated body be embalmed without any touch-ups and viewed in an open casket. Bradley claimed that she had insisted on the open casket, "so the world could see what they had done to my child." The media attention brought to the Till case—as a result of the open casket—awakened the American public both to the horrors of lynching and to the nascent civil rights movement. These are but a few examples of how African American funeral directors have acted both overtly and covertly to promote the political agendas of their communities.[24]

To conclude, African American funeral directors have "served the living" while burying the dead since the funeral profession first emerged after the Civil War. Their efforts to serve others have provided African American funeral directors with opportunities to engage with public culture and create a public identity by working for change at both the local and national level. Yet, the forces of the capitalist marketplace and the realities of racial discrimination throughout the United States have always complicated what this service entailed and whom it benefited most. For instance, in the early twentieth century, African American funeral directors were forced to create their own professional organization when they were excluded from membership in the National Funeral Directors Association. At the same time, these black entrepreneurs actively encouraged white funeral directors "to refuse to bury Negroes who seek their services, when Negro Funeral Directors [were] equipped to bury their own dead." Furthermore, in the 1920s individuals such as Charles C. Diggs Sr. established corporations such as the Detroit Memorial Park in an effort to give black Detroiters a dignified burial ground *and* a means to secure a home loan.

Put another way, when African American funeral directors "served the living" in the age of Jim Crow, it involved a very tricky dance between profit motives and the public good. As businesspeople, they recognized that racial segregation could be helpful to private enterprise and minority entrepreneurs. As civic leaders and civil rights activists, they were also well aware of the harm it inflicted on their communities and on society at large. As a result, these funeral directors walked a fine line when they used their status as successful business owners to become public leaders who worked to fight racial discrimination in their own neighborhoods through direct political action and infrapolitics as well. In the end, their efforts to end racial injustice in the public sphere always threatened their ability to maintain the stable minority market that a racially segregated society insures. The fight to end de jure racial segregation, of course, was a compelling one that took precedence over other business motives in the end. The continued existence of de facto racial segregation today, however, continues to provide African American funeral directors with a primarily minority consumer base and attests to the reality that the fight for both racial and economic equality for African Americans still continues.[25]

Chapter 11
Denizenship as Transnational Practice

Rachel Ida Buff

The city of Toledo is in northwest Ohio. Situated just south of Detroit, the Glass City, as it's called, has been in the Motor City orbit as long as there have been cars assembled in the region. Workers from western, central, and eastern Europe, the Middle East, Mexico, Indian reservations, and the American South gravitated to these cities throughout the great surge in automobile manufacturing that powered the national economy throughout the twentieth century. Michael Moore has illustrated the dramatic local effects of the eventual downturns in this industry in his documentary *Roger and Me.* Speaking in Toledo, Moore once proposed a tourist exchange between the exhausted denizens of Toledo and those of his nearby hometown of Flint, Michigan.

As a Rust Belt city, Toledo's history traces a specific and familiar arc: first world industrialization fueled by the labor immigration and migration (im/migration) of workers from less developed regions. As we slide down the far side of this arc, first world capital is, increasingly, exported to less developed regions in the third world, to take advantage of the cheap labor provided by free trade agreements, economic development zones, and the restrictions on organizing provided by repressive governments that have often been backed by U.S. foreign policy. And so, on a windy day in March, two Nicaraguan women stood in front of our local Kohl's to explain how a job making jeans in their home country did not pay them enough to afford milk for their children.

Such stories, and the relationships they sketch between first and third worlds, will likely be familiar to you. As will, perhaps, some tales of northwest Ohio as I continue, and ask you to drive south with me, to the small college town where I used to teach, about twenty miles from Toledo. Every morning, I would cross an invisible boundary, between the deindustrialized Rust Belt where I live, and the Farm and Bible Belt, where Bowling Green, Ohio, is.

Toledo and Detroit are working-class cities, with strong im/migrant institutions, such as churches and social organizations. They have Democratic, if conservative, politics. In contrast, small towns like Bowling Green define themselves with memories of much earlier migrations. Mad Anthony Wayne's rout of the pan-Indian coalition led by Shawnee brothers Tecumseh and Tenskwatawa cleared this part of the country for settlement by the marginal Euro-American settlers pushed west just after the American Revolution. (One way to get from Toledo to Bowling Green is to follow the county highway known as the Anthony Wayne Trail.) As local Indians were forced west, to Kansas and Oklahoma, these settlers were joined by Irish and German immigrants.

These im/migrant Euro-Americans drained the Great Black Swamp. The resulting landscape, one of the places in the entire world most transformed by human agency, yielded no hiding places for recalcitrant Indians, imagined or real, and provided rich, if completely flat, farmland. With strong histories of Klan activity, from the rise of the second Klan in the 1920s on, these flat counties seem entirely white and Christian, vote Republican, and profess a republicanism based on affinity to locale and suspicion of foreign ideas and influences.

This too, is a familiar story: the clearing of New World land and the removal of its indigenous inhabitants allowed for the building of small towns, each of which, in some ways, imagines itself as the true "City on the Hill" of American exceptionalism. And of course, like most familiar stories, it is not quite true. As agribusiness has replaced small farming, many white farmers in the region have been reduced to doing farm work on factory farms; many others have sought employment in a motley assortment of factory labor available in the region. Migrant workers from Mexico and farther south in Central America now do most of the farm work here. These workers arrive in late spring and work in tomatoes, pickling cucumbers, and other local crops until the fall. Most migrate seasonally, moving north with the warm weather, and then returning to Texas or farther south as winter approaches.

First World, Third World, New World

These worlds—first, third, new—are not geographically distinct entities. The presence of the third world in the first is the result of so-called "free" trade and labor migration. And the idea of a "new world," an empty frontier landscape, has persisted, from the fifteenth century on, despite immediate evidence that this New World had long been inhabited and cultivated, and despite technology that can map the world into meters or fly an unoccupied drone to a deadly errand in the desert. These worlds constantly overlap, providing the sociological and visual juxtapositions that have led to descriptions of our current era as "postmodern."

It is possible, in northwest Ohio, to stand in a field worked by Mayan-speaking im/migrants from Chiapas or Guatemala, regarding their slickers hanging to dry from the rain and the pesticides, from which they lack any legal protection, and to see across the field the half-million-dollar houses being constructed for suburban residents of Perrysburg, named for Commodore Oliver Hazard Perry, who helped defeat the British and their native allies here during the War of 1812. Or to drive in the shadow of the Davis-Besse nuclear power plant, which came within 3/8 of an inch of melting down in March of 2002, into the marshes of Maumee Bay as it meets Lake Erie. Sport fishermen intent on re-creating that New World feeling of solitary contact with the wild drive these roads, bypassing the shacks that house migrant workers, stopping in diners whose bathrooms sport racist, anti-immigrant graffiti. In Wauseon, near the Indiana line, the mayor in 1998 supported a local English-only proposition by arguing, "It's like going to a football game and rooting for our team." Lawyers for Toledo's Farm Labor Organizing Committee recently won a case against the state highway patrol for racial profiling, arguing that the patrol could not stop vans with southwestern license plates for speeding and then ask for everyone's immigration papers.[1] Such niceties are quickly becoming extinct in the post-PATRIOT Act era. In Detroit's "Mexican-town," Chicano Brown Berets work with Arab American organizers to proclaim an "INS-free zone," where im/migrants can be safe from deportation.

It is my contention that these worlds—first, third, new—have long been adjacent and entwined, as they are in northwest Ohio; that the project of American Empire has always been both far-flung and intimate. Connections between these worlds complicate the cultural constructs that shape public policy and our visions of public culture.

Recent work, particularly in Asian American studies, shows the ways that citizenship has long been racialized by law and by public practice. Scholars have argued that if Asians were denied access to citizenship as "aliens ineligible for naturalization" from 1790 through the early 1940s, then this history of exclusion must transform not only the struggles of Asian American communities, but the category of citizenship itself. Lisa Lowe and other scholars have argued that citizenship for all is defined, and delimited, by the policies that police citizenship at the margins. Asian immigration has been the ground on which the state has attempted to resolve the inequalities of capitalist democracy and a multiracial workforce.[2] Yen Le Espiritu quotes Stuart Hall arguing that citizenship is one of "those images, concepts and premises which provide the frameworks through which we represent, interpret, understand and 'make sense of' some aspect of social existence."[3]

Legal scholar John S. W. Park has written eloquently about the contradiction in American political thought "between principles of equality and fairness on the one hand, and principles of national sovereignty with bounded political communities on the other."[4] This contradiction is as evident at the walls being built at the U.S.-Mexico border as it is in our public culture. Tensions between liberalism's commitment to equality and justice for all and the necessity of reinforcing national boundaries accelerate in an increasingly transnational global political economy, intensifying a long-running culture war over the position of "aliens" in the national community. On the one hand, free trade agreements secure the mobility of capital, while the enduring clamor for immigration reform and immigrant responsibility limit the movement of people across borders and, increasingly, within the nation-state.

These contradictions produce a class of semipermanently stateless low-wage workers. Immigrant rights' advocates speak of "globalization from below," in which workers would migrate freely, transforming the definitions of citizenship itself as they do so, but national policies have tended to reinforce militarized borders and increasingly limited definitions of citizenship.[5] This contradiction also generates a conflict between the lived experiences of these workers and their legal status. Their legal status might be described as denizenship, rather than citizenship—as a category that describes the legal and cultural condition of people proscribed from citizenship, but perhaps no less engaged in the process of what generations of scholars and reformers have called "Americanization."

The historical evolution of citizenship has always entailed the existence of those who do not benefit from its protections and rights—denizens, who inhabit a nation, sometimes for generations, without the benefit of political representation or cultural recognition. Where American public culture has been premised on the Jeffersonian notion of engaged citizenship, many people without access to the legal protections of citizenship practice what might be called engaged denizenship: they are involved in their communities and loyal to their countries. While citizenship confers official rights of representation, its absence has not meant a historical lack of political subjectivity on the part of denizens. Instead, denizens have constantly challenged the boundaries of citizenship, in many cases expanding them, and in other cases, forcing the state to publicly articulate its justification for their ongoing exclusion. In what follows, I want to trace the entwining of worlds and categories of identity, as it has shaped the post–1945 period, a time that we really can no longer call the "postwar period" (post which war would that be?), but that is, nonetheless, crucial to the shaping of our current moment.

The Imperial Order and the National Family

In the period immediately following World War II, the United States consolidated a global empire of political and economic alliances, as well as social and cultural influence. Seen through the American Cold War prism, the world was a turbulent and menacing place, fraught with expansionist Soviet totalitarianism and a newly decolonizing third world likely to fall prey to it. Based on their earlier adventures with imperial and domestic frontiers, Cold War politicians colored the world into black-and-white distinctions: good and evil, freedom and slavery, democracy and totalitarianism, and capitalism and socialism. These distinctions, in turn, mobilized discourses of race, gender, and sexuality to domesticate both national and international spheres. The inevitable colonial interventions abroad were contiguous with the disciplining of bodies at home.

While foreign policy and immigration had long been entwined prior to the Cold War, the regulation of aliens entering the civic body became something of a political obsession, in light of contemporary concerns for subversion and infiltration. The transformation of aliens into citizens was a central issue in public policy. Whether they were domestic dissenters, native "communalists," or immigrants at specific risk for being foreign agents, aliens to the social body needed transformation. A gendered ideology of a national family helped to organize social politics in this period. Threatening aliens could become cheerful citizen-family members by passing through state-mediated rituals of naturalization. And, in the prevailing patriarchal order of the day, those allowed into the family, as wives, children, and stepchildren, were compelled to adopt its ways. As anthropologist Ann Stoler has noted, managing the "conjugal relations of empire" has always entailed the regulation of citizen and foreign bodies, and any possible relations between them.[6]

This imperial public policy had specific implications for the relationships between first, third, and new worlds. Domestic policy toward Indian

nations, "the nations within," as Vine Deloria has called them, paralleled immigration and foreign policy in important ways.[7] Indian *people* were redis-
covered as a national problem in the wake of their heroic and disproportionate
service in World War II, represented most vividly in the popular imagination
by the story of Ira Hayes. Communalist Indian *nations*, however, were viewed
as antagonistic to the project of Cold War democracy. To marry into the national family, to be eligible for the benefits as well as depredations of citizenship, immigrants, Indians, and other internal aliens had to change.

Consider the year 1952. Congress overrode presidential vetoes to pass
the McCarran-Walter Immigration Act. This act reinstated race-based national origins quotas at the same time that it ended the long-standing ban on
the naturalization of Asians. It also implemented a distinction, still on the
books and very much central to our understanding of immigration and
refugee politics to this day, between "economic" and "political" refugees: essentially, those fleeing regimes more and less friendly to the United States. It
has been true since that time almost without exception, that lighter skinned
immigrants turn out to be more eligible for consideration as "political"
refugees, deserving asylum, while darker ones are deemed "economic" and
undeserving, even if they are fleeing national economies shuddering from
the ravages of U.S.-backed World Bank economic policy. Think about
Haitians and Cubans, Hondurans and Nicaraguans; Guatemalans or Sal-
vadorans during their long, CIA-inspired civil wars; think about black Cuban
"Marielitos" or Bush's recent statement on Haitian boat people.

The fact that McCarran-Walter was racially restrictive legislation that at
the same time ended the long-standing ban on the naturalization of Asian
immigrants has presented an interesting paradox for historians. Was this a
part of a broader, civil rights moment represented by the historic *Brown v.
Board* decision? The law set tiny quotas for immigrants from Asia and newly
decolonized nations in Africa and mobilized potent distinctions between deserving and undeserving refugees. We can resolve this seeming paradox by
thinking globally rather than nationally. It's key that Asian exclusion ended
at a time of escalating U.S. military involvement in Asia, and also that the
McCarran-Walter Act of 1952, while reasserting national origins as an important way of screening new immigrants, institutionalized the war brides programs of World War II and Korea as a permanent feature of immigration law.
The wives of GIs were seen as particularly desirable, tractable immigrants;
and the necessity of bringing these women in would be a permanent feature
of a militarized postwar order. In general, immigrants, the great majority of
whom would be women in the postwar period, entered the nation as femi-

nized partners, subject to wifely transformation to become a member of the family. Immigration and foreign policy mediated the boundaries of the Cold War imperial order.

Congress also implemented Public Law 280 in 1953. This law, unironically called "termination policy," sought to end the trust relationship between Indians and the federal government. Under termination, land claims would be individualized, Indians would, in the language of the time "become citizens"—even though they had been considered such since 1924—and reservations would disappear into local counties. The dual claims of Indian people to citizenship in the United States and their own Indian nations had been a crucial component of federal jurisprudence since Justice John Marshall deemed Indians "domestic, dependent nations" in 1831. But termination policy twisted the rhetoric of the African American civil rights movement to argue that their loyalty to tribal nations impeded the access of Indian people to full citizenship. Thus, the "nations within" were also subject to the project of regulating "the conjugal relations of empire."[8]

Termination was to complete the "break up of the tribal land mass" begun by the Dawes Allotment Act in the late nineteenth century. In addition, the termination project included a relocation program, which was to bring Indians off reservations, relocate them into cities, and, hopefully, naturalize them into life as American consumer-citizens. While these policies intended to "bring Indians in" to the national family, the implementation of termination and relocation proposed great losses for Indian people, both in terms of their land and their own family arrangements.[9] In Menominee, Wisconsin, for example, the Bureau of Indian Affairs focused on teaching Indian women how to cook and garden in preparation for termination and relocation. Not, presumably, because Indian women didn't know how to prepare food for their families, but because the ways that they prepared it, who did the cooking and gardening and hunting, were not deemed appropriate for life as American citizens. Citizenship holds the possibility for not only enfranchisement, but for coercion, for loss.

As proffered by postwar public policy, citizenship represented a narrowing of identity for many people. In the stories I have presented here, immigrants and Indians, two groups of people whose complex cultural loyalties challenged a political identity predicated on a narrow, national model, came in for scrutiny and transformation into manageable citizen-subjects, compliant wives of the Cold War order. Because it was so crucial to Cold War policy to divide and map the world into first, third, and New World constituencies, these new citizens were asked to choose and publicly ratify their alliances. This historic moment has clear parallels with our own, in which those with complex political, cultural, or national loyalties are subject to scrutiny, incarceration, deportation, and other forms of coercion. And, as our current conditions so sharply remind us, such narrowing of citizenship and loyalty is rarely liberating.

Citizenship became a contested terrain in this period, a culture war, in historian Nikhil Singh's term.[10] At the same time that federal policy makers set out to create a safe way of filtering the addition of internal and external aliens into the national body, Indian and immigrant groups organized to press for inclusion on their own terms. As a result of this pressure, the politics of transformation would yield to new definitions of citizenship and political identity. Just as the world does not divide so easily into the Cold War order of first and third, free and unfree, good and evil, resistance to the coercive aspect of citizenship has often taken the form of insisting on alternative identities.

Immigrants and Indians retained cultural and political connections to their homelands, despite the clear implication of public policy that they become politically monogamous from this moment forward. Their political struggles allied them with other groups working for social change, often defining themselves as much by culture or neighborhood as by nation. In the following section, I want to explore the politics and practices of denizenship in a contemporary context.

Denizenship in a Time of Crisis

Let's return to the location of northwest Ohio. The Farm Labor Organizing Committee (FLOC) succeeded in 1998 in putting legal opposition on the books to the very common practice of racial profiling. The scenario usually went something like this: a highway patrol officer pulls over an older vehicle, say a van with Texas plates, for speeding or for having out-of-date tags. After issuing the ticket for whatever the appropriate infraction, the officer then asks to see everyone's immigration papers. Before the Federal Sixth Circuit, lawyers for FLOC successfully argued that this practice constitutes racial profiling, since highway patrol officers rarely ask for the immigration papers of white folks with similar traffic infractions.

This case was initiated in 1998, and concluded before September 11, 2001. In our current time of national and international crisis, however, the significance of this precedent is likely to be minimal. The PATRIOT Act passed in late 2001 abridges many constitutional protections of civil liberties and gives the federal government the right to scrutinize everyone, in particular, immigrants who are legal residents but not citizens, even at the risk of racial profiling.[11] What are the politics of denizenship at such a moment of crisis?

The trend in immigration and naturalization policy since the mid-1980s has been to put pressure on noncitizens to naturalize and to diminish the rights of those who do not or cannot do so. As with termination policy, the stated goal here is for everyone possible to enjoy the rights of citizenship. But, looking at northwest Ohio and the rest of the nation, we can see that resident but noncitizen and undocumented im/migrants are here for a reason. The pressure on their home economies from free trade and the need for workers in the United States ensures the continued migration of people with complex loyalties and, increasingly, lack of access to citizenship rights in this country. Campbell, Del Monte, Mount Olive, and Heinz need Mexican, Guatemalan, Honduran and Salvadoran workers, and they get them.

In 2003, Toledo City Council member Louis Escobar, working with Baldemar Velasquez, the head of the Farm Labor Organizing Committee, introduced a motion to allow denizens to use foreign ID cards to obtain gas and electrical accounts and register their kids for school. At a hearing in August, other council members and the city police chief voiced their concerns that allowing noncitizens this kind of access could pose security risks. Using such denizenship rights, they argued, noncitizens might set up vast crime networks; they might slip by police undetected, as the hijackers of 9/11 did. There was vigorous debate in an open session. Two-thirds of the city council chambers were filled with FLOC members, Latino and Latina workers who took days off from the harvest to come speak about the importance of this motion to them, or, for the many people who did not speak English, to stand witness. There were lots of kids there.

The motion eventually passed council unanimously. This means that migrant workers in Toledo can put their kids in school, rent an apartment, or get a bank account, without coming up against the everyday segregation imposed on those without citizenship rights. It does not, of course, protect them from being stopped on the highway or subject to so much of the rest of the racial harassment that has become legitimate in this PATRIOT Act era. Nor will it necessarily stand up against the specifications mandated by the REAL ID Act, a component of the Emergency Supplemental Appropriations Act for Defense, the Global War on Terror, and Tsuami Relief Act of 2005.[12] The very name of the legislative package in which the REAL ID Act was bundled elucidates the contradictions of public culture in our current era. In order to become more global and address catastrophes and risks like terrorism and tsunamis, the rights of denizens to carry out vital daily activities like driving a car and taking the kids to school are curtailed. Access to a public culture containing libraries, schools, and highways is increasingly delimited. What effect might this segregation have on our public culture?

Acting to allow noncitizens more expanded rights is not a retreat from the crucial struggle to protect constitutional rights for citizens. Rather, it is an acknowledgment that the fates of citizens and denizens have always been entangled and mutual; that the boundaries we draw between worlds, while having their own reality and force, do not accurately describe the im/migrant, multiply connected realities that continue to constitute everyday life.

Conclusion

I have argued that the idea of first, third, and new worlds organizes a specific map of the world. And that this map is useful, but it fails to describe the complex history of any given county, province, reservation, or borough. Further, that the term "im/migration," as an imaginative turn, might help us to see the parallels between, for instance, Indians moving from sovereign reservations to cities, and Latino/Latina undocumented workers spending much of their lives in places where they are perceived and legally limited to being foreigners.

Particularly at this historical moment, it is important that we recognize how crucial the struggle for full citizenship within the nation-state has been to so many people. At the same time, though, citizenship also describes a limited map of the world. In this "free trade" era, capital is free to move across borders. Workers follow. In order to conceive of how these workers might have access to political power and social enfranchisement, we can retrieve a notion of "denizenship," a word often used to describe the inhabitants of scary, border spaces—Nayan Shah describes the way nineteenth-century reformers viewed denizens of Chinatown as living in a dirty, opium- and vice-ridden shadow city to San Francisco.[13] But we are all denizens—we all struggle locally for full rights. The idea that we might be denizens as well as citizens of various official nations can aid us in uniting locally and globally. Recognition of the public culture of denizenship allows for a transnational public culture that brings together denizens of variously imagined first, third, and new worlds.

Chapter 12

The Queen's Mirrors: Public Identity and the Process of Transformation in Cincinnati, Ohio

Mary E. Frederickson

On a warm summer night in late August 2004, a candlelight procession of seven hundred men, women, and children walked slowly across the 140-year-old suspension bridge that spans the Ohio River between Covington, Kentucky, and Cincinnati, Ohio. Their voices raised in song, the Freedom Center Choir retraced the route followed by generations of enslaved Americans who had crossed that "River Jordan" in search of freedom. The procession filed onto a wide stage where an array of national, state, and local public officials, together with representatives from Cincinnati's largest corporations waited to speak at the public dedication of the newly opened National Underground Railroad Freedom Center, widely acclaimed as the latest jewel in the Queen City's crown.[1]

For government and corporate leaders in Cincinnati the Freedom Center represents a fervent hope for civic transformation. In recent years the city's reputation for intolerance has spread throughout the country. In 2000, the Census Bureau declared Cincinnati the eighth most segregated city in the nation. Riots broke out in the city in 2001, as thousands protested deeply entrenched police brutality. After years of intense racial conflict, the NAACP in 2002 declared Cincinnati "ground zero for race relations in America." In November 2004, three months after the National Underground Railroad Freedom Center opened, Cincinnati was ranked as one of the top three "meanest" cities in the nation, based on public policies regarding the homeless.[2]

The development of this new museum in a community with a long history of racial and ethnic conflict reflects the conscious use of culture to transform public identity. This essay examines the processes of negotiation, confrontation, and cooperation through which public institutions compromise with diverse public constituencies to define and control a shared urban identity. Public identity is often thought of in terms of individuals in relation to their social identities. Public identities, therefore, are social identities that get defined and negotiated through the intersections of history and culture, an idea reinforced by the predominance of identity politics.[3] This essay suggests that public identity applies not only to citizens within a community, but also to the places they inhabit. Recent scholarship in public memory and the invention of tradition corroborates this conception. Dolores Hayden's *Power of Place* makes this point strongly, arguing that "public processes that recognize both the cultural and the political importance of place" can "nurture citizens' public memory." The collective nature of this memory encompasses, in Hayden's words, "shared time in the form of shared territory." The interrelationship between public space, memory, and identity underscores the connection between personal memories and collective or social memories held by families, neighbors, groups of workers, and communities.[4]

In American cities like Cincinnati a recognition of shared history has the potential of conveying a sense of collective civic identity. But this can happen only after institutions have consciously engaged diverse publics in a process of negotiation; or conversely, after various constituencies of citizens have used whatever means at their disposal to make their ideas known to public institutions. These forms of negotiation and engagement focus on how culture, in the form of patterns of meanings explicitly or implicitly embedded in signs, symbols, languages, and codes, can shape a shared public identity.[5] Building on Dolores Hayden's work, "The Queen's Mirrors" demonstrates how public identity is constructed along a continuum that ranges from individual to collective identities. This essay suggests that the concept of public identity focused on individual, collective, and civic identities needs to be expanded to incorporate the intersection between publics and the locales they inhabit.

In the nineteenth century Americans hailed Cincinnati as "the fair Queen of the West: distinguished for order, enterprise, public spirit, and liberality."[6] For almost two hundred years, the city has embraced this noble designation, incorporating a crown into its civic flag and emblazoning its police cars with a coronet. But the city was also the site of intense divisions between abolitionists and pro-slavery activists in the years before the Civil War. Both in the antebellum period and in the decades that followed the war, riots caused by racial oppression and ethnic discrimination erupted on a regular basis in Cincinnati: in 1829, in 1841 and 1884, throughout the twentieth century, and most recently in 2001. In a city shaped by commercial competition, divisive class-based politics, and racial, ethnic, and religious diversity, cultural institutions have long been used to project different facets of a shared public identity.[7]

The Freedom Center, conceptualized by executive director Spencer Crew, as a "museum of conscience," openly challenges us to explore the processes of negotiation and transformation that can take place in contemporary museums. In 1930, French philosopher Georges Bataille described the modern museum as a "colossal mirror" in which the residents of a city can find themselves admirable. Bataille's observation affirms the theoretical role of the Freedom Center in contemporary Cincinnati, but also raises questions about the process of negotiating public identities in the United States. Is Bataille's description of the modern museum as a "colossal mirror" reflecting civic virtue still applicable in an age that museum scholar Neil Harris sees as one of continuous "existential scrutiny?" Ivan Karp argues that Harris is correct when he asserts that in recent decades "the relations between museums and audiences have . . . taken on more overtly political overtones." In 1991, philosopher Denis Dutton argued when reviewing Ivan Karp and Stephen D. Lavine's *Exhibiting Cultures*, that "museums . . . have become battlegrounds." Few disagree: "Politics has erupted publicly into the imagined sanctity of . . . museums," writes social anthropologist Sharon Macdonald, while political scientist Timothy Luke echoes Karp and Harris when he contends that museums are "frontline emplacements for competing classes, groups, or regions."[8]

In this environment, museums and other central institutions of civil society, defined by Benedict Anderson as "institutions of power," perform the work of social reproduction, but at the same time are subject to ongoing cultural deconstruction. Clearly, contemporary museums struggle to manage political relationships with an increasing number of communities and constituencies. In "The Queen's Mirrors" I argue that these negotiations took place in the past as well as the present, and that eighteenth- and nineteenth-century Americans, like their counterparts in the twentieth and twenty-first centuries, also struggled to create civic institutions that reinforced a particular public identity. How have Americans, over time, consciously and unconsciously transformed public identity in response to multiple voices contesting for influence? How have museums used their power to classify, define, and represent? Through which processes of negotiation do museums, in anthropologist Ivan Karp's words, "reproduce structures of belief and experience through which cultural differences are understood?"[9]

The history of the American city chosen as the site of the National Underground Railroad Freedom Center, offers some answers to these questions, particularly regarding how communities use museums to engage in the process of negotiating public identity, and how this process has changed over time. Beginning in the late 1810s, when Cincinnati was the largest hub of American culture west of the Alleghenies, the city crowned itself the "Queen City," and then spent almost two centuries defending that title. Marked by growth and progress, as well as by loss and decline, this city, like others in the United States, has used public identity in three transformative ways: first, to restore what has been lost; second, to celebrate its history; and third, to incorporate repressed aspects of civic life. The process of using culture to negotiate public identity is highlighted in Cincinnati's history, but it is woven into the fabric of every American city, for as cultural theorist Michel de Certeau has argued, the city always functions as a place of "transformations and appropriations."[10]

Many American cities have followed trajectories like Cincinnati's: rapid growth in the years after their founding, followed by a plateau and then a slow decline. Before the Civil War, location and rich natural resources lured people and industry to Cincinnati; commercial jobs drew immigrants and migrants until the city's population ranked among the highest in the nation. By 1840, Cincinnati's cultural reputation was well recognized and the "Western Metropolis" was hailed as the "Paris of America." Then as trade routes shifted and railroads replaced steamboats, first St. Louis and then Chicago became the premier city of "inland America," leaving Cincinnati in a distant third place.[11] Cincinnati is interesting, not because it remained the biggest or the best, like New York, Chicago, or Los Angeles, but because it did not. Most important, it was when the city failed to keep pace in terms of industry, commerce, and finance, that it sought most vigorously to establish prowess as a cultural center and to use public culture to transform its identity. As Mary Kupiec Cayton argues in this volume, "[t]he problem of defining public culture . . . depends on identifying where contestations for meaning take place and . . . what form those contestations may take." Cayton underscores the importance of both place (where contestation for meaning happens) and process (what forms the contestation takes, who participates, and the actions taken). All of these, Cayton tells us, "are historically contingent and contested questions." As such they help us think about problems of cultural identity, power, and the contestation of meaning in a postmodern world in which talking about American culture, past or present, involves discussing "an open-ended set of meanings or processes which, far from being agreed upon and uncontested, are negotiated, disputed, accommodated, and modified over time."[12]

Construction of the National Underground Railroad Freedom Center is Cincinnati's most recent attempt to show a better face to the nation and the world, but this effort to redefine the city's character is but one in a long series of similar undertakings. The metaphor for Cincinnati has always been a queen, and if we think of a queen not as a static entity, but as what it is, a personification of the city, then this metaphor has a life cycle that illuminates the process of urban cultural transformation.[13] In Cincinnati's case, the Queen's reign follows this pattern: the late eighteenth century witnessed a Virgin Queen who ruled over a forest and green hills untouched by Europeans; in the nineteenth century we see a Reigning Monarch whose wealth and power waxed in glory days and then declined. The early twentieth century Queen fades into an aging dowager, basking in past glories. In the later part of the twentieth century the image of the Queen turns queer, exposing the contradictions, dualities, and heterogeneities of civic culture, and the repressed underside of city life. At the beginning of the twenty-first century the Queen's heirs struggle to unite their disparate identities. The city's major museums bear witness to each of these stages of cultural transformation. Moreover, the history of these institutions reveals a common pattern: each was founded to transform the public identity of the city in specific ways in the eyes of both local residents and the outside world.

Taken together the city's museums reflect multiple aspects of the Queen City's public identity; however, each institution also reproduces a dominant cultural memory. The city's "museumizing imagination," as Benedict Anderson has described the profoundly political process of museum formation, has resulted in the establishment of five major institutions built over a time span of almost two hundred years.[14] The Natural History Museum, founded as the "Western Museum" in 1818, tells the story of the land before the city, of the river and the ancient people who lived nearby. The Cincinnati Art Museum contains highly valued artifacts, paintings, prints, sculpture, pottery, and textiles that connect the city to its European roots. The Taft Museum, housed in an early nineteenth-century mansion, mirrors elite style during the city's heyday. The Contemporary Arts Center reflects the Queen as queer and a controversial culture that blurs the boundaries of sexualities, races, and classes. The dedication of the National Underground Railroad Freedom Center in the summer of 2004 culminated over a decade of civic regeneration during which the National History Museum moved to a new building, the Cincinnati Art Museum added a new wing, the Taft underwent a major renovation, and the Contemporary Arts Center constructed "the most important American building to be completed since the end of the cold war," designed by Iraqi-born architect Zaha Hadid.[15] Cincinnati's newest museum, the Freedom Center, faces the river, symbolically forming a new front door to the city as it bears witness to the legacy of American slavery. Construction, controversy, and renovations have transformed the institutions that Cincinnatians often refer to as the "jewels in the Queen's crown." As it turns out, these recent quests for cultural transformation as a way of redefining the city's identity fit into a repeating pattern of shaping public culture that stretches from the late eighteenth century to the present.

The Virgin Queen: A Natural History

The Western Museum opened its doors in Cincinnati in 1818, the first natural history museum west of the Allegheny Mountains. John J. Audubon worked there as a taxidermist, and a few years later, noted sculptor Hiram Powers got his start there too, carving wax figures for the exhibits. From its inception the founders of the Western Museum conflated the land, an extensive array of wildlife, and the indigenous Indian population under the broad canopy of "Nature." Like other European settlers in the New World, some of the city's early citizens shared this perspective on the environment and sought to preserve Nature herself within the walls of the city's first museum. The Western Museum has changed locations and names several times since 1818, but the collective memory that it protects has scarcely changed at all. In 2006, the Natural History Museum drew a direct connection between the "First People," who came to the Ohio Valley thousands of years ago and contemporary Cincinnatians. The museum's narrative asserts that Cincinnati's public identity as a city built on sacred ground, on a "well-omened spot" in the midst of an unsurpassed natural environment, preordained the city's greatness.

By the time the Natural History Museum was built in 1818, the natural world that it described had largely disappeared. Explorers in the 1750s and the 1780s had described the region in admiring detail, writing that the land is "well timbered with large Walnut, Ash, Sugar Trees, Cherry Trees &c, it is well watered with a great Number of little Streams or Rivulets, and full of beautiful natural Meadows, covered with wild Rye, blue Grass and Clover, and abounds with Turkeys, Deer, Elks and most Sorts of Game."[16] The early nineteenth century brought dramatic changes: General Anthony Wayne's defeat of the Delaware and Shawnee at the Battle of Fallen Timbers resulted in an exodus of the region's native population. Once European settlers moved into the area, a wave of deforestation swept across the Ohio Valley. In 1822, a visitor reported that "all of the land in the immediate neighborhood of Cincinnati is without a tree upon it." Steep hillside forests were cut for firewood and lumber. The city's thriving leather industry created a huge demand for tanbark, resulting in the "ruthless slaughter" of oak timber within a hundred-mile radius of the city. As environmentalist Stanley Hedeen recounts, by 1881 "deforestation had reduced the woodland in Hamilton County's Mill Creek Township to 15 percent of its original coverage." Once the forests were gone, the black bear, gray wolf, and mountain lion disappeared as well. Turkeys, grouse, the passenger pigeon and Carolina parakeets followed suit, as did multiple species of fish.[17]

Over the years, the Natural History Museum carefully preserved as part of the city's identity what Cincinnatians had lost when they destroyed the natural environment to build the city. In defiance of deforestation, the exhibits recreate scenes that are heavily wooded. Stuffed black bears are on view, along with replicas of the now extinct passenger pigeon. And for years when Cincinnati schoolchildren toured the museum, a diorama of Tecumseh overlooking the Ohio River dominated one room. Tecumseh stood his ground there in the museum for decades as part of an origin narrative in which the Delaware and Shawnee were sacrificed for "progress" and the greater good of white settlement. Cincinnatians viewing this exhibit saw the proud Indian chief, but no evidence of the massacre of Indians that followed Tecumseh's stand.

The museum's organizing theme articulates a story as teleological as the nineteenth-century science on which it is based. Nevertheless, as Georges Bataille suggests, those who go to the museum and hear these stories can feel themselves in touch with the natural world in important ways. The message it delivers transforms the meaning of the everyday natural world into something special, sacred, outside the ordinary. Visitors leave the museum with a new, or renewed, sense that the very land they walk upon, the hills and forests that surround the city, and the river that flows along its southern edge have a rich, interconnected history. This is an inclusive history that goes far back in time, but ends in the present, with the Cincinnatians of today who live in the "well-omened spot" chosen so long ago as a place favored by nature.

Contemporary exhibits in the Natural History Museum no longer feature the wax carvings of Hiram Powers's day. Instead, touch-screen computer monitors introduce visitors to the Mound Builders, who once populated the Ohio Valley and constructed an intricate series of geometric earthworks and burial mounds throughout the region. A map on the museum's computer screen outlines the location of these mounds. Another screen overlays a map of the twenty-first century city. With eerie precision, one ancient mound lines up directly underneath the city's Central Parkway; another exactly where early Cincinnatians built the city's first market. The market was closed in 1871 when an ornate fountain was built on the same spot. This urban plaza, known as "Fountain Square," has long been regarded as the city's spiritual center. The museum's display ends with a film clip of contemporary Cincinnati residents enjoying Fountain Square on a sunny day, with a voice-over concluding that: "Ancient monuments brought people together for festivals, rituals, trade, and pleasure, a process we repeat today among newer monuments."

In 1992, Cincinnati's Natural History Museum moved into the old Union Terminal building, a massive 1934 art deco train station, built of concrete and steel. As in the days of John Audubon and Hiram Powers, contemporary museum curators keep their patrons in touch with a carefully restored history preserved in images of an earlier and lost natural landscape. The museum's narrative makes no attempt to disclose the ruthless role that the city's founders played in destroying nature—the land, the forest, the animals, and the Indians. The illusion that contemporary Cincinnatians live in harmony with nature, as their ancestors did before them, is the museum's most carefully preserved artifact.

The Reigning Queen's "Art Palace of the West"

The Natural History Museum helped early Cincinnati residents preserve the idea of the city's relationship to nature, and as the city grew, street names like Walnut, Vine, Orchard, Plum, and Cherry recalled for local residents the sidehills and fields that once "clothe[d] themselves with luxurious vegetation."[18] In the 1850s, wealthy Cincinnatians began to move out of the city basin, an area by then choked with coal smoke, smog, and incessant noise, to settle in the lush landscape of the hills that overlooked the river. Nicholas Longworth, one of the richest men in the city, purchased an estate in 1831, that spanned both of these worlds, stretching from a Pike Street mansion four blocks from the Ohio River to the top of Mount Adams. Longworth cultivated extensive vineyards and called his domain the "Garden of Eden." In 1865, the city council purchased Longworth's estate for a public park, a place soon considered by local observers "to surpass Nature itself." For Cincinnatians "Eden Park" restored and even improved upon the original "charmed garden" that the city's founders had discovered when they rounded that gentle bend in the Ohio.[19] It was in the midst of this new garden of Eden that a group of wealthy Cincinnatians chose in the 1880s to construct the "Art Palace of the West." The impetus for an "art palace" came from the Women's Centennial Executive Committee, an influential group of female art patrons and artists who worked together to organize the well received "Cincinnati Room" in the Women's Pavilion at the 1876 Centennial Exhibition in Philadelphia and afterward as the Women's Art Museum Association. This group argued that establishing a museum and a training school to prepare a new generation of artists was essential to Cincinnati's future.[20]

After the Civil War, Cincinnati lost its position as the nation's third largest manufacturing city, dropping to seventh by 1880. Chicago, not Cincinnati, emerged as the "Rome of the Railroads," and the new commercial center of "inland America." Critics referred to Cincinnati as the "fallen monarch" and routinely depicted the Queen City as a "dumpy and comic figure." Moreover, the city's reputation as a pork-butchering center inspired writers to refer to it as "the city of the unclean beast." Other epithets targeted the large German population and depicted the city as a "beer-guzzling metropolis," where cultural leaders were on a "Quixotic mission . . . to establish classical music amongst pork-packers." In many ways its reputation as a second-rate metropolis was undeserved for as Chicago took over the lead in pork packing, Cincinnati emerged from the depressions of the 1870s as the most diverse industrial center in the West. By the mid-1880s Cincinnati ranked first in the production of a broad range of manufacturing goods, from carriages to coffins, furniture to whiskey; it was second in shoes, boots, and clothing, and a stiff competitor in books, leather, paints, glassware, and bricks.[21]

Civic elites clung during these years to the city's public identity as the "Queen of the West," and stressed that Cincinnati was involved in a new stage of industrialization, one emphasizing not traditional pork packing or iron manufacturing, but industries and inventions that reflected the beauty and practicality of the mechanical arts. Beginning in 1870, Cincinnati manufacturers hosted annual industrial expositions to promote this new public identity. Crowds of 200,000 to 300,000 from across the region attended these extravagant affairs to view the latest labor-saving machinery displayed next to elaborately framed paintings, sculpture, photographs, and engravings. In 1877, the city built Music Hall, an enormous public facility designed to house both industrial expositions and musical events. Exposition president Edmund Pendleton spelled out Cincinnati's commitment to a different industrial paradigm when he emphasized that "Nowhere were 'Art and her twin sister Industry'—the two forces that 'civilize the world'—joined in a more graceful and productive alliance than in the form of modern technology."[22]

No cultural institution in the city was more committed to the ideal of merging art and industry than the Women's Art Museum Association. The wives and daughters of Cincinnati's wealthiest families, led by their president, Mrs. A. F. Perry, a woman known for "taking the bull by the horns,"[23] established a sweeping agenda of reform and uplift that addressed what they saw as the city's major economic and social problems. In their view the promotion of the "industrial arts" would negotiate a new public identity for the city, simultaneously relieving an ongoing economic depression and helping bridge class divisions in Cincinnati. They mobilized support for building an art museum that would itself become "an educator," which would teach Cincinnatians about the relationship between art and industry, and train new generations of artists to create products that would stimulate the city's economy. The local pottery industry that burgeoned in the 1850s, expanded into the "art pottery" market in the 1860s, and attained international acclaim after 1880, exemplified to them the benefits of artistic inspiration and industrial pragmatism. These products were designed in accord with John Ruskin's philosophy that "beautiful surroundings make people virtuous." Practical stoneware and decorative pottery would make a home "beautifully appointed," one in which, by extension, "the family would benefit greatly in moral aptitude."[24] Cincinnati's potteries, the most famous of which was Rookwood, founded in 1880 by Maria Longworth Nichols, employed hundreds of workers, predominantly women, for whom a steady wage not incidentally reduced the risk of prostitution. For the members of the Women's Art Museum Association who initiated plans to build an "art palace" in the city, and for the wealthy male art patrons who later assumed control of the art museum project, the connection between moral uplift and public identity was central.[25]

The Cincinnati Art Museum opened on May 18, 1886. The crowd assembled on that brilliant sunlit afternoon heard the opening prayer: "Bless our land with honorable industry, sound learning, pure manners." The museum was dedicated "to art in its various uses and applications, to science, to natural history, and to kindred subjects." Heralded as "a gift by the people to the people," the "Art Palace of the West" opened as an "art industry museum" that would benefit all classes. The *Commercial Gazette* headline read: "A Noble Gem Added to the City's Crown of Hills," and asked, "May not Cincinnati boast of this as the fairest jewel in her crown?" Mayor Amor Smith emphasized the museum's role as "a generous leaven," lifting, teaching, and cultivating both art and commerce. "Standing as it does with majestic presence," he said to the crowd, "high above the valley where move the industrial masses, like a sentinel of thought, silent and ever present, it beckons us to its halls and galleries."[26]

But the mayor's florid prose did not reflect how the industrial masses in the valley below Eden Park felt about the new museum on the top of the hill. That very afternoon thousands of Cincinnati workers were in the midst of the largest strike in the history of the city. On May Day 1886, organized and unorganized workers throughout the city had joined some 340,000 U.S. workers and walked off their jobs to force manufacturers to adopt a universal eight-hour workday. Over the next week, one-third of the Cincinnati workforce, some 32,000 men and women demonstrated remarkable unity across ethnic, religious, racial, gender, and occupational lines and joined the May Day strikes, the most dramatic American working-class protest of the nineteenth century. Cincinnati workers shut down every industry in the city for over two weeks. The black smoke that usually poured from the city's factories faded away; the incessant noise stopped. Mayor Amor Smith, himself one of Cincinnati's leading candle and soap manufacturers, called in 1,000 special police and militia regiments, totaling 1,400 soldiers. Fears of anarchy and violence reached a fever pitch in the two weeks before the "Art Palace" opened. Seamstresses, waitresses, laundresses, barbers, cracker bakers, pick and shovel men, undertaker carriage drivers, and grocery clerks had organized new unions during the first eleven days of May. By the third week in May, as opening ceremonies began in Eden Park for the city's new art museum, manufacturers had hurriedly reached settlements with their workers and the number of strikers had dropped from a peak of over 30,000 to around 5,000. Well-organized, militant, and confident in their roles as workers and citizens, factory artisans and laborers throughout the city had won major gains, including shorter hours and wage increases of 10–20 percent.[27]

Standing high above the city basin, the "Art Palace of the West" became a powerful symbol of growing class division in a community in which manufacturers and merchants constantly emphasized the connection between art and industry, but remained bewildered and shocked by increasing collective activism and militant responses by workers who over the previous decade had routinely worked twelve-hour shifts as their wages declined. Two years earlier, in 1884, tensions that had simmered for years had erupted in the city when a crowd of several thousand rallied in Music Hall to protest the light sentences given two accused murderers, then marched to the county courthouse and jail in furious protest against political and judicial corruption.

Local police could not contain the rioting crowd and before the night was over the courthouse and jail had burned to the ground, and seven thousand state militiamen had been moved into the city. The next two nights thousands of workers shouting for "true justice" battled with militiamen and police. Cincinnati elites had feared then that the "Paris of America" was on the brink of a European-style revolution.[28]

In the wake of these riots, the city's "Art Palace" was dedicated to art and industry in the hope of using culture to transform the city's public identity from that of a community besieged by striking mobs to a place of order and calm. The museum was open to all, as long as they paid the twenty-five-cent admission charge, a sizable sum for skilled workers whose daily wages averaged less than two dollars. Attendance by "the masses" was sparse the first six weeks after the museum opened, and officials announced Sunday hours to accommodate "those large numbers who by force of circumstance are prevented from coming during the week."[29] After 1900, fears of a workers' revolution subsided and the museum's emphasis gradually shifted from its original mission of merging art and industry to the collection of great works of art. The name changed as well, from the "Art Palace" to the more republican Cincinnati Art Museum. For well over a century, Cincinnatians have been able to slip through the door of the museum in Eden Park, and look into a colossal mirror that refracted not local "industrial arts," but five thousand years of Western history.

From the beginning the Cincinnati Art Museum constructed a cultural memory of Cincinnati as an urban center that unstintingly support the arts from its founding in 1788, although little evidence exists to support that idea. Curators in the "Art Palace" placed the art produced in the city in the context of European culture. The new "Cincinnati Wing," which opened on May 17, 2003, brought the museum full circle, back to its dedication on another May afternoon, 117 years earlier, when both workers and elites were engaged in transforming the city's public culture, one group of citizens by striking for "true justice," and the other by opening an "art palace" that would "bless the land with honorable industry, sound learning and pure manners." In 2003, Cincinnati Art Museum trustees were still trying to draw "the masses" to the museum, just as they had in 1886. After the dedication of the "Cincinnati Wing," the museum finally realized its promise to be open to all by eliminating the general admission charge with the help of an endowment from the Rosenthal Foundation. "Our foundation is committed to fostering social change in Cincinnati," the Rosenthals said, "and we feel this donation will certainly do that for the Museum and our city."[30]

The Cincinnati Art Museum promoted and celebrated Cincinnati as the "Paris of the West," a city worthy of the title of queen, a forward-looking monarch in the full power of her reign. Yet as the nineteenth century turned to the twentieth, the Queen began to age and her powers wane. The city's Taft Museum, the home and art collection of Charles P. and Anna Sinton Taft, evokes the image of a still magnificent but aging dowager holding forth under a portrait of her youthful self, illuminated by past glories.

An Aging Dowager in a Federal Villa

The most aggressive procurers of European cultural artifacts in Cincinnati after the turn of the century were not adding to the collections in the Cincinnati Art Museum, but building one of their own. The marriage of Anna Sinton and Charles P. Taft on December 4, 1873, merged the industrial wealth of Anna's father, iron magnate David Sinton, with the intellectual ideals and ambitions of the Tafts, a well-educated family dedicated to public service. The young couple lived in the Sinton home, a federal mansion on Pike Street, four blocks from the Ohio River. Built by Cincinnati merchant Martin Baum, and expanded by its second owner, Nicholas Longworth, the house is now one of the oldest surviving wooden structures in Cincinnati. When David Sinton, one of the founders of the Cincinnati Art Museum, died in 1900, his only child, Anna Sinton Taft, became the wealthiest woman in Ohio. Within two years she and her husband began to travel extensively, and over the next twenty-five years they purchased a broad range of nineteenth-century American paintings, over a hundred European Old Masters, numerous European sculptures, an extensive array of European decorative arts, and several hundred Chinese ceramics. Charles Taft died in 1929; Anna two years later. Their wills established the Taft home as a public museum and endowed the Cincinnati Institute of Fine Arts to administer it.[31]

Charles and Anna Taft let their personal tastes guide the expansion of their collection. Works they acquired had to appeal to their developing sense of aesthetics, complement the other pieces they owned, and have educational value, in their view, for Cincinnati artists. Their intention to share their collection was evident from the outset. Charles Taft believed in the educational and instructive value of the arts, and speaking in 1878 to the Women's Art Museum Association, he argued that art should be collected "for the inspiration of artists in one's own time."[32] Art patrons, local artists, and amateurs were regularly invited to the Taft's elegant mansion on Pike Street to discuss their work, study the collection, or to admire a recent acquisition. The Tafts had an active social life, and as Charles rose to prominence in publishing and politics they became renowned for entertaining an array of distinguished guests. Charles's brother William Howard Taft was a frequent visitor and announced his run for president from their front steps in 1908.

The objects the Tafts amassed predated the Civil War, harking back to the era when the Pike Street house was constructed, and even earlier to the years before Cincinnati was founded. Their repeated travels to New York and London, Paris, Brussels, Germany, and Holland yielded European treasures from the seventeenth, eighteenth, and early nineteenth centuries. The Tafts became discriminating critics and obtained good advice regarding their purchases. But Anna Taft was in her forties and Charles in his fifties when they started their collection and their acquisitions reflect a long-gone world captured in sublime landscapes and elegant portraits, an elite premodern world of formality and respectability. The Tafts had some interest in the impressionists, ignored the development of modernism, and paid scant attention to contemporary art. During the years they traveled to Europe on a regular basis, between 1902 and 1927, they met few, if any, of the broad range of working artists who were experimenting with new forms and techniques in painting and sculpture. They disregarded post-impressionist painters Gauguin and Cézanne, and sculptors Rodin and Degas, not to mention Klee, Matisse, and Picasso.

Nevertheless, the art works the Tafts brought back to Cincinnati made for lively conversation on Sunday afternoons when they opened their home to visitors. They had portraits painted of themselves by Spanish artist Raimundo de Madrazo, and commissioned a much loved painting of President Taft by Joaquin Sorolla. William Howard repeatedly had urged Charles and Anna to move to Washington where they would be closer to him and could build an appropriate house to hold their collection, away from the soot-laden air of Cincinnati, where they had to keep their paintings under glass to protect them. The once elegant Pike Street neighborhood had changed dramatically by 1900, when most of the city's elite had moved out to fashionable suburbs on the hills above the basin. When the American Book Company built a large factory just south of the Taft home, workmen walked on their roof and swung cables across the top of the house. But as William Howard Taft put it, Charles and Anna "stuck to the old place with a cat-like love for the situation."[33]

Inside the Pike Street mansion remarkably few modifications took place. Charles and Anna Taft grew older as they carefully maintained their treasures, generously supported the Cincinnati Art Museum, the Cincinnati Symphony Orchestra, and the Zoological Gardens. In 1927, they donated their house and art collection to the city of Cincinnati, with the stipulation that they live there for the remainder of the lives. After Charles died, Anna held forth for another two years in the rambling mansion that her father had purchased over half a century earlier. Once the Taft home became a public museum, in 1932, Cincinnatians moved easily through the rooms in which Charles and Anna had so frequently entertained. Nothing was roped off, and the likenesses of the Tafts by Raimundo de Madrazo kept watch from the Music Room walls. The Taft Museum is frozen in time, and more than any other institution in the city celebrates the collective memory of Cincinnati's early history. The city's Dowager Queen anchors Cincinnatians in the past, to a lost world where immigrants like David Sinton became unbelievably rich during a period of concentrated industrial and political power in a society rigidly segregated by class, ethnicity, race, and gender.

Over the years various restorations of the Taft Museum have uncovered evidence of the mélange of architectural styles used in early Cincinnati, as well as the expertise of builders, carpenters, and plasterers in the city in 1820. Shortly before her death, Anna Taft revealed a well-kept secret about the old house when she casually mentioned that mural decorations, which she had never seen, were hidden under the wallpaper in the entrance halls. When the city acquired the house in 1931, the wallpaper was removed and eight landscape murals, more stunning than any artifacts collected by the Tafts, were carefully uncovered. Painted in the early 1850s by Robert S. Duncanson, a New York native who had made his way to Cincinnati, the murals had been commissioned by Nicholas Longworth. Hidden for more than six decades, these large six-by-nine foot panels were created at a formative stage in Duncanson's development as an artist, a period when Longworth's confidence in him made an enormous difference in the trajectory of his career. Duncanson started out as a house painter and glazier, and later gained a national and international reputation as a landscape painter, the first African American to do so. At the time he painted the distinctive mural sequence for Longworth, the rich tones and calm pastoral scenes in his work belied the turmoil of Duncanson's existence as a free black man in a country shaped by slavery. In 1841, twenty-year-old Duncanson and his mother had settled in the Cincinnati area, the same year a massive race riot in the city caused half of the free black population to migrate to Canada. Turning his back, at least publicly, to abolitionism and the racial ferment that gripped the city in the 1850s, Duncanson declared: "I am not interested in colour, only paint." Soon afterward he left Ohio for England and Europe, where he stayed until the Civil War began.[34]

The multilayered irony of Charles and Anna Taft's long search for artistic validation in the art brokerage houses of New York and Europe, when all the while these exceptional murals remained covered up in their own house, parallels the suppressed lives, thwarted talent, and unrealized potential of African Americans in Cincinnati and throughout the United States. Duncanson's antebellum murals romanticized the Ohio Valley landscape in a style that built on and then departed from the Hudson River School. Reflecting the cultural memory contained in the Natural History Museum, in Duncanson's paintings the natural world is depicted in gently flowing rivers, waterfalls, trees, rolling hillsides, and golden light that recreated for nineteenth-century Cincinnatians the 'charmed garden' and the well-omened spot discovered by the city's founders. Covered over in the years following the Civil War, Duncanson's work remained as concealed and elusive as the pledges of equality and justice that followed Reconstruction. The Promised Land so vibrantly depicted in each of the eight murals Duncanson painted for Longworth was cast in shadow, literally and metaphorically. The Tafts and the hundreds of guests they welcomed to the Pike Street house in their attempt to enrich the artistic life of the city never knew that the possibility of cultural transformation was right before them, not in plain sight, but hidden by their own adornments.

In the spring 2004, the Taft Museum completed a major renovation that restored the original house to the grandeur of the 1820s, making it look even more elegant than it did in Longworth's day. The new Taft reflects an idealized past, and many Cincinnatians feel good about themselves when they visit the new museum: "The first look and I was in love with it. It really is a crown jewel of our city now," said Indian Hill socialite Maddy Gordon. After a $22.8 million face-lift, Taft director Phillip C. Long reported that "the grand lady of Pike Street is back in action." But Jim Knippenberg of the *Cincinnati Enquirer* sounded a different note when he reported that the real "crown jewel is the series of pre-Civil War murals by African-American landscape painter Robert S. Duncanson."[35] In the restored Taft, Robert Duncanson's work dominates the building's first floor. The eight elaborate murals he spent two years painting so long ago have undergone six years of delicate inch by inch reconditioning. Moreover, an Ohio Bicentennial historical marker honoring Duncanson stands at the Taft's front door; the Duncanson Society, established in 1986, to "affirm an ongoing African-American presence within the structure of the Taft Museum," supports the Duncanson Artist-in-Residence. In 2004, that post was held by Melvin Grier, a renowned African American photojournalist whose work has received worldwide acclaim.[36]

In 2005, Grier's provocative photographs of contemporary urban life were displayed in the new "Education Room" of the renovated Taft Museum. Over the mantel, the words of twentieth-century African American writer James Baldwin, who like Robert S. Duncanson fled to Europe in disgust over America's racial injustice, offer a different perspective on the seeming permanence of the Baum-Sinton-Taft House and the history it celebrates and preserves. "Nothing," Baldwin writes, "is fixed, forever and forever and forever, it is not fixed; the earth is always shifting, the light is always changing, the sea does not cease to grind down rock."[37]

Anna Sinton Taft would probably not have chosen Baldwin's quotation, given its subversive repudiation of her commitment to preserving the Queen City's past glories, to adorn a mantel in her house. Yet it reflects other currents at play in the cultural milieu of the city, undercurrents more complex and heterogeneous than the public identity promoted by the city's establishment. This hidden history of the city finds its expression in contemporary forms of civic culture that emerged in the latter part of the twentieth century. Here then, the Queen turns queer.

A Queer Queen: The Contemporary Arts Center

Despite the effort of civic leaders to exert control over cultural representation, the collective unconscious also plays a part in the transformation of public culture, whether recognized or not. The repressed feelings and desires, the unspoken proclivities, the hidden aspects of the city that are not part of the civic persona promoted by the established community, nevertheless emerge in the public and private actions of the populace. Here then, the Queen City is revealed not as a virgin, nor a reigning monarch or aging dowager, but as queer. This Queen can assume changeable and mixed identities that transcend categories of race, ethnicity, gender, and body image, in keeping with queer theory's assertion that every part of an identity, whether individual or collective, is fluid and heterogeneous, and therefore capable of transformation.[38] In the Contemporary Arts Center, representations of the Queer Queen give Cincinnatians an opportunity to look at different sides of themselves and their community, and to consider the possibility of embracing something new. This prospect is for some exciting and refreshing, for others deeply disturbing and threatening.

Distinctly different from the city's older museums, the Contemporary Arts Center has never reflected the grandeur of the city's past; it is not a museum that Cincinnatians frequent in order to feel good about themselves. Rather, from its inception, the Contemporary Arts Center has mirrored the civic unconscious of a city that throughout the twentieth century became increasingly intolerant of difference. In stark contrast to its nineteenth-century image as a community known for its "public spirit and liberality," by 1920 Cincinnati had changed dramatically as a result of Prohibition and a broad range of Americanization projects aimed at purging German influence during and after World War I. As the city expanded outside of the basin, that "charmed garden" first settled by European pioneers in the 1780s, race, ethnicity, class and religion increasingly segregated the population. In the years before and after World War II this trend only grew more intense as thousands of southern African American and white Appalachian migrants moved into the city in search of employment and educational opportunities for their children. The flight of upper- and middle-class, predominantly white Cincinnatians out of the city began in earnest after the Civil War, gained momentum in the 1920s, reached a peak in the decades of the civil rights movement, and continues still, in the twenty-first century.[39]

In the 1930s as Americans became increasingly aware of the rising tide of fascism, antisemitism, ethnic cleansing, and war in Europe, three Cincinnati women, Peggy Frank, Betty Pollack, and Rita Rentschler, looked for ways to use culture to transform public perceptions of world affairs. Assuming a role similar to that played by the Women's Art Museum Association in an earlier era, they founded the Cincinnati Modern Art Society, one of the first modern art societies in the United States, in 1939. The new organization opened its first exhibition, *Modern Paintings from Cincinnati Collections*, in the basement of the Cincinnati Art Museum. Three years later, in 1942, as the United States mobilized for war and sent thousands of troops abroad, the society brought Pablo Picasso's *Guernica* to Cincinnati. Painted during the Spanish Civil War, this devastating critique of war, deeply disturbing in peacetime, had a major impact on Cincinnatians who saw it on the dark threshold of World War II. Throughout the 1940s the Modern Art Society used public culture to provide alternative narratives to contemporary events and to speak to the city of the generativity that comes from crossing boundaries. Local exhibitions of the art of Paul Klee, Alexander Calder, Henri Rousseau, and Le Corbusier introduced a range of modernists whose work had been deemphasized by curators at the Cincinnati Art Museum, who preferred impressionist works, and of course by the Tafts, whose collection focused on romantic landscapes.⁴⁰

Even as Cincinnati became more politically and socially conservative in the 1950s and 1960s, membership in the Modern Art Society doubled and the organization voted to change its name to the Contemporary Arts Center (CAC). As the Cincinnati Art Museum had done in an earlier era, the CAC increased the city's visibility in the art world on a national and international level. The center organized a major exhibition of David Smith's work, invited John Cage to perform and opened one of the first museum exhibitions in the United States of pop art, *An American Viewpoint 1963*, with Roy Lichtenstein and Andy Warhol. By 1970, the CAC had moved to bigger venues twice and its exhibition space was one of the largest devoted to the contemporary arts in the United States.⁴¹

Despite the controversial nature of many of its exhibitions and its growing collection, the CAC managed for almost half a century to operate in plain sight but remain unnoticed by those in the city who preferred representational art, eschewed alternative political narratives, and abhorred the idea of crossing boundaries of any kind. Granted, fund-raising to support the development of contemporary art in the city was never easy. The CAC, as one observer put it, was "still eyed with suspicion in some quarters, like a foreign in-law." Nevertheless, since its founding in 1939, the Contemporary Arts Center had enjoyed a comfortable respectability and acceptance. This quiescent era ended in 1988, the year of Cincinnati's Bicentennial, when the CAC triggered a national controversy as it commissioned artist Andrew Leicester to create a public sculpture for the entrance to the newly built Sawyer Point Park on the riverfront. Leicester's fanciful design of flying pigs, recalling the city's nineteenth-century role as the world leader in pork packing, drew harsh criticism and became part of an ongoing national debate about the nature of public art. Cincinnati mayor Charlie Luken found the representations inappropriate for his "vision of a modern metropolis." The mayor argued that the swine were insulting and "would make the city a laughingstock."⁴² A media blitz ensued over several months, ending in a town hall debate over "enshrining the swine." Pro-pig forces won a raucous victory after a full-size hog and several beribboned piglets ran through the city council chambers. Eventually four bronze-winged "angelic porkers" were installed along the riverbank, in Leicester's words, "sing[ing] the praises of all their brethren who died so the city may prosper."⁴³

The furor over the CAC's commission focused on public art that explored repressed aspects of civic life, rather than celebrating the prevailing historical narrative. This episode revealed a myriad of deep-seated feelings on the part of Cincinnatians about, as Leicester put it, "this kind of undefinable thing—people's notion of what represents them."[44] Leicester's art provoked debate, raised questions, and was not easily understandable, and it revealed a broad range of values, tastes, and beliefs within the city. These different ways of seeing were not about race, religion, morality, or gun control, but about public identity and the nature of civic life. Since 1988, the "flying pigs" have become the unofficial political symbol of the city and a cottage industry has grown up around them with books, food, and an annual "Flying Pig Marathon." Most significantly, in 2000, a year-long public art event call the "Big Pig Gig" showcased the work of local artists who decorated dozens of full-sized fiberglass pigs, which were then prominently displayed throughout the city.[45]

Although initially controversial, once in place along the riverfront Leicester's "flying pigs" had a tremendously positive effect. Civic leaders opposed the winged swine out of fear that the bronze creatures would revive the sordid nature of Cincinnati's pork-packing past—the pigs running in the street, the streams running with blood, the squeals, smells, and the offal cast into the river. This image of the city had been repressed since the 1870s, when civic leaders eschewed the title "Porkopolis" and emphasized the beauty and practicality of the mechanical "arts." But instead, Leicester's pigs worked transformative magic, lightening the mood of civic life, making people laugh, and unleashing a tremendous amount of creative energy. Like a patient in psychoanalysis, Cincinnati was able to embrace its past by dealing with it openly, rather than being ashamed of it. Leicester's art indeed functioned as Bataille's "colossal mirror" in which the residents of the city were able to find themselves admirable after all.

As complex as the Leicester affair turned out to be for the CAC, it was a prologue to an even more multifaceted drama that developed two years later when the Contemporary Arts Center decided to exhibit Robert Mapplethorpe's *The Perfect Moment*, a traveling retrospective of 175 photographs depicting life in New York and San Francisco gay subculture during the AIDS epidemic in the 1980s, as well as flowers, portraits, and still lifes. Nine photographs in the collection depicted overtly sexual or sadomasochistic acts. The exhibit had already been shown to critical acclaim at the Whitney Museum in New York and in Philadelphia; Cincinnati was to be the fifth stop on a six-city tour during 1989–90. While the exhibit was in Chicago, Robert Mapplethorpe died of AIDS at age forty-two. The show then moved to Washington, D.C., where Senator Jesse Helms, Republican from North Carolina, with support from many others, used the explicit content of the exhibit to fuel his campaign to cancel federal funding for the National Endowment for the Arts (NEA). In an effort to tamp down the furor and support the NEA, the Corcoran Museum canceled the exhibit. This strategy backfired as museum directors and artists from across the country criticized the Corcoran for "caving in" to Helms. The publicity surrounding Mapplethorpe's death and the Corcoran cancellation put the four remaining cities on the Mapplethorpe tour, Hartford, Berkeley, Cincinnati, and Boston, on notice that their museums could become casualties in the opening salvos of a growing culture war. Out of the four museums left to exhibit *The Perfect Moment*, the Contemporary Arts Center in Cincinnati became the perfect target for conservatives determined to take a stand on public censorship.[46]

Right-wing forces in Cincinnati were well equipped to disrupt the Mapplethorpe exhibit, with support coming in from across the United States, as well as strong ties to local law enforcement, to the Republican Party that dominated city politics, and to the news media. Before the exhibit opened, a 16,000-member group in Cincinnati called Citizens for Community Values encouraged its membership to wage an anti-Mapplethorpe letter-writing campaign targeting Contemporary Arts Center members and staff, local newspapers, the employers of the CAC board, and corporations and individuals connected to the exhibit. On the national level the development of anti-obscenity SWAT training for local police forces under the direction of Attorney General Edwin Meese and a reactionary political agenda focused on a broad range of morality issues, including abortion, pornography, homosexuality, and sex education, had created a climate that emboldened local supporters of censorship.[47]

As the Contemporary Arts Center prepared to open the Mapplethorpe exhibit, CAC director Dennis Barrie received support from other museum directors, both within the city and across the United States. Local religious leaders from Protestant and Jewish congregations stood firmly with the CAC, as did members of the Cincinnati Symphony Orchestra, the Ohio Arts Council, and the Cincinnati Ballet. In response to public concerns about the show, the museum separated the more explicit photographs, including three with a man's anus being penetrated with various objects; one of a man urinating in another man's mouth; one showing a finger inserted in a penis; and two of children with their genitals exposed. These works became known as the "X, Y, and Z portfolios" and were displayed in a separate corner of the exhibition space. The decision was made to admit no one under eighteen to the exhibit. In a preemptive move, the CAC's curator invited Cincinnati police in to view the photographs and discuss Mapplethorpe's work. Two days before the exhibit opened, a crowd of one thousand rallied on Fountain Square in a show of support for the CAC and artistic freedom. Concerned about the city's reputation, the *Cincinnati Enquirer* published an editorial recommending "a calm resolution to the all-too-public feud." It argued that the "Mapplethorpe mess . . . was giving Cincinnati a bad name nationally."[48]

The Perfect Moment opened to the public on the morning of April 7, and at 2:30 p.m. police sirens could be heard coming down Fifth Street to the CAC. More than twenty uniformed police and plainclothes officers walked into the Center for Contemporary Art and presented director Dennis Barrie and the CAC board with four indictments against the exhibit. Barrie argued later that "the police had symbolically walked into every arts institution in the country." The police cleared the building and closed the CAC while they videotaped each photograph. The tapes would later be used as evidence in criminal cases against Barrie and the center. As hundreds of people waited outside, the crowd became agitated, chanting and booing the police. "When they demanded that we take the photos down they had found offensive," Barrie stated, "they were seeking the censorship of all *art* that was challenging, provocative or not politically correct." The CAC had anticipated trouble for months and on April 7, 1990, Cincinnati became the first American city in which an art museum was entered by uniformed police and placed on trial for obscenity.[49]

The story of what followed is a complicated narrative involving court trials; 81,000 Cincinnatians waiting in line to see *The Perfect Moment*; the doubling of CAC membership; Hamilton County Sheriff Simon Leis, who wanted to "smash the photographs" but didn't; worried members of the Mapplethorpe Foundation and the artist's estate who thought the photographs might be destroyed; harsh criticism for "Censornati"; pro-CAC protestors in Fountain Square; and death threats against director Dennis Barrie and his family. In the case of art versus obscenity in Cincinnati in 1990 (*Cincinnati v. Cincinnati Contemporary Arts Center*, 566 N.E. 2d/207 214 [1990]), art carried the day in court when a ten-day trial ended with a jury of eight deliberating less than two hours to acquit the Center for Contemporary Art and Dennis Barrie. Mapplethorpe's photographs provided Cincinnatians with a multifaceted set of reflections and challenged traditional cultural assumptions about gender, sexuality, race, and the body. Columnist Ellen Goodman referred to the trial as "Soho meets Cincinnati" or "a tale of two tongues" in which an insular and esoteric art world was forced to interact with citizens who did not speak their private language.[50] As with Andrew Leicester's "flying pigs," public opinion in the city eventually turned toward acceptance: of the CAC's right to exhibit controversial art, of the broad parameters of the First Amendment, and of the importance of a local case in the context of the ongoing national debate over cultural politics. The jury, described as "not museum goers" and "non artists" repeatedly said that they saw no problem with people seeing or reading things, as long as they were adults. And that included the offending photographs from *The Perfect Moment*. The jury saw the museum as "protected turf" in the legal battle over obscenity. Cincinnatians seemed relieved over the Mapplethorpe decision. When the verdict was announced by a local radio station broadcasting a Cincinnati Reds baseball game, people in the stadium stood up and cheered. A *Cincinnati Post* editorial argued that the jury's decision "saved Cincinnati from becoming the first city to convict an art museum of pandering obscenity." That, the *Post* argued, "would have been a difficult distinction to live down."[51]

In the end, both sides appropriated the Mapplethorpe case as a victory. Citizens for Community Values grew in size and continues to actively pursue obscenity issues. They quite rightly see what happened in Cincinnati in 1990, as having had a powerful effect on artists and museums throughout the country who have responded to the threat of prosecution and high-cost legal fights with self-censorship. A year after the trial ended, the CAC board quietly removed Dennis Barrie as director, a move that Citizens for Community Values interpreted as an accomplishment. On the other hand, from the CAC's perspective, the proponents of censorship received a severe blow in Cincinnati. They lost face on both the national and local level when they were rejected by the very citizenry they saw themselves as serving. *The Perfect Moment* transformed the CAC, from a local institution with an interesting past, to a national arts center with an international reputation and a promising future. As a consequence of the Mapplethorpe case, the CAC also broadened its support base within the city. Since 1970, the Contemporary Arts Center had rented exhibition space above a Walgreen's store in the downtown Mercantile Building, but soon after Mapplethorpe, plans were put on the table to construct a new building. The Rosenthal Foundation, ever committed to "fostering social change in Cincinnati," provided funding and the CAC commissioned Baghdad-born, London-based architect Zaha Hadid, nicknamed "the reigning queen of the avant garde," to design a new and different jewel for the city's crown.[52]

The building Hadid created confirms Certeau's observation that the city always functions as a place of "transformations and appropriations." Hadid appropriated Cincinnati as a city that had the ability to "believe in the fantastic." In turn, she transformed the landscape of the downtown and changed the cultural work that happens there. The CAC panel that hired Hadid wanted her to perform magic and to create, in the words of CAC director Charles Desmarais, "a unique place so that we will be able to do things no one else will be able to do." This "diva of design," a queer queen in her own right who regularly moves back and forth across cultural, geographic, and gendered boundaries, constructed a building that put a face on the collective unconscious of the city, and in so doing changed Cincinnati's persona from that of a dowager to that of a queen who can assume different and changing identities that offer the possibility of accepting something new.[53] After Mapplethorpe, the CAC and the city began to think more expansively; as Charles Desmarais told reporters, "We want to change the whole concept of what a museum can be with this building." Once the building opened reaction was predictably mixed: "I love it; I hate it," CAC associate curator Matt Distel told a reporter. Like a relationship with a challenging family member, Distel described his feelings about the new CAC as marked by loyalty and "a certain amount of conflict and growth."[54] The new Contemporary Arts Center encourages Cincinnatians to integrate conflicting feelings and negotiate boundaries in ways they have not thought of before, to remember of lessons of *Guernica* and Mapplethorpe, and to stay open to the fluidity and heterogeneity of human experience. In Cincinnati, in 2004, opportunities for this type of civic practice increased dramatically with the opening of the National Underground Railroad Freedom Center.

The Queen and the Freedom Center

Let us return to that warm August evening in 2004, when a chorus of Cincinnatians traversed the bridge across the Ohio and stepped onto the grounds of the new Freedom Center to participate in the building's public dedication. As a "museum of conscience" the Freedom Center is central to the process of civic transformation in which Cincinnati is once again engaged. Cincinnati wants something very specific from the Freedom Center. When asked the key word used by the city in connection with this new institution, Mayor Charlie Luken responded: "Growth." Luken argues that "racial polarization makes it difficult to succeed" in Cincinnati, and he sees the Freedom Center, together with police reform, new stadiums, and a convention center, as providing the city with ways "to attract diverse populations, income levels, ages, sexual orientation."[55] Housed in a warm brownstone building with copper trim and sides that curve like the currents of the river, Cincinnati's newest museum stands between two new stadiums—football to the west; baseball to the east. The Freedom Center offers something completely different: a state-of-the-art facility run by nationally known scholars, a trained staff of guides and docents, galleries, theaters, and an interactive learning library for children and adults. The Freedom Center has generated new forms of civic engagement, from community outreach, to work with local schools, to a successful collaboration with opera companies in Cincinnati, Detroit, and Philadelphia, to produce *Margaret Garner: A New American Opera* by Richard Danielpour and Toni Morrison, which opened in 2005. The 158,000-square-foot museum is carefully designed to teach "the powerful and courageous lessons of history," encouraging patrons to both engage the history of American slavery and the Underground Railroad and to stand up for what they think is right in the contemporary world.

The Freedom Center is an ambiguous space into which visitors project their own ideas about history and enslavement, about race and the meaning of freedom. Museum patrons who identify racially as "white," and want to "see themselves as admirable" in the reflection that the museum provides have to struggle to come to terms with the history that confronts them. The Underground Railroad was itself a hidden network of interconnecting relationships that crossed well-fortified political, geographical, psychological, and racial boundaries. The narrative told in the Freedom Center makes it impossible to ignore the ways in which slavery and a culture of racism shaped the history of Cincinnati and that of the nation. Visitors frequently compare the Freedom Center to the U.S. Holocaust Memorial Museum in Washington, D.C., a place where the horror of human cruelty is inescapable. African American visitors to the museum can pay homage to the strength of ancestors who withstood the horror of the middle passage, survived the harsh injustice of slavery, and lived to know emancipation. Regardless of racial identity many who visit the museum go through the exhibits, view the films, stand in the main hall, and silently look out across the Ohio River; and then circle back and go through the entire museum again.

No exhibit in the Freedom Center is more powerful than the large jail or slave "pen" that dominates the main floor of the building. Enslaved men and women were routinely warehoused in this structure on a northern Kentucky farm less than fifty miles from the Freedom Center before being sold farther south. Standing inside the slave pen even for a few moments, it is impossible not to feel the weight of the past; yet this jail is also one of those ambiguous spaces where one encounters not only the past, but also the present. Critics who opposed the building of a National Underground Railroad Museum and Freedom Center with its $110 million price tag argued that making a slave jail the museum's central display, one clearly visible from outside of the museum, sends a powerful message and an ominous reminder to the significant number of destitute men and women on Cincinnati's downtown streets. In 2002, Harry Belafonte spoke out against local leaders in Cincinnati whom he accused of perpetuating ongoing oppression. He argued that "plantations exist all over America [and] if you walk into L.A., into Watts, or to Over-the-Rhine in Cincinnati, you'll find people whose lives are as degrading as anything slavery's ever produced. They live in economic oppression in a very disenfranchised way."[56] Some Cincinnatians say they will never visit the Freedom Center, that it represents just another effort by the power structure to use culture to transform the city's image. "The museum doesn't help its own cause . . . identifying itself as the 'crown jewel' of a $2 billion redevelopment of Cincinnati's central riverfront," writes Gregory Flannery in Cincinnati's alternative newspaper *CityBeat*.[57] For others, the twelve-dollar-per-person entrance fee forms a barrier more prohibitive proportionally than the twenty-five cents the "Art Palace of the West" charged in 1886. Many local citizens ask why so much money was spent building a place for Procter and Gamble, the Chamber of Commerce, city officials, and local universities to have expensive gatherings in a grand space overlooking the river. How can this be done, critics charge, when anger and rage run so deep in the city, when local, state, and federal resources are scarce, unemployment high, and poverty rampant? Isn't this, they ask, another example of the white majority appropriating black history, this time in the name of freedom and the sacred narratives of emancipation? Ambivalence still hangs in the air.

Thousands of people from Cincinnati and beyond toured the Freedom Center in the first weeks after it opened to the public, but few left the two-acre site and walked north from the river's edge through the streets of downtown Cincinnati to Over-the-Rhine. This is the neighborhood where German immigrants to the city settled in the nineteenth century, where anti-German sentiment swept through during World War I, resulting in German street names being changed to "Republic" and "Liberty," where Appalachian migrants rented homes in the 1920s and 1930s, and where African Americans displaced by urban "renewal" in the 1960s and 1970s found housing they could afford. This is the neighborhood where Timothy Thomas, an unarmed nineteen-year-old African American, was shot and killed by Officer Stephen Roach in the early morning hours of April 7, 2001. Thomas was the fifteenth black man killed by Cincinnati police since 1995. Following

Thomas's death, hundreds of protesters from Over-the-Rhine and other city neighborhoods took to the streets, marching and carrying signs, and also breaking windows and setting fire to stores and cars. By 2006, most of the buildings in Over-the-Rhine had been repaired, but if you look closely, you will still see evidence of the chaos that consumed the neighborhood in the three days following Thomas's death: boarded-up windows, cracked glass, and burned-out buildings.[58]

Walk twelve blocks north from the Freedom Center on Race Street, or Vine, and you traverse a neighborhood where a majority of the population lives below the poverty line, the average median household income is less than $10,000 a year, the population is 80 percent African American and unemployment is over 50 percent. Turn right when you come to Liberty Street and walk three blocks east, and you will come to a place called the "Free Store." One of Cincinnati's most respected charities, the Free Store and Food Bank was established after riots racked the city in 1967, when the civil rights movement raised hopes of social and economic justice that the city quickly dashed. In recent years during the holiday season the Free Store has a long line outside, much like in Margaret Bourke-White's 1937 photograph "At the Time of the Louisville Flood." The walk from the Freedom Center to the Free Store is short, but the distance in terms of public identity and economic signification could not be greater. These two institutions form an important axis of identification along which theoretical concepts about gentrification, globalization, and freedom fragment into pragmatic concerns about housing, jobs, and safety. The Free Store operates completely outside of that commercial world where Sharon Zukin argues that "quests for unfulfilled desires take place in a dream world of public identities shaped in relation to commodities."[59] The Freedom Center, on the other hand, was created by that commercial world and is central to the city's plans for economic regeneration and a transformed public identity in the twenty-first century.

At the National Underground Railroad Freedom Center dedication in 2004, city, state, and national officials celebrated the museum's power to transform Cincinnati and the nation, to inspire a racially divided citizenry, and spread a message of freedom throughout the world. As they spoke, each dignitary, including First Lady Laura Bush, had to raise his or her voice to be heard over the chants of activists from nearby Over-the-Rhine. Officials spoke that summer night of freedom and hope, while protestors yelled from a nearby street: "No justice, no peace. No justice, no peace. No justice, no peace." If you listened carefully, you could hear the echo of other urban voices: from 1884, when thousands of Cincinnati workers took to the streets chanting "True justice, true justice, true justice"; from 2001, when crowds called: "No justice, no peace, no racist police."[60]

The greatest challenge facing the National Underground Railroad Freedom Center is to avoid being appropriated by powerful corporate interests and by politicians on the local, state, and national level who co-opt the meaning of freedom for their own agendas. At the Freedom Center dedication, Laura Bush made it clear that the administration sees the Freedom Center nationally as a "cornerstone of the American conscience" and globally as "a source of inspiration on our continuing journey toward freedom for all."[61] What exactly does this mean in terms of public identity in post-9/11 America? Which voices will define and control the meaning of freedom, justice, peace, and democracy in a period of renewed American imperialism?

The Freedom Center is just downriver from the city's nineteenth-century public landing in the charmed garden tended on that "well-omened" spot that drew the eye of the city's first settlers. But from the windows of this carefully crafted building, Cincinnatians can see their city and the river from new perspectives. The Freedom Center openly encourages Cincinnatians to restore the lost histories of enslaved Americans and to explore long repressed aspects of civic life. This "museum of conscience" allows visitors to construct their own versions of the past, celebratory for some, shameful for others, and facilitates the understanding of mixed and changeable identities that never matched the fixed coordinates of race, gender, class, and body most frequently represented in American culture. As a public institution, the Freedom Center provides a new space where, at least theoretically, citizens can actively negotiate a public identity that represents the diverse public constituencies in the city.[62]

History weighs heavily on Cincinnati and every American city. That is one reason why cities constantly remake themselves, reshaping civic spaces, shifting the boundaries of private and public, transforming their public identity, and as part of that process, building museums that "have the power to represent and reproduce, as well as to restore what has been lost, to celebrate particular constructions of civic, state, and national history, and to incorporate repressed memories of civic life."[63] Change itself provides a way to reconfigure what has come before, altering the environment, tearing down what is no longer desirable, rerouting roads, and erecting new buildings and bridges. This process allows people to focus on the new and forget the less admirable parts of their history. The year the Civil War ended, Cincinnatians did not look back at the bloody struggle over slavery that had long divided the city, but forward to completing the suspension bridge across the Ohio

River, a powerful symbolic connection between the North and South. In the same spirit, two years after the 1884 Courthouse Riots, Cincinnatians opened the "Art Palace of the West." And it was no accident that the concept of the Freedom Center grew out of the tumult of the mid-1990s when Cincinnati reeled from violent confrontations between the police and members of the African American community, and Marge Schott, owner of the Cincinnati Reds, made a series of public comments that were widely regarded as racist. The opening of the National Underground Railroad Freedom Center in 2004 was seen by many citizens and public officials as a positive antidote to the city's tarnished reputation following the riots of April 2001.[64]

Museums have the potential to lighten the burden of the past and point us in the direction of a shared public identity. Nineteenth-century Cincinnatians considered museums the "ornaments of an enlightened community," or as one Cincinnati newspaper put it: "the heart of the city's best life." Twenty-first-century American museumgoers make strikingly similar comments. When the newly renovated Museum of Modern Art reopened in New York City in November 2004, *New York Times* columnist Michael Kimmelman wrote: "Obviously the Modern matters deeply, to the city, to our psyche. It is part of our identity. We have missed it."[65] Public institutions throughout the United States constantly negotiate with diverse constituencies, the stakeholders in the construction of public identity. The design for a new museum that will house the International Freedom Center at Ground Zero was described by Nicolai Ouroussoff in 2005 as "a temple of contemplation and conflict." It is "more about politics," he wrote, "than architecture."[66] In Cincinnati, when the National Underground Railroad Freedom Center opened and that seven-hundred-member Freedom Center Chorus crossed the Ohio River, conflicts about the relevance of this new institution and its willingness to deal with the long repressed history of slavery were still being negotiated. "I don't know if a comfy, cozy trip through a museum that doesn't literally show the blood, literally the sweat and literally the separation of the African-American family is going to do it," one radio commentator warned.[67] For others, the Freedom Center, like museums built in earlier periods in the city's history, held out the promise of transformation: a belief that perceptions about the past have the potential to change, that racial conflicts might be resolved, and that the civic identity of Cincinnati could be restored to the "public spirit and liberality" that once made the Queen City the fairest of them all.

As various constituencies work to incorporate this new museum into the life history of the city, they will infuse the Freedom Center with meaning, both individual and collective, personal and civic. Like the city itself, the museum is a space where cultural construction can take place. As Sharon Macdonald argues, museums are "key cultural loci . . . symbols and sites for the playing out of social relations of identity and difference, knowledge and power, theory and representation."[68] The building and rebuilding of memories in relationship to such a public space continues a process that generations of citizens have engaged in before, that of defining and negotiating public identities through the intersections of memory and culture. Museums are sites where cultural transformations can and do occur. Place matters, and so do representations of memory. But the use of culture to shape a shared public identity has been and remains a complicated process. When successful, it is marked by consensus and conflict. Meaningful cultural transformation takes place when the work of civic engagement is ongoing and uneven, political, and most probably contentious. The middle ground reached after such contemplation and negotiation is a hallowed place, one that reflects, like the Queen's mirrors, the committed work of an admirable citizenry.

Epilogue
Pitfalls and Promises:
Whither the "Public" in America?

Sheila L. Croucher

The terrorist attacks of September 11, 2001, and the war on terror that ensued, energized an ongoing debate over civic engagement in America and led many scholars to speculate about the potential for civic revitalization in the United States. Would this conflict, like others in America's past, mobilize the citizenry, increase volunteerism, and enhance community sentiment?[1] Political scientist Robert Putnam, who not long before 9/11 had famously warned of a decline in civic engagement in the United States illustrated by the tendency of Americans to "bowl alone," saw in 9/11 a potential for Americans to begin "bowling together." He wrote: "In the aftermath of September's tragedy, a window of opportunity has opened for a sort of civic renewal that occurs only once or twice a century."[2] Indeed, Americans generously donated money and blood, adorned their homes, cars, and clothes with American flags, and, according to some indicators, experienced an increase in trust of neighbors and national pride.[3] Given the degree of political and cultural divisiveness present in the United States on September 10, 2001, this response may suggest, as Edward Linenthal does in Chapter 2, "Remembrance, Contestation, Excavation," that "Bereavement, perhaps, is one of the only ways Americans can imagine themselves as one. It trumps, for a time anyway, the many ways we are divided." The extent to which the opportunity for civic revitalization was seized, however, remains unclear.

Most measures subsequent to the immediate aftermath of 9/11 indicate that any increase in civic vitality in the United States was minimal and short-lived. Putnam's own research revealed that occasional volunteering was up only slightly after 9/11, and regular volunteering remained unchanged.[4] Theda Skocpol also analyzed public reaction to 9/11 and concluded that official efforts to mobilize citizens in a civic fashion have been only sporadic and weak, and much more commercial than civic. She attributes the minimal increase in public engagement to the fact that existing civic organizations provide few outlets or arenas for group involvement: "Churches remain vital centers of membership activity in many United States communities, but other kinds of membership associations have dwindled or disappeared."[5] "How Americans Respond" (HAR), a large-scale, longitudinal survey organized by the Institute for Social Research, attempted to gauge social trust in the United States and concluded that Americans did rally around each other in a show of patriotism and mutual support. The flip side, however, of trust in neighbors and fellow Americans was distrust of some groups of foreigners, immigrants, and some ethnic groups in the United States.[6] This distrust calls into question, as does Linenthal's analysis, the notion of a "seamless bereaved community," and suggests, as Linenthal does, that "perhaps such events both bring communities together and tear them apart simultaneously."

September 11 became a touchstone in American public life, but another date, the November 2, 2004, United States presidential election ("11/2") provided another more recent opportunity to assess the state of the public realm in America.[7] The good news, in terms of what Mary Kupiec Cayton characterizes as the *political* or *civic* public, is that the turnout of eligible voters who went to the polls was the heaviest it has been since 1968. Additionally, a number of new organizations emerged as key social and political actors such as ACT and MoveOn.org—attesting and contributing to an energized civil society in the United States. The troubling news is that the form and content of the public debate during the 2004 election was simultaneously more restrictive and more divisive. The range of possible policy options and political viewpoints in areas ranging from education to foreign affairs to economic policy was quite narrow and polarized. Meanwhile, the political "dirty tricks," the overwhelming influence of money, and the invocation of moral values as a justification for using state and federal constitutions to deny, rather than guarantee, civil rights for some citizens casts a long shadow on the democratic public sphere. Moreover, 11/2/04 revealed the now infamous divide between "Blue" and "Red" America.

In a post-9/11/01 and post-11/2/04 era, the time is ripe for a reconsideration of the notion of the public in America. The contributors to this volume have provided a range of analyses on the theories, history, evolution, and contemporary manifestations of public culture. From the Los Angeles Plaza of the eighteenth century to the Mexican migrant workers in northwest Ohio now negotiating transnational forms of belonging, these authors present a variety of perspectives on how individuals and groups have created and debated shared public meanings and identities. Certain common themes and concerns are threaded throughout the volume. Many contributors address the inequalities of power that affect democratic participation in, and access to, the public realm—calling into question the actual "publicness" of the public. Several authors grapple with the implications of a public defined and characterized increasingly by commercialization and consumption. To what extent, their analyses ask, are we a nation of citizens, shoppers, or both? And throughout the volume it becomes clear that the cultural, political, and geographic contours of public identities are in a state of flux. Nationhood has and continues to be central to how "we" is constructed and defined, but alternative forms of identity and belonging are emerging that transcend, subdivide, and challenge the hegemony of the nation-state.

Overall, the contributors to this volume offer different perspectives on the vitality, significance, and form of a public realm in the United States. Together their empirical analyses contribute to the conceptualization of the notion of public culture as a way to advance long-standing debates about democracy and identity and to situate those debates in the context of a rapidly globalizing world. From Aristotle to Mill to Tocqueville, political theorists have emphasized the importance of public deliberation to democracy and liberty. Aristotle rejected Plato's commitment to rule by philosophers and advocated that experts be replaced by ordinary citizens who would engage in public deliberation. John Stuart Mill strongly supported the development of civil society as a sphere of voluntary association that would exist between individuals and states and depend upon widespread public discussion. For his part, Tocqueville saw the abundance of voluntary association and pervasive public deliberation as central to America's burgeoning democracy. Contemporary scholars like Putnam and Skocpol continue these discussions in their focus on how civic engagement in the United States can be revitalized. As the authors in this volume engage with the concept of public culture, they contribute important practical, political, and scholarly insights to this historical discussion. They remind us to pay attention to how public the public really is, to whether what we are witnessing in the contemporary era qualifies as civic culture or consumer culture, and to how the contours of the debate are affected by shifting forms of identity and belonging in a postmodern, possibly postnational, world.

How Public Is the Public Realm?

As Mary Kupiec Cayton points out in this volume, some calls for civic engagement fail to acknowledge or address the inequalities of cultural power that flow from and are deeply enmeshed in economic, political, and social structures. At the same time, totalizing rhetorics of citizenship that pervade liberal democratic theory tend to erase other and multiple identities and attachments, as well as the ways in which the very notion of "citizen" is linked to and rooted in the inequalities noted above.[8] Hal Rothman, in Chapter 9, "Gates, Barriers, and the Rise of Affinity," applies this critique specifically to Putnam, whose vision of an ideal American past of front-yard culture and neighborhood block parties ignores that this was also a world "where social control stemmed from power relationships, where kin, culture, and caste defined boundaries that were understood by all." Throughout the volume, the authors take note of and expose cultural, political, and economic inequalities in the public realm, while grappling with the potential for human agency and resistance. As Cayton notes, the question that underlies all others about the nature and constitution of public culture is: "What viable forms of political and cultural intervention exist in a world where systemic forces play a huge role in determining social, political, economic, and cultural outcomes?"

Mary Ryan, in Chapter 1, "Looking for the Public in Time and Space," celebrates the diversity and community that characterized life in the Los Angeles Plaza in the early nineteenth century. She is also careful to note, however, and her analysis skillfully illustrates, that public culture, even if diverse, is not necessarily just and is often built upon hidden exclusions of gender, race, and ethnicity. Ultimately, Ryan sees hope in the example of the Los Angeles Plaza, and concludes: "Diversity per se is not necessarily corrosive of a common culture: it can, as seen in the parades and festivals of the nineteenth century, become its very substance." She cautions, however, that the expectations for social harmony that often attach to the language of public culture are utopian at best and authoritarian at worst as notions of public civility can become rugs under which to sweep injustice and inequity. Edward Linenthal's and Mary Frederickson's analyses of memorials, museums, and historical memory as sites of contestation also illustrates that public spaces and public culture, although permeated by discourses and realities of inequality, can offer the potential for open dialogue.

In Chapter 6, "Screening Pornography," Wendy Chun's sees in new technologies, namely the Internet, the opportunity for new arenas of public space. "The Internet is public," she argues, "*because* it allows individuals to speak in a space that is fundamentally indeterminate." And, because public space belongs by rights to no one, "the Internet can enable something like democracy." Chun's analysis of pornography also seems to confirm Ryan's caveat that public culture may not and should not be expected to conform to social expectations for harmony, decorum, and polite behavior.

Hal Rothman is perhaps the least optimistic of the contributors in terms of the contemporary promise or potential of public space: "What we once did in public we now do in private space; what was once free now has an admission charge." Rothman attributes the fact that "there's little shared space left in American society," to the willingness of Americans to abdicate rights in favor of a perception of safety. This willingness and the dangerous implications that flow from it have, arguably, become even more pronounced after 9/11. Rothman, Chapter 9, also identifies a troubling tendency to use or confuse private commercial space—whether airports, casinos, or malls—with public space. This use of private space permits a sense of security and attempts to evoke the comforts of a shared past that was, and now in renewed form continues to be, propped up by exclusion. He reminds us again, as did Ryan and Chun, that in truly free and open public space "all kinds of obnoxious behaviors . . . are legal and widely tolerated."

Suzanne Smith and Rachel Ida Buff offer slightly more sanguine analyses of the promise of the public in the United States. Smith's historical analysis of African American funeral directors reminds us to be open to and aware of political engagement that occurs in spaces or through mechanisms not conventionally recognized as political. It is likely that James C. Scott's concept of the "infrapolitics" of oppressed groups, which informs Smith's research, can not only illustrate the covert ways that black funeral directors furthered the political agenda of their respective communities, but can also reveal similar forms of engagement and resistance among marginalized groups in contemporary national and transnational contexts. Buff's examination of denizenship points in such a direction. Even in a post-9/11 era and even in a small, relatively conservative Midwestern city, immigrants, citizens, politicians, and community advocates united to pass local legislation extending certain rights to noncitizens. This move suggests, as does Buff in Chapter 11, "an acknowledgment that the fates of citizens and denizens have always been entangled and mutual; that the boundaries we draw between worlds, while having their own reality and force, do not accurately describe the im/migrant, multiply connected realities that continue to constitute everyday life." Buff's analysis also attests to the need to situate our understanding of public culture and public action in a changing and increasingly global context—a topic addressed in greater detail below.

Citizen Shoppers?

Throughout this volume, the contributors call attention to a close and complex relationship between public culture and consumer culture. They tend to agree that public space is now largely defined and encapsulated by commercial space. Mary Frederickson, in Chapter 12, explains that "The greatest challenge facing the National Underground Railroad Freedom Center is to avoid being appropriated by powerful corporate interests and by politicians on the local, state, and national level who co-opt the meaning of freedom for their own agendas." Similarly, for Catherine Gudis (Chapter 7) the billboard war "reveals the permeability of what are often considered separate realms of public and private, nature and the market." Yet, whether it is the billboards that Gudis analyzes, or medicine shows, radio, television, and the Internet, these chapters reveal how the commercialization and commodification of public spaces have evolved steadily over a long period of time. Less unanimous agreement exists among the contributors with regard to how this reality is to be evaluated. To what extent does the contemporary context confirm Adorno and Horkheimer's critique of public culture as essentially consumerism and the culture industry as one that insures capitalist hegemony, undermines critical thinking, and deceives consumers into thinking they are making choices when the slate of options is actually quite narrow. Or, for example, as Lynn Spigel avers with respect to television, can media technologies be effective vehicles for counternarratives and resistance?

Susan Strasser (Chapter 4) states unequivocally that "American culture, at home and across the globe, is corporate culture." Her focus on medicine shows of the late 1800s illustrates how Americans have for centuries adjusted to the constant encroachments of sponsorship. Strasser avoids taking an explicitly normative position with respect to this reality. Somebody, she recognizes, has to "pay the piper," and, in much the same way that we now sit resigned through advertisements for cell phone service and cars in the movie theater, earlier audiences accepted that if you want to hear the banjo player, you have to sit through the medicine pitch. Strasser's research offers an early example of how Americans have been habituated to the evolving world of sponsored public culture, and Gudis's study of billboards turns to a subsequent phase in that evolution. What, after all, is more genuinely or inherently public than the landscape, and it too has been thoroughly commodified as outdoor advertising has transformed public highways into commercial "buyways." Like Strasser, Gudis (Chapter 7) chooses not to conclude on a pessimistic note. If public space is defined by "that which is exempt from commerce," she writes, "we are bereft." However, if public space is defined by the mobility of the masses, "we are indeed well endowed." This potential promise of mobility is what Spigel (Chapter 5) seems to refer to when she concludes her analysis of television by stating that "the presence of multiple media platforms holds out hopeful possibilities for increased expression," though she is also right to caution that "what this will amount to in terms of democracy and citizenship remains a complex historical question."

Finally, Sharon Zukin's contribution on the social space of shopping returns, in a manner, to a question posed by Ryan in Chapter 1. Ryan challenged the commonplace assumption that commerce is antithetical to civic-mindedness, asking: "Is the public enemy the bad taste that pervades the shopping mall . . . ? Or is it the fact that unalloyed and unquestioned commercialism surrenders the public good to the free play of the market, with the imbalance of power it entails?" For Ryan, then, commerce is not necessarily corrosive of civic engagement, and Zukin (Chapter 8) says: "The diamond ring in the display case, the red stiletto heels in the plate-glass window, and the racks of CDs enclosed in plastic boxes embody dreams of possession, perfection, and self-improvement. Stores provide a public space to pursue private dreams, while offering a common experience of public culture."

Of course, shopping and shops in America, as Zukin carefully notes, are not now and have never been free of the divisions that permeate society at large. Zukin is also concerned that shopping has in recent decades become less local, more abstract, and less of a civic activity. Even the Internet, and sites like eBay and Amazon that held out the promise of democratizing shopping and broadening the public sphere, have had the opposite effect–not simply by commodifying public culture, but by concentrating power in a relatively small number of sites. Nonetheless, Zukin is cautiously hopeful that collective strategies—ranging from antiglobalization movements to support for local farmers—do exist for making shopping a more social, more democratic public sphere, and that shopping can remain an opportunity not just for buying, but for conversation.

By referencing antiglobalization movements and support for local farmers (and implicitly paraphrasing the message of a popular bumper sticker "Think Globally, Act Locally") Zukin suggests another important point with regard to contemporary understandings of the public. What the slogan on the bumper sticker conveys, and several contributors to this volume demonstrate, is that the concentration of power and the political engagement with or resistance against it cannot be conceptualized in purely national terms.

Shifting Contours

The nation and national identity, as Marguerite Shaffer notes in her preface to this volume, have been and continue to be dominant narratives of American studies. Various contributors invoke the discourse of nation, but they also reveal many contemporary complexities surrounding it. This is significant because globalization and the rise of transnationalism, both in theory and practice, have affected the conceptual reliance on and privileging of the nation-state as both a unit of analysis and an arena of action.

As American studies takes seriously the issue of public culture, a question to be considered is: How can we reflect on common endeavors and the possibility of common cultural meaning when meaningful identities seem increasingly to be associated with valuing different and particular histories, experiences, and conceptions of the self? The "we" in this case refers to the American nation, and the dilemma described is one that has been central to social, political, and public policy analyses of the past decades that focus on cultural diversity in the United States. On one side of the debate are critics of multiculturalism such as Arthur Schlesinger Jr. and John J. Miller who bemoan how multiculturalism and a "cult of ethnicity" have led to the "disuniting" and "undermining" of America.[9] Disputing these claims are scholars like historian Ronald Takaki who sees and celebrates America as multicultural from it inception.[10] Joining Takaki are political theorists such as Will Kymlicka, who views multiculturalism as perfectly reconcilable with liberal democracy, and Anne Norton, who details the virtues of multiculturalism as public policy.[11]

Reconciling diversity and public culture within the context of the United States continues to be a central concern for American studies scholars, but so too must the question of which "public" or "publics" constitute the appropriate point of reference or arena of action and engagement. Shared culture, as Cayton acknowledges, can be nationalist in orientation, but more often than not, the nature of "cultural identity proves far more complex than any simple reference to national identity or citizenship can capture." Increasingly, this complexity is evident not only in the form of subnational attachments and identities addressed by the scholarship on multiculturalism, but in transnational ones as well. Several contributors to this volume take into account the growing transcendence of national borders and the potential challenges of globalization. Understanding these shifting contours of cultural and political belonging will be central to engaging politically and theoretically with issues of public action, image, identity, and space.[12]

Globalization, in the most basic sense, can be defined as the compression of time and space; or in greater specificity as "neither a singular condition nor a linear process. Rather, it is best thought of as a multidimensional phenomenon involving diverse domains of activity and interaction, including the economic, political, technological, military, legal, cultural and environmental."[13] A central dimension of this phenomenon involves states, as administrative governing units, losing their autonomy in the international system, and as a result their capacity to manage the well-being of their constituencies. Rothman (Chapter 9) for example, incorporates Christopher Lasch's concept of "a transnational class of monied individuals who are essentially stateless, without an evident sense of national obligation." Borders, geographic, cultural, and political are becoming more permeable as people, ideas, goods, and services move more freely across them. This affects not only large urban areas or border regions in the United States, like Los Angeles, but also, increasingly, small Midwestern towns as is illustrated in Buff's chapter on northwest Ohio.

It is important to note that amid these forces of global change, the nation-state continues to be powerful—politically and symbolically—even as it is increasingly contested. Analyzing the powerful resurgence of American nationhood after 9/11, Spigel (Chapter 5) writes that "the . . . will to remember was connected to the resuscitation of national culture in a country heretofore divided by culture wars and extreme political partisanship." Since 9/11 we have also experienced something similar to what John Bodnar describes in Chapter 3, on the American remembrance of World War II: "Public commemorations have been punctuated by calls to honor and emulate the good behavior of the wartime generation with its presumed commitment to patriotism and conventional values such as marriage and capitalism." We have also seen how romantic forms of nationalism "can lift people from the frustrations of everyday life. . . . They offer hope and a sense of collective and individual empowerment." Nevertheless, for the purposes of this volume assessing the persistence or decline of the nation-state is less important than considering how contemporary challenges to the national form affect issues of public action, image, space, and identity. This consideration is particularly important given the extent to which the nation continues to be a common referent for the "public."

Nationhood, from one perspective, can be viewed as a force for unity and commonality, a basis for democracy, and a source of material and psychological security for those included within its boundaries.[14] It is on this basis that some observers view the declining power and centrality of nation-states as problematic. Charles Taylor, for example, insists that democracies require strong common identification on the part of their citizens and, hence: "we cannot do without patriotism in the modern world."[15] In a similar vein, Kwame Anthony Appiah emphasizes the need for rootedness and the capacity of nations and states to provide that. He challenges the cosmopolitan critique of states, asserting that many of the values of cultural pluralism that cosmopolitanism celebrates depend on the existence of and protections afforded by states: "It is because humans live best on a smaller scale that we should defend not just the state, but the county, the town, the street, the business, the craft, the profession, and the family, as communities . . . that are appropriate spheres of moral concern."[16]

Nevertheless, nationhood and nationalism are also notorious forces of exclusion and oppression. Even the most civic of nations, a status the United States proudly proclaims for itself, rely heavily on "others"—both internal and external—to construct and maintain an "us." Notably, Ryan's history of the Los Angeles Plaza seems to reveal that diversity and public culture coexisted much more comfortably in Southern California prior to the expansion and consolidation of the American nation. Similarly, since 9/11 foreign and domestic policy in the United States has been dominated by the "celebration of American cultural superiority" that Spigel discusses in Chapter 5 on entertainment wars. For ethnic, racial, religious, and sexual others in the United States, the limitations of American nationhood as an arena of public action and identity have been highlighted post-9/11. For these individuals and groups, globalization, to the extent that is represents a challenge to the hegemony of nationhood as a form of attachment and a site of engagement, might be viewed as emancipatory. Several contributors to this volume see in the fragmentation of the postmodern era the potential for counternarratives of resistance (Chun, Cayton, Spigel, Zukin). Moreover, Bodnar's analysis in Chapter 3 reminds us that linking democracy to love and loyalty of the nation-state can be misguided: "Patriotism is almost always demonstrated in military terms and almost never within an older (progressive) frame of citizen engagement in genuine civic or social reform."

Ultimately, Spigel's emphasis on the contemporary limitations of nationalist myths seems accurate. These myths are and will likely continue to be mobilized, as has been the case in post-9/11 America. However, because the economic and cultural practices of the twenty-first century United States society, media or otherwise, are not conducive to unifying narratives of patriotism, these myths are not likely to work indefinitely. If globalization can be conceptualized as a proliferation in sites and spaces of public action and identity, then the future may be promising in terms of democratic practice. Postnational scholars like Yasemin Soysal make this claim with regard to the growing international human rights regime that protects individuals irrespective of their membership in a state.[17] And communitarian Amitai

Etzioni sees in the emergence of transnational organizations and networks the potential for a United States foreign policy devoted to building global community, not empire.[18] If, on the other hand, globalization represents greater centralization of power and the further commodification of the public sphere, then the future looks much more dim. Either way, in the realm of political engagement it makes sense to think globally, while paying closer attention, as Ryan and Zukin suggest, to opportunities for acting locally. And in the realm of analysis, scholars must stay open to ways in which shifting contours are reconfiguring public action, image, space, and identity.

Notes

Preface

1. Terry Eagleton, *After Theory* (New York: Basic Books, 2003), 1.
2. Hannah Arendt, *The Human Condition* (Garden City, N.Y.: Doubleday, 1959), 48.
3. Ibid., 53.
4. Harry C. Boyte, *Everyday Politics: Reconnecting Citizens and Public Life* (Philadelphia: University of Pennsylvania Press, 2004), xvii.
5. Jürgen Habermas, *The Structural Transformation of the Public Sphere: An Inquiry into a Category of Bourgeois Society*; trans. Thomas Burger with the assistance of Frederick Lawrence (Cambridge, Mass.: MIT Press, 1989).
6. Boyte, *Everyday Politics*.
7. Michael Frisch, "Prismatics, Multivalence, and Other Riffs on the Millennial Moment: Presidential Address to the American Studies Association, 13 October 2000," *American Quarterly* 53 (June 2001): 193-231.
8. Ibid., 205.
9. Ibid., 206.
10. George Sanchez, "Working at the Crossroads: American Studies for the 21st Century Presidential Address to the American Studies Association November 9, 2001," *American Quarterly* 54 (March 2002): 207.
11. Boyte, *Everyday Politics*; Robert D. Putnam, *Bowling Alone: The Collapse and Revival of American Community* (New York: Simon and Schuster, 2000).
12. Arendt, *The Human Condition*; John Dewey, *The Public and Its Problems* (Athens, Ohio: Ohio University Press, 1954); Boyte, *Everyday Politics*; Clifford Geertz, *Interpretation of Cultures: Selected Essays* (New York: Basic Books, 1973); Habermas, *The Structural Transformation of the Public Sphere*; Stuart Hall, ed., *Representation: Cultural Representations and Signifying Practices* (London: Sage, 1997); Michael Warner, *Publics and Counterpublics* (New York: Zone Books, 2002).
13. Dewey, *The Public and Its Problems*, 13.
14. Eagleton, *After Theory*, 7.
15. Ibid., 21.
16. For the final report, see http://www.units.muohio.edu/americanstudies/projects/neh/index.php.
17. For a historiographical overview of the field, see Gene Wise, " 'Paradigm Dramas' in American Studies: A Cultural and Institutional History of the Movement, *American Quarterly* 31 (June 1979): 293–337.
18. Arendt, *The Human Condition*, 52.

What Is Public Culture?

1. Robert Putman's *Bowling Alone: The Collapse and Revival of American Community* (New York: Simon and Schuster, 2000) is perhaps the best known of scholarly studies that document a lack of civic engagement as a hallmark of contemporary American culture and which urge its revival. His Saguaro Seminar on Civic Engagement in America at Harvard University is an ongoing initiative that "focuses on expanding what we know about our levels of trust and community engagement and on developing strategies and efforts to increase this engagement" (http://www.ksg.harvard.edu/saguaro/).

2. Robert I. Rotberg, "Social Capital and Political Culture in Africa, America, Australasia, and Europe," in *Patterns of Social Capital: Stability and Change in Historical Perspective*, ed. Robert I. Rotberg (Cambridge and New York: Cambridge University Press, 2001), 1.

3. See, for example, Thomas Bridges, *The Culture of Citizenship: Inventing Postmodern Civic Culture* (Albany: State University of New York Press, 1994), 4.

4. Hannah Arendt, *The Human Condition* (Garden City, N.Y.: Doubleday, 1959), 25, quoting Werner Jaeger, *Paideia* (1945), III, 111.

5. On Arendt, see Seyla Benhabib, "Models of Public Space: Hannah Arendt, the Liberal Tradition, and Jürgen Habermas," in *Feminism, the Public and the Private*, ed. Joan B. Landes (New York: Oxford University Press, 1998), 65–99.

6. John Locke, *The Second Treatise of Civil Government* (1690), chap. 9, sec. 131.

7. For a history of the notions of public and private in Western political thought, especially as they pertain to the role of women in society, see Jean Bethke Elshtain, *Public Man, Private Woman: Women in Social and Political Thought* (Princeton, N.J.: Princeton University Press, 1981).

8. Gramsci's model is most thoroughly laid out in his *Prison Notebooks*. See *Selections from the Prison Notebooks of Antonio Gramsci*, ed. and trans. Quintin Hoare and Geoffrey Nowell Smith (London: Lawrence and Wishart, 1971).

9. *Dialectic of Enlightenment* (London: Verso, 1979), 120–67 (originally published as *Dialektik der Aufklärung* [Amsterdam: Querido, 1947]).

10. Theodor W. Adorno, "Resignation," in *Critical Models: Interventions and Catchwords*, trans. Henry W. Pickford (New York: Columbia University Press, 1998), 293.

11. Jürgen Habermas, *The Theory of Communicative Action*, trans. Thomas McCarthy, vol. 1, *Reason and the Rationalization of Society*, and vol. 2, *Lifeword and System: Critique of Functionalist Reason* (Boston: Beacon Press, 1984, 1985).

12. See Jürgen Habermas, "The Public Sphere: An Encyclopedia Article," in *Critical Theory and Society: A Reader*, ed. Stephen Eric Bronner and Douglas M. Kellner, trans. Sara Lennox and Frank Lennox (New York: Routledge, 1989), 136–42. In addition, much of my reading of Habermas is informed by Martin Morris's incisive *Rethinking the Communicative Turn: Adorno, Habermas, and the Problem of Communicative Freedom* (Albany: State University of New York Press, 2001).

13. On the concept of Habermas's public sphere, see Craig Calhoun, ed., *Habermas and the Public Sphere* (Cambridge, Mass.: MIT Press, 1992).

14. Habermas, *Theory of Communicative Action*, 2:232.

15. See Ljubia Mitrovi, "New Social Paradigm: Habermas's Theory of Communicative Action," *Philosophy and Sociology* 2 (1999): 220.

16. Habermas, *Theory of Communicative Action*, 2:355.

17. Jüeaen Habermas, *Between Facts and Norms: Contributions to a Discourse Theory of Law and Democracy*, trans. William Rehg (Cambridge, Mass.: MIT, 1996), 367.

18. Carl Boggs, *The End of Politics: Corporate Power and the Decline of the Public Sphere* (New York: Guilford Press, 2000), 208–42.

19. This in essence is Michel Foucault's argument in his *History of Sexuality*, trans. Robert Hurley (New York: Pantheon, 1978).

20. A decade and a half's worth of his essays on various topics related to the public are collected in *Publics and Counterpublics* (New York: Zone Books, 2002).

21. Warner, *Publics and Counterpublics*, 8, 11–12.

22. Ibid., 55.

23. Nancy Fraser, "Rethinking the Public Sphere: A Contribution to the Critique of Actually Existing Democracy," in Calhoun, *Habermas and the Public Sphere*, 109–42. See also Benhabib, "Models of Public Space."

24. Warner, *Publics and Counterpublics*, 122.

25. See ibid., 21–124.

26. Fraser, "Rethinking the Public Sphere," 116–20.

27. Mary P. Ryan, "Gender and Public Access: Women's Politics in Nineteenth-Century America," in Landes, *Feminism, the Public and the Private*, 204. See also her *Civic Wars: Democracy and Public Life in the American City during the Nineteenth Century* (Berkeley: University of California Press, 1997).

28. Madan Sarup, *Identity, Culture and the Postmodern World*, ed. Tasneem Raja (Athens: University of Georgia Press, 1996), 48.

29. Wendy Brown, "Wounded Attachments: Late Modern Oppositional Political Formations," in Landes, *Feminism, the Public and the Private*, 460. Indeed, Kwame Anthony Appiah, "Identity: Political Not Cultural," in *Field Work: Sites in Literary and Cultural Studies*, ed. Marjorie Garber, Paul B. Franklin, and Rebecca C. Walkowitz (New York and London: Routledge, 1996), 34–40, argues that all identities, because they are contrastive, are political in nature.

30. Fraser, "Rethinking the Public Sphere," 122. Among those in addition to Fraser and Warner who have theorized that identity is constructed by discourse rather than as an essential property of subjects, see Peter Uwe Hohendahl, "The Public Sphere: Models and Boundaries," in Calhoun, *Habermas and the Public Sphere*, 99–108; Gust A. Yep, "My Three Cultures: Navigating the Multicultural Identity Landscape," in *Readings in Cultural Contexts*, ed. Judith N. Martin, Thomas K. Nakayama, and Lisa A. Flores (Mountain View, Calif.: Mayfield Publishing, 1998), 79–85; and Nancy Whittier, "Meaning and Structure in Social Movements," in *Social Movements: Identity, Culture and the State*, ed. David S. Meyer, Nancy Whittier, and Belinda Robnett (Oxford and New York: Oxford University Press, 2002), 289–307.

31. Iris Marion Young, "Impartiality and the Civic Public: Some Implications of Feminist Critiques of Moral and Political Theory," in Landes, *Feminism, the Public and the Private*, 424; Warner, *Publics and Counterpublics*, 121–24.

32. Warner, *Publics and Counterpublics*, 119.

Notes to Pages 21–33

33. Lauren Berlant, *The Queen of America Goes to Washington City: Essays on Sex and Citizenship* (Durham, N.C.: Duke University Press, 1997), especially "Introduction: The Intimate Public Sphere," 1–24.

34. Nancy Fraser, "A Future for Marxism," *New Politics* 6, no. 4 (n.s.), whole no. 24 (Winter 1998); repr. http://www.wpunj.edu/~newpol/issue24/fraser24.htm.

35. Warner, *Publics and Counterpublics*, 11–12.

36. It may be worth noting that my choice of the term "sexual orientation" already implies a position vis-à-vis the discursive world in which the conversation with respect to identity and sexuality is positioned—and unavoidably so. I have already indicated my sense of my own discursive position; it makes a difference in the working concept I choose here. Were I positioned differently, I almost certainly would have chosen to cast the conversation in different terms because the public(s) invoked would have been different ones.

37. George Chauncey, *Gay New York: Gender, Urban Culture, and the Making of the Gay Male World, 1890–1940* (New York: Basic Books, 1994). Chauncey's historically contingent narrative rests, of course, on the discursive model of sexuality developed by Foucault in his *History of Sexuality*.

Chapter 1. Looking for the Public in Time and Space

1. "At Mayor Villaraigosa's Inauguration," *Los Angeles Times*, July 2, 2005, A1, A30.

2. The lines of the debate were first posed in Calhoun, *Habermas and the Public Sphere*. More recently the issues are best articulated in Warner, *Publics and Counterpublics*, especially chapters 1 and 2.

3. John Dewey, *The Public and Its Problems* (Chicago: Swallow Press, 1954); Mary P. Ryan, *Civic Wars: Democracy and Public Life in the American City during the Nineteenth Century* (Berkeley: University of California Press, 1997), 6. Quotations are from *John Dewey: The Political Writings*, ed. Debra Morris and Ian Shapiro (Indianapolis: Hackett, 1993), 174, 242.

4. Neal Harlow, *Maps and Surveys of the Pueblo Lands of Los Angeles* (Los Angeles: Dawson's Book Shop, 1976), 14–15; W. W. Robinson, *Maps of Los Angeles from Ord's Survey of 1849 to the End of the Boom of the Eighties* (Los Angeles: Dawson's Book Shop, 1966).

5. Douglas Monroy, *Thrown Among Strangers: The Making of Mexican Culture in Frontier California* (Berkeley: University of California Press, 1990), chap. 3.

6. Harris Newmark, *Sixty Years in Southern California . . . Reminiscences of Harris Newmark*, ed. Maurice Newmark and Marco Newmark (New York: Houghton Mifflin, 1930), 101–2, 49, chap. 7.

7. W. W. Robinson, *Los Angeles from the Days of the Pueblo: A Brief History and Guide to the Plaza Area*, revised with an introduction by Doyce B. Nunis (San Francisco: California Historical Society, 1981), chap. 3.

8. Monroy, *Thrown Among Strangers*, 101–2.

9. Ibid., 108

10. Robinson, *Los Angeles*, 51.

11. Ibid., chap. 4; Antonio Maria Osio, *The History of Alta California: A Memoir of Mexican California*, trans. Rose Marie Beebe and Robert M. Senkewicz (Madison: University of Wisconsin Press, 1996), 238–45.

12. Newmark, *Sixty Years in Southern California*, chap. 8; John McGroaty, *Los Angeles from the Mountains to the Sea* (New York and Chicago: American Historical Society), 1: 59.

13. Ludwig Louis Salavator, *Los Angeles in the Sunny Seventies* (Los Angeles: Callster and Zeitlin, 1919), 125.

14. McGroaty, *Los Angeles from the Mountains to the Sea*, 30–31.

15. Leonard Pitt, *The Decline of the Californios: A Social History of Spanish-Speaking Californians, 1846–1890* (Berkeley: University of California Press, 1999).

16. Puck Collection, album 1 "Los Angeles Long Ago," Huntington Photographic Collections, Huntington Library, San Marino, Calif.

17. Jean Bruce Poole and Tevvy Ball, *El Pueblo: The Historic Heart of Los Angeles* (Los Angeles: Getty Conservation Institute and the J. Paul Getty Museum, 2002), 110–12, 123; Pitt, *Decline of the Californios*; Dolores Hayden, *The Power of Place: Urban Landscapes as Public History* (Cambridge, Mass.: MIT Press, 1995), 138–67.

18. Newmark, *Sixty Years in Southern California*, 296, 338.

19. Richard A. Warren, *Vagrants and Citizens: Politics and the Masses in Mexico City from Colony to Republic* (Wilmington, Del.: SR Books, 2001).

20. Newmark, *Sixty Years in Southern California*, 43–49.

21. J. Gregg Layne, "Annals of Los Angeles," *California Historical Society Quarterly* 13 (September 1934): 195–223, quotation on 220.

22. For the urban violence coincident with the expansion of democracy in the United States, see Paul Gilje, *Rioting in America* (Blomington: Indiana University Press, 1996); David Grimsted, *American Mobbing, 1828–1861* (New York: Oxford University Press, 1998); and Ryan, *Civic Wars*.

23. Monroy, *Thrown Among Strangers*, 186–222; Lawrence E. Guillow, "Pandemonium in the Plaza: The First Los Angeles Riot, July 22, 1856," *Southern California Quarterly* (1995): 183–97.

24. William Deverell, *White-Washed Adobe: The Rise of Los Angeles and the Remaking of Its Mexican Past* (Berkeley: University of California Press, 2005); Richard White, *The Middle Ground: Indians, Empires and Republics in the Great Lakes Region, 1650–1815* (London: Cambridge University Press, 1991).

25. Newmark, *Sixty Years in Southern California*, 417.

26. Ibid., 428–33; Marco R. Newmark, "Calle de los Negros and the Chinese Massacre of 1871, *Historical Society of Southern California Quarterly* 26, nos. 2 and 3 (1944): 97–98.

27. *The City Beautiful, Suggestions by Charles Mulford Robinson: Report of the Municipal Art Commission for the City of Los Angeles* (Los Angeles: William J. Porter, 1901), 1–4.

28. Gregory Hise and William Devereux, *Eden by Design: The 1930 Olmsted-Bartholomew Plan for the Los Angles Region* (Berkeley: University of California Press, 2000); "Report of the Allied Architects Associations of Los Angeles on an Administration Center for the County of Los Angeles and the City of Los Angeles," December 31, 1924, submitted to the Board of Supervisors, Huntington Library.

29. Marco Newmark, "La Fiesta de Los Angeles of 1894," *Historical Society of Southern California Quarterly* 29 (June 1947): 106; Christina Wielus Mead, "Las Fiestas de Los Angles: A Survey of Yearly Celebrations, 1894–1898," *Historical Society of Southern California Quarterly* 31 (June 1949): 61–114.

30. Rodney Steiner, *Los Angeles: The Centrifugal City* (Dubuque, Iowa: Kendall Hunt Publishing, 1981), 125.

31. Robinson, *Maps*, no. 44.

32. Samuel Storrow, "The North End or So-Called Plaza Site," *Los Angeles Municipal League Bulletin*, January 3, 1926.

33. Dana W. Bartlett, *The Better City: A Sociological Study of a Modern City* (Los Angeles: Neuner Company Press, 1907), 87–106.

34. Mark Wild, *Street Meeting: Multi-Ethnic Neighborhoods in Early Twentieth-Century Los Angeles* (Berkeley: University of California Press, 2005), chaps. 6 and 7, p. 151.

35. Ricardo Romo, *East Los Angeles: History of a Barrio* (Austin: University of Texas Press, 1983), 103, 105–8; Phoebe S. Kropp, "Citizens of the Past: Olvera Street and the Construction of Race and Memory in 1930s Los Angeles," *Radical History Review* 81 (Fall 2001): 35–60.

36. Henri Lefebvre, *The Production of Space*, trans. Donald Nicholson-Smith (Oxford: Blackwell, 1991); Henri Lefebvre, *Critique of Everyday Life*, trans. John Moore (London: Verso, 1991).

Chapter 2. Remembrance, Contestation, Excavation

Edward Linenthal delivered a shorter version of this essay at the Seventeenth Annual Oklahoma Lecture in the Humanities on February 28, 2002, in Tulsa, Oklahoma. An edited version of that lecture appeared in the Oklahoma Humanities Council's publication, *Humanities Interview* 20, no. 2 (Spring 2002): 3–6.

1. Quoted material from Fei Xiaotong in following paragraphs from Fei Xiaotong, "The Shallowness of Cultural Tradition," in R. David Arkush and Leo O. Lee, eds., *Land Without Ghosts: Chinese Impressions of America from the Mid-Nineteenth Century to the Present* (Berkeley: University of California Press, 1989), 177ff.

2. Patricia Nelson Limerick, *Something in the Soil: Legacies and Reckonings in the New West* (New York: W. W. Norton, 2000), 33.

3. Paul A. Hutton, "Washita Past," in *Washita Symposium: Past, Present, and Future* (Washita Battlefield National Historic Site: National Park Service, 2001), 21–22.

4. Lawrence H. Hart, "Legacies of the Massacre and Battle at the Washita," *Oklahoma Today* (May/June 1999): 60.

5. Ibid., 61; Bob Blackburn, "Washita Future," in *Washita Symposium*, 83.

6. Quoted material in previous three paragraphs from "Battle or Massacre?" in *Washita Symposium*, 42–51.

7. Quoted material from Sarah Craighead's presentation at the National Park Service workshop "The National Park Service and Civic Engagement," December 6–8, 2001. Text of presentation in author's files, and I thank Sarah Craighead for providing me with the text.

8. Nathan Irvin Huggins, *Black Odyssey: The African-American Ordeal in Slavery* (New York: Vintage Books, 1990), xii–xiii. A valuable set of essays exploring the rapidly changing historic landscape of slavery is James Oliver Horton and Lois E. Horton, eds., *Slavery and Public History: The Tough Stuff of American Memory* (New York: New Press, 2006).

9. John Hope Franklin and Scott Ellsworth, "History Knows No Fences: An Overview," in *Tulsa Race Riot: A Report by the Oklahoma Commission to Study the Tulsa Race Riot of 1921*, February 28, 2001, 22–23.

10. James S. Hirsch, *Riot and Remembrance: The Tulsa Race Riot and Its Legacy* (Boston: Houghton Mifflin, 2002), 323.

11. Quoted material in previous two paragraphs from Danny Goble, "Final Report of the Oklahoma Commission to Study the Tulsa Race Riot of 1921," in *Tulsa Race Riot*, 7.

12. Leon Litwack, *Trouble in Mind: Black Southerners in the Age of Jim Crow* (New York: Alfred A. Knopf, 1998), 281.

13. There is, of course, a rich and ever-expanding multiracial historical landscape, and at least eight communities are actively engaged in recalling lynching through, for example, erection of memorials, cleaning of grave sites, rituals of reconciliation, books, educational centers, and community forums. A whole new generation of scholars are at work on the horrific reality of lynching. In October 2002 at Emory University in Atlanta, Georgia, a conference, "Lynching and Racial Violence in America: Histories and Legacies," brought together many of these scholars. There were, for example, panels on the history of lynching, artistic responses to lynching, political and intellectual response, the history of race riots, legal perspectives, histories of the antilynching movement, and media responses. Participants also visited the "Without Sanctuary" exhibition at the Martin Luther King Jr. National Historic Site. See Mark Auslander, "'Return to Sender': Confronting Lynching and Our Haunted Landscapes," *Southern Changes* (Spring/Summer 2002): 4–7. For some examples of community remembrance, see http://www.mooresford.org.

14. First quote from Leon Litwack, "Hellhounds," in James Allen, Hilton Als, John Lewis, and Leon F. Litwack, *Without Sanctuary: Lynching Photographs in America* (Santa Fe, N.M.: Twin Palms Publishers, 2000), 11; second quote from back of postcard, fig. 26 in Allen, et. al., *Without Sanctuary*.

15. Quoted material in previous two paragraphs from James H. Madison, *A Lynching in the Heartland: Race and Memory in America* (New York: Palgrave, 2001), 118, 149.

16. Mark Curriden and Leroy Phillips Jr., *Contempt of Court: The Turn-of-the-Century Lynching That Launched a Hundred Years of Federalism* (New York: Anchor Books, 1999), 286, 347, xvii.

17. See, for example, Laura Wexler, *Fire in a Canebrake: The Last Mass Lynching in America* (New York: Scribner, 2003).

18. Lawrence H. Hart, "Testimony on 'Washita Battlefield National Historic Site Act of 1996,' before the House Subcommittee on National Parks, Forests, and Public Lands," n.d. (I thank Bob Blackburn for providing me a copy of the text.)

19. Edward T. Linenthal, *The Unfinished Bombing: Oklahoma City in American Memory* (New York: Oxford University Press, 2001), 233–34.

20. Falwell quoted, among many other places in Michael E. Naparstek, "Falwell and Robertson Stumble," *Religion in the News* 4, no. 3 (Fall 2001): 5; Arendt's powerful words are from her essay on Isak Dinesen in *Men in Dark Times* (New York: Harcourt, Brace and World, 1968), 104. It should come as no surprise that there were a number of "razor's edge" issues at the World Trade Center site, among them the appropriate role of firemen and workers from other agencies in recovery operations, the treatment of symbolically—and materially—charged debris, and the accusations by journalist William Langewiesche of rescue workers looting at the site, an accusation met by bitter denials. See William Langewiesche, *American Ground: Unbuilding the World Trade Center* (New York: North Point Press, 2002).

21. Paul Fussell, *Wartime: Understanding and Behavior in the Second World War* (New York: Oxford University Press, 1989), ix.

Chapter 3. Public Sentiments and the American Remembrance of World War II

I would like to thank Robb Westbrook, Peggy Shaffer, and anonymous readers for critical comments on a draft of this essay.

1. Jay Winter, *Sites of Memory, Sites of Mourning: The Great War in European Cultural History* (Cambridge: Cambridge University Press, 1995), 1–26, 115; Paul Fussell, *The Great War and Modern Memory* (New York: Oxford University Press, 1975). Michael Kammen, *Mystic Chords of Memory: The Transformation of Tradition in American Culture* (New York: Knopf, 1991), 533–44, also discusses the tension between traditional and modern forms of remembrance after 1945. On the return of "normalcy" to Europe, see Richard Bessell and Dirk Schumann, eds., *Life After Death: Approaches to the Cultural and Social History of Europe during the 1940s and 1950s* (Washington, D.C.: German Historical Institute, 2003). Jay Winter and Emmanuel Sivian, "Setting the Framework," in *War and Remembrance in the Twentieth Century*, ed. Winter and Sivian (Cambridge: Cambridge University Press, 1999), 6–39, offers a more complex view of the process of remembering war by indicating that it is a public activity involving a "dialogue between agents" and an exchange of views and positions in rituals, monuments, film, art, and fiction. As such they suggest that it is "messy" and always susceptible to alteration. Individual memories do not get translated directly into collective memory, which is more likely to result from some agreement of what can be shared and not from any simple transfer of the personal into the public. The metaphor of "exchange" implies that collective remembrance is formed in society and does not emanate simply from the power and interests of states or the psychological processes of individuals. For a critique of Winter's position on the healing aspects of traditional language in Europe after World War I, see Susan Kingsley Kent, "Remembering the Great War," *Journal of British Studies* 37 (January 1998): 105–10. Kent suggests that Winter's view of mourning as a universal reaction to the ruptures of the Great War that crossed national and state boundaries ignored the level of pain and suffering that families and wounded veterans carried with them every day for the rest of their lives. And she raised questions about his failure to note the political goals behind the promotion of certain forms of remembrance—goals that this

essay attempts to reveal. For an important discussion on trauma as a sense of "utter powerlessness," see Jenny Edkins, *Trauma and the Memory of Politics* (Cambridge: Cambridge University Press, 2003), 4–5, 13, 57–70.

2. Archibald MacLeish, *Collected Poems, 1917–1982* (Boston: Houghton Mifflin, 1985), 341, 611.

3. Donald L. Miller, *Lewis Mumford: A Life* (New York: Weidenfeld and Nicolson, 1989), 424–27; Studs Terkel, *The Good War: An Oral History of World War II* (New York: Pantheon Books, 1984), 3–39; John R. Satterfield, *We Band of Brothers: The Sullivans and World War II* (Parkersburg, Iowa: Mid-Prairie Books, 1995), 203; Paul S. Boyer, *By the Bomb's Early Light: American Thought and Culture at the Dawn of the Atomic Age* (Chapel Hill: University of North Carolina Press, 1994); Lary May, *The Big Tomorrow: Hollywood and the Politics of the American Way* (Chicago: University of Chicago Press, 2000), 283–84; John Bodnar, *Blue-Collar Hollywood: Liberalism, Democracy, and Working People in American Film* (Baltimore: Johns Hopkins University Press, 2003), 94.

4. Norman Mailer, *The Naked and the Dead* (New York: Rinehart, 1948); James Jones, *From Here to Eternity* (New York: Scribner, 1951).

5. See Patrick Joyce, *Democratic Subjects: The Self and the Social in Nineteenth-Century England* (Cambridge: Cambridge University Press, 1994), 156, for an account of how some citizens in nineteenth-century England imagined their lives as tied to a larger project of nationalism and liberal democracy that allowed them a "final liberation" from the more troubled and uncertain world of experience and the idea that evil might triumph over good. Tom Brokaw, *The Greatest Generation* (New York: Random House, 1998), xiv–xxx, 43–51, 268, 329–31. Information on the Library of Congress's oral history project with veterans throughout the United States can be found at http://www.loc.gov.folklife/vets-portal.html.

6. Stephen Ambrose, *Band of Brothers: E Company, 506 Regiment, 101st Airborne from Normandy to Hitler's Eagle Nest* (New York: Simon and Schuster, 2001), 2–11, 82. The HBO television series based on this book actually presents the anguish of the individual soldier in greater detail. Part 7 of the televised series, "The Breaking Point," opens, for instance, with a direct recollection of a veteran in our times noting that everywhere he looked at times he saw dead people—"ours, theirs, civilians." Another veteran interview recalled that he "had a lot of trouble in later life" when he recalled all the dying. This particular episode also allows for more of the "soldier's story" of the war with accounts that are critical of some officers and a portrait of the men without strong political ideologies as they simply fight to survive.

7. Ambrose, *Band of Brothers*, 218–19, 402–3.

8. James Bradley, *Flags of Our Fathers* (New York: Bantam, 2001); William Manchester, *Goodbye Darkness* (Boston: Little Brown, 1979), 127, 232–33, 250.

9. *Save Our History: The World War II Memorial*, videocassette produced by the History Channel, 1999; Richard Kohn, "History and the Culture Wars: The Case of the Smithsonian's Enola Gay Exhibition," *Journal of American History* (December 1995): 636–63; Bob Greene, *Duty: A Father, His Son, and the Man Who Won the War* (New York: HarperCollins, 2001), 19. For an effort of the American government to preempt any discussion of the trauma inflicted on the Japanese by the dropping of the atomic bombs, see Robert Jay Lifton and Greg Mitchell, *Hiroshima in America: Fifty Years of Denial* (New York: G. P. Putnam, 1995), especially 33–37.

10. Omer Bartov, *Mirrors of Destruction: War, Genocide and Modern Identity* (New York: Oxford University Press, 2000), 14–16. On the failure of romantic myths to contextualize the past, see Paul Hamilton, *Historicism* (London: Routledge, 2002), 1–5. See Jonathan M. Hansen, *The Lost Promise of Patriotism: Debating American Identity* (Chicago: University of Chicago Press, 2003), 157. Melinda Lawson, *Patriot Fires: Forging a New American Nationalism in the Civil War North* (Lawrence: University of Kansas Press, 2002), 14–16, suggests a similar experience from Civil War times in which the postwar era seemed to celebrate the "sanctification of the nation-state through sacrifice." During the war she noticed a heightened concern for celebrating the soldiers and sympathizing with their suffering displacing from public attention other issues such as free labor, slavery, and emancipation. We also know that veterans groups—from both the North and the South—dominated the public commemoration of the Civil War and fostered ideals of male valor in battle more than sentiments of pain and suffering in war and the politics of slavery. See David Blight, *Race and Reunion: The Civil War in American Memory* (Cambridge, Mass.: Belknap Press of Harvard University Press, 2001).

11. See John Bodnar, "Saving Private Ryan and Postwar Memory," *American Historical Review* 106 (June 2001): 805–17; Winter and Sivian, "Setting the Framework," 27–32; Judith Herman, *Trauma and Recovery: The Aftermath of Violence from Domestic Abuse to Political Terror* (New York: Basic Books, 1992), 2-3, 133–36. Lifton and Mitchell, *Hiroshima in America*, 345–46.

12. Pieter Lagrou, "The Nationalization of Victimhood: Selective Violence and National Grief in Western Europe, 1940-1960," in Bessel and Schumann, *Life after Death*, 243–57; Nina Tumarkin, *The Living and the Dead: The Rise and Fall of the Cult of World War II in Russia* (New York: Basic Books, 1994), 127–40; Henry Rousso, *The Vichy Syndrome: History and Memory in France since 1944* (Cambridge, Mass.: Harvard University Press, 1991), 15–70; Lisa Yoneyama, *Hiroshima Traces: Time, Space, and the Dialectics of Memory* (Berkeley: University of California Press, 1999); Robert Moeller, *War Stories: The Search for a Usable Past in Germany* (Berkeley: University of California Press, 2001). See Eric L. Santer, *Stranded Objects: Mourning, Memory, and Film in Postwar Germany* (Ithaca, N.Y.: Cornell University Press, 1993), 1–19, for a discussion of how some Germans still held onto the dream of collective power through Hitler after the war instead of confronting the tragedy of the Nazism. See also Alan Mintz, *Popular Culture and the Shaping of Holocaust Memory in America* (Seattle: University of Washington Press, 2001), 14–15.

13. George H. Roeder, *The Censored War: American Visual Experiences during World War Two* (New Haven, Conn.: Yale University Press, 1993), 25, 29. I differ from Tom Engelhardt, *The End of Victory Culture: The End of Cold War America and the Disillusioning of a Generation* (New York: Basic Books, 1995), 10, who argues that a "heroic war ethos" eroded only gradually after 1945. On the difficulty of reconciling the bombing of Hiroshima with our self-image as "decent people," see Lifton and Mitchell, *Hiroshima*, 1–5.

14. Louis B. Sohn, *The Human Rights Revolution: From Roosevelt's Four Freedoms to the Independence of Peace, Development and Human Rights* (Cambridge, Mass.: Harvard Law School Human Rights Program, 1995). See Elizabeth Borgwardt, *A New Deal for the World: America's Vision for Human Rights* (Cambridge, Mass.: Harvard University Press, 2005), 3–4.

15. Clayton R. Koppes and Gregory D. Black, *Hollywood Goes to War: How Politics, Profits, and Propaganda Shaped World War II* (Berkeley: University of California Press, 1987), 66–70; Henry A. Wallace, *Century of the Common Man* (New York: International Workers Order, 1943); Mark L. Kleinman, *A World of Hope, World of Fear: Henry Wallace, Reinhold Niebhur and American Liberalism* (Columbus: Ohio State University Press, 2000), 7.

16. Alan Winkler, *The Politics of Propaganda: The Office of War Information, 1942–1945* (New Haven, Conn.: Yale University Press, 1978); Thomas Fleming, *The New Dealer's War: Franklin D. Roosevelt and the War within World War II* (New York: Basic Books, 2001), 192–93. Allan Nevins, "What Did the American People Think Once It Was in Process," in *While You Were Gone: A Report on Wartime Life in the United States*, ed. Jack Goodman (New York: Simon and Schuster, 1946), 17.

17. Godfrey Hodgson, *The World Turned Right Side Up* (Boston: Houghton Mifflin, 1996), 14, 33; Robert Westbrook, "In the Mirror of the Enemy: Japanese Political Culture and the Peculiarities of American Patriotism in World War II," in *Bonds of Affection: Americans Define Their Patriotism*, ed. John Bodnar (Princeton, N.J.: Princeton University Press, 1996), 213–18; Westbrook, "Fighting for the American Family: Private Interests and Political Obligation in World War II," in *The Power of Culture*, ed. Richard Wightman Fox and T. J. Jackson Lears (Chicago: University of Chicago Press, 1993), 195–211. Candace Vogler and Patchen Markell discuss the problem of violence for the liberal state in "Introduction: Violence, Redemption and the Liberal Imagination," *Public Culture* 15 (2003): 1–10.

18. Eric Sevareid, *Not So Wild a Dream* (Columbia: University of Missouri Press, 1946), 213–16. For a fictional discussion of cynicism in America over homefront activities during the war, see the novel by Irwin Shaw, *The Young Lions* (New York: Random House, 1948).

19. Peter Fritzsche, "Spectres of History: On Nostalgia, Exile, and Modernity," *American Historical Review* 106 (December 2001): 1587–1618; Jody Rosen, *White Christmas: The Story of an American Song* (New York: Scribner, 2002), 137–60; Glenn Hendler, *Public Sentiments: Structures of Feeling in Nineteenth-Century American Literatures* (Chapel Hill: University of North Carolina Press, 2001), 3–22. See also Lawson, *Patriot Fires*, 5–11.

20. Ernie Pyle, *Brave Men* (New York: Grosset and Dunlap, 1944), 3, 32, 106–7, 124–40.

21. John Hersey, *A Bell for Adano* (New York: Knopf, 1944), 45–47, 67, 87, 116, 248. For a further discussion of the sentimental view of American men during and after the war that moves in less democratic directions, see Christian G. Appy, " 'We'll Follow the Old Man': The Strains of Sentimental Militarism in Popular Films of the Fifties," in *Rethinking Cold War Culture*, ed. Peter Kuznick and James Gilbert (Washington, D.C.: Smithsonian Institution Press, 2001), 74–105.

22. Samuel Hymes, *The Soldier's Tale: Bearing Witness to Modern War* (New York: Penguin Books, 1997), 11, 111–13; Gerald F. Linderman, *The World Within War: America's Combat Experience in World War II* (Cambridge, Mass.: Harvard University Press, 1999), 3–4.

23. Mancheser, *Goodbye Darkness*, 391.

24. J. Glen Gray, *The Warriors: Reflections on Men in Battle* (New York: Harcourt,

Brace, 1959); Joanna Bourke, *An Intimate History of Killing: Face to Face Killing in Twentieth Century Warfare* (New York: Basic Books, 1999), 13, 53, 169; E. B. Sledge, *With the Old Breed at Peleliu and Okinawa* (Novato, Calif.: Presidio Press, 1981), 120–23.

25. Samuel Stouffer, et al., *The American Soldier* (Princeton, N.J.: Princeton University Press, 1949), 1:286–87, 298, 2:149, 167, 588; Manchester, *Goodbye Darkness*, 391.

26. Edward Scheiberling, "A New Birth of Americanism," *American Legion Magazine* 38 (August 1945): 6; Jennifer E. Brooks, "Winning the Peace: Georgia Veterans and the Struggle to Define the Political Legacy of World War II," *Journal of Southern History* 66 (August 2000): 563–93; Mary Ann Glendon, *A World Made New: Eleanor Roosevelt and the Universal Declaration of Human Rights* (New York: Random House, 2000), 9, 19, 150–56. Samuel Moyn, "Two Regimes of Memory," *American Historical Review* 103 (October 1998): 1182–86, discusses the tension between universal and more particularistic forms of memory. Wendy Brown, *Politics Out of History* (Princeton, N.J.: Princeton University Press, 2001), 9, explains the historical transformation from a more universal liberal politics to one centered on demands for group rights. She suggests that dreams of universal and individual rights were held together for a time by a general faith in progress. Both sets of rights could advance together. If the experience of war tended to upset the faith in the idea of human progress—as I suspect it did—the demands for group or victim rights may have superseded more universal calls. If group demands proved more powerful than universal ones—as implicated in the democratic idealism of the four freedoms—then the settlement of group needs tended to end political action.

27. Sharon K. Krause, *Liberalism with Honor* (Cambridge, Mass.: Harvard University Press, 2002), 5, 32–33.

28. Stouffer et al., *American Soldier*, 2:597, 622. Jennifer D. Keene, *Doughboys, the Great War, and the Remaking of America* (Baltimore: Johns Hopkins University Press, 2001), 200–212, discusses how World War I–era veterans pushed through the G.I. Bill for those who fought in World War II.

29. G. Kurt Piehler, *Remembering War the American Way* (Washington, D.C.: Smithsonian Institution Press, 1995), 136, 143; Philip Jenkins, *The Cold War at Home: The Red Scare in Pennsylvania, 1945–1960* (Chapel Hill: University of North Carolina Press, 1999), 55–56; Joseph Walwik, *The Peekskill, New York Anti-Communist Riots of 1949* (Lewistown, N.Y.: Edwin Mellen Press, 2002), 2–3, 30–36, 63–68; Thomas Rummer, *The American Legion: An Official History, 1919–1968* (New York: M. Evans, 1990), 302–03, 327; Richard M. Fried, *The Russians Are Coming! The Russians Are Coming! Pageantry and Patriotism in Cold-War America* (New York: Oxford University Press, 1998), 22–23.

30. Robert J. Havighurst, et al., *The American Veteran Back Home: A Study of Veteran Readjustment* (New York: Longmans, Green, 1951), 51, 142–43, 206–14; Mark Grandstaf, "Making the Military American: Advertising Reforms and the Demise of an Antistanding Military Tradition," *Journal of Military History* 60 (April 1996): 299–324.

31. Phil Melling, "War and Memory in the New World Order," in *War and Memory in the Twentieth Century*, ed. Martin Evans and Ken Lunn (Oxford, U.K.: Berg, 1997), 257.

32. See William Reddy, "Sentimentalism and Its Erasure," *Journal of Modern History* 72 (March 2000): 109–52, for an account of a transition from democratic sentiments to military ones during the era of the French Revolution. On the way in which commemorations of individual deaths can be used to sustain the national or collective memory of a war and on the way the listing of war dead need not represent a form of resistance to "totalizing discourses" as is often inferred in accounts of the Vietnam Veterans Memorial, see Daniel Sherman, "Bodies and Names: The Emergence of Commemoration in Interwar France," *American Historical Review* 103 (April 1998): 443–47.

Chapter 4. Sponsorship and Snake Oil

Many thanks to Wendy Gamber, Bob Guldin, Lewis Hyde, Phyllis Palmer, Ann Romines, and Michael Sappol for helpful comments.

1. See Susan Smulyan, *Selling Radio: The Commercialization of American Broadcasting, 1920–1934* (Washington, D.C.: Smithsonian Institution Press, 1994).

2. Nancy Tomes, "The Great American Medicine Show Revisited," *Bulletin of the History of Medicine* 79 (2005): 636.

3. Fred "Doc Foster" Bloodgood, "Pitching on the Physic Opera," http://www.pbs.org/willa/pages/page49.html.

4. Brooks McNamara, *Step Right Up,* rev. ed. (Jackson: University Press of Mississippi, 1995), 19, 54.

5. On the Wizard Oil shows, see ibid., 61–72; on Kickapoo, ibid., 73–95.

6. Ibid., 55–59, 178.

7. On courting the customer, see Susan Strasser, *Satisfaction Guaranteed: The Making of the American Mass Market* (New York: Pantheon Books, 1989).

8. McNamara, *Step Right Up,* 54.

9. James Harvey Young, *The Toadstool Millionaires: A Social History of Patent Medicines in America before Federal Regulation* (Princeton, N.J.: Princeton University Press, 1961), 40–41. On the development of trademark, see Strasser, *Satisfaction Guaranteed,* 44ff.

10. James Harvey Young, in Guenter B. Risse, Ronald L. Numbers, and Judith Walzer Leavitt, eds., *Medicine Without Doctors: Home Health Care in American History* (New York: Science History Publications, 1977), 96.

11. T. J. Jackson Lears, *Fables of Abundance: A Cultural History of Advertising in America* (New York: Basic Books, 1994), 97.

12. Pamela Laird, *Advertising Progress: American Business and the Rise of Consumer Marketing* (Baltimore: Johns Hopkins University Press, 1998), 18–19. In "Developing the Brand: The Case of Alcohol, 1800–1880," *Enterprise & Society,* 4 (September 2003): 405–41, Paul Duguid makes a persuasive case that the brand concept was developed earlier.

13. Daniel Pope, *The Making of Modern Advertising* (New York: Basic Books, 1983), 232.

14. Young, *Toadstool Millionaires,* vii–viii.

15. McNamara, *Step Right Up*, 34; Lears, *Fables of Abundance*, 43.

16. *Oxford English Dictionary*, 2nd ed. online.

17. Suzanne White, "Medicine's Humble Humbug: Four Periods in the Understanding of the Placebo," *Pharmacy in History* 27 (1985): 51.

18. John Uri Lloyd, Wolfgang Ostwald, and Walter Haller, "A Study in Pharmacy," *Journal of the American Pharmaceutical Association* 19 (October 1930): 1081. See also John Uri Lloyd, "Eclectic Fads, No. 2—Alcohol Not 'An Eclectic Fad,'" *Eclectic Medical Journal* 80 (March 1920): 1–8.

19. See Lorine Swainston Goodwin, *The Pure Food, Drink, and Drug Crusaders, 1879–1914* (Jefferson, N.C.: McFarland & Company, 1999), 88–130.

20. Quoted in McNamara, *Step Right Up*, 81.

21. Sarah Stage, *Female Complaints: Lydia Pinkham and the Business of Women's Medicine* (New York: W. W. Norton & Company, 1979), 167–68.

22. Edward Bok, "A Few Words to the W.C.T.U.," The *Ladies' Home Journal*, (September, 1904): 16.

23. Peter Temin, *Taking Your Medicine: Drug Regulation in the United States* (Cambridge, Mass.: Harvard University Press, 1980), 27, 32.

24. James Harvey Young, *The Medical Messiahs: A Social History of Health Quackery in Twentieth-Century America* (Princeton, N.J.: Princeton University Press, 1967; new ed. 1992), 44.

25. Rufus King, "'The American System': Legal Sanctions to Repress Drug Abuse," in *Drugs and the Criminal Justice System*, ed. James A. Inciardi and Carl D. Chambers (Beverly Hills, Calif.: Sage Publications, 1974), reprinted at http://www.druglibrary.org/special/king/king3.htm.

26. On small business record-keeping, see Strasser, *Satisfaction Guaranteed*, 231–35.

27. On domestic medicine, see Risse, Numbers, and Leavitt, *Medicine Without Doctors*; Lamar Riley Murphy, *Enter the Physician: The Transformation of Domestic Medicine, 1760–1860* (Tuscaloosa: University of Alabama Press, 1991); Emily K. Abel, *Hearts of Wisdom: American Women Caring for Kin* (Cambridge, Mass.: Harvard University Press, 2000).

28. Charles E. Rosenberg, "Medical Text and Social Context: Explaining William Buchan's Domestic Medicine," *Bulletin of the History of Medicine* 57 (1983): 22–42; see also Charles E. Rosenberg, introduction to John C. Gunn, *Gunn's Domestic Medicine: A Facsimile of the First Edition* (Knoxville: University of Tennessee Press, 1986).

29. Robert S. Lynd and Helen Merrell Lynd, *Middletown: A Study in Modern American Culture* (New York: Harcourt, Brace and World, 1929), 436.

30. Norman Gevitz, "Domestic Medical Guides and the Drug Trade in Nineteenth-Century America," *Pharmacy in History*, 32 (1990): 52.

31. Edward Bok, "The 'Patent-Medicine' Curse," *Ladies' Home Journal* (May 1904): 18.

32. There are a number of methods for calculating relative value; a useful calculator for six of them may be found at http://measuringworth.com/calculators/uscompare/http://www.eh.net/hmit/compare. Using the unskilled wages method, the best way to determine costs of goods in terms of the amount of work it took to earn

the money, $2 in 1904 is equivalent to $206 in 2006 dollars; the other estimates range from $375 to $1028.

33. Quoted in Abel, *Hearts of Wisdom*, 73.

34. David L. Dykstra, "The Medical Profession and Patent and Proprietary Medicines during the Nineteenth Century," *Bulletin of the History of Medicine* 29 (1955): 408–409.

35. Temin, *Taking Your Medicine*, 29.

36. James Harvey Young, *American Self-Dosage Medicines: An Historical Perspective* (Lawrence, Kans.: Coronado Press, 1974), 4.

37. Merck & Co., *Merck's 1901 Manual of the Materia Medica; A Ready-Reference Pocket Book for the Practicing Physician and Surgeon* (New York: Merck & Co., 1901), in Collection 101, Box 55, Lloyd Library, Cincinnati, Ohio.

38. See Caroline Jean Acker, "From All Purpose Anodyne to Marker of Deviance: Physicians' Attitudes towards Opiates in the U.S. from 1890 to 1940," in *Drugs and Narcotics in History*, ed. Roy Porter and Mikuláˇs Teich (Cambridge: Cambridge University Press, 1995), 114–132.

39. Stage, *Female Complaints*, 27–31.

40. "Who Was Henry Helmbold?" reprinted "(with slight editing)" from the November, 1912 *Druggists' Circular* at http://www.bottlebooks.com/helmboldstory/Helmbold.htm and http://www.glswrk-auction.com/023.htm.

41. Daniel J. Boorstin, *The Image: A Guide to Pseudo-Events in America* (New York: Atheneum, 1978), 213–14.

42. Bloodgood, "Pitching on the Physic Opera." See also Fred Bloodgood, in Brooks McNamara, ed., *American Popular Entertainments* (New York: Performing Arts Journal Publications, 1983), 49, quoted and cited in McNamara, *Step Right Up*, 229.

43. "Who Was Henry Helmbold?"

44. Winifred Johnston, "Medicine Show," *Southwest Review* 21 (July 1936): 397.

45. On Helms, see McNamara, *Step Right Up*, 159–81.

46. Prof. Harry Helms, "How to Be Your Own Doctor," Harry Houdini scrapbook collection, Library of Congress, Scrapbook 96, microfilm reel 21. The scrapbook is not paginated; like Brooks McNamara, I do not believe that it is possible to create accurate page references for these scrapbooks. See McNamara, *Step Right Up*, 228.

47. Lears, *Fables of Abundance*, 100.

48. Herman Melville, *The Confidence-Man: His Masquerade*, ed. by Harrison Hayford, Hershel Parker, and G. Thomas Tanselle (Evanston, Ill.: Northwestern University Press, 1984), 81.

49. Karen Halttunen, *Confidence Men and Painted Women: A Study of Middle-Class Culture in America, 1830–1870* (New Haven, Conn.: Yale University Press, 1982), 1–8.

50. Lears, *Fables of Abundance*, 43.

51. Lewis Hyde, *Trickster Makes This World: Mischief, Myth, and Art* (New York: Farrar, Straus and Giroux, 1998), 10.

52. "The Indians of New York City," *New York Times*, September 12, 1897, SM6.

53. "In Love with a Kickapoo," *New York Times*, February 4, 1893, 8; "Silly Stella Brightman," *New York Times*, February 7, 1893, 3.

54. Winifred Johnston, "Medicine Show," *Southwest Review* 21 (July 1936), 392.

55. Philip J. Deloria, *Playing Indian* (New Haven, Conn.: Yale University Press, 1998), 7.

56. Quoted in Strasser, *Satisfaction Guaranteed*, 129; see also James Harvey Young, *American Self-Dosage Medicines: An Historical Perspective* (Lawrence, Kans.: Coronado Press, 1974), 3.

57. "Hires Root Beer History," http://www.dpsu.com/hires_root_beer.html; this is the official history from Dr Pepper/Seven Up, Inc., which owns Hires.

58. "Dr Pepper History," http://www.dpsu.com/dr_pepper.html http://www.brandspeoplelove.com/csab/Brands/DrPepper/HistoryofDrPepper/tabid/147/Default.aspx. This official company history does not discuss the product's name; for one version of the myth, see "Dublin Dr Pepper History," http://www.drpep.com/history.htm.

59. M. D. Deiver, for Thomas Holloway, to Calvin Cowles, March 9, 1857, Cowles Papers no. #3808, Folder 461A, Southern Historical Collection, Manuscripts Department, Wilson Library, University of North Carolina at Chapel Hill. "New-York City," *New York Daily Times*, December 20, 1856, 8. On the counterfeiting of proprietary medicines and their trademarks, see Elysa Ream Engelman, " 'The Face That Haunts Me Ever': Consumers, Retailers, Critics, and the Branded Personality of Lydia E. Pinkham" (unpublished Ph.D. dissertation, Boston University, 2003), 72–95.

60. "Special Notices," *The New York Times*, March 14, 1857, 5.

61. "The Ville Du Havre Disaster," *New York Times*, December 9, 1873, 8.

62. "Who Was Henry Helmbold?"

63. I am indebted to Stephen Mihm and Kathleen Brown for this insight. Mihm's paper "Ghosts in the Machine: Counterfeiters, Bank Notes, and the Industrialization of Engraving in Antebellum America," Research Seminar Paper #95, The Center for the History of Business, Technology, and Society, Hagley Museum and Library, December 12, 2002, contains some reference to the patent medicine connection; Brown's excellent comment at the seminar extended the comparison.

64. John Uri Lloyd, "Spurious Drugs," reprint from *The Druggists Circular*, (February 1915), n.p. Lloyd Library, Collection 1, Box 54, Folder 755. On endangered golden seal, see J. U. Lloyd and C. G. Lloyd, *Drugs and Medicines of North America* (Cincinnati: J. U. and C. G. Lloyd, 1884), 1:83.

65. "Medical Frauds Arrested," *New York Times*, May 5, 1897, 1.

66. "Big Hunt Now on for Drug Swindlers," *New York Times*, October 9, 1904, 1.

67. "Against Counterfeit Preparations," reprinted from The *Chicago Tribune*, *New York Times*, November 2, 1898, 5.

68. McNamara, *Step Right Up*, 69.

69. On Riley, see Lears, *Fables of Abundance*, 40–43; McNamara, *Step Right Up*, 70–72.

70. George Jean Nathan, "The Medicine Men," *Harper's Weekly*, September 9, 1911, 24.

71. For *Dangerous Nan McGrew*, see "Medicine Show in Talkie," *New York Times*, June 21, 1930, 20; for photographs from the other films, see McNamara, *Step Right Up*, 141, 148, 150, 158.

72. On consumer activism, see Nancy Tomes, "Merchants of Health: Medicine and Consumer Culture in the United States, 1900–1940," *Journal of American History*, (September 2001): 538ff.

73. Lears, *Fables of Abundance*, 100.

74. For the best discussion of the background to that story, see the two articles by Nancy Tomes cited above.

Chapter 5. Entertainment Wars

Thanks to Marita Sturken, Jeffrey Sconce, Jan Olsson, Chris Berry, and four anonymous readers for their help with this essay.

1. "Disaster Programming," *Variety.com*, September 21, 2001, 1. For more on TV network cancellations of violent movies, see John Dempsey, "Cable Nets Nix Violent Pix in Wake of Tragedy," *Variety.com*, September 16, 2001, 1–2, http://www.variety.com/article/VR1117852717.html?categoryid=14&cs=1; Joe Flint and John Lippman, "Hollywood Revisits Terrorism-Related Projects" *Wall Street Journal*, September 13, 2001, B2; Joe Flint, "TV Programmers Avoid All Allusions to Attacks," *Wall Street Journal*, September 28, 2001, B6.

2. For speculations on the "end of irony," see Jeff Gordinier, "How We Saw It," *Entertainment Weekly*, September 28, 2001, 12; Peter Bart, "Where's the Snap and Crackle of Pop Culture?" *Variety.com*, September 30, 2001, 1–2, http://www.variety.com/article/VR1117853369.html?categoryid=1&cs=1. Note, however, that a counterdiscourse popped up immediately in venues like the *Onion* and *Salon*, which used irony early on. In an online essay, James Der Derian noted some of the inconsistencies in what he called the "protected zones of language" after 9/11, pointing out, for example, that irony was in some venues under attack: "President Bush was given room to joke in a morale-boosting visit to the CIA, saying he's 'spending a lot of quality time lately' with George Tenet, the director of the CIA." Der Derian also took on *New York Times* reporter Edward Rothstein for taking an "opportunist shot at postmodernists and postcolonialists" by "claiming that their irony and relativism is 'ethnically perverse' and produces 'guilty passivity.'" See Der Derian's "9.11: Before, After, and In Between," Social Science Research Council, After September 11 Archive, SSRC.org, 5 (the original posting date is no longer on the site).

3. Jennifer Netherby, "Renters Flock to Video Stores," *VideoBusiness.com*, September 21, 2001, 1–2, http://www.videobusiness.com/article/CA619433.html. *Video on Line* reported that "Wal-mart stores asked the studios for a list of their titles that contain scenes of the World Trade Center, presumably to take some merchandising action on those movies" (Jennifer Netherby, "World Trade Center on Wal-Mart's Minds, *VideoBusiness.com/news*, September 13, 2001, 1, http://www.videobusiness.com/article/CA619425.html).

4. "Domain Names Grow after Attacks," *Variety.com*, September 25, 2001, 1.

5. Even while cable outlets are not regulated by the Federal Communications Commission to the extent that the broadcast networks are, they still are widely perceived as "service" industries and protectors of public safety in times of crisis (obviously, this is the platform of cable news outlets like CNN, which dramatically increased its viewership after 9/11).

6. I am borrowing Raymond Williams's phrase "a whole way of life," which he

used to define culture. See his *Culture and Society, 1780–1950* (1958; New York: Columbia University Press, 1983), 325.

7. More generally, 9/11 disrupted the familiar/consumer uses of a host of communication technologies, from cell phones to television to satellites to video games, all of which now resonated in an uncanny sense with the militaristic/wartime uses for which their basic technology was developed.

8. Mary Anne Doane, "Information, Crisis, Catastrophe," in *Logics of Television: Essays in Cultural Criticism*, ed. Patricia Mellencamp (Bloomington: Indiana University Press, 1990), 222–39.

9. Vanessa O'Connell, "TV Networks Cut $320 Million of Ads in Crisis," *Wall Street Journal*, September 19, 2001.

10. *Variety* reported that "commercial breaks were back across the board Monday [September 17]" (Rick Kissell, "TV Getting Back to Biz and Blurbs," *Variety.com*, September 17, 2001, 1, http://www.variety.com/article/VR1117852805.html?categoryid=14&cs=1).

11. Jack Valenti, "Hollywood, and Our Nation, Will Meet the Test," *Variety.com*, September 27, 2001, 1–2, http://www.variety.com/article/VR1117853266.html?categoryid=9&cs=1.

12. The president said this in a televised address he delivered at Chicago O'Hare Airport with the aim of convincing people to return to plane travel. Note, too, that in subsequent months various advertisers linked their promotional discourses to 9/11 and the idea of patriotic consumption. (For example, ads for United and American Airlines as well as financial corporations did this.)

13. For examples of literature on TV news, 9/11, and Afghanistan, see *Television and New Media* 3 (May 2002); Daya Kishan Thussu and Des Freedman, eds., *War and the Media* (Thousand Oaks, Calif.: Sage, 2003); Stephen Hess and Marvin Kalb, eds., *The Media and the War on Terrorism* (Washington, D.C.: Brookings Institute, 2003); Barbie Zelizer and Stuart Allan, eds., *Journalism after September 11* (New York: Routledge, 2002).

14. As other scholars have argued, we should not accept at face value the information/entertainment binary that underpins the ideological logic of mainstream media systems. This binary—and the related binaries of important/trivial, private/public, masculine/feminine, and high/low—not only elide the fact that news is also narrative (and increasingly entertaining) but also fail to acknowledge that entertainment also serves to provide audiences with particular ways of knowing about and seeing the world. See, for example, Richard Dyer, *Only Entertainment* (New York: Routledge, 1992); John Fiske, "Popular News," chap. 8 in his *Reading the Popular* (Boston: Unwin and Hyman, 1989); James Freedman, ed., *Reality Squared: Televisual Discourse on the Real* (New Brunswick, N.J.: Rutgers University Press, 2002).

15. Der Derian, "9.11," 2.

16. For an interesting discussion of media references to Pearl Harbor and the rerelease of the film after 9/11, see Cynthia Weber, "The Media, the 'War on Terrorism' and the Circulation of Non-Knowledge," in Thussu and Freedman, *War and the Media*, 190–99.

17. This kind of coverage is, of course, symptomatic of the general rise of "infotainment" in the climate of media conglomeration and a ratings-driven commercial

ethos. For speculation on the social/political effects of the news coverage of 9/11 in terms of "infotainment," see Daya Kishan Thussu, "Live TV and Bloodless Deaths: War, Infotainment, and 24/7 News," in Thussu and Freedman, *War and the Media*, 117–32. There is much additional literature on issues of infotainment. See, for example, Leonard Downie Jr. and Robert G. Kaiser, *The News about the News: American Journalism in Peril* (New York: Knopf, 2002); and Pierre Bourdieu, *On Television*, trans. Priscilla Parkhurst Ferguson (New York: New Press, 1998). For analysis of the effect that round-the-clock coverage of "real time" wars has on foreign policy, see Piers Robinson, *The CNN Effect: The Myth of News, Foreign Policy, and Intervention* (New York: Routledge, 2002).

18. Claude Brodesser, "Feds Seek H'wood Help," *Variety.com*, October 7, 2001, http://www.variety.com/article/VR1117853841.html?categoryid=18&cs=1; Michael Schneider, "Fox Salutes Request by Bush for 'Wanted' Spec," *Variety.com*, October 10, 2001, http://www.variety.com/article/VR1117854100.html?categoryid=14&cs=1.

19. Michel de Certeau, "History: Science and Fiction," in *Heterologies: Discourse on the Other*, trans. Brian Massumi (Minneapolis: University of Minnesota Press, 1986), 199–221.

20. Roland Barthes, *Mythologies*, trans. A. Lavers (London: Cape, 1972); Marita Sturken, *Tangled Memories: The Vietnam War, the AIDS Epidemic, and the Politics of Remembering* (Berkeley: University of California Press, 1997). For more on the role of memory/nostalgia in film, television, and other popular media, see, for example, the Cahiers du Cinéma interview with Michel Foucault, reprinted in *Edinburgh Magazine* 2 (1977): 19–25; Patrick Bommes and Richard Wright, "Charms of Residence," in *Making Histories: Studies in History Writing and Politics*, ed. Richard Johnson et al. (London: Hutchinson, 1982); George Lipsitz, *Time Passages: Collective Memory and American Popular Culture* (Minneapolis: University of Minnesota Press, 1989); Robert Rosenstone, *Visions of the Past: The Challenge of Film to Our Idea of History* (New York: Belknap Press, 1996); Robert Rosenstone, *Revisioning History: Film and the Construction of a New Past* (Princeton, N.J.: Princeton University Press, 1994); Marcia Landy, ed., *The Historical Film: History and Memory in Media* (New Brunswick, N.J.: Rutgers University Press, 2000); "Special Debate," *Screen* 42 (Summer 2001): 188–216 (this is a series of short essays on trauma and cinema); David Morley and Kevin Robins, "No Place Like Heimet: Images of Homeland," in *Spaces of Identity: Global Media, Electronic Landscapes, and Cultural Boundaries* (New York: Routledge, 1995), 85–104; Purnima Mankekar, *Screening Culture, Viewing Politics: An Ethnography of Television, Womanhood, and Nation in Postcolonial India* (Durham, N.C.: Duke University Press, 1999).

21. Louis Chunovic, "Will TV News—or Its Audience—Finally Grow Up?" *TelevisionWeek*, September 24, 2001, 15. Note that news executives responded to such criticism. For example, CBS's Mel Karmizan and Fox News Channel's Roger Ailes promised to upgrade news programs and to cover more international issues.

22. So, too, this ABC lineup followed the logic of what Daniel Dayan and Elihu Katz see as integral to media events more generally, namely, a "neo romantic desire for heroic action by great men followed by the spontaneity of mass action" (*Media Events: The Live Broadcasting of History* [Cambridge: Harvard University Press, 1992], 21).

23. Some people have told me that they found it a useful source of "modeling" for their own conversations with their children.

24. Several other series also created special episodes about the attacks or else planted references to 9/11 in preexisting episodes. NBC's *Third Watch* began its season on October 29 with a documentary in which real-life emergency workers recalled their experiences on 9/11. ABC's *NYPD Blue* added two scenes acknowledging the attack into its season opener on November 6. As *New York Times* critic Caryn James pointed out, "The creators of 'Third Watch' and 'N.Y.P.D. Blue' have said they felt a responsibility to deal with the events, but the decision was practical, too. Their supposedly realistic characters would have seemed utterly unbelievable if they had ignored such an all-consuming tragedy" ("Dramatic Events That Rewrite the Script," *New York Times*, October 29, 2001, E7).

25. Josh lists many of the same Taliban injustices that President Bush listed in his first televised speech to Congress after the attacks.

26. Edward W. Said, *Orientalism* (New York: Vintage Books, 1979), esp. 284–328.

27. Ibid., 291.

28. Lauren Berlant, *The Queen of America Goes to Washington City: Essays on Sex and Citizenship* (Durham, N.C.: Duke University Press, 1997).

29. As Slavoj Žižek wrote just days after the attacks, this sense of a pure "evil Outside" was the response of a public living in a fake "Matrix"-like existence, a public that had for so long considered itself immune to the suffering endured on a daily basis by other world populations and, in any case, in no way responsible for its own perpetuation of violence around the world. Slavoj Žižek, "Welcome to the Desert of the Real!" posted on Re: Constructions.mit.edu, September 15, 2001 at http://web.mit.edu/cms/recon structions/interpretations/desertreal.html. The title is taken from a line in the film *The Matrix*. Žižek's short essay was later developed in a book. See his *Welcome to the Desert of the Real* (London: Verso, 2002). Der Derian's "9.11," 4–5, similarly evokes *The Matrix*.

30. Jack Lule, "Myth and Terror on the Editorial Page: The *New York Times* Responds to September 11, 2001," *Journalism and Mass Communication Quarterly* 29, no. 2 (2002): 275–93.

31. Yet, as Marita Sturken argues, this "end of innocence" theme is common to the stories spun around national disasters (for example, the same language was used after JFK's assassination). See Sturken, *Tangled Memories*, chap. 1.

32. Justin Lewis, "Speaking of Wars . . . ," *Television and New Media* 3 (May 2002): 170.

33. In this sense, it is interesting to note how television created a *continuous past*, particularly with regard to World War II and Vietnam. In place of the grave generational divides these wars had previously come to signify, television presented unifying narratives that bridged the gap between the self-sacrificing "Greatest Generation" and baby-boomer draft dodgers. This was most vividly displayed when Vietnam POW/Senator John McCain met 1960s youth rebel Stephen Stills on the *Tonight Show*, reconciling their differences.

34. Jayne Rodgers, "Icons and Invisibility: Gender, Myth, and 9/11," in Thussu and Freedman, eds., *War and the Media*, 206, 207.

35. Linda Williams, *Playing the Race Card: Melodramas of Black and White from Uncle Tom to O. J. Simpson* (Princeton, N.J.: Princeton University Press, 2001), 24.

36. One month after the attacks, *Variety* reported, "A rash of documentaries—some put together in a hurry—that aim to explain terrorism is a hot property" (Andrea R. Vaucher, "Arab, Terror Docus Heat Up the Market," *Variety.com*, October 10, 2001, 1, http://www.variety.com/article/VR1117854033.html?categoryid=1089&cs=1).

37. U.S. and British air strikes on Afghanistan began on October 7, 2001, and American warplanes attacked the Taliban in the field on October 10, 2001.

38. Saira Shah, cited in Janelle Brown, "Beneath the Veil' Redux," *Salon.com*, November 16, 2001, 1–2, http://archive.salon.com/mwt/feature/2001/11/16/veil_two/index.html.

39. Rick Kissell, "Bush Speech, Telethon Both Draw Record Auds," *Variety.com*, September 23, 2001, 1–2, http://www.variety.com/article/VR1117852982.html?categoryid=14&cs=1.

40. As one of the readers for this article suggested, the telethon's aura of liveness might have also helped to stave off the fear that TV and commercial culture were themselves "dead." To be sure, live "call-in" donations to stars ensured that money was still circulating through the media wires (here, not through the crass commercialism of TV as usual, but through the exchange economies of charity).

41. He said this on the broadcast. *The Fifty-third Annual Primetime Emmy Awards*, Sunday, November 4, 2001.

42. Gary Smith, cited in Joseph Adalian, "Show Finally Goes On and TV Biz Takes Heart," *Variety.com*, November 4, 2001, 1, http://www.variety.com/article/VR1117855304.html?categoryid=14&cs=1.

43. Underscoring the show's global impact, later in the ceremony there is a video montage of leaders from around the globe offering their condolences to the American public.

44. Sigmund Freud, "The Uncanny," in *Studies in Parapsychology* (1919; New York: Collier Books, 1963), 19–60. Freud discusses his lack of bibliographical references vis-à-vis the war in Europe on page 20.

45. When I delivered an earlier draft of this essay at a conference at the University of California, Berkeley, Ratiba Hadj-Moussa pointed out that this dynamic of national performance doesn't necessarily suggest that people don't in some way believe in the performance. I want to thank her for this observation. Clearly, through the act of national performance, it is possible to actually believe in the role you are playing—and even to believe in it more than ever!

46. Note, too, that "America the Beautiful" replaced the actual national anthem after 9/11 because no one seemed to be able to remember the words to the "Star-Spangled Banner."

47. Even news is now a matter of taste and "branded" by networks in ways that appeal to consumer profiles. For example, the news on Fox (especially its markedly conservative talk shows) attracts one of cable TV's most loyal publics, but many on the left mock its pretense of "Fair and Balanced" reporting. Al Franken's best-seller *Lies and the Lying Liars Who Tell Them: A Fair and Balanced Look at the Right* (New York: E. P. Dutton, 2003) and his lawsuit with Fox obviously drew on the more left associated taste publics that define themselves in distinction—in Bourdieu's sense—not only to Fox News but also to the viewers who (they imagine) watch it. For his discussion of taste as social distinction, see Pierre Bourdieu, *Distinction: A Social Critique of*

the Judgement of Taste, trans. Richard Nice (Cambridge, Mass.: Harvard University Press, 1984).

48. Even before the attacks, patriotic symbols were reemerging as a fashion fad. Corporations such as Tommy Hilfiger, Polo Ralph Lauren, and the Gap Inc.'s Old Navy sported the flag trend, while European haute couture designer Catherine Malandrino unveiled her flag-motif fall collection in the summer of 2001 (which included a skirt that Madonna wore on her concert tour). See Teri Agins, "Flag Fashion's Surging Popularity Fits with Some Fall Collections," *Wall Street Journal*, September 19, 2001, B5. According to Agins, the post-9/11 flag fashions were an extension of this trend, not an invention of it.

49. In 1992 Dayan and Katz speculated on the fate of television, nationalism, and media events in what they saw to be an increasingly multichannel and segmented television system. They argued that while the old three-network or public broadcast systems "will disappear," television's previous functions of "national integration may devolve upon" media events. Their speculation now seems particularly apt. They also predicted that with new technologies and possible erosion of the nation-state, "media events may then create and integrate communities larger than nations." See Dayan and Katz, *Media Events*, 23.

50. Fredric Jameson, "The Dialectics of Disaster," *South Atlantic Quarterly* 101 (Spring 2002): 300.

51. According to *Variety*, news organizations were "furious that CNN wouldn't forego competition" and "rallied against exclusives, saying that they don't serve the public's interest during a time of national crisis." ABC news spokesperson Jeffrey Schneider disputed any exclusivity deal by arguing fair use. He said, "There was no question in anybody's mind that these images from Al Jazeera were of compelling national interest," and "We felt we had a duty to broadcast them to the American people which far outweighed whatever commercial agenda CNN was attempting to pursue in this time of war." Meanwhile, Walter Isaacson, CEO of CNN News Group, told *Variety* that CNN had a "reciprocal affiliate deal" with Al Jazeera and that "it's Al Jazeera's material and we don't have a right to give it away." Isaacson did admit, however, that "in a time of war, we won't make a big deal about this sort of thing." See Paul Bernstein and Pamela McClintock, "Newsies Fight over Bin Laden Interview," *Variety.com*, October 7, 2001, 1–2, http://www.variety.com/article/VR1117853835 .html?categoryid=14&cs=1.

52. John Dempsey, "Invite to Cablers to Join Telethon Irks Affils," *Variety.com*, September 20, 2001, 1, http://www.variety.com/article/VR1117852947.html?catego ryid=19&cs=1. The underlying reasons for the broadcasters' concern had to do with issues of East Coast-West Coast transmission times. The big four networks—ABC, CBS, NBC, and Fox—aired the telethon at 9:00 p.m. eastern time, and because they wanted to make it seem like a simultaneous nationwide event, they also showed it taped via a dual feed at 9:00 p.m. on the West Coast. Some single-feed cable networks such as TBS and the National Geographic Channel, however, planned to show the telethon live at 6:00 p.m. on the West Coast, and thereby preempt the 9:00 p.m. taped West Coast network broadcast. Some network affiliates and owned and operated stations were simply unhappy that any cable networks were airing the telethon, even if cablers showed it simultaneously (at 9:00 p.m.) with the Big Four.

53. David Kissinger, cited in Rick Lyman with Bill Carter, "In Little Time, Pop Culture Is Almost Back to Normal," *New York Times*, October 4, 2001.

54. See, for example, Jostein Gripsrud, ed., *Television and Common Knowledge* (New York: Routledge, 1999), esp. Graham Murdock, "Rights and Representations," 7–17; James Curran, "Mass Media and Democracy Revisited," in *Mass Media and Society*, ed. James Curran and Michael Gurevitch, 2nd ed. (London: Arnold, 1996), 81–119.

55. See, for example, Vance Kepley Jr., "The Weaver Years at NBC," *Wide Angle* 12 (April 1990): 46–63, and "From 'Frontal Lobes' to the 'Bob and Bob Show': NBC Management and Programming Strategies, 1949–65," in *Hollywood in the Age of Television*, ed. Tino Balio (Boston: Unwin Hyman, 1990), 41–62; Lynn Spigel, "The Making of a Television Literate Elite," in *The Television Studies Book*, ed. Christine Geraghty and David Lusted (London: Arnold, 1998), 63–85.

56. Laurie Ouellette, *Viewers Like You? How Public TV Failed the People* (New Brunswick, N.J.: Rutgers University Press, 2002).

57. ABC is now owned by Disney (which owns or partially owns, for example, the Disney theme parks, radio stations, cable networks like ESPN and Lifetime, retail outlets, feature film companies, newspapers, and magazines); CBS, once owned by Viacom and now split with its parent company, holds Showtime and CBS-Paramount, while Viacom owns, for example, Paramount Pictures as well as cable networks like MTV and Nickelodeon; NBC is part owned by Vivendi and General Electric (which entered into a joint venture with Microsoft and owns MSNBC); and Fox is owned by Rupert Murdoch's News Corp. (which owns, for example, Fox Broadcasting; Fox News Channel; Fox Sports Net; motion picture companies; magazines like *TV Guide*; book publishers; and numerous newspapers and delivers entertainment and information to at least 75 percent of the globe). Meanwhile, media conglomerate Time Warner owns a large number of cable channels, production companies, home video, magazines, music companies, and book publishers (for example, HBO, CNN, the WB Network, Castle Rock Entertainment, Warner Books, Time Warner Cable, Warner Bros. Television, and *Time* magazine, and its notorious deal with America Online). With telephone and cable operators acquiring and partnering with media corporations and moving into content, the synergy among these sectors is even more pronounced. These ownership structures make these media organizations more like vertically integrated movie studios of the classical period, as they have controlling stakes in all sectors of their industry—production, distribution, and exhibition—in addition to obvious benefits of owning multiple and related companies that reduce risk and increase opportunities for synergy between different companies in the umbrella corporation. Note, however, that the great instability of the technologies market begs us to ask new questions regarding the future of media conglomeration and convergence.

58. Media conglomerates often say that consolidation of ownership leads to more choice (for example, some media conglomerates claim that consolidation of business holdings allows them to use income from their mainstream media outlets to launch minority channels). A variety of media activists, industry executives, media scholars, and government officials have, however, sharply attacked conglomeration and questioned the degree to which freedom of speech and diversity of representation can exist in a

deregulated media system in which just a few major corporations own most of the media sources. See, for example, Patricia Aufderheide, *Communications Policy and the Public Interest: The Telecommunications Act of 1996* (New York: Guilford Press, 1999); Patricia Aufderheide, ed., *Conglomerates and the Media* (New York: New Press, 1997); Robert McChesney, *Corporate Media and the Threat to Democracy* (New York: Seven Stories Press, 1997); Ben H. Bagdikian, *The Media Monopoly*, 6th ed. (Boston: Beacon Press, 2000); Dean Alger, *Megamedia: How Giant Corporations Dominate Mass Media, Distort Competition, and Endanger Democracy* (New York: Rowman and Littlefield, 1998).

59. Dayan and Katz, *Media Events*, 20.

60. Bruce A. Williams, "The New Media Environment, Internet Chatrooms, and Public Discourse after 9/11," in Thussu and Freedman, *War and the Media*, 183. It should be noted that the Pew Research Center found that nine out of ten Americans were getting their news primarily from television after the 9/11 attacks. See "Troubled Times for Network Evening News," *Washington Post*, March 10, 2002. Citing an ABC News poll, however, Williams claims that "almost half of all Americans now get news over the Internet, and over a third of them increased their reliance on online sources after September 11" ("New Media Environment," 176).

61. Williams, "New Media Environment," 182. Although Williams cites various online attempts to draw ideological boundaries, he doesn't necessary view this as a bad thing. While he admits that some such attempts were disturbing, he also argues that "insular conversations that are not easily accessible to the wider public play a positive role by allowing marginalized groups to clarify their distinct values in opposition to those of the society-at-large within the safety of a sympathetic and homogeneous group" (184). Despite his pointing to the insular nature of the Web and the desire of some groups to draw ideological boundaries, Williams also argues that there was a general air of civility on the Internet (188–89).

62. The administration viewed the presence of Al Jazeera's graphic war footage and bin Laden's videotapes (which were aired around the world) as a grave problem. On October 3, 2001 (a few days before the bombings began), Secretary of State Colin Powell asked the Qatari emir, Sheikh Hamad bin Khalifa, to "tone down" Al Jazeera's inflammatory rhetoric, and the Bush administration specifically requested that the tapes be taken off the network. The International Press Institute sent a letter to Colin Powell, stating that Powell's tactics had "serious consequences for press freedom." Al Jazeera journalists defended their coverage of graphic images by stating that they were trying to cover the war objectively, from both sides (Mohammed El-Nawawy and Adel Iskandar, *Al Jazeera: The Story of the Network That Is Rattling Governments and Redefining Modern Journalism*, updated ed. [Cambridge, Mass.: Westview Press, 2002], 176–81). See also El-Nawawy and Iskandar's discussion of Europe's and Al Jazeera's coverage of Afghanistan (ibid., 186–89).

63. Jonathan Burston, "War and the Entertainment Industries: New Research Priorities in an Era of Cyber-Patriotism," in Thussu and Freedman, *War and the Media*, 163–75. For more, see James Der Derian, *Virtuous War: Mapping the Military-Industrial Media Entertainment Network* (Boulder, Colo.: Westview, 2001). At ICT, technologies such as immersive simulation games are being developed simultaneously for entertainment and military uses.

64. A member of the Bush administration met with Hollywood studio chiefs

and network executives in Beverly Hills on October 18, 2001 to discuss efforts to "enhance the perception of America around the world." See Peter Bart, "H'wood Enlists in War," *Variety.com*, October 17, 2001, 1–3, http://www.variety.com/article/VR1117854476.html?categoryid=1064&cs=1. A few weeks later, they gathered in what was referred to as a "summit" to discuss more detailed plans for Hollywood's participation in the war effort. See Rick Lyman, "White House Sets Meeting with Film Executives to Discuss War on Terrorism," *Variety.com*, November 8, 2001, 1–3. See also Pamela McClintock, "Nets Rally Stars around Flag," *Variety.com*, December 3, 2001, 1–2, http://www.variety.com/article/VR1117856708.html?categoryid=19&cs=1.

65. Meanwhile, in a connected fashion, Al Jazeera's presence also threatens the hegemony of Western global news sources. Driven by fierce competition for Arab audiences, in January 2002 CNN officially launched its Arabic Web site, CNNArabic.com. See Noureddine Miladi, "Mapping the Al Jazeera Phenomenon," in Thussu and Freedman, *War and the Media*, 159. Note that CNN launched the Web site at the same time (January 2002) that Al Jazeera withdrew its exclusivity agreement with CNN because of the dispute over a tape CNN aired without its approval.

66. In a provocative thesis, Bret Maxwell Dawson argues that while TV returned to much of its previous content, television's temporal and narrational forms were "traumatized" by 9/11. He argues that the effects of this trauma can be seen in the way that elements of catastrophe television (e.g., live broadcasts, an aura of authenticity, and an obsession with time) have appeared with increasing popularity in reality TV and programs like Fox's *24*. See his "TV since 9/11" (master's thesis, University of New South Wales, Sydney, Australia, 2003). While I would not posit such deterministic notions of trauma, it does seem useful to think about how 9/11 relates to a particular historical conjuncture in aesthetic ideals of TV realism, and in particular TV's obsession with the reality genre and real time (which, as Dawson admits, began before 9/11).

67. This cycle of memorializing documentaries began with CBS's *9/11* (aired March 10, 2002), which was followed by *Telling Nicholas* (HBO, May 12, 2002), *In Memoriam: New York City, 9.11* (HBO, May 26, 2002), and others. For a seminar I taught at UCLA, Sharon Sharp wrote a very interesting paper, "Remembering 9/11: Memory, History, and the American Family," which considers how these documentaries used sentimental images of the family in crisis to tell histories of 9/11.

68. Baudrillard and Virilio both have published monographs on 9/11. See Jean Baudrillard, *The Spirit of Terrorism and Requiem for the Twin Towers*, trans. Chris Turner (London: Verso, 2002); Paul Virilio, *Ground Zero*, trans. Chris Turner (London: Verso, 2002).

Chapter 6. Screening Pornography

1. Al Gore, "Remarks Prepared for Delivery," International Telecommunications Union, Monday March 21, 1994, http://www.goelzer.net/telecom/al-gore.html.

2. The U.S. District Court for the Eastern District of Pennsylvania, Adjudication on Motions for Preliminary Injunction (hereafter referred to as Preliminary Injunction), *ACLU v. Reno*, 929 F.Supp. 824 (E.D. Pa 1996), Judge Dalzell's opinion, at sec. E

"Conclusion," in *American Civil Liberties Union v. Reno*, no. 99–1324 (hereafter referred to as *Preliminary Injunction*).

3. Bill Gates, *The Road Ahead* (New York: Vintage, 1995).

4. See Wendy Chun, "Scenes of Empowerment," in *Control and Freedom* (Cambridge, Mass.: MIT Press, 2006), 129–70.

5. Mike Godwin, "Journoporn: Dissection of the Time Scandal," *Hotwired*, http://hotwired.wired.com/special/pornscare/godwin.html.

6. Philip Elmer-Dewitt, "On a Screen Near You: Cyberporn," *Time*, July 3, 1995, 38–45.

7. Ibid., 38.

8. Quoted in "Cybersex: Policing Pornography on the Internet," *ABC Nightline*, June 27, 1995.

9. Elmer-Dewitt, "Screen," 40.

10. Ibid., 40. Many commentators argued that although these images could not be found on the average magazine rack, they did not compare with the pornography available in specialty shops since they were readily available and since many of the images online were scans.

11. According to Whitfield Diffie and Susan Landau in their description of National Security Agency intercept machines, "if an intercepted message is found to be encrypted, it is automatically recorded. This is possible because at present only a small fraction of the world's communications are encrypted" (*Privacy on the Line: The Politics of Wiretapping and Encryption* [Cambridge, Mass.: MIT, 1998], 91).

12. Michel Foucault himself calls Jeremy Bentham's belief that opinion was always "good" an optimistic illusion: the utilitarians "overlooked the real conditions of possibility of opinion, the 'media' of opinion, a materiality caught up in the mechanisms of the economy and power in its forms of the press, publishing and later the cinema and television." Michel Foucault, "The Eye of Power," in *Power/Knowledge: Selected Interviews and Other Writings, 1972–1977*, trans. Colin Gordon (New York: Pantheon Books, 1980), 146–65.

13. Thomas Keenan, *Fables of Responsibility: Aberrations and Predicaments in Ethics and Politics* (Stanford, Calif.: Stanford University Press, 1997), 201.

14. Not accidentally, this process of re-creation parallels the process of paranoid recovery. As "the paranoiac builds [the world] again, not more splendid, it is true, but at least so that he can once more live in it," the inmate/student/worker is called to rebuild his or her own interior world. If the paranoiac "builds [his/her world] up by the work of his delusions," the inmate/student/worker rebuilds his or her world by work of the delusion of constant surveillance. As with the paranoiac, "the delusion-formation, which we take to be a pathological product, is in reality an attempt at recovery, a process of reconstruction." Sigmund Freud, "Psychoanalytic Notes upon an Autobiographical Account of a Case of Paranoia (Dementia Paranoides)," in *Three Case Histories* (New York: Collier Books, 1963), 147. Rehabilitation becomes paranoid reconstruction.

15. Jeremy Bentham, "Panopticon; or, The Inspection-House," in *The Panopticon Writings* (London and New York: Verso, 1995), 34.

16. In England and the United States, law enforcement officers do not need a search warrant in order to determine the sending and receiving locations of one's e-mail; but a search warrant is needed in order to read them.

17. David S. Armagh, Nick L. Battaglia, and Kenneth V. Lanning, *Use of Computers in the Sexual Exploitation of Children* (Washington, D.C.: Office of Justice Programs, U.S. Department of Justice, 1999), 4.

18. United States House of Representatives, 104th Congress, *Cyberporn: Protecting Our Children from the Back Alleys of the Internet* (Washington, D.C.: Government Printing Office, 1995), 80.

19. Elmer-Dewitt, "Screen," 40.

20. Ibid., 40–42.

21. These images—produced by the same artist that "darkened" O. J. Simpson's face—provoked much controversy.

22. According to MacKinnon, pornography is "constructing and performative rather than . . . merely referential or connotative. The message of these materials, and there is one, as there is to all conscious activity, is 'get her,' pointing at all women, to the perpetrators' benefit of ten billion dollars a year and counting. This message is addressed directly to the penis, delivered through an erection, and taken out on women in the real world" (*Only Words* [Cambridge, Mass.: Harvard University Press, 1993], 21). In terms of its effect on women, "as Andrea Dworkin has said, 'pornography is the law for women.' Like law, pornography does what it says. That pornography is reality is what silenced women have not been permitted to *say* for hundreds of years" (ibid., 41).

23. Jean Baudrillard, *The Ecstasy of Communication*, trans. Bernard Schutze and Caroline Schutze (Brooklyn, N.Y.: Semiotext(e), 1988), 35.

24. For more on the relationship between pornographic images and reference, see Lucienne Frappier-Mazur, "The Truth and the Obscene Word in Eighteenth-Century French Pornography," in *The Invention of Pornography: Obscenity and the Origins of Modernity, 1500–1800*, ed. Lynn Hunt (New York: Zone Books, 1993), 203–21.

25. U.S. Congress, House Report 105–775, "Child Online Protection Act," 105th Cong., 2nd Sess., 1998, available online at http:// www.congress.gov/cgi-bin/cpqery/ R?cp105:FLD010:@1(hr775)/ or at http://www.access.gpo.gov/congress/105hrept.html.

26. Armagh, Battaglia, and Lanning, *The Use of Computers*, 6.

27. Ibid., 5.

28. As one convicted pedophile put it, "on the computer, the search for a victim is an arduous task that's fraught with danger due to the intensity of law enforcement. . . . Besides . . . victims are too easy to find in other places [Successful pedophiles] are better with your children than you are. They give them more attention. They are your swim coach, your Sunday school teacher—people you trust to come into contact with your child every single day" (as quoted by Bob Trebilcock in "Child Molesters on the Internet," *Redbook*, April 1997, 100–107).

29. Jean Baudrillard and Paul Virilio view cybersex more generally (not online child pornography) as a substitute for sex and thus a form of species suicide.

30. For a provocative case regarding the relationship between Internet regulation, surveillance, and pornography, see Laura Kipnis's analysis of *United States v. Depew*. In this case, two men (one a pedophile and the other a "top," the active role in sadomasochism) were contacted over the Internet by an undercover San Jose police officer who suggested they make a snuff film. Although no child was ever kidnapped or killed, although DePew himself withdrew from the project, and although the lines between fantasy and intent were extremely difficult to draw, Depew was sentenced to thirty-

three years in prison for intent to kidnap, in part due to videotapes of his violent and potentially life-threatening S/M encounters with willing partners (hanging, electrocution, and so on). Laura Kipnis, *Bound and Gagged: Pornography and the Politics of Fantasy in America* (Durham, N.C.: Duke University Press, 1999), chap. 1.

31. The obverse of this is Paul Virilio's fear in *Open Sky* that cybersex will lead to uncontrollable masturbation and the end of physical sex; Virilio compares cybersex to AIDS. Paul Virilio, *Open Sky*, trans. Julie Rose (London and New York: Verso, 1997).

32. *New York v. Ferber*, 458 U.S. 747m 757 (1982) (quoting *Globe Newspaper Co. v. Superior Court*, 457 U.S. 596, 607 [1982] and *Sable v. FCC*, 492 U.S. [1989] at 126).

33. In terms of pornography legislation, in 1957 (*Roth v. United States*), the Supreme Court decided the First Amendment did not extend to "obscenity," but the Court also defined obscenity to be materials that are "utterly without redeeming social importance," which to "the average person, applying contemporary local standards, the dominant theme taken as a whole appeals to prurient interests" (354 U.S. 1957). As Frederick Lane has argued, although the Roth decision upheld Samuel Roth's indictment for mailing what we would now consider to be "fairly mild sexual materials," it also enabled the genesis of magazines such as *Playboy* and *Penthouse*, as well as the distribution of literary works such as *Lady Chatterley's Lover* and *Memoirs of a Lady of Pleasure*, because of the phrases "local standards," "taken as a whole" and "utterly without redeeming social importance." Frederick S. Lane III, *Obscene Profits: The Entrepreneurs of Pornography in the Cyber Age* (New York: Routeledge, 2000), 25. This decision was revised by *Miller v. California*, 413. U.S. 15 (1973), so that the new three-pronged test for obscenity became "(a) whether the average person, applying contemporary community standards, would find that the work, taken as a whole, appeals to the prurient interest; (b) whether the work depicts or describes, in a patently offensive way, sexual conduct specifically defined by applicable state law; and (c) whether the work, taken as a whole, lacks serious literary, artistic, political or scientific value." The "*Miller* test" made more explicit the relation between pornography (as the depiction of sexual acts) and obscenity, and it took "sexual conduct" outside of considerations applied to the work taken as a whole. It also moved from local to community standards, thus implying that something like a "community" with appropriate standards existed. Lastly, its narrowing of "utterly without redeeming social importance" to lacking "serious literary, artistic, political or scientific value" further restricted "free speech." Although *Miller* is still arguably the text for "print obscenity," each new communications medium required a "new" decision in order to demarcate the "unspeakable," and thus speakable words/images. For instance, the question of "community standards" becomes a key point of contention in defining online obscenity. The CDA sought to avoid this by simply taking out community standards; COPA reintroduced them. For more on the limits of the speakable, see Judith Butler *Excitable Speech: A Politics of the Performative* (New York: Routledge, 1997).

34. 336 U.S. (1949).

35. See *Sable v. FCC*, 492 U.S. (1989), *FCC v. Pacifica*, 438 U.S. (1978), *Red Lion Broadcasting Co. v. FCC*, 395 U.S. 367 (1969), *Turner Broadcasting Systems v. FCC*, 114 S.Ct. 2445 (1994), *Miami Herald Publishing Co. v. Tornillo*, 418 U.S. 214 (1974).

36. For more on this, see Paula Findlen, "Humanism, Politics, and Pornography in Renaissance Italy," in Hunt, *The Invention of Pornography*, 49–108.

37. http://www.fcc.gov/Reports/tcom/1996.txt.

38. *Department of Justice Brief, Reno v. ACLU*, filed with the Supreme Court on January 21, 1997 (http://www.ciec.org/SC_appeal/979121_DOJ_brief.html.; hereafter referred to as *DOJ Brief*), Sec. C. "The Display Provision Is Facially Constitutional, 1.a."

39. *DOJ Brief*, "Summary of Argument."

40. Ibid., "Statement, 2."

41. As cited in ibid.

42. *DOJ Brief*, "Summary of Argument, B."

43. In legislation designed to protect minors, there is some tradition of strict liability. For instance, "reasonable belief" that your wife was over sixteen is not a defense against a statutory rape charge. According to Amy Kapczynski, "this negligence standard embodies a certain kind of Foucauldian regulation—you have to imagine what the 'reasonable person' would do to keep this stuff from kids, and are thus allowed a certain discretion to self-regulate, as opposed to having definitive rules that were imposed by the state" (personal correspondence, 24 June 2003).

44. According to Senator Charles Grassley, it is not fair for parents to have "the sole responsibility to spend their hard-earned money to ensure that cyberporn does not flood into their homes through their personal computers" (as quoted in *DOJ Brief* "E. There Are No Alternatives That Would Be Equally Effective in Advancing the Government's Interests").

45. *DOJ Brief*, "Statement, 2."

46. The government thus works to ensure that public spaces are legally available to all, without addressing issues of fair access (just as after the battle over civil rights, it ensured that race-based barriers were taken down, but did not address inequalities in income and opportunity in a manner that would guarantee fair access to these public sites).

47. The zoning argument did, however, win over Justice O'Connor and Chief Justice Rehnquist. In their concurrence, O'Connor explains: "I write separately to explain why I view the Communications Decency Act of 1996 (CDA) as little more than an attempt by Congress to create 'adult zones' on the Internet. Our precedent indicates that the creation of such zones can be constitutionally sound. Despite the soundness of its purpose, however, portions of the CDA are unconstitutional because they stray from the blueprint our prior cases have developed for constructing a 'zoning law' that passes constitutional muster" (*Concurrence by O'Connor/Rehnquist, (Reno v. ACLU*, 521 U.S. 844 [1977], 886). http://www.ciec.org/SC_appeal/concurrence.html.

48. Ibid., 845.

49. In response to the government's precedents, the Supreme Court stated:

a close look at the precedents relied on by the Government—*Ginsberg v. New York*, 390 U.S. 629; *FCC v. Pacifica Foundation*, 438 U.S. 726; and *Renton v. Playtime Theatres, Inc.*, 475 U.S. 41—raises, rather than relieves, doubts about the CDA's constitutionality. The CDA differs from the various laws and orders upheld in those cases in many ways, including that it does not allow parents to consent to their children's use of restricted materials; is not limited to commercial transactions; fails to provide any definition of "indecent" and omits any requirement that "patently offensive" material lack socially redeeming value; neither limits its broad categorical prohibitions to particular times nor bases them on an evaluation by an agency familiar with the medium's unique characteristics; is punitive; applies to a medium that, unlike radio, receives full

First Amendment protection; and, cannot be properly analyzed as a form of time, place, and manner regulation because it is a content based blanket restriction on speech. (Ibid.)

50. Dalzell's opinion, *Preliminary Injunction*, sec. D.3, "The Effect of the CDA and the Novel Characteristics of Internet Communication."

51. Ibid., sec. E, "Conclusion."

52. *Abrams v. United States*, 250 U.S. 616, 630 (1919) (Holmes, J., dissenting).

53. *Preliminary Injunction*, Dalzell, sec. D. 4, "Diversity and Access on the Internet."

54. Ibid.

55. Ibid., sec. 5, "Protection of Children from Pornography."

56. Ibid., sec. 3.

57. Ibid., sec D. 4.

58. U.S. Supreme Court, *Supreme Court Opinion (n.o 96–511): Reno v. ACLU*, 521 U.S. 844 (1997), 885 at http://www.ciec.org/SC_appeal/opinion.html or U.S. Supreme Court (see http://supremecourtus.gov/opinions/) (hereafter referred to as *Supreme Court Opinion*).

59. Ibid., 847.

60. Ibid., 854.

61. Chief Judge Sloviter's opinion, sec. C, "Applicable Standard of Review," *Preliminary Injunction*.

62. "Findings of Fact," no. 84, *Preliminary Injunction*.

63. Senior Circuit Judge Leonard J. Garth, writing the opinion of the court, affirming the District Court's order dated February 1, 1999, issuing a preliminary injunction. U.S. Court of Appeals for the Third Circuit. No. 99-1324. *ACLU v. Reno*, 217 F. 31 162, 7000 U.S. App. LEXIS 14419 (3rd Cir. Pa. 2000) (http://www.doask.dotell.com/contnet/copaapel.htm), Decision to Uphold Preliminary Injunction No. 99–1324, 30.

64. Ibid., 34.

65. Thomas Weber, "The X Files: For Those Who Scoff at Internet Commerce, Here's a Hot Market—Raking in the Millions, Sex Sites Use Old-Fashioned Porn and Cutting-Edge Tech—Lessons for the Mainstream," *Wall Street Journal*, August 20, 1997, A1. The threat of legislation has had a profound impact on Web sites. For instance, Altern.org, a large alternative network in France, closed down in June 2000 after France passed a law making Web hosting services responsible for their users' content. The owner, Valentin Lacambre, did not wait to see if the law would pass through the French courts; http://www.nettime.org/Lists-Archives/nettime-1-0007/msg00064.html.

66. A Justice Department memo to the legislature stated that it believed the CDA unconstitutional. ACLU, "Defending Reproductive Rights in Cyberspacce" 10/31/1996, http://www.aclu.org/reproductiverights/gen/16532res19961031.html.

67. See http://yro.slahsdot.org/article/pl?sid=03/03/13/2215207.

68. *Supreme Court Opinion*, 521 U.S. 844 (1997), 853.

69. *U.S. Code*, sec. 2251, "Congressional Findings," *United States Code*.

70. Kipnis, *Bound and Gagged*, 161.

71. Fredric Jameson, *Signatures of the Visible* (New York: Routledge, 1992), 1.

72. Butler, *Excitable Speech*, 77.

73. Thomas Keenan, "Windows: of vulnerability," in *The Phantom Public Sphere*, ed. Bruce Robbins (Minneapolis: University of Minnesota Press, 1993), 133–34.

74. Claude Lefort, *Democracy and Political Theory*, trans. David Macy (Minneapolis: Minnesota University Press, 1988).

Chapter 7. The Billboard War

Portions of this essay are from part 3 of my book *Buyways: Billboards, Automobiles, and the American Landscape* (New York: Routledge, 2004), 163–246.

1. The phrase "billboard war" was commonly used to describe roadside reform efforts, as is noted by James P. Taylor in his address to the Vermont Federation of Women's Clubs, *Hospitality de Luxe: Pomp of Highways and Glory of Roadsides* (Burlington, Vt.: Lane Press, 1929), n.p., and in Albert S. Bard's overview of the movement, "Winning the Billboard War," *National Municipal Review* 30 (July 1941): 2.

2. On the earlier history of resistance to outdoor advertising, see Gudis, *Buyways*, 26–29, 166–71. Also see Quentin Schultz, "Legislating Morality: The Progressive Response to American Outdoor Advertising, 1900–1917," *Journal of Popular Culture* 17 (Spring 1984): 37–44; William H. Wilson, "J. Horace McFarland and the City Beautiful Movement," *Journal of Urban History* 7 (May 1981): 315–34, and "The Billboard: Bane of the City Beautiful," *Journal of Urban History* 13 (August 1987): 394–425; Ernest Morrison, *J. Horace McFarland: A Thorn for Beauty* (Harrisburg, Pa.: Commonwealth of Pennsylvania, Pennsylvania Historical and Museum Commission, 1995); and Michele H. Bogart, "Posters versus Billboards," *Artists, Advertising, and the Borders of Art* (Chicago: University of Chicago Press, 1995), 79–124.

3. For more on the role of women in civic improvement organizations and in the City Beautiful movement, see Bonj Szczygiel, " 'City Beautiful' Revisited: An Analysis of Nineteenth-Century Civic Improvement Efforts," *Journal of Urban History* 29 (January 2003): 107–32; Eugenie Ladner Birch, "From Civic Worker to City Planner: Women and Planning, 1890–1980," in *The American Planner: Biographies and Recollections*, ed. Donald A. Krueckeberg (New York: Methuen, 1983), 398–99; Susan Marie Wirka, "The City Social Movement: Progressive Women Reformers and Early Social Planning," in *Planning the Twentieth-Century American City*, ed. Mary Corbin Sies and Charles Silver (Baltimore: Johns Hopkins University Press, 1996), 55–76; Jon A. Peterson, "The City Beautiful Movement: Forgotten Origins and Lost Meaning," *Journal of Urban History* 2 (August 1976): 421–23; Karen Blair, *The Torchbearers: Women and Their Amateur Arts Associations in America, 1890–1930* (Bloomington: Indiana University Press, 1994), 94–102; and Daphne Spain, *How Women Saved the City* (Minneapolis: University of Minnesota Press, 2001), 54–57.

4. "Official Minutes of the Board of Directors Meeting, General Federation of Women's Clubs, Washington, D.C., Wednesday, January 9, 1924," 370, "Big Advertisers Drop Billboards as Public Indignation Gains Force," *American Press*, March 1924, 5, and "Report by Mrs. Elizabeth B. Lawton, Seventeenth Biennial Convention," 415, all in the Outdoor Advertising Archives, John W. Hartman Center for Sales, Advertising, and Marketing History, Duke University, Durham, N.C. (hereafter OAA/Duke); "Billboards on the Move," *Civic Comment* (published by the American Civic Association) 8 (June 28, 1924), 12; Elizabeth Lawton, "Protecting the Scenery from Billboards," in

American Civic Annual, ed. Harlean James (Washington, D.C.: American Civic Association, 1929), 144. On the GFWC: Blair, *Torchbearers*, 39; Anne M. Evans, "Women's Rural Organizations and their Activities," *United States Department of Agriculture Bulletin No. 719* (Washington, D.C.: Government Printing Office, 1918), 1.

5. "Funeral Services Conducted for Mrs. Elizabeth Lawton," *Glens Falls, N.Y., Times*, July 8, 1952, and other untitled obituaries, OAA/Duke; Roger William Riis, "The Billboards Must Go—II," *Reader's Digest*, November 1938, 81; Birch, "From Civic Worker to City Planner," 414.

6. "Report by Mrs. Elizabeth B. Lawton, Seventeenth Biennial Convention, Los Angeles, 1924," 415, "Women's Clubs Against Billboards," *American Magazine of Art*, July 2, 1922, "To Eliminate Billboards," *Paterson Press Guardian*, August 1, 1922, and *American Magazine of Art*, November 1922, OAA/Duke; *General Federation News* 3 (July–August 1922): 22.

7. *Roadside Bulletin* 2 (October 1934): 1. Hereafter, the *Roadside Bulletin* will be abbreviated to *RB*; please note that this journal was not published with regularity and often did not print the month or year of publication.

8. With her husband, Lawton conducted at least twenty-two state and four regional surveys. "Funeral Services Conducted for Mrs. Elizabeth Lawton," letter from George Kleiser, president, Outdoor Advertising Association of America, to I. W. Digges, Secretary, Outdoor Advertising Inc., August 8, 1931, and August 19, 1931, and National Roadside Council, *What It Is—What It Does*, December 1938, n.p., OAA/Duke; "The Federal City Roadside Campaign," *Civic Comment* 32 (January-February 1931): 3.

9. William C. Hunt recognized the threat posed by Mrs. Lawton, whom he described as "a human comet," for her use of the "powerful agencies of publicity." Hunt, "Popularization of Poster Advertising," *Outdoor Advertising Association News* (hereafter *OAA News*) 14 (August 1924): 9.

10. This comment was scrawled on a page with obituary clippings dated July 1952, OAA/Duke. Edward C. Donnelly described Lawton's activities as "pernicious, unfounded and constantly harassing" (letter to H. E. Fisk, July 23, 1941) while J. B. Stewart called her the "arch enemy" of outdoor activities (letter to Tom Griffith, Griffith Advertising Agency, May 3, 1940), OAA/Duke.

11. Letter from Mrs. C. Oliver Iselin, National Roadside Council, to Library of the Department of City Planning and Landscape Architecture, Harvard University, February 1955, Loeb Library, Harvard University. The dissolution letter claimed that state garden clubs and Keep America Beautiful were doing the same work, so the NRC was no longer necessary.

12. *The National Committee for Restriction of Outdoor Advertising: What It Is and What It Seeks to Do* (New York: National Committee for Restriction of Outdoor Advertising, n.d.), n.p.; *Save the Beauty of America: The Landscape Is No Place for Advertising* (Washington, D.C.: General Federation of Women's Clubs, Department of Art, Billboard Restriction Committee, n.d.), n.p.; "Billboards on the Move," 12.

13. Mrs. W. L. Lawton, *Digest of Address on Billboard Campaign, Delivered at the Biennial (Los Angeles, Cal.) Art Day, June 11, 1924* (Washington, D.C.: General Federation of Women's Clubs, 1924), n.p.

14. "Recent Roadside Improvement," in *American Civic Annual*, ed. Harlean James, vol. 3 (Washington, D.C.: American Civic Association, 1931), 162; "What Is the

Policy of the General Federation of Women's Clubs on Billboard Restriction," Box 21, Albert Sprague Bard Papers, New York Public Library (hereafter Bard Papers).

15. James P. Karp, "The Evolving Meaning of Aesthetics in Land-Use Regulation," *Columbia Journal of Environmental Law* 15, no. 2 (1990): 310.

16. *City of Passaic v. Paterson Bill Posting, Advertising & Sign Painting Co.*, 72 N.J.L. 285, 62 A. 267 (1905); *Varney & Green v. Williams*, 155 Cal. 318 (1909); *St. Louis Gunning Advertising Co. v. St. Louis*, 231 U.S. 761 (1913); *Thomas Cusack Co. v. City of Chicago*, 242 U.S. 526 (1917). Dozens of articles published by the NRC and American Civic Association (ACA) bemoan the courts' shortsightedness in granting aesthetics primary attention. Articles that spell out the legal limitations include Everett L. Millard, "Legal Handicaps in the Billboard Problem," *American City* 12 (March 1915): 254–55; "Aesthetic Considerations and Billboard Zoning," *Journal of Land and Public Utility Economics*, May 1931, 208–10; Andrew Wright Crawford, *Important Advances Toward Eradicating the Billboard Nuisance*, 2nd ed. (Washington, D.C.: American Civic Association, 1920), 10. As a way around the exclusion of aesthetics from the police power, the ACA suggested that each state amend its constitution so that the " 'rule of reason' now applicable to legislation under the police power for the protection of the ear and nose to be likewise applicable to acts for the protection of the eye." "If we can get rid of John Barleycorn by a constitutional amendment, we can similarly get rid of Billy Billboard. Indeed, John used to be one of Billy's best customers . . . !" Crawford, *Important Advances*, 14–15; "Fairfield County," 5, Box 20, Bard Papers.

Aesthetics, standing alone, was the basis for the exercise of the police power beginning with the Supreme Court's decision in *Berman v. Parker*, 348 U.S. 26 (1954), which authorized urban renewal projects based on the idea that "the concept of public welfare is broad and inclusive. The values it represents are spiritual as well as physical, aesthetic as well as monetary." *People v. Stover*, 191 N.E. 2d 272 (1963), continued the trend. Secondary sources on the legal regulation of outdoor advertising include: John Costonis, "Law and Aesthetics: A Critique and a Reformulation of the Dilemmas," *UMKC Law Review* 48, no. 2 (1980): 126–66; J. Barry Cullingworth, "Aesthetics in U.S. Planning: From Billboards to Design Controls," *Town Planning Review* 62 (October 1991): 399–413; Daniel R. Mandelker and William R. Ewald, *Street Graphics and the Law* (Washington, D.C., and Chicago: Planners Press, American Planning Association, 1988). A philosophical and legal overview of aesthetics, zoning, and planning is Samuel Bufford, "Beyond the Eye of the Beholder: A New Majority of Jurisdictions Authorize Aesthetic Regulation," *Michigan Law Review* 80 (January 1982): 355–461; Karp, "Evolving Meaning of Aesthetics," 307–28.

17. "Big Advertisers Drop Billboards," 5, and reprint of Mrs. W. L. Lawton, "Rural Billboard Advertising Increasingly Viewed as Menace to Outdoor Beauty," *General Federation News*, March 1929, OAA/Duke.

18. "Knocking a Nuisance—Signboards or Scenery, Which?" *Philadelphia Record*, April 13, 1924, 8–9.

19. *RB* 2, no. 1 (n.d.): 4; *RB* 1, no. 4 (February 1931): 3; *RB* 1, no. 6 (c. 1931): 17; *RB* 1, no. 2 (c. 1930): 16; *RB* 1, no. 6 (c. 1931): 17; *RB* 1, no. 2 (c. 1930): 16.

20. "Billboards on the Move," 12; Taylor, *Hospitality de Luxe*, n.p.; "Is an Assault on Advertising Under Way?" *Printers' Ink*, April 17, 1924, 54.

21. See, for instance, Kathryn Kish Sklar, "The Consumers' White Label Cam-

paign of the National Consumers' League," in *Getting and Spending: European and American Consumer Societies in the Twentieth Century*, ed. Susan Strasser, Charles McGovern, and Matthias Judt (Cambridge: Cambridge University Press, 1998), 17–35; Lizabeth Cohen, *A Consumers' Republic: The Politics of Mass Consumption in Postwar America* (New York: Alfred A. Knopf, 2003), 22, 31–41, 50–53.

22. Lawton, "Protecting the Scenery from Billboards," 145–46.

23. Blair, *Torchbearers*, 101; *The National Committee for Restriction of Outdoor Advertising*, n.p.; *RB* 1, no. 4 (February 1931): 3.

24. *RB* 1, no. 4 (February 1931): 3; *RB* 1, no. 3 (n.d.): 23; "Another Sticker Joins the Ranks," *Civic Comment* (March–April 1931), and "Topics of the Times: A Buyers' Strike Against Billboards," *New York Times*, November 19, 1929, OAA/Duke.

25. They published this "Honor Roll," as it was sometimes called, in the *Roadside Bulletin* and publicized it through garden clubs, the American Civic Association, the American Federation of Arts, the American Institute of Architects, and the American Nature Association, along with other affiliated GFWC groups. See, for instance, "A White List," *Garden Glories* (Garden Club of Illinois, Inc.) 4 (September 1932), OAA/Duke.

26. "Standard Oil Quits Billboards in East and 2,200 in the West," *American Press*, May 1924, 1–2; "Big Advertisers Drop Billboards," 5; "Knocking a Nuisance," 8–9; "Standard Oil Champions Beauty," *Brooklyn Eagle*, April 13, 1924, 2.

27. Mrs. Charles N. Felton, "Keep Scenic Highways Scenic," *California Highways and Public Works*, February 1930, 15, 17; C. C. Carleton, "Zoning for Control of Building Along the California State Highway System," *California Highways and Public Works*, January 1936, 16; George B. Ford, "A Program for Roadside Improvement," in *American Civic Annual*, ed. Harlean James, vol. 2 (Washington, D.C.: American Civic Association, 1930), 184–87; Birch, "From Civic Worker to City Planner," 491. Years later another Rockefeller—Laurence—would offer support for another incarnation of the same cause, Lady Bird Johnson's beautification campaigns. Lewis Gould, *Lady Bird Johnson and the Environment* (Lawrence: University Press of Kansas, 1988), 69–70.

28. "Is an Assault on Advertising Under Way?" 54–55, 61, 64.

29. *Los Angeles Herald Examiner*, July 6, 1951, Regional History Center, University of Southern California, Los Angeles; Alice Spalding Brown, *History of the Outdoor Circle* (Honolulu, 1962); Josephine L. Campbell, *How Hawaii Erased a Blot* (Honolulu: Outdoor Circle, n.d.); Fred C. Kelly, "How Hawaii Abolished Objectionable Signs: Boycott versus Billboard," *Reader's Digest*, February 1937, 39; typescript of speech and slide show by Frank C. Balfour, "Battle of the Billboards in California," presented before the Right of Way Committee, American Association of State Highway Officials' Thirty-seventh Annual Convention, Omaha, Nebraska, October 23–26, 1951, 14–16, Regional History Center, University of Southern California, Los Angeles.

30. See www.outdoorcircle.com. The other states to ban billboards are Alaska, Maine, and Vermont.

31. *Progress in 1925: National Committee for Restriction of Outdoor Advertising* (New York: National Roadside Council, 1925), 3–4.

32. *An Appeal to Chambers of Commerce and Civic Organizations* (New York: National Roadside Council, n.d.), n.p.

33. *Save the Beauty of America*, n.p.

34. In the narratives accompanying her surveys, Lawton articulated her aesthetic

standards; other articles in the *Roadside Bulletin* did likewise. See, for instance, *RB* 1, no. 2 (ca. 1930): 2; *RB* 1, no. 3 (n.d.): 6.

35. Thomas Cole, "Essay on American Scenery" (1835), in *The American Landscape: A Critical Anthology of Prose and Poetry*, ed. John Conron (New York: Oxford University Press, 1973), 568–78. On landscape painting, the picturesque, and the sublime, see: *American Iconology*, ed. David Miller (New Haven, Conn.: Yale University Press, 1993); William H. Truettner and Alan Wallach, eds., *Thomas Cole: Landscape into History* (New Haven, Conn.: Yale University Press; and Washington, D.C.: Smithsonian Institution, National Museum of American Art, 1994); Barbara Novak, *Nature and Culture: American Landscape and Painting, 1825–1875*, rev. ed. (New York: Oxford University Press, 1995); George A. Thompson, ed., *Landscape in America* (Austin: University of Texas Press, 1995). On ideas about nature and industrial technology, see John Kasson, *Civilizing the Machine: Technology and Republican Values in America* (New York: Grossman Pubs., 1976); Leo Marx, *Machine in the Garden: Technology and the Pastoral Ideal in America* (London: Oxford University Press, 1964).

36. Billboard and Roadside Committee, *Calendar 1928: The Garden Club of America*, OAA/Duke; Lawton, "Protecting the Scenery from Billboards," 143, 146; *Save the Beauty of America*, cover; *The State Highways: The Lesson of the Mohawk Trail* (Boston: Massachusetts Forestry Association, n.d.), n.p.

37. On the cultural construction of nature and wilderness, see Roderick Nash, *Wilderness and the American Mind* (New Haven, Conn.: Yale University Press, 1967); James L. Machor, *Pastoral Cities: Urban Ideals and the Symbolic Landscape of America* (Madison: University of Wisconsin Press, 1987); Michael Rogin, "Nature as Politics and Nature as Romance in America," *Ronald Reagan, the Movie* (Berkeley: University of California Press, 1987), 169–89; Richard Slotkin, *Regeneration through Violence: The Mythology of the American Frontier* (Middletown, Conn.: Wesleyan University Press, 1973); Henry Nash Smith, *Virgin Land* (Cambridge, Mass.: Harvard University Press, 1950); Perry Miller, *Errand into the Wilderness* (Cambridge, Mass.: Harvard University Press, 1964); and Miller, *Nature's Nation* (Cambridge, Mass.: Belknap Press of Harvard University, 1967).

38. "Forum on Roadside Beauty," 26; *RB* 2, no. 4 (May 1933): 3.

39. Ralph Waldo Emerson, "Nature" (1836), in Conron, *American Landscape*, 580.

40. "Who Owns the Landscape," *New York Herald Tribune*, quoted in *RB* 1, no. 6 (ca. 1931): 1; Charlotte Rumbold, "Beyond the Billboards Lies America," *Clevelander* 6 (June 1931): 2.

41. Many have addressed the idea of vision as appropriative, "empiric," or "magisterial" especially in terms of art and photography. For instance, John Berger, *Ways of Seeing* (London: Penguin Books, 1972); Susan Sontag, *On Photography* (New York: Farrar, Straus and Giroux, 1977); Albert Boime, *Magisterial Gaze: Manifest Destiny and the American Landscape Painting* (Washington, D.C.: Smithsonian Institution, 1991); Angela Miller, *The Empire of the Eye: Landscape Representation and American Cultural Politics, 1825–1875* (Ithaca, N.Y.: Cornell University Press, 1993); Mary Louise Pratt, *Imperial Eyes: Travel Writing and Transculturation* (New York: Routledge, 1992). Alan Trachtenberg addresses this in terms of Clarence King's descriptions of the Sierra Nevadas in *Reading American Photographs: Images as History* (New York: Noonday Press, 1990), 119–63. Dona Brown addresses the way in which

tourism helped to spread market relations "into the landscape, and even into regions of human consciousness" (*Inventing New England: Regional Tourism in the Nineteenth Century* [Washington: Smithsonian Institution Press, 1995], 10), and Marguerite S. Shaffer expands upon the role of tourism and commodification of the landscape in *See America First: Tourism and National Identity, 1880–1940* (Washington, D.C.: Smithsonian Institution Press, 2001).

42. *RB* 2, no. 4 (May 1933): 26.

43. Lawton, *Digest of Address on Billboard Campaign*, n.p.

44. For more on the strategies employed by outdoor advertisers, see Gudis, *Buyways*, chap. 3, "Producing Mobile Audiences and Corridors of Consumption," 49–65.

45. "Ten Ways to Sell the Poster Idea," *The Poster* 12 (December 1921): 18. A similar point is the subject of W. Livingston Larned, "Posters and the Winter Tourist," *The Poster* 11 (February 1920): 1.

46. *RB* 1, no. 2 (ca. 1930): 2; *RB* 1, no. 3 (n.d.): 6.

47. On fears of overproduction and underconsumption, and attempts to "rationalize" distribution in the 1920s and 1930s, see Benjamin Kline Hunnicutt, "The New Economic Gospel of Consumption," *Work Without End: Abandoning Shorter Hours for the Right to Work* (Philadelphia: Temple University Press, 1988), 37–65; Gary Cross, *Time and Money: The Making of Consumer Culture* (New York: Routledge, 1993), 15–46; Daniel Horowitz, *The Morality of Spending: Attitudes Toward the Consumer Society in America, 1875–1940* (Baltimore: Johns Hopkins University Press, 1985), 135ff.

48. F. T. Hopkins, *The Roadside Advertising Controversy* (Chicago: National Outdoor Advertising Bureau, 1938), n.p.

49. "To the Ladies," *Printers' Ink*, May 8, 1924, OAA/Duke.

50. *100 Reformers versus 25,000 Wage Earners* (New York: OAAA, ca. 1936), n.p.

51. Lavinia Engle, "Billboard Tax Law in Maryland," in James, *American Civic Annual*, vol. 3 (1931), 199.

52. *Association News* 22 (July 1932): 38–39; Hopkins, *Roadside Advertising Controversy*. "Don't forget, ladies," another billboard advocate wrote, in case the reformers were not sympathetic to farmers, that "in about 80 per cent of cases these rentals are paid to women." S. N. Holliday, *The Story of Organized Outdoor Advertising* (n.d.), 5, OAA/Duke.

53. Franz Aust, "The Democratization of Art," *The Poster* 15 (December 1924): 8.

54. Holliday, *Organized Outdoor Advertising*, 4. On the broad reach of the medium to illiterate and immigrant populations, see "Ten Ways to Sell the Poster Idea," 17; Leonard Dreyfuss, "The Advertising and Marketing of Tomorrow," *The Poster* 14 (August 1923): 12; Arthur Acheson, "Poster Publicity in the States," *The Poster* 11 (February 1920): 21; "New Ideals in Poster Art," *The Poster* 11 (October 1920): 32; Leonard Dreyfuss, "A Brief Survey of Poster Advertising," *The Poster* 11 (February 1920): 35.

55. Bogart, "Posters versus Billboards," 114.

56. Aust, "Democratization," 8.

57. Loredo Taft, "Bring Art to the Home Towns," *The Poster* 15 (December 1924): 2; Aust, "Democratization," 4–5, 8.

58. *Foster and Kleiser Company Gardens* (San Francisco: Foster and Kleiser Co., 1930), n.p., and *"Come into the Garden with Us"* (San Francisco: Foster and Kleiser Co., 1930), n.p., Clear Channel Outdoor, History Archive, Los Angeles (hereafter Clear

Channel Archive). Other examples of sign parks nationwide are represented in *Beauty and Utility in Outdoor Advertising* (Chicago: Outdoor Advertising Association of America, n.d.); John Whitmer, "A Cooperative Community Development," *OAA News* 19 (October 1929): 26; "Landscaping the Panel Location," *OAA News* 16 (October 1926): 10.

59. "*Come into the Garden with Us*," n.p. The "lizzies" were produced between 1923 and 1931, when the cost became prohibitive. TAB Annual Meeting and Management Conference, January 1978, file: Bulletin Structures, Clear Channel Archive.

60. "Wilder Aids Civic Plans," *OAA News* 13 (January 1923): 21; "How Association Members Improve Rundown and Unsightly Sections," *The Poster* 14 (February 1923): 20–21; Harris Wescott, "If Standardized Outdoor Advertising Did Not Exist!" *The Poster* 19 (March 1928): 8–11; *5,743*; *Victory Gardens* (General Outdoor Advertising Co., ca. 1944), n.p., OAA/Duke.

61. Aust, "Democratization," 4–5.

62. Unsigned, unattributed letters from Johnstown, Pa., to Gordon H. Seymour, Springfield, Mass., November 13, 1920, and to J. H. Brinkmeyer, president of Poster Advertising Association, April 29, 1922, OAA/Duke. Leonard Dreyfuss also proposed the formation of a "Sisterhood of the Poster Advertising Association," in an article by that name. He thought that if all else failed, the women would at least enhance the "entertainment features" of association meetings. *OAA News* 10 (December 1920): 10.

63. Letter to Brinkmeyer, April 29, 1920.

64. Ibid.; Minutes, Thirty-sixth Annual Convention, OAAA, Atlanta, October 18–23, 1926, vol. 1, 41–46, OAA/Duke.

65. In 1940 Lilly formed the Women's Fact-Finding Roadside Association. The group's early activities included lobbying the New York City Planning Commission to express their opposition to proposed zoning resolutions. See *Woman's Fact-Finding Roadside Association* (n.d), OAA/Duke. A variant of the fact-finding group was formed in the early 1960s as the women's division of the OAAA, called the Outdoor Advertising Women of America. Letter from Freda Dixon, director, Women's Division, OAAA, to the Committee Members of the Outdoor Advertising Women of America (n.d.), membership pamphlet *Outdoor Advertising Women of America* (Chicago: OAAA Women's Division, n.d.), and issues of *Newsletter of the Outdoor Advertising Women of America*, 1961–63, OAA/Duke.

66. Their success may be judged by the comments of Elizabeth Lawton, who, in describing the strength of the billboard lobby, claimed it "had many friends in court," was firmly entrenched in "practically every civic group of prominence" and chambers of commerce, and had infiltrated all of the garden and women's clubs ("where, in some cases, the wives of billboard men, or of large billboard users, hold key positions and influence club policies"), to the extent that many legislators and club members were afraid to raise the subject of roadside control. Elizabeth Lawton, "Florida Behind the Billboards," *Nature Magazine* (May 1940): 283.

67. Letter to George Kleiser, president, OAAA, from J. B. Stewart, vice president, Legal and Legislative Division, OAAA, April 25, 1933, and letter from Herbert Fisk to George Kleiser, April 18, 1933, OAA/Duke; *RB* 2, no. 3 (ca. 1933): 19.

68. Clubwomen acknowledged their lobbying for license fees and enforcement of existing regulations would drive the small, independent operators out of business, perhaps to the advantage of the largest outdoor advertisers. "Shall Our Roadsides Be

Scenic or Signic," *Billboards Destroy Motoring Joy: Billboard Primer* (Garden Club of Virginia, ca. 1936), Stella Minick, "Report of Work Done by the Garden Club of Waynesboro in Reference to Roadside Improvement," October 2, 1939, OAA/Duke. Also see the transcripts of "Conference on Roadside Business and Rural Beauty," Chamber of Commerce, Washington, D.C., January 8, 1931, 29, OAA/Duke.

69. *1912–1952 Federal Litigations*, a compiled record of all litigations between the United States and the Outdoor Advertising Association of America, distributed by OAAA, Chicago, September 30, 1952. The consolidation of the outdoor advertising industry is similar to many other industries at the height of the trade association movement in the 1920s. See Ellis W. Hawley, "Herbert Hoover, the Commerce Secretariat, and the Vision of an 'Associative State,' 1921–1928," *Journal of American History* 61 (June 1974): 116–40.

70. *RB* 1, no. 3 (n.d.): 12.

71. Lawton, *Digest of Address on Billboard Campaign*, n.p.

72. Struthers Burt, "Beauty and Billboards Are Not Compatible," in James, *American Civic Annual*, vol. 3 (1931), 184.

73. On the zoning plans the NRC put forth, see *National Roadside Council: What It Is—What It Does* (New York: National Roadside Council, ca. 1939), n.p.; Bard, "Winning the Billboard War," 1–4; RB 2, no. 3 (ca. 1933): 55–60.

74. *Roadside Improvement*, supplement to *Planning and Civic Comment* 4 (October–December 1938): 20. Also see Edward Bassett, "Billboards," *Planning and Civic Comment* 1 (April–June 1935): 18.

75. Daniel M. Bluestone, "Roadside Blight and the Reform of Commercial Architecture," in *Roadside America: The Automobile in Design and Culture*, ed. Jan Jennings (Ames, Iowa: Iowa State University Press and Society for Commercial Archeology, 1990), 170–83.

76. *The Roadside Advertising Controversy* (New York: New York City Federation of Women's Clubs, 1939), n.p.

77. Letter from Elizabeth Lawton to Arthur Pack, American Nature Association, April 22, 1932, General Correspondence 1932 file, Box 20, Bard Papers.

78. For instance, the National Association of Real Estate Boards supported the outdoor advertising industry in the 1920s and 1930s. That ended in 1940 when they joined the NRC, partly because they feared that billboards were contributing to ribbon developments that would depreciate property values in both urban and ex-urban areas. Letter from Herbert Nelson to Elizabeth Lawton, October 21, 1939, reproduced as "Do Billboards Depreciate Real Estate Value?" *National Roadside Council News Letter*, and letter from A. E. Germer, manager, Department of Public Relations, to members of the OAAA, January 3, 1940, OAA/Duke; Bard, "Winning the Billboard War," 2, 4; Thomas C. Desmond, "Women at Work: Cleaning Up the Roadsides," *Bulletin: National Council of State Garden Clubs*, November 1941, 22; *Decentralization: What Is It Doing to Our Cities?* (Chicago: Urban Land Institute, 1940). The Automobile Club of America also drafted a model roadside zoning bill that borrowed greatly from 1931 proposals of the NRC. *Roadside Protection, A Study of the Problem and a Legislative Guide* (Washington, D.C.: American Automobile Association, 1941), 12–13; *America's Roadsides: A Practical Program for Replacing Confusion and Chaos with Sane and Orderly Development* (Washington, D.C.: American Automobile Association, 1940).

79. William Kaszynski, *The American Highway: The History and Culture of Roads in the United States* (Jefferson, N.C.: McFarland, 2000), 170–71. Was the largest, most

costly public works program ever undertaken in the United States to be the "greatest giveaway of all time," "a huge theft from the public," and "a subsidy to the billboard industry," critics asked, as they envisioned thousands of miles of open highways converted into billboard alleys? *Advertising Agency Magazine*, January 17, 1958, 15; Robert Moses, "Salvo in the Billboard Battle," *New York Times Magazine*, March 16, 1958, 16.

80. Gould, *Lady Bird Johnson*, 167.

81. Ibid., 142, 157.

82. Even Ada Louise Huxtable, who was supportive of reform efforts, commented that the White House Conference on Natural Beauty sounded like a "tea party for little old ladies devoted to the cause of simple pastoral pleasures." "Planning for Beauty," *New York Times*, May 24, 1965, 28.

83. Gould, *Lady Bird Johnson*, 153, 188. Gould describes the discomfort that Lady Bird Johnson and male members of the administration felt with "feminine aura" of beautification, which sounded "cosmetic and trivial and . . . prissy" (60–61).

84. Elizabeth Brenner Drew, "Lady Bird's Beauty Bill," *Atlantic Monthly*, December 1965, 68–71; "LBJ's Plan for Roads: Beauty—or No Money," *U.S. News and World Report*, June 7, 1965, 62–77.

85. Gould, *Lady Bird Johnson*, 150ff.

86. Shelby Scates, "Billboards—Great Society Grapples Great Issues," *Argus* (Seattle, Washington), June 25, 1965, 1; reprint of "What President Johnson's Proposed Federal Billboard Control Bill Will Mean to the Standardized Outdoor Advertising Medium," *Advertising Age*, May 31, 1965, OAA/Duke; Gould, *Lady Bird Johnson*, 144, 152; Philip Tocker, transcript of interview by Lewis Gould, July 3, 1984, 16, and August 1, 1984, 1–2, OAA/Duke.

87. The Highway Beautification Act withheld funds to states that did not comply. *Highway Beautification Act of 1965* (San Francisco: Foster and Kleiser Co., 1965), n.p.

88. Tocker interview, August 1, 1984, 2.

89. Letter from John W. Primrose, West Kentucky Advertising Company, to Frank Blake, OAAA, June 1, 1965, OAA/Duke.

90. "Getting into Outdoor," *Marketing Week*, January 30, 2003, 39. New digital-ink billboards can be networked together and changed instantly to take into account viewer reaction, time of day, location, sales results, or current events. "Ford Tests Digital Ink Billboards in Clear Channel Tie," *Marketing* (London), April 3, 2003, 7; Chris Powell, "Digital Ink Makes Billboards Flexible," *Marketing Magazine* (Toronto), April 14, 2003, 4; "Magink Digital-Ink Billboards Heralded as the Future of Outdoor Advertising," *Business Wire*, April 30, 2003; Kathy Prentice, "Taxi! Taxi! I Have a Message for You!," *Media Life*, April 16, 2001 (http://www.medialifemagazine.com/news2001/apr01/apr16/1_mon/news5monday.html).

Chapter 8. *The Social Space of Shopping*

1. Alex Witchel, "He Changed the Way America Cooks," *New York Times*, February 11, 2004, F4.

2. Raymond Williams, *The Country and the City* (New York: Oxford University

Press, 1973), 297; cf. George Ritzer, *The McDonaldization of Society* (Thousand Oaks, Calif.: Pine Forge Press, 1996).

3. On childhood memories of shopping, see Sharon Zukin, *The Cultures of Cities* (Cambridge, Mass. and Oxford: Blackwell, 1995), 192–207.

4. Grace Elizabeth Hale, *Making Whiteness: The Culture of Segregation in the South, 1890–1940* (New York: Pantheon, 1998), 173–78; Elizabeth Chin, *Purchasing Power: Black Kids and American Consumer Culture* (Minneapolis: University of Minnesota Press, 2001), 91–115; Pyong Gap Min, *Caught in the Middle: Korean Communities in New York and Los Angeles* (Berkeley: University of California Press, 1996); Jennifer Lee, *Civility in the City: Blacks, Jews, and Koreans in Urban America* (Cambridge Mass.: Harvard University Press, 2002).

5. Cf. Michelle de la Pradelle's insightful analysis of the public space created by a local market in France, where vendors and shoppers purposely forget or deny their obligations and social status from outside the market situation. *Market Day in Provence*, trans. Amy Jacobs (Chicago: University of Chicago Press, 2006). Debate over Americans' supposed loss of collective social action was sparked by Robert D. Putnam, *Bowling Alone: The Collapse and Revival of American Community* (New York: Simon and Schuster, 2000), which curiously doesn't consider shopping as the source of a different form of public life.

6. See Sharon Zukin, *Point of Purchase: How Shopping Changed American Culture* (New York: Routledge, 2004).

7. Lizabeth Cohen, *A Consumers' Republic: The Politics of Mass Consumption in Postwar America* (New York: Knopf, 2003).

8. Don Slater, *Consumer Culture and Modernity* (Cambridge: Polity, 1997).

9. Walter Benjamin, *The Arcades Project*, trans. Howard Eiland and Kevin McLaughlin (Cambridge, Mass.: Belknap Press, 1999). On "mobilization" rather than "manipulation" of consumers' desires, see Peter Miller and Nikolas Rose, "Mobilizing the Consumer: Assembling the Subject of Consumption," *Theory, Culture and Society* 14, no.1 (1997): 1–36.

10. This is the point made more broadly about all of nineteenth-century Paris by David Harvey, *Paris, Capital of Modernity* (New York: Routledge, 2003).

11. On the Palais Royal as a heterotopic modern space, see Kevin Hetherington, *The Badlands of Modernity* (London: Routledge, 1997).

12. For a complementary view comparing the gaze of the mobile shopper with movie viewing, see Anne Friedberg, *Window Shopping: Cinema and the Postmodern* (Berkeley: University of California Press, 1993).

13. On B. Altman see, http://www.nypl.org/research/sibl/altman/tcont.html. On department stores see, Rosalind H. Williams, *Dream Worlds: Mass Consumption in Nineteenth-Century France* (Berkeley: University of California Press, 1982); William Leach, *Land of Desire: Merchants, Power, and the Rise of a New American Culture* (New York: Pantheon. 1993).

14. Leach, *Land of Desire*.

15. Alison Isenberg, *Downtown America* (Chicago: University of Chicago Press, 2004).

16. On suburbanization of shopping and public life, see Cohen, *A Consumers'*

Republic, 257–89; Zukin, *Point of Purchase*. On malls as dystopic dreams, see Lauren Langman, "Neon Cages: Shopping for Subjectivity," in *Lifestyle Shopping: The Subject of Consumption*, ed. Rob Shields (London: Routledge, 1992), 40–82.

17. Colin Campbell, *The Romantic Ethic and the Spirit of Modern Consumerism* (Oxford: Basil Blackwell, 1987), 77–95.

18. Daniel J. Boorstin, *The Americans: The Democratic Experience* (New York: Random House, 1973), 90.

19. Information on Woolworth's from Zukin, *Point of Purchase*, 70–76.

20. Information on Wal-Mart from Zukin, *Point of Purchase*, 80–85. For an examination of how Wal-Mart's strategy to keep prices low affects suppliers, see Charles Fishman, *The Wal-Mart Effect* (New York: Penguin, 2006), and how it affects labor policies, see Nelson Lichtenstein, ed., *Wal-Mart: The Face of 21st Century Capitalism* (New York: New Press, 2006).

21. Thomas Frank, *The Conquest of Cool* (Chicago: University of Chicago Press, 1997).

22. Branded stores from Zukin, *Point of Purchase*; organization of diversity from Kalman Applbaum, *The Marketing Era: From Professional Practice to Global Provisioning* (New York: Routledge, 2003).

23. Zukin, *Point of Purchase*, 124–39.

24. On Wal-Mart's strategies as an employer, see Barbara Ehrenreich, *Nickel and Dimed* (New York: Metropolitan Books, 2001), 121–91; Steven Greenhouse, "Suit by Wal-Mart Cleaners Asserts Rackets Violation," *New York Times*, November 11, 2003, A12; Nancy Cleeland and Abigail Goldman, "California's Unions Fight Hard to Keep Wal-Mart Out of Town," *Los Angeles Times*, November 29, 2003, at http://seattle times.nwsource.com/html/businesstechnology/2001803437_walmart290.html.

25. On the suburbanization of shopping and the evisceration of urban public life, see Douglas Rae, *City: Urbanism and Its End* (New Haven, Conn.: Yale University Press, 2003).

26. Zukin, *Point of Purchase*, 227–52.

27. *New York Times*, February 19, 2004, December 6, 2002, December 25, 2002, July 27, 2003.

28. The most influential book along these lines has been Naomi Klein, *No Logo* (New York: Picador, 1999).

29. On buying locally grown foods, and reducing greenhouse gases released in transportation, see Michael Pollan, *The Omnivore's Dilemma* (New York: Norton, 2006).

Chapter 9. Gates, Barriers, and the Rise of Affinity

Hal Rothman originally presented a condensed version of this essay at The Transformation of Public Culture Symposium at Miami University, Oxford, Ohio, in March 2004. In 2005, Hal was diagnosed with Lou Gehrig's disease. He revised this essay to the best of his abilities as he struggled with the muscular degeneration caused by the disease, but he chose not to include note references. He died February 25, 2007. The material in this essay is derived from his book *Neon Metropolis: How Las Vegas*

Started the Twenty-first Century (New York: Routledge, 2002) and also the many columns he wrote for a range of newspapers and magazines.

Chapter 10. To Serve the Living

1. James C. Scott, *Domination and the Arts of Resistance* (New Haven, Conn.: Yale University Press, 1990), 18–19.

2. Ibid., 199.

3. For more detailed discussion of these changes, see James J. Farrell, *Inventing the American Way of Death, 1830–1920* (Philadelphia: Temple University Press, 1980), 147–48, 176–77; and Gary Laderman, *The Sacred Remains: American Attitudes Toward Death, 1799–1883* (New Haven, Conn.: Yale University Press, 1996), 30–38.

4. Laderman, *The Sacred Remains*, 104–5.

5. Robert W. Habenstein and William M. Lamers, *The History of American Funeral Directing*, 5th ed. (Brookfield, Wis.: Burton and Mayer, 2001), 205–18.

6. Ibid., 211.

7. For a more detailed description and analysis of Lincoln's funeral, see Laderman, *The Sacred Remains*, 157–63.

8. For detailed information about the evolution of the casket industry, see Habenstein and Lamers, 157–96.

9. For additional information about the history of burial leagues, see Roberta Wright Hughes and Wilbur B. Hughes III, *Lay Down Body: Living History in African American Cemeteries* (Detroit: Visible Ink Press, 1996), 267–90; Karla F. C. Holloway, *Passed On: African American Mourning Stories* (Durham, N.C.: Duke University Press, 2002), 33–36; and Langston Hughes and Arna Bontemps, *The Book of Negro Folklore* (New York: Dodd Mead, 1958), 105.

10. Evidence of the early integration of the Rochester School of Embalming can be found in graduation photographs from the school from the turn of the century.

11. *Constitution of the National Funeral Directors Association, October 4, 1912*, National Funeral Directors Association Archives, Brookfield, Wisconsin.

12. Farrell, *Inventing the American Way of Death*, 156–57.

13. Ibid., 172–77.

14. "Our 1929 Program," *The Colored Embalmer* 2, no. 8 (February 1929): 4.

15. "Race Chauffeurs Block a Funeral Procession," *Cleveland Advocate*, November 16, 1918, 1.

16. "Proceedings of the Eigthy-ninth Annual Convention of the National Funeral Directors Association," Wednesday morning session, October 28, 1970, National Funeral Directors Association Archives, Brookfield, Wisconsin, 11; "NFDA Hits Racial Bar," *Casket and Sunnyside* (December 1970): 22–25.

17. Keith Weldon Medley, *We as Freemen: Plessy v. Ferguson* (Gretna, La.: Pelican, 2003), 89.

18. "Family Proud of 126-Year-Old Business Tradition," *Times-Picayune* (New Orleans), August 23, 1998, 10–11.

19. For more details about the Citizens Committee, see Medley, *We as Freemen*, 111–37.

20. For more details about Charles C. Diggs Sr.'s career, see Richard W. Thomas, *Life for Us Is What We Make It: Building Black Community in Detroit, 1915–1945* (Bloomington: Indiana University Press, 1992), 265–69.

21. Roberta Hughes Wright, *Detroit Memorial Park: The Evolution of an American Corporation* (Southfield, Mich.: Charro Book Company, 1993), 24–25.

22. For recent information on this practice, see Jeremy Olshan, "May You Vote in Peace: Funeral Directors Offer Ride to the Polls in Limos," *Press of Atlantic City*, August 6, 2002, C.1.

23. For specific examples, see Timothy B. Tyson, *Radio Free Dixie: Robert F. Williams and the Roots of Black Power* (Durham: University of North Carolina Press, 1999), 232; and James Farmer, *Lay Bare the Heart: An Autobiography of the Civil Rights Movement* (Fort Worth: Texas Christian University Press, 1998), 246–54.

24. For further discussion of the political significance of the Till funeral, see Holloway, *Passed On*, 25, 129–30, 136; and Christine Harold and Kevin Michael DeLuca, "Behold the Corpse: Violent Images and the Case of Emmett Till," *Rhetoric and Public Affairs* 8, no. 2 (2005): 263–86. For other examples of black funeral directors working actively to support local civil rights struggles, see Matthew C. Whitaker, *Race Work: The Rise of Civil Rights in the Urban West* (Lincoln: University of Nebraska Press, 2005), which profiles the Ragsdale family in Phoenix, Arizona.

25. For recent coverage about racial segregation in the funeral industry, see Matthew Mogul, "Race Lines Continue to Divide Augusta, Georgia-Area Funeral Home Sector," *Augusta Chronicle*, February 23, 2004.

Chapter 11. Denizenship as Transnational Practice

1. *Farm Labor Organizing Committee v. Ohio State Highway Patrol et al.*, 308 F.3d 523 (6th Cir. 2002).

2. See Lisa Lowe, *Immigrant Acts: On Asian American Cultural Politics* (Chapel Hill, N.C.: Duke University Press, 1996), 18–30; Bill Ong Hing, *Making and Remaking Asian America through Immigration Policy, 1850–1990* (Palo Alto, Calif.: Stanford University Press, 1993).

3. See Yen Le Espiritu, *Asian American Women and Men: Labor, Laws and Love* (Thousand Oaks, Calif.: Sage Publications, 1997), 17.

4. John Sung Woo Park *Elusive Citizenship: Immigration, Asian Americans, and the Paradox of Civil Rights* (New York: New York University Press, 2004), 5.

5. Robert Lovato, "Envisioning Another World: Integración Desde Abajo," *The Nation*, March 6, 2006, 22–26; see also Tim Costello, Jeremy Brecher, and Brendan Smith, *Globalization from Below* (Boston: South End Press, 2000).

6. Ann Laura Stoler, *Carnal Knowledge and Imperial Power: Race and the Intimate in Colonial Rule* (Berkeley: University of California Press, 2002).

7. Vine Deloria Jr. and Clifford Lytle, *The Nations Within: The Past and Future of American Indian Sovereignty* (New York: Pantheon, 1984).

8. See my *Immigration and the Political Economy of Home: West Indian Brooklyn and American Indian Minneapolis, 1945–1992* (Berkeley: University of California Press, 2001), particularly chapter 3.

9. On termination, see Donald Fixico, *Termination and Relocation: Federal Indian Policy, 1945–1960* (Albuquerque: University of New Mexico Press, 1986); Nicholas C. Peroff, *Menominee DRUMS: Tribal Termination and Relocation, 1954–1974* (Norman: University of Oklahoma Press, 1982). Specifically on relocation policy, see Joane Nagel, *American Indian Ethnic Renewal: Red Power and the Resurgence of Identity and Culture* (New York: Oxford University Press, 1996).

10. Nikhil Pal Singh, "Culture/Wars: Recoding Empire in an Age of Democracy," *American Quarterly* 50, no. 3 (September 1998): 471–522.

11. See, in particular, David Cole, *Enemy Aliens: Double Standards and Constitutional Freedoms in the War on Terror* (New York: New Press, 2003).

12. "The Real ID Act: National Impact Analysis," presented by National Governors' Association, National Conference of State Legislatures and American Association of Motor Vehicle Administration, http://www.nga.org/Files/pdf/0609REALID.pdf.

13. Nayan Shah, *Contagious Divides: Epidemics and Race in San Francisco's Chinatown* (Berkeley: University of California Press, 2001).

Chapter 12. The Queen's Mirrors

Special thanks to Peggy Shaffer, Susan Boydston, Delores Walters, and Clint Joiner for their insights, interest, and expertise.

1. "Luminaries Attend Opening," *Cincinnati Post*, August 21, 2004; Edward Rothstein, "Slavery's Harsh History Is Portrayed in Promised Land," *New York Times*, August 18, 2004, 1; "National Underground Railroad Freedom Center Opens in Cincinnati," *Jet*, September 13, 2004.

2. *Cincinnati CityBeat*, vol. 9, no. 43, September 3–9, 2003.

3. See Benedict Anderson, "Census, Map and Museum," in *Imagined Communities* (London: Verso, 1991); Catherine Cocks, *Doing the Town: The Rise of Urban Tourism in the United States* (Berkeley: University of California Press, 2001); Ivan Karp and Steven D. Lavine, eds., *Exhibiting Cultures: The Poetics and Politics of Museum Display* (Washington, D.C.: Smithsonian Institution Press, 1991); Ivan Karp, Christine Mullen Kreamer, and Steven D. Lavine, eds., *Museums and Communities: The Politics of Public Culture* (Washington, D.C.: Smithsonian Institution Press, 1992); Richard Handler, *Nationalism and the Politics of Culture in Quebec* (Madison: University of Wisconsin Press, 1988); and Mary Kupiec Cayton, "What Is Public Culture? Agency and Contested Meaning in American Culture—An Introduction," in this volume.

4. Dolores Hayden, *The Power of Place: Urban Landscapes as Public History* (Cambridge, Mass.: MIT Press, 1995), 9–11.

5. Cayton, "What Is Public Culture?" 1.

6. B. Cooke writing in *Inquisitor and Cincinnati Advertiser*, May 4, 1819.

7. Cincinnati's history is recounted in Henry Louis Taylor, ed., *Race and the City: Work, Community and Protest in Cincinnati, 1820–1970* (Urbana: University of Illinois Press, 1993); Zane Miller and Bruce Tucker, *Changing Plans for America's Inner Cities: Cincinnati's Over-the-Rhine and Twentieth Century Urbanism* (Columbus: Ohio State University Press, 1998); David Stradling, *Cincinnati: From River City to Highway Metropolis* (Mt. Pleasant, S.C.: Arcadia Publishing, 2003); Nikki Marie Taylor, *Frontiers of Freedom: Cincinnati's Black Community, 1802–1868* (Athens: Ohio University Press, 2005).

8. Fergus M. Bordewich, "Free at Last," *Smithsonian Magazine*, December 2004; Georges Bataille, "The Museum," in *Rethinking Architecture: A Reader in Cultural Theory*, ed. Neil Leach (London: Routledge, 1997), 22–23; Ivan Karp, "Introduction: Museums and Communities: The Politics of Public Culture," in Karp, Kramer, and Lavine, *Museums and Communities*, 10–11; Denis Dutton, "Decontextualized Crab," *Philosophy and Literature* 16 (1992): 239; Sharon Macdonald, "Exhibitions of Power and Power of Exhibition: An Introduction to the Politics of Display," in *The Politics of Display: Museums, Science, Culture*, ed. Sharon Macdonald (London: Routledge, 1998), 1; Timothy Luke, *Museum Politics: Power Plays at the Exhibition* (Minneapolis: University of Minnesota Press, 2002), xvi.

9. Anderson, *Imagined Communities*, 163; Karp, "Introduction: Museums and Communities," 1–2.

10. Michel de Certeau, "Walking in the City," in *The Cultural Studies Reader*, ed. Simon During (London: Routledge, 1999), 155.

11. William Cronon, *Nature's Metropolis: Chicago and the Great West* (New York: Norton, 1991), 42.

12. Cayton, "What Is Public Culture?" 4, 2–3.

13. I am grateful to Susan Boydston for suggesting that I use the queen metaphor to illustrate the process of urban cultural transformation in Cincinnati.

14. Anderson, *Imagined Communities*, 178.

15. Herbert Muschamp, "Zaha Hadid's Urban Mothership," *New York Times*, June 8, 2003, Arts and Leisure, 1.

16. Christopher Gist, journal entry, February 17, 1751, as quoted in Stanley Hedeen, *The Mill Creek* (Cincinnati: Blue Heron Press, 1995), 9.

17. Hedeen, *The Mill Creek*, 30–31.

18. *History of Cincinnati and Hamilton County, Ohio: Their Past and Present* (Cincinnati: S.B. Nelson, 1894), 61. Available online at http: //www.heritagepursuit.com/Hamilton/HamtiltonIndex.htm. This nostalgic history of the city's founding recounts the story of the Roman farmer Cincinnatus, for whom the city was named, adding that "[i]t is impossible to conceive a more purely bucolic community than that which founded Cincinnati. An Ohio poet, John J. Piatt, in a poem called 'The Lost Farm,' surprises the reader by revealing in the closing line of his story that: 'The lost farm underneath the city lies.'"

19. Ibid., 81.

20. Robert C. Vitz, *The Queen and the Arts: Cultural Life in Nineteenth-Century Cincinnati* (Kent, Ohio: Kent State University Press, 1989), 214.

21. Cronon, *Nature's Metropolis*, 42; Vitz, *The Queen and the Arts*, 115.

22. Steven J. Ross, *Workers on the Edge: Work, Leisure, and Politics in Industrializing Cincinnati, 1788–1890* (New York: Columbia University Press, 1985), 233–34.

23. Women's Art Museum Association Papers (WAMA) Cincinnati Historical Society, box 4, item 358a.

24. Julie Aronson, ed., *Cincinnati Wing: The Story of Art in the Queen City* (Athens: Ohio University Press, 2003), 106.

25. Vitz, *The Queen and the Arts*, 197–204, 216.

26. "A Noble Gem Added to the City's Crown of Hills," *Cincinnati Commercial Gazette*, May 18, 1886.

27. Ross, *Workers on the Edge*, 289.

28. Ibid., 264.

29. *Cincinnati Commercial Gazette*, July 2, 1886.

30. *Cincinnati Enquirer*, November 6, 2002.

31. Ruth Krueger Meyer, "An Introduction to the Art Collection of Charles Phelps and Anna Sinton Taft," in *The Taft Museum: The History of the Collections and the Baum-Taft House*, ed. Edward J. Sullivan and Ruth Krueger Meyer (New York: Hudson Hills Press, 1995), 20.

32. Charles P. Taft, "The South Kensington Museum: What It Is; How It Originated; What It Has Done and Is Now Doing for England and the World; and the Adaptation of Such an Institution to the Needs and Possibilities of This City," WAMA Papers.

33. Meyer, "An Introduction," 25.

34. Joseph D. Ketner, "The Robert S. Duncanson Murals at the Taft Museum," in Sullivan and Meyer, *The Taft Museum*, 61–72; Duncanson quote in Vitz, *The Queen and the Arts*, 29.

35. Jim Knippenberg, "The Taft Reopens in Style: A Crown Jewel of Our City," *Cincinnati Enquirer*, May 14, 2004, http://www.enquirer.com/editions/2004/05/14/loc_taftopen14.html.

36. Taft Museum of Art, Duncanson Artist-in-Residence, http://www.taftmuseum.org/artist_in_residence.htm.

37. James Baldwin and Richard Avedon, *Nothing Personal* (New York: Atheneum, 1964).

38. Sally Miller Gearhart, "Foreword: My Trip to Queer," *Queer Theory and Communication: From Disciplining Queers to Queering the Discipline(s)*, ed. Gust A. Yep, Karen Lovaas, and John P. Elia (Binghamton, N.Y.: Haworth Press, 2004), xxi–xxii.

39. Ken Alltucker et al., "Cincinnati's Decline Leads Ohio Cities: Census Shows Suburbs Booming," *Cincinnati Enquirer*, March 17, 2001, http://www.enquirer.com/editions/2001/03/17_loc_cincinnatis_decline.html.

40. Information from the CAC Website at http://www.contemporaryartscenter.org/history.

41. Ibid.

42. John Johnston, "The Story Behind the Name," *Cincinnati Enquirer*, May 7, 1999, http://www.enquirer.com/editions/1999/05/07/spt_the_story_behind.html.

43. "Andrew Leicester, Public Artist," at http://www.andrewleicester.com/process/process.htm.

44. Johnston, "Story Behind the Name."

45. See Rick Pender, ed., *The Big Pig Gig* (Wilmington, Ohio: Orange Frazer Press, 2000); and Erika Lee Doss, *Spirit Poles and Flying Pigs: Public Art and Cul-*

tural Democracy in American Communities (Washington, D.C.: Smithsonian Books, 1995).

46. William Messer, "The Perfect Place for the Imperfect Moment," *Images Ink* 5, nos. 3/4 (1990): 26.

47. Ibid.

48. John Fox, "Then and Now: Mapplethorpe CAC," *Cincinnati CityBeat*, March 30–April 5, 2000, at http://citybeat.com/2000-03-30/cover.shtml.

49. Ibid.

50. Ellen Goodman, "A Warning from the Mapplethorpe Trial," quoted in "Afterword on the NEA Debate (House of Representatives—October 11, 1990)," available at http://thomas.loc.gov/cgi-bin/query/z?r101:H11OC0-911: (June 2005).

51. Debra Dennis, "Photo Show Verdict: Not Guilty," *Cincinnati Post*, October 6, 1990, 1A; baseball game source: Joan Altabe, "The Mapplethorpe Ruling," *Sarasota Herald-Tribune*, May 26, 2000, 25; Editorial, *Cincinnati Post*, October 6, 1990, 10A.

52. See http://www.arcspace.com/architects/hadid/ordrupgaard/.

53. Barry M. Horstman, "Diva of Design," *Cincinnati Post*, May 17, 2003, at http://www.cincypost.com/2003/05/17/zaha051703.html.

54. Abraham Orden, "Queen City," at http://www.artnet.com/Magazine/reviews/orden/orden4-22-05.asp.

55. Cincinnati Mayor Charlie Luken, Editorial, *Cincinnati Enquirer*, August 29, 2004, at http://www.enquirer.com/editions/2004/08/29/editorial_ed1a1luken.html.

56. *CNN Larry King Live* interview with Harry Belafonte aired on October 15, 2002 at http://transcripts.cnn.com/TRANSCRIPTS/0210/15/lkl.00.html.

57. Gregory Flannery, "Are We Free Yet?" *Cincinnati CityBeat*, August 8, 2004.

58. Thomas A. Dutton, " 'Violence' in Cincinnati," *The Nation*, June 18, 2001.

59. Sharon Zukin, "Shopping and Public Culture," Conference on Public Culture and Democracy, Miami University (Ohio), March 2004.

60. " 'People's Freedom Center' Event to Protest 'Watered Down' Freedom Center," *Cincinnati Enquirer*, August 18, 2004; Rev. Damon Lynch III and Thomas A. Dutton, "Cincinnati's 'Beacon,' " *The Nation*, January 10, 2005.

61. Laura Bush speech at Freedom Center dedication available at http://usinfo.state.gov/scv/Archive/2005/Jun/30-552138.html.

62. The Freedom Center has established a "Dialogue Zone" within the museum. Staffed by professional social workers and psychologists, it is designed to create a space where visitors can have an "inclusive, facilitated encounter" during which they can debrief, talk in small groups, and respond to what they have experienced at the Freedom Center.

63. Karp, "Introduction: Museums and Communities," 10–11.

64. Bordewich, "Free at Last," 2.

65. Vitz, *The Queen and the Arts*, 221; Michael Kimmelman "Art Review: Racing to Keep Up with the Newest," *New York Times*, November 19, 2004, at http://www.ny-times.com/2004/11/19/arts/design/19kimm.html.

66. Nicolai Ouroussoff, "A Temple of Contemplation and Conflict," *New York Times*, May 20, 2005 at http://www.nytimes.com/2005/05/20/arts/design/20free.html.

67. Nichelle M. Bolden, "Tell It Like It T-I-S," *Cincinnati CityBeat*, August 18, 2004.

68. See Sharon Macdonald, ed., *Theorizing Museums* (Oxford, U.K.: Blackwell Publishing, 2004), 2.

Epilgoue: Pitfalls and Promises

1. Theda Skocpol, "Will 9/11 and the War on Terror Revitalize American Civic Democracy?" *PS: Political Science and Politics* 35, no. 3 (September 2002): 537–40.

2. Robert Putnam, "Bowling Together," *The American Prospect*, February 11, 2002, 22.

3. Michael Traugott et al., "How Americans Responded: A Study of Public Reactions to 9/11/01," *PS: Political Science and Politics* 35, no. 3 (September 2002): 511–16.

4. Putnam, "Bowling Together," 20–21.

5. Skocpol, "Will 9/11," 539.

6. Traugott et al., "How Americans Responded."

7. I first heard Marguerite Shaffer make this reference to a "post-11/2 era" during her paper presentation at the 2004 meetings of the American Studies Association in Atlanta, Georgia.

8. Carole Pateman, *The Sexual Contract* (New York: Polity Press, 1988).

9. Arthur Schlesinger Jr., *The Disuniting of America: Reflections on a Multicultural Society* (New York: W. W. Norton, 1992); John J. Miller, *The Unmaking of Americans: How Multiculturalism Has Undermined the Assimilationist Ethic* (New York: Free Press, 1998).

10. Ronald Takaki, *A Different Mirror: A History of Multicultural America* (Boston: Little, Brown and Co., 1993).

11. Will Kymlicka, *Multicultural Citizenship* (Oxford: Clarendon Press, 1995); Anne Norton, "The Virtues of Multiculturalism," in *Multiculturalism and American Democracy*, ed. Arthur Melzer, Jerry Weinberger, and M. Richard Zinman (Lawrence: University of Kansas Press, 1998), 130–38.

12. Sheila Croucher, *Globalization and Belonging: The Politics of Identity in a Changing World* (Lanham, Md.: Rowman and Littlefield, 2003).

13. David Held, "Democracy and Globalization," in *Re-imagining Political Community*, ed. Danile Archibugi, David Held, and Martin Köhler (Stanford, Calif.: Stanford University Press, 1998) 13. E.g., see David Harvey, *The Condition of Postmodernity* (Oxford: Blackwell, 1990), on time/space compression.

14. For a fascinating and wide-ranging discussion of the pros and cons of patriotism versus cosmopolitanism, see Martha Nussbaum, *For Love of Country: Debating the Limits of Patriotism* (Boston: Beacon Press, 1996).

15. Charles Taylor, "Why Democracy Needs Patriotism," in Nussbaum, *For Love of Country*, 119.

16. K. Anthony Appiah, "Cosmopolitan Patriots," in Nussbaum, *For Love of Country*, 29.

17. Yasemin Soysal, "Citizenship and Identity: Living in Diasporas in Post-War Europe," *Ethnic and Racial Studies* 23, no. 1 (2000): 1–15.

18. Amitai Etzioni, *From Empire to Community* (New York: Palgrave, 2004).

Contributors

John Bodnar is a Chancellor's Professor in the Department of History and the codirector of the Center for the Study of History and Memory at Indiana University, Bloomington. He is the author of *Blue-Collar Hollywood: Liberalism, Democracy, and Working People in American Film* (2003), *Our Towns: Remembering Community in Indiana* (2000), *Bonds of Affection: Americans Define Their Patriotism* (1996), *Remaking America: Public Memory, Commemoration, and Patriotism in the Twentieth Century* (1992), and *The Transplanted: A History of Immigrants in Urban America* (1985).

Rachel Ida Buff is an associate professor in the Department of History and coordinator, Comparative Ethnic Studies, at the University of Wisconsin, Milwaukee. She is the author of *Immigration and the Political Economy of Home: West Indian Brooklyn and American Indian Minneapolis, 1945–1992* (2001), and the editor of *Immigrant Rights in the Shadows of U.S. Citizenship* (forthcoming, 2008).

Mary Kupiec Cayton is professor of history and American studies and chair of the Department of History at Miami University, Oxford, Ohio. She is the author of *Emerson's Emergence: Self and Society in the Transformation of New England, 1800–1845* (1989) and coeditor with Elliott Gorn and Peter Williams of *The Encyclopedia of American Social History* (1993) and *The Encyclopedia of American Cultural and Intellectual History* (2001).

Wendy Hui Kyong Chun is an associate professor of modern culture and media at Brown University. She is the author of *Control and Freedom: Power and Paranoia in the Age of Fiber Optics* (2006) and coeditor with Thomas Keenan of *New Media, Old Media: A History and Theory Reader* (2005).

Sheila L. Croucher is the Paul Rejai Professor of Political Science; she is jointly appointed in the American Studies Program at Miami University, Oxford, Ohio. She is the author of *Globalization and Belonging: Identity Politics in a Changing World* (2003) and *Imagining Miami: Ethnic Politics in a Postmodern World* (1997).

Mary E. Frederickson is an associate professor of history and affiliate in women's studies and American studies at Miami University, Oxford, Ohio.

She is the coeditor with Joyce L. Kornbluh of *Sisterhood and Solidarity: Work-ers' Education for Women, 1914–1984* (1984).

Catherine Gudis is an associate professor of history at the University of California, Riverside. She is the author of *Buyways: Billboards, Automobiles, and the American Landscape* (2004) and coeditor with Elspeth Brown and Marina Moskowitz of *Cultures of Commerce: Representation and American Business Culture, 1877–1960* (2006).

Edward T. Linenthal is a professor of history at Indiana University, Bloomington and the editor of the *Journal of American History*. He is the author of *The Unfinished Bombing: Oklahoma City in American Memory* (2001), *Preserving Memory: The Struggle to Create America's Holocaust Museum* (1995), *Sacred Ground: Americans and Their Battlefields* (1991), and *Symbolic Defense: The Cultural Significance of the Strategic Defense Initiative* (1989); and coeditor with Tom Engelhardt of *History Wars: The Enola Gay and Other Battles for the American Past* (1996), with David Chidester of *American Sacred Space* (1995), and with Ira Chernus of *A Shuddering Dawn: Religious Studies and the Nuclear Age* (1989).

Hal Rothman passed away on February 25, 2007, after a yearlong battle with Lou Gehrig's disease while this book was in process. He was a professor of history at the University of Nevada, Las Vegas. He was the author of *Neon Metropolis: How Las Vegas Started the Twenty-first Century* (2002), *Devil's Bargains: Tourism in the Twentieth Century American West* (1998), *Saving the Planet: The American Response to the Environment in the Twentieth Century* (2000), *LBJ's Texas White House: "Our Heart's Home"* (2001), *The Greening of a Nation? Environmentalism in the U.S. since 1945* (1997), *"I'll Never Fight Fire with My Bare Hands Again": Recollections of the First Forest Rangers of the Inland Northwest* (1994), *On Rims and Ridges: The Los Alamos Area since 1880* (1992), and *Preserving Different Pasts: The American National Monuments* (1989). He was the editor of *The Culture of Tourism, the Tourism of Culture* (2003) and *Reopening the American West* (1998), and coeditor with Mike Davis of *The Grit Beneath the Glitter: Tales from the Real Las Vegas* (2002) and with Char Miller of *Out of the Woods: Essays in Environmental History* (1997).

Mary P. Ryan is the John Martin Vincent Professor of History at Johns Hopkins University. She is the author of *Mysteries of Sex: Tracing Women and Men through American History, 1500 to 2000* (2006), *Civic Wars: Democracy and Public Life in American Cities during the Nineteenth Century* (1997), *Women in Public: Between Banners and Ballots, 1825–1880* (1990), *Cradle of the Middle Class: The Families of Oneida County New York 1790–1865* (1981), and *Womanhood in America* (1975).

Marguerite S. Shaffer is an associate professor of American studies and history and director of the program in American studies at Miami University, Oxford, Ohio. She is the author of *See America First: Tourism and National Identity, 1880–1940* (2001).

Suzanne Smith is an associate professor of history at George Mason University. She is the author of *Dancing in the Streets: Motown and the Cultural Politics of Detroit* (1999) and is currently working on her new book, *To Serve the Living: A Cultural History of African American Funeral Directing.*

Lynn Spigel is a professor in the School of Communications at Northwestern University. She is author of *TV by Design: Modern Art and the Rise of Network Television* (2008), *Welcome to the Dreamhouse: Popular Media and Postwar Suburbs* (2001), and *Make Room for TV: Television and the Family Ideal in Postwar America* (1992); and coeditor with Jan Olsson of *Television after TV: Essays on a Medium in Transition* (2004).

Susan Strasser is a professor of history at the University of Delaware. She is the author of *Waste and Want: A Social History of Trash* (1999); *Satisfaction Guaranteed: The Making of the American Mass Market* (1989); and *Never Done: A History of American Housework* (1982). She is the editor of *Commodifying Everything: Relationships of the Market* (2003) and coeditor with Charles McGovern and Matthias Judt of *Getting and Spending: European and American Consumer Societies in the Twentieth Century* (1998).

Sharon Zukin is the Broeklundian Professor of Sociology at Brooklyn College and the Graduate Center of the City University of New York. She is the author of *Point of Purchase: How Shopping Changed American Culture* (2004), *The Cultures of Cities* (1995), *Landscapes of Power: From Detroit to Disney World* (1991), *Industrial Policy: Business and Politics in the United States and France* (1985), *Loft Living* (1982); and *Beyond Marx and Tito* (1975); and coeditor with Michael Sorkin of *After the World Trade Center* (2002) and with Paul DiMaggio of *Structures of Capital* (1990).

Index

Acknowledgments

This book has been a collective effort from the start. I am grateful to the many people who helped bring it to fruition.

My colleague Andrew Cayton sowed the seeds for this project when he encouraged me to develop a symposium related to the work I had been doing in American studies and pointed me to a number of funding sources. Support from the McClellan Lecture Fund and the Manning Morgan Memorial Lecture Fund from the Department of History as well as additional funding from the Center for American and World Cultures and the John B. Altman Fund for the Humanities at Miami University made the symposium that led to the publication of this book possible. I would like to thank Charlotte Newman Goldy, former chair of the Department of History, Mary Jane Berman, director of the Center for American and World Cultures, and John Skillings, then dean of the College of Arts and Science, for their early support of this project.

Many Miami University faculty also contributed to the symposium. Richard Benjamin, Robert Benson, Mary Jane Berman, Andrew Cayton, Mary Kupiec Cayton, Sheila Croucher, Curtis Ellison, Mary Frederickson, and Peter Williams served as chairs and commentators. Their comments and suggestions greatly added to the conversation and the conceptualization of this volume. In addition, Phoebe Kropp of the University Pennsylvania joined us for the symposium and provided invaluable comments both at the symposium and later as reader for the volume.

Monique Brooks, then a student at Miami, was instrumental in making the symposium happen. She single-handedly organized, promoted, and handled all the local arrangements for the symposium. I am deeply in her debt. Finally, Angela Weaver, a graduate student at Miami, assisted in pulling together the visual images for this volume and securing all the necessary permissions.

Edward Linenthal delivered a shorter version of his essay at the Seventeenth Annual Oklahoma Lecture in the Humanities on February 28, 2002 in Tulsa, Oklahoma. An edited version of that lecture appeared in the Oklahoma Humanities Council's publication *Humanities Interview* 20, no. 2

(Spring 2002): 3–6. Lynn Spigel's essay, "Entertainment Wars: Television Culture after 9/11," is reprinted with permission from the Johns Hopkins University Press (Lynn Spigel, "Entertainment Wars: Television Culture after 9/11," *American Quarterly* 56, no. 2 [2004]: 235-70. © The American Studies Association). Wendy Hui Kyong Chun's essay, "Screening Pornography," is a revised version of chapter 2 from her book *Control and Freedom: Power and Paranoia in the Age of Fiber Optics* (Wendy Hui Chun, *Control and Freedom: Power and Paranoia in the Age of Fiber Optics*, 9,665-word excerpt from chapter 2, © 2005 Massachusetts Institute of Technology, published by MIT Press).